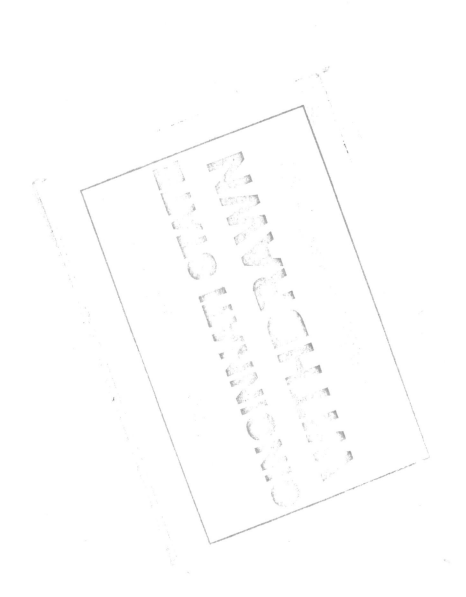

CINCINNATI

Praise for *Peer to Peer*

"The author has given a well-written and comprehensive overview of several representative peer-to-peer technologies. It is diligently researched and gives a lot of insights into a little-understood subject."
—**Erik Möller, Scientific Review Service and infoAnarchy.org**

"Interesting topic, well organized, engagingly written, excellent illustrations; a good read. I think it does a particularly good job of balancing technical, functional, business, and legal information, and presenting it in a way that is useful for both executive and technical people (which is no mean feat)."
—**Mitchel Ahern, Director, Business Development, AdTools Inc./SonyMusic**

"It is technical enough that the reader can actually implement or model the methods used in the text. However, it is not presented at such a high level that nontechnical users would get lost in the math."
—**Austin David, Sr. Systems Architect, Wink Communications, Inc.**

"*Peer to Peer* offers a contemporary and intelligent insight into the popular technologies that are the building blocks of p2p. It cuts through the media controversy and is a useful resource for exploring these technologies. This book was a pleasant change of pace from my day-to-day technical reading."
—**John Wegis, Engineering Manager, Kana Software, Inc.**

PEER TO PEER

PEER TO PEER

Collaboration and Sharing over the Internet

BO LEUF

♦ Addison-Wesley

Boston • San Francisco • New York • Toronto • Montreal
London • Munich • Paris • Madrid
Capetown • Sydney • Tokyo • Singapore • Mexico City

The publisher offers discounts on this book when ordered in quantity for special sales. For more information, please contact:

Pearson Education Corporate Sales Division
201 W. 103rd Street
Indianapolis, IN 46290
(800) 428-5331
corpsales@pearsontechgroup.com

Visit Addison-Wesley on the Web: www.awprofessional.com

Library of Congress Cataloging-in-Publication Data
Leuf, Bo.
  Peer to peer : collaboration and sharing over the Internet / Bo Leuf.
   p. cm.
  Includes index.
  ISBN 0-201-76732-5
  1. Peer-to-peer architecture (Computer networks) 2. Internet. I. Title.

TK5105.525 .L48 2002
004.6'8—dc21   2002024937

ISBN 0-201-76732-5
Text printed on recycled paper
1 2 3 4 5 6 7 8 9 10—HT—0605040302
First printing, June 2002

I dedicate this book to the many visionaries, architects, and programmers, who made the Internet an interesting place to "live" and work in.

And especially to Therese.

—Bo Leuf

Contents

Foreword

L ike the **Web**, peer to peer (p2p) networking grew rapidly out of user desire. Whether sharing music, pictures, or conversation, the user urge to connect on a one-to-one basis, without the intervention of a centralized governing authority, seems to express a fundamental human need.

Again like the Web, the initial growth of peer technologies came from mainly non-commercial motivations. Indeed, in for instance the case of Napster, it came from downright *anti*-commercial motivations! Now, p2p comes to the range of its adoption curve where many of the most egregious excesses of file swapping are being tamed, and the business community is trying to figure out how to take advantage of the tremendous natural energy that's apparent in the millions of swappers, chatters and hosters in p2p communities.

The trouble is, unlike the Web, p2p networking is not a single, simple communication protocol. It's not even a single networking structure. Most peer implementations don't particularly concern themselves with any clearly defined content types, nor is the technology normally targeted for specific business or personal purposes. The p2p model crops up in a variety of applications: file sharing, instant messaging, and resource allocation, to name a few. In all these cases, we see a similarity of application, but there are many differences in specific implementation.

Bo Leuf's book, *Peer to Peer: Collaboration and Sharing over the Internet*, comes along at a very good time for those of us actively looking to adapt our current business practices to the peer-to-peer model, or looking to develop next generation peer tools.

The book is interesting, well organized, informatively illustrated, and engagingly written. It especially well balances technical, functional, business, and legal information, and presents the material in a way that is useful for both the executive and technical reader—no mean feat.

Although his initial deconstruction of the p2p hype might tempt you momentarily to conclude, in the words of Gertrude Stein, that "there is no there there", this drastic approach allows for a more meaningful definition of what p2p is, based on first principles. As we are shown in the process, peer to peer is both less and more than you may have been led to believe. It is less, in that there is no short and simple defined protocol and tool suite for you to jump in and use. It is more, in that the shape of peer-to-peer relationships is rapidly becoming a new and fundamental means for users and machines to communicate. This relationship can be powerfully transformative, as the music industry has already discovered.

Mitchel Ahern
Director, Business Development
AdTools Inc., A SonyMusic Company

Preface

WHY THIS BOOK?

The idea of writing this book, *Peer to Peer: Collaboration and Sharing over the Internet*, seemed in several ways a natural and complementary progression from the previous one, *The Wiki Way* (Addison-Wesley, 2001). Subtitled *Quick Collaboration on the Web*, that book explored the client-server peer-collaborative world of WikiWiki. In that server-centric situation, there were even then hints of a wider peer perspective for applications, for example interlinking different wiki servers in a peer-to-peer kind of network to transparently exchange content and extend search capabilities across multiple sites.

The main thrust of this book, however, is to explore what, at its extreme, becomes the complete *opposite* of server-centric communication: when individual user applications connect "end-to-end" with each other across the network for various purposes. One significant and popular reason for such connectivity is to share content (file swapping), but beyond that, the full potential lies in the broader purpose of communicating and collaborating between endpoint applications, as well as between the users who sit at their respective computers or carry the appropriate network-aware devices.

P2P: The Journey

In *Peer to Peer*, you are invited to a guided journey through a hitherto arcane field, mostly known so far from the hype and controversy surrounding what is only a limited part of a much broader field of network distributed application.

You'll learn about an innovative emerging technology that not only can change, but is in fact already revolutionizing the way we use the Internet. Peer technology is at the heart of the efforts to build the next-generation Internet, what in some contexts is referred to as "Internet 3.0".

Because we are dealing with *peer* technology, it means that the practical **implementation** for the most part will be near to each of us, the users. For this reason, and the fact that an individual selects and deploys these implementations on a local machine, comparative descriptions of the technologies are needed in a format that not only techno-nerds can comprehend. And they are needed now, because an informed user base must be able to influence everything from corporate policy to legislative proposals. It's not just on an idle whim that significant sections of the text in this book deal with both the social and legal ramifications of p2p.

Therefore, read *Peer to Peer* with a mind open to exploring simple yet powerful networking tools that you can completely control. Play with the concepts, try the implementations, tweak the open sources, and see where it all takes you. Above all, contemplate the implications of the technology, both in terms of your own convenience and a broader social change.

WHO SHOULD READ THIS BOOK

This book targets primarily three groups of readers:

- Any reader who wants to explore new peer-based ways to communicate, collaborate, publish, and share over the Internet in ways independent of the usual content providers (traditional Web sites). To this end, the overall style and structure of the book is mainly held at a light-to-moderate level of technical difficulty, and all technojargon terms are explained early.

- Industry professionals, such as managers or technical responsibles, who need to get up to speed on distributed tools for messaging or collaboration, or for publishing, storing, sharing, and securing content. Typically, they want both a general technology overview and a how-to-implement guide in order to make informed decisions. These readers would inherently be inclined to focus mainly on the core implementation chapters, but shouldn't neglect the more general chapters.

- Researchers and students in academic settings who both study the design and implementation of p2p technology tools, and use them to great advantage in their day-to-day collaboration work.

As this book shows, "peer to peer" is not a new concept; only the form and medium change over time. The recent hype and controversy has also obscured much of the technology's potential—and additionally, its problems. In fact, a number of the problems confronting the current crop of peer implementations are well-known in older networking contexts, with solutions that can be adapted to the new.

BOOK STRUCTURE

... pier-to-pier ...

Peer to Peer is a combined exposition, guide, and tutorial. The ambition is to provide a single volume replete with historical background, state of the art, and some of the vision. Melding practical information and hints with in-depth analysis, all in an easy-to-read informal and personal style, the result is even entertaining—*a damn good read*, as the technical reviewers reassured the author.

The mix includes conceptual overviews, philosophical reflection, and contextual material from professionals in the field—in short all things interesting. You might consider this a tall order to fill for a single book. Assuredly, but it worked for the previous book, and was fun (if hard work) trying to do it once again with this new subject matter.

The book is organized into three parts, each catering to different needs and interests. There is some overlap, but you should find that each part approaches the various manifestations of the peer-to-peer concept from complementary directions, with a tone and depth appropriate to each. No matter the level of detail and involvement desired, a reader should always find something worthwhile to focus on.

Part I

Part I sets the foundations for the later discussions.

- The first chapter starts with the basics and defines what, exactly, p2p is— the term has come to mean many different things to different people. Getting familiar with a concept often requires some background and an examination of its origins, so the chapter looks at the history of telephony and of the early Internet to draw parallels and properly set the stage.

- Chapter 2 introduces the architectural models relevant to a discussion of peer technologies and defines important terminology.

- Chapter 3 introduces the implementations that are covered later, and examines some major performance issues common to most implementations, such as search and content management.

- Finally, Chapter 4 tackles security and legal issues, two difficult concern areas also common to most implementations. The intent here is to highlight what usage questions might become sensitive or critical when p2p technologies are deployed in a network.

Part II

Part II focuses on practical implementation examples. These core chapters explore representative implementations for each of the chosen implementation areas, providing an in-depth mix of both well-known and lesser-known solutions that illustrate different ways of achieving similar functionality.

- Chapter 5 provides a managerial overview and guide to deployment issues, an important complement to implementation-specific technical detail. It also covers technology selection and examines the factors that determine the scalability of a particular solution based on its architectural model.

- Chapter 6 highlights messaging technologies, showing the trade-off factors inherent in each example, and noting why the most popular implementations might be less suitable for corporate use.

- Chapter 7 progresses to file-sharing solutions, again with a special view to explaining the concepts behind some of the more popular implementations.

- Adopting a broader network perspective, Chapter 8 studies two peer solutions that approach distributed storage and content distribution from different requirements.

- Chapter 9 explains in considerable detail an important evolving technology for secure, anonymous publishing of content. Of particular interest is an analysis of the adaptive storage mechanism.

- Chapter 10 broadens the perspective to that of collaborative spaces in general, examining a couple of new infrastructure solutions that might define the Internet of the future.

Part III

Part III elevates the discussion into the higher realms of analysis and speculation.

- Chapter 11 provides the "insights" segment and looks at some of the assumptions and implications highlighted by peer technologies. From community building to legal concerns, from payment mechanisms to trust systems, peer solutions have shown a knack for raising controversy while suggesting innovative ways of working together.

- Chapter 12, intended as a case study section, summarizes the practical sides of working in a p2p environment and suggests where the current infrastructures might not yet be fully up to expectations.

- Chapter 13 voices both opinion and speculation on a grander scale. Visions of the future can just as easily be dark as light, and the text attempts to show why this is especially true for p2p.

Finally, three *appendixes* supplement the main body of the book by collecting terminology, references, and resources—providing additional detail that while valuable did not easily fit into the flow of the main text.

Navigation

This book is undeniably filled with a plethora of facts and explanations, and it is written more in the style of narrative rather than of mere reference-volume itemization. Despite the narrative ambitions, texts like this require multiple entry points and quick ways to locate specific details, for example a carefully crafted *index*. To further help you navigate, as a complement to the detailed *table of contents*, each *chapter at a glance* introduction provides a quick overview of the main topics covered in that chapter. Words marked in **bold** are *glossary* terms explained in Appendix A.

Scattered throughout the text you will find the occasional highlighted and numbered "*Bit*" where some special insight or factoid is singled out and presented in a shaded box. However, as a technical reviewer rightly quibbled, the template's original "Tip" context label for such elements was less applicable to this book. Taking the unorthodox approach of instead calling the element a "Bit" seemed to convey about the right level of unpretentious emphasis—they're often just my two-bits worth of insightful comment. Bits do serve the additional purpose of providing content locators for the reader and are therefore given their own *List of Bits* in Appendix C. Sadly, a full infrastructure of hyperlink cross-referencing is not possible in a printed book, which would be of great reader convenience, but perhaps a future e-edition....

When referencing Web resources, I use the convention of omitting the "http://" prefix, since modern Web browsers will accept addresses typed in without it.

THE AUTHOR

 Extensive experience in technical communication and teaching coupled with a deep understanding of cross-**platform** software product design, user interfaces, and usability analysis—all provide a unique perspective to writing technical books. I maintain several professional and recreational Internet Web sites, including one that provides commercial webhosting and wiki services for others.

An independent consultant in the computing sector in Sweden for some 25 years, I've been responsible for software development and localization projects. Training issues came to the foreground during a number of years as head of a language school specializing in an immersive teaching methodology. Currently a freelance consultant and technical writer, I specialize in software documentation, translation, and design-team training, with regular contributions to a major Swedish computer magazine. Authoring books is an activity that rather unexpectedly came to dominate the past few years. I also do occasional speaking engagements at technology conferences.

CONTRIBUTORS AND COLLEAGUES

A great many people helped make this book possible by contributing their enthusiasm, time, and effort—all in the spirit of the collaborative peer community that the Internet and publishing encourages.

Technical review is a time-consuming and demanding activity, ensuring that an author's worst slip-ups, omissions, and mistakes are caught before committing to paper. The technical reviewers are, in order of incoming review returns: Austin David, Mitchel Ahern (who also graciously contributed the foreword), John Wegis, and Erik Möller. These very knowledgeable professionals and colleagues helped make this book a better one and I express my profound gratitude for their efforts. I hope they enjoy the published version.

Finally, I would have been helpless without the encouragement, assistance, and resources provided by executive editor Mary T. O'Brien and her staff, and the support of the Addison-Welsey production team. A special thanks goes to the people at Studio B Literary Agency for their unstinting author support and encouragement.

Personal thanks go to supportive family members for enduring the long months of what to them must seem like endless research and typing, reading, editing, and general mental absentness at all hours of the day and night.

ERRATA AND OMISSIONS

There are assuredly mistakes and errors of omission in this book; it's unavoidable, despite (or sometimes because of) the many edit passes, proofing, and the excellent efforts of editors and technical reviewers. We all hope they are very few.

However, getting a book out is a complex process with numerous deadlines, and a finished book (any book) is neither "finished" nor perfect, just (hopefully) the best that could be done within the constraints at hand. We have all taken great care to get things right with multiple reviews and proofing. Nevertheless, some things might be overly simplified, or statements made that someone, somewhere, will be able to point to and say "Not so!" That may be; not everything can be fully verified, and sometimes the simple answer, correct in its place, is good enough for the focus at hand. The hardest mistakes to catch are the things we "know", because some of these unquestioned truths can be wrong, have changed since we learned them, or have more complex answers than we realize.

Omissions are generally due to the fact that the author must draw the line somewhere in terms of scope and detail. I've tried in the text to indicate where and why. The technical reviewers, drawn from various professional fields and with different perspectives and complementary expertise, made valuable suggestions as to where this selection process might be improved.

The bottom line in any computer-related field is that any attempt to make a definitive statement about such a rapidly moving target is doomed to failure. During the course of writing, *things changed!* All the time. In the interval between final submission and the printed book, not to mention by the time you read this, they've likely changed even more. Not only does the existing software continue to evolve, or sometimes disappear altogether, but new implementations can suddenly appear from nowhere and change the entire landscape. The biggest headache is to provide useful resource links—as Web sites change or disappear, some resources mentioned in the text might not be found and others not mentioned might be better.

Your feedback, positive and negative, is always appreciated. Comments and factual corrections will be used to improve future editions of the book and to identify where the writing was not as clear as intended. Such information will be regularly compiled and published on the support Web site (www.leuf.com) and complement the discussions that hopefully appear there.

The Internet has made up-to-date reader support a far easier task than it used to be, though I fear this makes some authors and publishers take woefully insufficient care in getting the paper effort right to begin with.

CONTACTING THE AUTHOR OR PUBLISHER

Authors tend to get a lot of correspondence in connection with a published book. Please be patient if you write and don't get an immediate response—with many professional commitments and the pressures of book deadlines to consider, immediate response might not be possible. However, my intention is always to at least acknowledge received reader mail quickly, even if a more personal response may at the time not be possible.

Better than sending e-mail might be to first visit the collaborative wiki at www.leuf.net/ww/wikidn?PeerToPeer, where you can meet an entire community of readers. This is an open support site for this book, where you can find updates and discussions about the book and about using peer-to-peer software. The main attraction of such a collaborative support Web site is the contacts you can form with other readers of the book. Collectively, the readers of such a site always have more answers and wisdom than any number of authors.

Otherwise, the arguably easiest way to reach me is by sending e-mail to bo@leuf.com. But before writing with specific questions, visit the Web site where you can find much information and further links, and very likely some immediate answers to common questions.

While the natural assumption is that you, the reader, have Internet connectivity, and can both visit the Web and send e-mail, this is not always true. You may therefore also contact me through the publisher by ordinary surface mail:

Bo Leuf
c/o Addison-Wesley Editorial Department
Pearson Technology Group
75 Arlington Street, Suite 300
Boston, Massachusetts
USA 02116

The publisher's Web site is www.awprofessional.com. You may contact the publisher to learn information about other published books, for example. Send an e-mail to info@awl.com, or use the previous surface mail address after the "c/o".

Thank you for buying *Peer To Peer*. I hope you enjoy reading this book as much as I enjoyed researching and writing it.

– Bo Leuf, February 2002

PART I

Peer to Peer Overview

Introduction to Peer to Peer

Achieving "buzz factor" is basically the same process in any field—it's about saying something that at least *appears* to be new about any, often old concept. And then with luck, something happens to attract broader attention. A particular subject can become hot and sexy overnight without anyone actually realizing why, and before you know it, all the trendsetters are hyping their version of it.

The bottom line in all the peer-to-peer (p2p) buzz during the past year is that much (most?) of it had relatively little substance or relevance. Under the hype:

- A lot of self-styled "peer-to-peer" technology wasn't, really, very much about that at all.

- Some implementations would probably have been better if attempted in some other technology.

- Much of the hype was locked into mistaken or incomplete preconceptions about what peer-to-peer can and can't do.

So, to clear the air, this chapter intends to tell it like it is. In simple terms.

The technologically savvy reader will surely now be tempted to skip an introductory chapter such as this. Yes, the explanations and figures can at first glance seem simplistic and may provoke the usual dismissive response of "Yeah, sure, I know all that!" But do read on. As I worked with the book, I found that the popular buzz had instilled even in me several misconceptions about the technology. It took considerable research and thought to distill out the essentials of p2p. I hope you'll glean some new insight as well.

CHAPTER 1 AT A GLANCE

The purpose of these chapter overviews, which you find on the back of each chapter's opening page, is to indicate the order in which material is presented and thus make it easier to find a particular section from its context. See it as a local subset of the table of contents, only with some contextual reference.

The highlighted words are the main headings in the chapter, which introduce second-level headings in the list items. Ideally, you would have the same hyperlink capability to jump directly to each section as I have on my screen, but *Alas, earwax....*

This overview chapter is designed to give a background in broad strokes on computer-mediated peer-to-peer systems. The goal is to find a workable and meaningful definition of the p2p concept, without which much of the later discussion could easily be misunderstood.

The Concept takes a hard look at the fundamentals of peer-to-peer as a meaningful term and attempts to strip away the hype.

- Next we consider *The Killer P2P Application* and how any such application must critically depend on how p2p can address both *The Bandwidth Factor* and *The Distribution Factor*. This leads to *A Common Denominator*, which summarizes the essential characteristics that define p2p as considered in this book.

Using *Historical Analogies*, this section attempts to nail down a useful technical definition along with criteria for evaluating different approaches.

- *Telephony* provides an illuminating analogy, not least because it laid the infrastructure on which networking was built. *Internet Infrastructure* next looks at how the Internet moved from its p2p roots to a more hierarchical structure.

Power to the People examines what p2p means for the individual, as an alternative to the now more common client-server architecture.

- *Virtual P2P* revisits the killer application theme and discusses how *Original Chat and IM* have been early contenders for that title.

THE CONCEPT

So, just what is "peer-to-peer" (*P2P, p2p, peer2peer*) anyway?

Unfortunately, the answer has been obfuscated by all the recent hype. "P2P" became a marketing label, or for some just a way to signal being attuned to the latest trends. To have an intelligent discussion about p2p and its real and potential uses, we need to be clear about what we mean—a definition of sorts. Otherwise this book will be no better than the ephemeral hype found elsewhere.

> **Bit 1.1 Some p2p technology is more about marketing than product.**
> A particular implementation or technology may or may not be in the p2p space at any given time, depending upon what mood the marketing people are in.

The term "peer-to-peer" was in fact used as far back as in the mid-1980s by local area network (**LAN**) vendors to describe their connectivity **architecture**. The concept applied to computers predates this by another couple of decades.

In essence, peer-to-peer simply means *equal communicating with equal*. That's pretty basic. So what was all the fuss about?

Peer-to-peer became a "buzz" concept in 2000, so much so that the label was (and often still is) gratuitously applied to anything that smacks of connecting or sharing. Suddenly p2p was the hottest subject around. That such a popular and controversial service as *Napster* took the public limelight was both a help and a hindrance to spreading the word, and popular perception suffers a distortion of the basic concept as a result. Music label corporations were driven to bring lawsuits, intense debate raged on both sides over the right to copy and the state of copyright, and all was due to this free p2p thing.

By early 2001, Napster claimed over 60 million registered users busy swapping terabytes of music files. Clearly, something significant had happened to bring at least one aspect of p2p to general public awareness—*everybody* knew about Napster p2p. Napster now attempted a skin change to become a legitimate commercial music outlet instead and began to filter the file sharing.

But by then, it seemed that nobody knew what p2p was any more. The thing is, p2p as a technology had developed from so many sources for so many different reasons, that there was little consensus about what it was supposed to be. Without a suitable, dominant definition, it's little wonder the term can seem hijacked.

> **Bit 1.2   There's far more to p2p than popularized MP3 file swapping.**
> As a well-known implementation of peer technology, Napster is used in several places to illustrate some p2p concepts, but this book is not about how to swap MP3 files in the post-free-Napster era.

Anyway, the buzz and hype are already receding—even some p2p conferences have been renamed to something with more perceived buzz appeal for 2002, perhaps a good thing. Fortunately, what's left are the practical implementations, the solutions and how people use them.

Beyond the hype, perhaps p2p is best described in terms of the *intent* of its supporters, as a set of technologies targeted at *better utilizing networked resources*. However, this definition is likely too broad for the purposes of this book, so we'll seek one with more practical focus in the following sections.

THE KILLER P2P APPLICATION

Hyped or not, and however unfocused the term, "p2p" quickly became much more than just one computer talking to another. Exactly what, has a lot to do with the available infrastructure, the context in which we apply the technology, and ultimately what people want to do with it.

Swapping music files turned out to be a killer application for p2p largely because that's what many people wanted to do. The coincidental availability of MP3 compression made this practical even for users with low-**bandwidth** connectivity, which was the majority of users at the time. Napster came to prominence by providing easy-to-use clients that could rapidly reach critical mass in terms of a user base large enough to be interesting. That Napster came to dominate the public conception of p2p is perhaps just a random conjunction of opportunity and timing.

An earlier large-scale file-sharing solution for general content, Scour, had already shut down after intense litigational pressure before the p2p term hyped fully. At its height, the Scour servers indexed around 40 TB of content—all kinds of files, not just MP3s. It was a huge community second only to Napster in number of users, and to this day, one can see nostalgic postings about "the good old days of Scour".

It's important to realize that although Napster quickly came to dominate the popular mind, it was only one p2p implementation among many. Like most such implementations, it was incomplete, idiosyncratic, and tightly focused on the particular service it provided—often to the exclusion of other, perhaps more interesting functionality. Napster achieved high visibility due to the controversial nature of freely swapping (copying) commercial music files. It was successful because of the way it could leverage off the new, widely available music compression technology, thus ensuring popularity among a broad class of new users with relatively low bandwidth. Numerous **clone** clients quickly arose, many of which remained compatible with the Napster protocol to increase client viability and so indirectly promote their own competing networks.

Another p2p implementation, instant messaging (IM), is at least as widespread as file sharing—but without all the buzz, perhaps because it became established before the controversy. However, IM exhibits a so-far enduring split into several proprietary and incompatible networks, mainly due to active resistance to interoperability by the currently dominating actor, America Online (AOL).

IM's fragmentation means that further incompatible implementations might yet arise and gain a significant market share. Through some combination of external factors, one of these implementations might reach a critical threshold in number of users and come to overshadow the existing systems. A proprietary IM client bundled with a common operating system might be one possible way this could happen.

This issue of critical threshold, very relevant to what becomes a killer application, can be seen as a result of Metcalfe's Law.

Bit 1.3 Metcalfe's Law: Network value rises by the square of the number of terminals.

Given the choice between joining a large existing network with many users or an incompatible new one with few users, new users will almost always decide that the bigger one is far more valuable.

This relationship is an important factor in the viability of any new technology, not just networks. The ratio is *geometric*, not linear, ensuring a runaway effect—the technology with the larger number of users soon comes to dominate. Metcalfe's Law is often used to explain the phenomenal growth of the Internet, often recast as: *The value of a network grows by the square of the processing power of all the computers attached to it.* Every new computer adds resources to the Net in a feedback spiral of ever-increasing value and choice.

Increasing at least a thousand times every five years, the trajectory of Internet traffic indicates that any user at any given time is confronting just *one tenth of one percent* of the potential expected in the network only half a decade on. This kind of growth is absolutely phenomenal.

The growth effect actually has little to do with how "good" or "smart" the technology is. Paramount is how many users it gains compared to other solutions. The more it gains, the more it will gain in future—it's that simple. This is a good reason to include compatibility with established standards in new technologies, or risk forever being at best just a marginal niche player.

One can quibble about the exact value factor and how to measure this, but the principle is fundamental—in both directions.

> **Bit 1.4   Fragmenting a network dramatically reduces the perceived value.**
> Divisive effects that break up a larger network make the value of the parts taken together far less than the value of the whole.

Speaking of directions, we should note that the value of fully *bidirectional* information flows is greater than when data flows in only one direction. Not only does it seem reasonable to factor in bidirectionality of connections into the value relationships between **nodes,** we might even state that Metcalfe's Law only applies to bidirectionally connected nodes. This qualification is especially relevant when considering the added value that new nodes bring to a network.

We can briefly examine some known connectivity factors on the Internet that would seem to confirm the divisive effect of unidirectional data flow:

- **Transient nodes and dynamic IP numbers.** Such nodes can reach the network but are usually unreachable by other nodes and so add little to the network's aggregate value.

- **Intranet nodes and network address translation (NAT).** The computers on an intranet LAN behind a NAT are generally not directly reachable from outside, thus they add little value to the larger Internet.

- **Firewalls.** Computers behind firewalls can usually not be contacted from outside; so as far as the outside network is concerned, they don't exist.

In all these cases, although the computers can see and use the Internet's resources using the normal protocols, the data flow is predominantly unidirectional, inwards. The net effect by their addition to larger networks is to *fragment*, not add value to the whole. Therefore, Metcalfe's Law as applied to the Internet should be seen as only valid when adding "open" nodes, freely reachable from other nodes.

For example, it's estimated that Web search engines index an ever smaller fraction of the total information held on the Internet as a whole, perhaps by now less than a tenth. At least part of the reason for this huge information store remaining unmapped is due to the fact that not all Internet-connected sites allow themselves to be indexed or even contacted directly from outside their particular barrier.

On the other hand, because p2p has at its core the concept of peer always being able to contact other peers freely, networks based on p2p will follow the value-added law. As later chapters show, p2p technologies are designed to actively circumvent the unidirectional barriers mentioned earlier, allowing otherwise insular nodes to participate freely in two-way conversations with other peers.

THE BANDWIDTH FACTOR

Any discussion of killer applications—past, present, or future—must also consider the issue of average available bandwidth. The kind of application that is interesting and practical for a large user base critically depends on both its bandwidth requirements and the average bandwidth available to the majority of potential users.

> **Bit 1.5   Gilder's Law: Bandwidth grows at least three times faster than computer power (both with regard to total network capacity).**
>
> This is a rough empirical average. Applying Moore's law for computer power (said to double roughly every 18 months), it means that network bandwidth can be expected on average to quadruple every year.

Gilder's Law is especially important during the threshold period when the technology is introduced. Thus it makes sense that the early popular p2p applications were the low-bandwidth e-mail and IM clients. File sharing in general might have been interesting, but large files were too costly in terms of the bandwidth (and online costs) this represented for the average user.

Later when higher bandwidth became more common, and when compression brought the size of a typical **CD**-quality music track down to a manageable average size of **4MB**, the viability of general p2p file sharing networks became manifest for the average user. This development was the window of opportunity that opened for Napster, along with the perceived added value of multi-peer access.

Further increases in bandwidth mean ever-lower costs for transporting ever-larger amounts of data. This situation leads to new opportunities for other kinds of applications, services on demand, and distributed computing—many of which we can't even begin to imagine yet. The trend increasingly favors p2p solutions.

Bit 1.6   The Black Box Law: Networks evolve towards high-bandwidth, dumb pipes, with intelligence spread to the machines at their peripheries.

As the cost of transporting information decreases with higher bandwidth, the most optimal configuration of network resources evolves towards a distributed, p2p one.

The Distribution Factor

Two problems turn up with the way the Web is currently organized with content servers; both are related to the demand for a particular piece of information.

- The more popular any information is, the less available it becomes as the demand saturates the capacity of the servers and network paths that provide it.

- Each user who accesses information will inefficiently consume a bandwidth corresponding to the entire content, often duplicating concurrent transfers of the very same information to other nearby users.

What p2p technology enables in this context is a combination of (often dynamically) distributed storage to meet peak demands without saturation and the replication of frequently requested information in locations nearer larger groups of users. Thus distribution is an important, albeit not necessarily defining characteristic of p2p technology. The implementation chapters describe some distribution examples.

A Common Denominator

The best place to begin the quest for a p2p definition is to find a common denominator for the p2p concept, even though some have come to question the relevance of a term that seems to have such a catch-all scope in common usage.

In that light, it's useful to temporarily reinterpret the term p2p as "person-to-person communication" and try to visualize the essential core of this concept and how it plays. Imagine, therefore, a room full of people. The thing most people want to do, most of the time, is communicate.

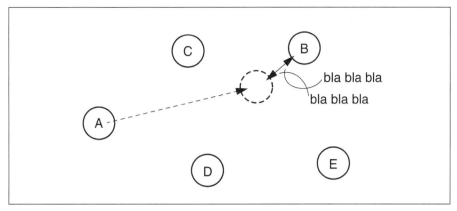

FIGURE **1.1** *P2P interpreted as "person-to-person". Person A in a room full of people wishes to communicate with B. A therefore locates and approaches B and establishes a direct connection.*

A simple diagram, such as that in Figure 1.1, can illustrate the situation. This trivial analogy is more useful than it may at first seem, because it moves our focus away from technological details and reminds us of some of the basic functionality that a p2p implementation must provide to support conversations. Consider: We generally prefer a *face-to-face* conversational mode without intermediaries, so that we are *aware* of the other person's presence and current state of receptivity, and we approach or face that person to "establish a connection" using particular social cues or *handshaking* protocols to start the conversation. Seen this way, many of the technical issues in p2p clients examined later take on an easy-to-grasp immediacy.

Bit 1.7   People talk—with each other, directly.

Conversation is pretty basic behavior. Almost quintessentially *human*. And very p2p.

Conversations Between Equals

One of the distinctive characteristics of any p2p system is what is often called direct *end-to-end* connectivity between equals.

This one-on-one property is distinctive, not exclusive; it does not preclude one-to-many broadcasts, nor have we at this stage specified what the end-points represent—people, machines, or software. Although not sufficient in itself, one-to-one connectivity can still be considered an essential hallmark of "pure" p2p.

> **Bit 1.8 P2P assumes some form of end-to-end connectivity.**
> Whether this connection is entirely unmediated, or partially assisted by centralized services, is irrelevant. At root, it's a "private" communication channel in a distributed network context.

In that light, early computer networks were eminently p2p at the machine level. For machine A to communicate with machine B, it established a direct connection. The connectivity technology used was secondary, either LAN or **modem**. The machines in the precursors to the Internet connected to each other by dial-up modem to exchange information. Later, workstations used LAN technology to maintain persistent local networking and again the initial model was p2p.

Today, the technology is different, and the physical connections with global reach are not fully p2p in themselves. Peer connectivity is instead accomplished in a different abstraction layer: a protocol suite known as **TCP/IP** that can connect together many separate internets on different machines and operating systems into a seemingly seamless whole—*the Internet*. We return to the Internet model in later discussions, because the experiences gained there are still surprisingly relevant to the "new" peer technologies.

Conversations Are Dynamic

When we see networks today, we commonly think of them as persistent connections, machine to machine. However, human conversations are dynamic, transient, and changing. These characteristics are true of modern p2p networks as well; their connectivity is constantly changing as nodes come and go.

> **Bit 1.9 Modern p2p connectivity is usually transient, not permanent.**
> Each p2p node "lives in the moment" and has an essentially random selection of other nodes as its neighbors at any given time. This topology may be slow to change, or more rapid, depending on other factors.

Mutable connectivity is easy to realize in the abstracted network, where although the physical connectivity is fixed, the protocol level of communication connectivity can assume any topology at all as long as abstract connections can be formed between arbitrary member nodes. This factor may have been a major

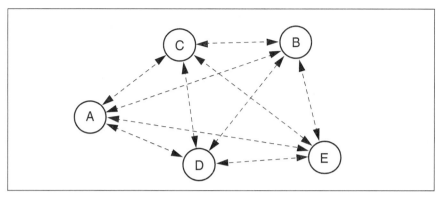

FIGURE **1.2** *Basic p2p connectivity implies each node can connect directly to any other. The number of possible connections increases rapidly with the number of nodes.*

consideration in making the communications field so expansive. Removing the requirements for end-to-end wiring for each connection, as was the case for the telegraph, a whole new kind of infrastructure could be created out of virtual connections. The cost of establishing new connections becomes essentially zero.

In our simple person-to-person network example, there are many possible connections, as shown in Figure 1.2. In general, the number of connections for n nodes is $(n^2-n)/2$. The math shows that possible direct connections increase geometrically as the network grows. When connections are physical, such as in computer networks, it quickly becomes unrealistic to provide for all of them. Instead, we use the concept of addressing and routing over a much smaller finite set of connections, such as seen in Figure 1.3 for the simple model. The full connectivity is then abstracted to some form of protocol layer.

Many topologies are possible for networks. Good design balances between simplicity, many redundant physical paths, avoidance of single points of failure, and given constraints. This subject is revisited later, especially in the context of the different implementations in Part II of this book, because it forms one of the critical factors for issues of scalability, performance, and reliability. Each design must assign priorities and make appropriate trade-offs to become practical and affordable.

It must be noted that for the Internet, any talk of a "direct" connection is a virtual construct only, conceptual rather than factual, because the basis for Internet connectivity is **packet**-switching router technology. Thus, a data stream sent from A to say E is chopped up into many discrete packets, each of which can be sent a physically different route whenever alternative choices exist along the way. The packets are

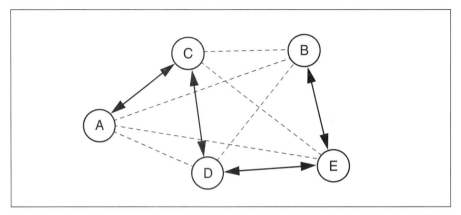

FIGURE 1.3   *In practical networks, direct p2p connectivity is usually consigned to an abstract routing layer, so that the physical connections (solid arrows) can be made much simpler and tractable.*

reassembled in the correct order at the destination, possibly individually requested again and resent if errors are detected or some packets never arrive.

Network Identities

So far, the focus is on physical and addressing connectivity, in a word: *infrastructure*. There is also the issue of addressing even in the simple person-to-person model; we use personal names. Named identities are crucial to conversations. That's probably why names were invented in languages (human-to-human protocol) in the first place, it's easier and more consistent to call someone "Joe", than "you over there by the table" or explicitly specify a coordinate set (x, y, z).

The perceptive reader may realize that **representational** addressing raises the issue of **directory services** to translate between naming and actual location. Internet IP addressing is fine for physical connections that persist. Internet domain addressing is better as a human-readable abstraction to represent such addresses, and it also enables a certain kind of relocation to occur behind the scenes.

However, even with the addition of dynamic Internet services to perform on-the-fly translation based on more transient connectivity, this kind of machine-oriented endpoint addressing is not well suited to the needs of p2p conversations. Keep this in mind, because it crops up again in the outline of different p2p models in Chapter 2.

If "direct" connectivity was all there was to peer networking (as it used to be known), we would be hard pressed to explain the subsequent buzz. However, most things go through cycles as they develop, various characteristics waxing and waning in importance. Only in the full historical context do we understand that some developments came as a reaction to something that happened earlier.

For our purposes, it's therefore useful to briefly discuss some of the historical points in the development of early networks that had peer aspects.

HISTORICAL ANALOGIES

Modern peer technologies owe much to what has gone on before, both directly and indirectly. This slight detour outlines some of the precursor technologies and attendant growth of communication infrastructure.

TELEPHONY

The **analog telephone** was an early extension to direct person-to-person connectivity. In fact, telephony could be considered the first large-scale peer network technology, developed in the dark ages before computers. Although the endpoints were the fixed telephone locations (homes and offices) of the people who wanted to connect, rather than the individuals themselves, most users easily accepted this accessibility limitation, and usage confounded the experts. After all, nobody would ever want to use a telephone to talk to another person. This view caused significant problems for the early advocates to raise capital to build the infrastructure.

At least one early metropolitan telephone network, created in 1893 by Tidvadar Puskás in Budapest, Hungary, was instead initially used as a broadcast system. (Puskás was a colleague to Thomas Edison, who returned to Hungary with broad rights to Edison inventions and with a bold vision to build a new infrastructure.)

In the Budapest system, the central exchange sent a simultaneous ring signal to all subscriber homes. People lifted their handsets or connected external speakers to listen; they didn't speak into the device at all. The exchange instead broadcast official announcements or news, or even live evening concerts—a very early example of what we now call streaming media!

As subscriber call usage later increased, this "talking newspaper" service was made optional and then moved to a separate line. This system is today cited as an early experiment in wire radio broadcasting, but it's seldom mentioned in telephony contexts. It never amounted to more than a passing curiosity, despite the grand visions expressed by Puskás during its early deployment.

The early history of the telephone tells us something important about how people use technology, especially new technology.

> **Bit 1.10 People use technologies to achieve their own goals.**
> The normal application of any given technology will probably arise more from unexpected user innovations, than from any explicit design intentions.

The rapid growth of person-to-person calls was an unexpected side effect of early telephony network growth. It developed spontaneously among users.

Informal ring protocols arose on the early "party line" connections where many devices shared and could listen in on the same line. Just as a central operator could use two signals to indicate that someone in say the Smith household should pick up to receive a call, anyone else on the line could also generate a similar ring pattern to originate a call. Reaching other "local networks" required the assistance of switchboard operators.

Development of automatic switching exchanges and the deployment of multiple virtual-pair lines later made "placing a person to person call" a matter of endpoint connections set up by just dialing a number. A more reliable privacy was also ensured, instead of the loose social convention that others on a shared line shouldn't listen in on "private" calls. New user services needed to be developed, such as subscriber directories, which further enhanced network usefulness to the user.

Early dismissal of telephony technology by the experts and caustic comments by contemporaries notwithstanding, telephones became ubiquitous, even essential, with transparent global direct dialing further contributing to its utility. Now, mobile phones are becoming just as common, and global roaming third-generation (3G) **24/7** Internet mobile connectivity is already being deployed in field trials. We are therefore on the verge of telephony as a true person-to-person network, the connectivity endpoints no longer tied to physical locations but to the bearer, anywhere. A merging of telephony and computer communication into the same device/infrastructure can't help but profoundly affect the future of p2p implementations.

The rapid development of national and global telephone infrastructures is fascinating in its own right, but it's high time to get back to the main purpose of this chapter. The point of this historical summary is to draw conceptual parallels with familiar technology and to point out that the same connectivity infrastructure can be used in different ways. How it is used can determine how future functionality will be enhanced. Virtual-pair switching exchanges and direct dialing ultimately depended on a user demand for more end-to-end direct connectivity. Its availability made the technology attractive for more users and thus drove greater demand. As the number of subscribers increased, so too did the perceived value of the network.

INTERNET INFRASTRUCTURE

In a way similar to telephony usage, the personal use of computer networks (for example, e-mail and chat) grew out of individual efforts to provide the software and protocols for it, frequently at variance with official design and intention.

Interestingly, although the official projects could fail, individual and unofficial experiments sometimes came to overshadow the original intentions. Contrary to popular myth, the precursor computer networks to ARPANET, eventually leading to our Internet, were in fact "failed" projects to share expensive contractor mainframe resources, for example to implement transparent process migration. The usually cited project motivation to create a decentralized, damage tolerant, post-apocalypse command network is nothing more than a retrofit misinterpretation. It probably stems from how the contractors motivated further funding when unintended aspects of the network showed greater promise than the original contract goal.

Functional automatic resource sharing did emerge but only later as an enhancement to an already extensive and global Internet infrastructure—I witnessed one early experiment in 1981. Even then, few could imagine that only a few decades later, a largely academic/corporate network would have turned into a global *public utility* for information transportation. No single entity planned the Internet that way—it just evolved from seemingly unrelated innovations and deployments.

Early connectivity design often relied on and was influenced by the existing telephony network and what had been learned from it. Later design and deployment has been a decentralized process—a curious blend of anarchy and consensus that remains even today. This makes researching the history of the Internet a daunting task, because the descriptions are so dependent on chosen focus and sometimes contradictory sources. Luckily, we need here only touch on a few significant issues relevant to overall development.

Initially, the early machines, large and at fixed locations, simply phoned each other as required to exchange information over modem. Some of these connections soon became permanent over dedicated leased lines. Packet switching later separated physical connectivity details from the logical data transmission layer.

Later developments added network-specific layers of addressing and resource-sharing capabilities. The machines already had local operator chat capabilities, so it wasn't long before "relay" programs were added to allow operators at remote sites to exchange **messages** between sites. When this started to interfere with file exchanging, because the 9600 bps channel bandwidth quickly got saturated by the higher priority chat relay, the new chat capability was deemed important enough that programmers reworked the code to be less obtrusive rather than lose it. In effect, this form of operator-to-operator relayed chat was the first p2p messaging system.

IP Addressing

When the *Internet Protocol* (IP) numbering scheme was designed as a way of addressing resources across the network, it was only natural that it was adapted to the then current shape of the network and its parts. The core of this scheme is a uniquely assigned 32-bit number, commonly written out as four dotted "class" components, as in "A.B.C.D", or "192.168.1.22" to give a typical LAN example.

Historically, these classes did represent the assignment of entire blocks of numbers to subnets with corresponding requirements on how many nodes they needed to support. This kind of wasteful correlation became impossible to sustain as demand for **IP numbers** soon outstripped availability.

Packets of data can be routed to the correct destination in an efficient and decentralized way by assigning address blocks to particular machines that in turn maintain lists of subgroups assigned at that level, and so on, until a list designates individual machines at the next subordinate level. For human ease of use, the Domain Name System (DNS) was added, a hierarchical naming system of Internet domains. Delegation of assigning and tracking name-number relationships within each level's subnet is handled with authoritative DNS servers at that level.

Let us compare telephone and Internet addressing. In Figure 1.4, the schematic diagrams show how a representational name is translated to a physical address in order to achieve direct connectivity.

- Landline telephone connectivity is currently based on subscriber number tied to a location (and local exchange), with added prefixes for region, operator and country. Mobile telephony is tied to either a particular handset or identity chip, not any fixed location. Telephone directory services are available to the subscriber in various forms: printed books, operator assistance, automated databases, and personal lists. It seems likely that future directory services will gain an extra abstraction layer to hide numbers and the functionality to autodial from a representational name. Mobile phones incorporate some of this functionality, translating from local names list to autodial number at the press of a button.

- Internet addressing is currently based on IP numbers that are tied to physical machines. More specifically, an IP number is tied to the machine's **network interface card** (NIC). The *Internet domain namespace* provides an

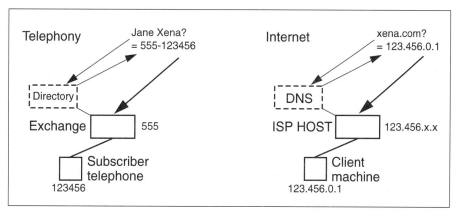

FIGURE 1.4   *Comparing infrastructure, telephony and Internet, with respect to how representational naming is used to address a given endpoint.*

abstract representational model with names that are easier to remember, and DNS servers on the Internet implement the directory service that automatically maps between the two.

Just as names can be reassociated to new telephone numbers, domains can also move to different IP numbers. Because DNS access is integrated with the use of client software, users need normally not concern themselves with the machine-level addressing when they use domain names.

These days, the most any user comes into contact with the "raw" IP numbers is when dealing with a LAN. Historically, certain blocks of the entire A.B.C.D range were reserved for local networks, and routers are (or should be) implemented so that packets addressed to one of these reserved IP numbers is never passed onto the general network. The most well-known IP addresses are 127.0.0.1 (loopback or localhost), 192.168.x.x (the most commonly used LAN range), and 10.x.x.x (used mainly within the networks of large corporations or **ISPs—Internet service providers**).

In person-to-person communication terms, we can note that e-mail addressing is firmly tied to domains, so users who own their own domains have permanent mailbox addresses no matter what their current location or Internet host. Users without their own domains are not so lucky, although knowing the IP of a mailbox server allows one to address an e-mail explicitly to that machine.

It's important for later discussion to note that current Internet domain addressing by definition maps to particular (permanent) resources, in practice host machines at known locations. DNS granularity does not resolve individuals and was never designed to do so. The closest thing to it is the e-mail address, which should be seen as just another resource on some host: a mailbox. Seen mailbox to mailbox, the Internet has long been a p2p network built on the e-mail transport protocol.

> **Bit 1.11 The Internet paradigm is addressing resources, not individuals.**
> Any p2p implementation that targets individual users must currently provide supplementary directory services with finer granularity than DNS.

Although Internet addressing can seem similar to how landline telephony maps numbers to individual households, a host machine with a single IP number might in some ways more resemble a public telephone in a village square. Reliably reaching a particular individual can be difficult. This caveat has had crucial impact on design decisions when implementing individual peer-to-peer technology over the Internet. We examine this topic and the issue of identity in more detail in Chapter 2.

A related constraint is the similarity to landline telephony in the assumption that the addressed is in a fixed location with continuous connectivity.

> **Bit 1.12 Domain addressing assumes static IP and constant connectivity.**
> In most cases, the unavailability of a particular resource on the Internet at any time is considered an "error condition". For most individuals, however, Internet connectivity remains by contrast a transient, exceptional state.

Internet and the Individual

The growth of the number of individuals with intermittent and variable PC connectivity has increasingly made the original addressing model inappropriate to the needs of the majority of Internet users.

The PC revolution, followed by the explosion in home Internet access, had immediate consequences for how connected machines were identified. Static addressing granularity is limited. ISP hosts own fixed IP number blocks and simply can't give all dial-up users their own IP number. Instead, each user is for the duration of a dial-up session allocated a different, dynamic IP number from a smaller, common pool of available numbers—known as **DHCP** allocation.

Therefore, IP addressing doesn't at present correlate reliably with either PC or individual identities—although this situation might change dramatically as the next standard, known as IPv6, is deployed to provide a vastly greater pool of numbers.

Currently, a particular IP number can easily represent many different users at different times, or even many different users at the same time. The former is true for dial-up, the latter for users on a LAN communicating with the Internet through a **gateway** or **firewall** machine. Even though each LAN computer has a unique local identity, all are identified from the Internet as having the same IP number, the public IP of the gateway machine. Multiple, unrelated Web sites with different domains might also share a common IP number, solely by being hosted on the same machine.

In addition, an individual might have several different access options—from home, from work, or on the road—and by extension, different Internet identities. From the *people point of view*—in other words, *usage*—it's the individual identity that's usually the most interesting or important property.

> **Bit 1.13 The p2p focus is mainly on individual or content identity.**
> Any p2p implementation that targets individual users must cope with shared IP, dynamic IP allocation, and erratic or roaming connectivity.

Identity resolution is one reason why p2p technologies hold such great appeal and promise; many of them do track individual identity in spite of the machine-bound granularity of IP addressing and the variable nature of a person's location. Others are designed to track or search for content, also irrespective of location.

This endpoint "delocalization" process is similar to what has already been happening in telephony. From a situation where you knew (or could derive from the number) an exact physical location for the person answering, but not necessarily the identity, phone numbers are today increasingly relocatable to arbitrary locations. In the case of a cell phone number in particular, you almost always know who will answer, but almost never from where—a complete reversal of the first paradigm.

The Internet has less attraction to individual users as a fixed infrastructure (traditional IP addressing) than as an overlay of a virtual infrastructure that is user-centric or content-centric and highly tolerant of arbitrary locality and presence—the p2p model. Some analysts therefore prefer to derive from this context an absolute defining requirement of variable connectivity for determining whether or not a given implementation is truly p2p. However, I believe that such a definition is overly simplistic. It's only a pragmatic reflection of the fact that intermittent connectivity and variable addresses describe how the current majority of p2p nodes connect.

> **Bit 1.14 (Current) p2p treats intermittent variable connectivity as the norm.**
> In effect, this requires reliable and persistent user identification through mechanisms
> other than the current DNS and IP addressing schemes.

This view of p2p wasn't true earlier, albeit many new p2p advocates don't seem
to consider the old technology worthy of the p2p moniker. Furthermore, the context
can change dramatically in the near future, as noted in the previous mention of IPv6,
when for instance 3G mobile connectivity could provide static, individual IP
addressing for any number of devices, irrespective of type, location, or motion—a
permanent mobile identity with a granularity far exceeding any requirements for
simply uniquely identifying individuals.

A new generation of p2p technologies might therefore revert to treating static IP
identities as the norm. Such a change would have a significant impact on many aspects
of p2p implementation in ways that are today considered unrealistic. Just think of the
changes that ubiquitous mobile phones have brought to telephony. Such speculations
properly belong to Part III of this book, however. For now, the focus must remain on
the historical facts in relation to the present.

Infrastructure Centralizes

The increasing load on what became the Internet, the explosive growth of its user base
and the emergence of its new face, the Web, were all factors that drove development
away from the early peer network to a more hierarchical infrastructure.

The resultant trend was towards **client-server** (cS) relationships where the great
majority of users were seen as passive recipients of static, server-stored information.
This trend also applied to e-mail, as mailboxes were centralized away from user
endpoints to main ISP server farms. In addition, it applied to the collectively posted
form of e-mail, newsgroups, a massive p2p network of servers for transport and
storage, where users hold traditional client-to-server sessions to read or post.

Parallel to this divisive trend, a tendency emerged in Internet connectivity to
funnel data transfers up to high-bandwidth (backbone) connections between top-level
servers, further distancing the Internet from its p2p roots. Figure 1.5 illustrates this
tendency as a comparison between simple structures. The recent deployment of
Internet2, a separate higher-capacity backbone network, added a further dimension of
segregation to the basic connectivity structure.

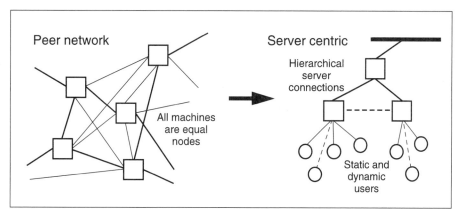

FIGURE 1.5   *Simple comparison of a true peer network (early Internet) to a more server centric model with hierarchical connectivity down to user clients (later Internet, especially the Web).*

Centralization introduces vulnerabilities and risks, or in some cases temptations. It's comparatively easy to corrupt or censor information that resides in well-defined, static locations or that travels predictable routes. Individuals can be tracked and profiles made of what they access, where and when they access it, who they contact, and what they write. Becoming the target of unwanted electronic advertising (spam) is a minor inconvenience compared to the full potential for misuse. It's also easier to disrupt functionality when the system is more centralized.

As always, when structures become more centralized, countering forces arise to promote a return to decentralized structures. In various contexts, this fueled attempts to use the existing Internet connectivity to realize virtual networks that would behave like p2p ones as far as their specific (user) functionality was concerned.

> **Bit 1.15   Internet p2p is a reaction to the server-centric structure.**
>
> Much of the impetus behind various Internet peer technologies can be seen as a reaction away from server-centric content and passive clients, back to free exchange between individual combined client-server nodes in the network.

Protocol Layers

Later discussions refer to "protocol layers". Putting this term in proper context requires at least some understanding of the implied abstraction model.

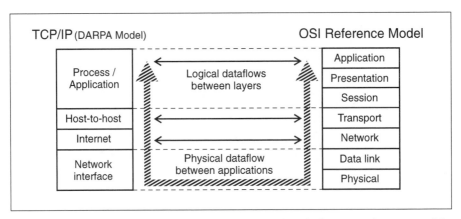

FIGURE 1.6   *Comparing the Internet TCP/IP model with the OSI reference model. While data physically flows between the physical layer, higher level layers logically appear to be directly interconnected.*

As a common base for discussion of networking interfaces, the **Open Systems Interconnect (OSI) reference model** was created. Although rarely used in practical implementations, mainly because of its perceived overkill, the seven-layer OSI model (an ISO standard) is commonly used when discussing other implementations. We might for instance in this light examine the four-layer Internet TCP/IP model, which predates OSI by many years and was originally known as the "DARPA model" after the US government agency that initially developed TCP/IP.

Comparing the TCP/IP and OSI models schematically, Figure 1.6 shows their relationship. Each layer defines a particular structure in the data flow. Physically, the network sees only bits flowing by, which is handled at the lowest level of protocol, the framed packets of data of a standard size that the network interface sends and receives. At this level, packets are packets, whatever they contain.

The next higher level is the network level, which defines the protocol used to handle the packets—for example, TCP/IP in the Internet. One can therefore see a virtual connection between the transport layers on either end of a communication and discuss how the devices communicate without needing to look at details of how packets are framed and sent. Above this, yet often considered in the same context, is the Internet host level, the transport layer that applications must communicate with in order to talk to other machines.

The top of the Internet stack is the application and process layer, which is the program code that wishes to connect and communicate over the network. Layer abstraction means that the application needs to know only about the program interface (API) to the transport layer, not the specifics of protocol or hardware.

This design approach all allows easy exchange of components at any level. One can recognize the same abstraction levels in the Windows network model, where the user configures the bindings (interfaces) by installing a NIC, a protocol, and a client, which represent none other than the three main layers of the model.

POWER TO THE PEOPLE

The "new" p2p technology is for many as much a "political" statement as a technological one. Perhaps this explains some of the buzz—it's a revolution of sorts.

> **Bit 1.16 P2P is about distributed ownership of resources.**
> Characteristic for current p2p networks is that the computing resources (PCs) are owned and managed by the users.

The issue has several aspects. At its most trivial level, any one entity bears few centralized investments and administrative costs. Even server-mediated solutions can be deployed with modest means, as numerous startups have shown. As nodes connect to the network, offering their resources, a computing entity on a larger scale emerges. This building of distributed supercomputers on a shoestring has been used to great effect with various distributed computing (DP) projects, although I hesitate to accept some of these shared resource and distributed processing implementations as valid examples of p2p technology (I'll explain why in Chapter 2).

On the other hand, corporate entities have made use of distributed PCs for various kinds of p2p solutions to allow local employee groups to actively retain and maintain resources, yet provide global access without the need for new central servers and storage. The bottom line here is better resource quality at a lower cost.

In the corporate world, control ultimately rests with the boss. For the public at large, control rests with the individual—at least that's the view of many.

> **Bit 1.17 P2P is about distributed control of resources.**
> The fact that the data and resources are controlled by the users is characteristic of and is the motivation for many current p2p networks.

A strong element of anarchy and "total freedom" characterizes p2p usage, not infrequently with considerable disregard for the commercial values of "ownership" and content control. This view largely fueled the Napster phenomenon: the *free* exchange of music tracks that otherwise everyone would have had to buy bundled on CD. The distributed control in p2p meant that it was exceedingly difficult for the commercial interests to stop the, as they saw it, illegal copying. The legal and moral issue is more complex than it might appear, and we deal with this in Chapter 4.

Related to this issue is the stance taken by, for example, Free Haven and Freenet, two p2p models that primarily intend to ensure that resources such as files or Web content are protected against censorship and forced site closure. Encrypted and distributed across a p2p network of independently managed nodes, the material becomes as persistent as the network itself.

> **Bit 1.18 P2P is often about persistent storage of content.**
> The fact that data and resources are controlled by the users, not censurable by any external authority, is characteristic of and motivation for many current p2p networks.

VIRTUAL P2P

Using existing Internet connectivity as a base for deploying a virtual p2p network leverages the reach and capabilities of the implementation enormously. To join such a network only requires the proper software and Internet access from anywhere.

It's interesting to note that e-mail was the "killer application" for the early Internet, which in its extended form includes newsgroups and mailing lists. The popularity of e-mail confirms the assumption that what people always want to do, whatever the technology, is communicate with each other. A major reason it became so popular is because the e-mail transport mechanism and domain addressing means that a sender needs to know only a person's permanent identity in order to contact that person—location doesn't matter.

Whether e-mail should still be considered p2p *technology* is an open question. Like a number of activities, it has a person-to-person appearance, whatever the technical infrastructure, but the actual implementations can vary greatly. For most people these days, their mailbox is not the endpoint of the connection. In the same way, much so-called p2p functionality can be implemented in different ways, with a varying amount of actual p2p technology and using different architecture models.

Few people today maintain 24/7 connectivity and run their own e-mail servers (although this is a p2p architectural possibility) but instead rely on the prevailing ISP and server-centric implementations. Most users can therefore retrieve or send mail only through their ISP mail servers, and they are often constrained to using ISP Internet access lines to do this—perhaps even "hard-wired" from home due to cable or other location-specific connectivity. For them, e-mail fails to be p2p technology, because of the indirectness of the transport and the reliance on remote server-hosted accounts to receive, process, and store content.

But this perspective is subject to change as the technology and architecture changes. Recall the telephony analogy for a moment; phone booth to phone booth between town squares, compared to individual roaming cellular handsets. The same individuals might be talking to one another in either case, but current cellular technology is more akin to what we'd care to call "p2p".

In any case, it's the experienced totality of the virtual connectivity model that determines the characteristic signature of the technology. The possible virtual models can be vastly different, yet use the exact same underlying physical transport infrastructure. Changing connectivity model is as easy as swapping out the software at the endpoints and can at least in theory be transparently moved across to different physical network technologies: standard phone lines, integrated digital service networks (**ISDN**) or digital subscriber lines (**DSL**), cable, wireless, satellite, optical fiber, power lines, and so on. The perceived network and its protocols don't change, only the packet transport medium.

Original Chat and IM

The first widespread virtual p2p technology to hit the Internet was *chat*, which is a method of establishing a typed conversation between two or more users in real-time. A natural evolution of the operator-to-operator chat relay mentioned earlier, this chat includes any Internet-connected PC in a client-server connectivity model.

Internet Relay Chat (IRC) evolved into server-mediated private or public virtual chatrooms, moderated or unmoderated, where many can converse at once. Thus it lost much of the original person-to-person aspect. Chatrooms are implemented by creating multiway connections from a hosting server and relaying any input to all clients participating on a named "channel" (a convention that allows IRC servers to selectively forward or not forward messages for different groups).

The original p2p functionality moved on into another technology, what is now called IM, although chat and IM modes are often combined in the same client software to the confusion of some due to the imprecise usage of the term "chat". From the multiperson discussions, people can pair off for private chats or shift to an alternate technology IM connection.

Server mediation in either technology provides the transport protocol details that at least in theory allow two clients to establish a direct connection and participate in a private conversation. As shown in Chapter 6, however, some IM implementations retain the IRC characteristic of relaying messages through the mediating server, even for private conversations that are perceived as being p2p-connected. Despite this confusion, I have arbitrarily drawn the defining p2p line between IRC and IM—only the IM implementations are considered in any detail in this book.

Today's chat and IM are perceived as p2p in the same way conversations on the telephone are, people talking to people—distinguishable in the strict p2p sense much as a rural-line, marketplace phone might be to personal cellular. The convenience of chat is significant to people who are nearby their computers, have an active (24/7) Internet connection and wish to exchange some quick words with someone. In addition, the social dimension that has grown up around chat is significant.

Chat technology resolves the individual addressing issue by maintaining a centralized directory to correlate a registered user identity with current online Internet address. This directory is automatically updated by the client software whenever the user connects to the Internet. Client update additionally resolves the issue of tracking user availability (actual and user-selectable) for messaging, notification, and other features particular to a given implementation.

IRC identity is essentially based on current IP and an arbitrary user "nick" (nickname or handle) that can be changed at whim as long as it is unique to a particular chatroom context. The main focus is on informal multiway conversations, not any lasting permanent network identity spanning different sessions. By contrast, the IM model relies on each user having a server-registered identity that persists across sessions, possibly supplemented with an arbitrary and visible handle chosen by the user. Chapter 6 examines a few IM implementations in detail, showing how their version of p2p works.

A probable convergence of text and voice messaging is on the horizon, as chat and IM merge with Small Message Service (SMS) in the next generation of 3G mobile services. Such a development is bound to have significant consequences for how people hold conversations, and we might well see a large-scale shift in some contexts from telephony to chat. Such a shift might critically depend on what kind of mobile user interfaces are designed for the devices—phone convenience aside, the typical cellular user interface is not pleasant to use for typing much of anything.

Peer
Architectures

With a clearer grasp of what the p2p concept means, we can now take on the task of classifying peer architectures. This analysis is fairly abstract and non-specific, at least to begin with, because any subsequent discussions of specific technologies and **implementations** must build on a common groundwork.

As a first step, we must define the fundamental terms and the basic p2p models. Including a summary of primary characteristics in this overview proves useful when comparing the functionality of different technologies, and also when we look in Part III at the future development of p2p applications.

We also need to discuss **protocols**, the "glue" that holds networks together. Later chapters dissect particular protocols in considerable detail, so this discussion is not made dependent on any particular implementation. It provides a familiar context in which to place the later specifics. In addition, it can serve as a map to help identify any omissions or simplifications in the protocol design of a particular implementation, which could otherwise be obscured in the mass of technical detail.

Finally, because the focus of the book is mainly from the **end user** perspective, and thus on application implementations where the p2p software is entirely or mostly administered by the user, this chapter is the appropriate place to summarize some of the peer implementations that aren't covered in other chapters. The final section therefore mentions a selection of common peer networking technologies native to different operating systems. These technologies often form the underlying transport layer in host systems that application p2p implementations depend on, yet transcend with their own protocols.

CHAPTER 2 AT A GLANCE

This chapter introduces the architectural models and fundamental terms used in peer-to-peer networking.

From Model to Reality starts with a summary of the conceptual models for p2p, before delving further into detailed terms.

- The *Protocol Types* section analyzes the basics of protocol to introduce some terms and concepts used later to describe particular implementations. *Network Purpose* adds a perspective often overlooked, that of suitability to a particular purpose.

Architectural Models provides an overview of the main types of p2p technologies based on their architecture.

- The models covered are *Atomistic P2P*, *User-Centric P2P* and *Data-Centric P2P*. The *Leveraged P2P* section discusses how distributed implementations might incorporate and blend aspects from these p2p models to improve functionality and performance.

Specific Architectures is mainly a background to Part II and gives an overview of some p2p possibilities not included elsewhere in this book.

- *Native Networking* describes common solutions already built into operating systems, while *Other Application Groups* zips through some p2p and p2p-related technologies not covered elsewhere.

FROM MODEL TO REALITY

First of all, let's summarize into a concise structure the conceptual models of p2p that were introduced in the historical overview in Chapter 1.

Of the many possible ways to structure the information about different conceptual models for information exchange using computers, Table 2.1 takes the perspective of client-server analysis. All the main client-server models are included to give context, while the shaded section in the middle of the table encompasses the established and accepted p2p architectures discussed in this book.

As used in the table, the term "index" means collections of logical links to distributed resources or data, while "directory" refers to collections of logical links to users. Not all applications or networks make this distinction between the two terms and services, but it is a useful one. In either case, this logical addressing is usually independent of the underlying addressing scheme for the network (for instance, the Internet). The latter just functions as a transport layer for the specific p2p protocols.

Although distributed resource sharing, or what might be called the computation-centric model, is often included as a p2p technology, its exchange model actually says nothing about the presence of any p2p architecture. A distributed computation-centric implementation might indeed include p2p characteristics from any of the table's preceding three p2p models, likely data-centric. Quite often, however, node communication is only with the central server that owns the data and distributes the tasks. Next-generation Web or a fully deployed .NET infrastructure, both still in the future, might also include many aspects of p2p but are unlikely as a whole to build on any one p2p architectural model.

> **Bit 2.1   Sharing distributed resources doesn't necessarily make it p2p.**
> The defining issues should instead be how these resources or network nodes communicate, and who owns and controls both them and the data.

The Table 2.1 summary also gives a chronological overview of popular trends in communication modes, even though the actual development and use of each listed technology is nowhere as linear and simple as the popularized "paradigm shifts" would suggest. In the earliest **dumb-terminal systems**, for example, the mainframe servers could be interconnected in an atomistic p2p model, refuting the impression that this model came later. Yet it's still true that the PC p2p model did.

TABLE 2.1 *Conceptual models for information exchange*

Conceptual model	Client-side	Server-side
Centralized processing (or "dumb terminal systems")	Display on many (local) dumb clients (terminals)	Data storage, processing, indexing, policies on one server "mainframe"
Client-server (such as corporate NT domain networks)	Processing and display on many smart clients (such as LAN PCs)	Data storage, processing, indexing, policies on one main server
Web server and browser (current paradigm)	Limited processing, display on many clients on WAN or Internet	Data storage and limited processing on many (distributed) servers
Atomistic P2P	**Peer-to-peer models:** The client-server distinction blurs in all these peer models. Data storage, processing, and display on many peers.	No separate servers
User-centric P2P		Directory services on one or few servers
Data-centric P2P		Indexing services on one or few servers
Computation-centric or distributed process	Processing on many distributed clients	Administration, storage, indexing, and display on one or few servers
Next-generation Web (and perhaps .NET)	Data, processing, co-authoring, and display on many clients	Many kinds of distributed services on many servers

The original vision of the World Wide Web by its "creator" Tim Berners-Lee and others was a predominantly data-centric p2p one—a globally hyperlinked content space where no single server had precedence over any other. This vision implied extensive co-authoring and open collaboration by all users. However, much to the disappointment of the first visionaries, the Web instead evolved to have overwhelmingly static and server-centric content, locked to the visitors. There came to be few actual content providers compared to the many users. With users constrained to the role of passive consumers, and little peer communication between them, functionality development of Web browsers focused mainly on snazzy presentation features, not user utility, nor for that matter many of the more basic navigational and collaborative improvements proposed from the very start.

Nevertheless, the importance and use of open p2p models has returned on a new level, user-to-user rather than machine-to-machine, making the developmental chronology implied by the previous table reasonably accurate in that sense.

Protocol Types

Protocol forms the "glue" that holds a network together by defining how nodes communicate with each other to achieve network functionality. We therefore need to examine the terms and concepts that are later used to describe how particular implementations function.

Protocols are specified at many different levels, but we can define some common characteristics concerning how a protocol is implemented. For example, we can consider the kind of *modality focus* of the communication:

- **Message-based** protocol, where the focus is on sending and receiving discrete, packaged and addressed messages. How the messages are carried between two parties is delegated to an autonomous agent, which is like a conversation with messages exchanged by courier, carrier pigeon, or mail.

- **Connection-based** protocol, where the focus is on establishing connections over which messages can be sent. This situation is more like a telephone conversation, where a dial-up connection allows "raw" messages (unpackaged and unaddressed) to be exchanged in real time.

Another, related aspect is the *relative timing* of messages:

- **Asynchronous** conversation, in which one side need not wait for the other side's response before sending another message.

- **Synchronous** conversation, where explicit or implicit dependencies exist between a message and its response. Additionally, there are often internal timing constraints between parts of the same message.

A third aspect is *state*, as applied to the network used for message transport:

- **Stateless** network, which treats all messages the same with no reference to previous messages. The same message will be processed and interpreted the same way every time it is sent.

- **State-aware** network, which exhibits dependencies. Processing one message can influence how a future message will be handled. Memory of past events is preserved—the same message can give different results at different times.

The current Internet TCP/IP connectivity model is connection-based, asynchronous, and inherently stateless. However, many message-based Internet applications introduce various *ad hoc* mechanisms and protocols to track state.

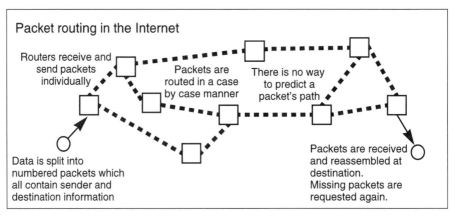

Packet routing in the Internet

Routers receive and send packets individually

Packets are routed in a case by case manner

There is no way to predict a packet's path

Data is split into numbered packets which all contain sender and destination information

Packets are received and reassembled at destination. Missing packets are requested again.

FIGURE 2.1 *Simple illustration of how data transfer between Internet routers is accomplished by asynchronous forwarding of individual packets along whatever path each router at that moment deems suitable*

Constraints of Internet Transport

Internet messages are packaged, addressed, and sent as a number of **packets** determined by underlying transport layers. The packets are routed by independent routers with locally determined priorities and paths. The "sockets" one sometimes sees reference to are logical abstractions of virtual endpoint connections between, for example, server and client, but have no correlation with how messages really travel between them. Figure 2.1 is a simple illustration of that concept.

There is little concern at higher or application levels for how the data transfer is accomplished. The requirement is only that all packets are received within a "reasonable" time, or can be requested again if missing so that the message can ultimately be reconstructed. Hence TCP/IP is characterized as a **reliable transport,** in that it implements handshaking to track and acknowledge packets received.

This pervasive and asynchronous nature of **packet transport** is not a problem unless dealing with various forms of "streaming" content, where packets must be received in a particular order. The severe timing constraints of "real-time" content mean that any missing packets can't easily be requested again. Generally speaking, implementing streaming media over the Internet requires both an acceptance of a buffering delay at the receiver and some tolerance for missing packets. Therefore, streaming connections rely on **UDP** (User Datagram Protocol) as transport, which doesn't try to guarantee packet reception in return for less overhead to manage.

Internet-based p2p applications must usually accept at least the constraint of the asynchronous and stateless nature of the underlying TCP/IP packet routing. They must also build on the current IP addressing model, even if they subsequently construct other directory services with different scope and resolution.

Conversational Modes

The current Internet paradigm, especially the Web, has for some time been predominantly unidirectional in its information flow—from content server to consumer client. This aspect has hampered the development of support at all levels for arbitrary *conversations*.

In the strict sense, most current Internet applications don't easily support real conversations, only requests for predetermined, static content at some more or less permanent address on the network. This is reflected in, for example, Web browser design, which for the sake of efficiency caches content locally but can have problems dealing with sites that generate dynamic content.

That's not to say it's impossible, or even necessarily hard, to support flexible conversations in the existing protocols—p2p applications are a case in point—only that the majority of deployed Internet applications tend to be very rigid and limited in this respect, or to ignore the conversational aspect altogether.

> **Bit 2.2   P2P innately supports natural, bidirectional conversational modes.**
> You could use this criterion as a quick litmus test to determine whether a particular technology lived up to its **market meme** of being p2p.

It's mainly for this reason that the deployment of *application talking to application* is still rare and limited in its scope. The vision of autonomous agents deployed to roam the Web, capable of gathering and filtering information according to rules relevant to the interests defined by the user, has long been a compelling one, yet remains largely unfulfilled. To achieve this, not only must bidirectional conversations be a natural mode in the infrastructure protocols, but the information must be accessible in a common structure or metastructure, and the various agents and servers fully interoperable.

Next-generation Web applications do promise a far greater degree of bidirectional conversation support, partly because of proposed extensions to the underlying Web transport protocols, and partly because of a whole range of services geared to distributed authoring and management of content, as exemplified by **DAV** (Distributed Authoring and Versioning). The other part of the equation is that newer content protocols such as eXtensible Markup Language (XML) are designed to meet the linked requirements of common structure, configurable functionality, and ease of extensibility for particular, perhaps unforeseen needs.

Until then, various protocol overlays in the form of existing p2p technologies allow users to retrofit at least some functionality that easily and transparently can support real conversations between nodes in all modes. Some of this is evident in the discussions of architecture models later in this chapter, and in Part II where practical implementations are examined in detail.

Protocols and infrastructure are only one part of the story. The technology must also have an aim, a reason for its design that manifests in the implementation.

NETWORK PURPOSE

Each implementation of a p2p network has a stated purpose or intent at some level. Usually, this implicit or explicit goal was made early in the design process and so to a great extent determines both just how and for what you can use it.

A given implementation might be admirable in many critical aspects, yet unsuited to the purpose you intend. Many current p2p architectures are relatively specialized. Some focus areas for current p2p implementations include

- Messaging
- File sharing and data sharing
- Content publishing
- Content retrieval (including search and distribution)
- Distributed storage
- Distributed network services
- Distributed processing (and presentation)
- Decentralized collaboration
- Content management/control
- General resource sharing

In addition, the prospective user must evaluate the impact of specific design decisions concerning scalability, **security**, reliability, storage model, and so on.

Actor Conversations

The network purpose also includes the dimension of **actors**, and it is common (and natural) to use the idiom of "conversation" when describing network interactions between peers. Looking at this idiom, we can more clearly see some useful ways of talking about the process of communicating over a p2p network, and some of the essential components of such architecture.

We see three communication situations in p2p network conversations.

- Person to person (P-P)

- Person to application (P-A)

- Application to application (A-A)

Peer applications such as messaging are of P-P type, while file-sharing nodes that automatically fulfill typed-in requests by remote users are basically P-A. Both P-A and A-A will likely grow in importance as we get better at designing automata that can interface with people in "normal" conversational contexts, and with each other to manage routine transactions for particular content or services on the network.

We've seen the same trend in telephony P-A, especially recently in the maturing field of advanced voice recognition services, where human operators are rapidly vanishing and becoming only instances of last resort for fulfilling user requests. Web-based customer care centers have also seen rapid deployment as cost-saving ways to allow customers to fulfill their own requests and manage their own accounts. Online Internet booking, shopping, and banking are other P-A technologies that have seen significant investments and deployment, albeit occasionally with mixed results. Online government, so far usually in the somewhat limited sense of requesting information, retrieving forms, and filing tax returns, is yet another P-A area.

Bit 2.3   A-A conversational modes are the next emergent technology.
Except in very limited or rare cases, there are few examples yet of automated agency that can interact with other agents to fulfill more complex user-delegated tasks.

It's been stated, probably correctly, that *the real transformation of the Internet will occur first when A-A conversations become commonplace*. This transformation would be at least as great a shift in communication patterns as when telephony (and especially cellular phones), e-mail, or instant messaging became popular.

Extensive use of A-A would probably imply an equally extensive deployment of P-A, where people communicate with the local client interfaces to the user applications implementing the delegated user authority—see the following section.

Anyone interested in seeing where both P-A and A-A implementations of p2p might lead should look more closely at the open, overtly protocol-based implementations discussed later in Part II, and at the speculations in Part III.

Properties and Components

Looking at conversation properties in general lets us identify some essential p2p properties and components more clearly. Defining these basic terms is important for later discussions.

- **Identity.** This property simply serves to uniquely identify any user, client, service, or resource, and is fundamental to any p2p context. The practical implementation of a network's identity namespace critically determines or limits the scope of application of the p2p network. Another critical identity issue deals with identifying and tracking individual messages.

- **Presence.** As a property, presence defines the arbitrary coming and going of actors in a dynamic conversation. As a component, it represents the mechanism by which users, applications, services, or resources can manage and communicate information about their current state. Note that "presence" can go beyond the simple state model to convey all manner of context-specific information for a particular conversation.

- **Roster.** One most often identifies roster as a list of frequently contacted identities. The corresponding component provides short-list entry points into a chosen peer community but is often underestimated in terms of its potential automation utility to the user—see "agency". In particular, applications and services can make use of a roster to intelligently share resources, filter conversations, and determine appropriate levels of trust automatically, without the user's constant attention and intervention.

- **Agency.** With relationships to both identity and roster, agency defines the ability for an application to act as an autonomous client. This can mean initiating, managing, coordinating, and filtering conversations that the user would be interested in or has set up rules for—e-mail filtering rule sets are but a simple precursor to agency. In some cases, the agent might act with vested formal authority on behalf of the user, probably leveraged with one or another form of digital signature or certificate.

- **Browsing.** As yet comparatively rare in p2p implementations, the ability to browse available peers, services, applications, resources, and relationships is an important but underrated feature that is only marginally supported in the current paradigm of searching the network or central user/resource database. We find its best known implementation in the form of the browser built into Microsoft Network Neighborhood.

- **Architecture.** In this context, architecture mainly denotes how messages are managed and passed between endpoints in a conversation. One dimension for describing this term is to locate the process somewhere on the scale of client-server to atomistic peer. Another is degree of distribution of services and storage. The relevance of any description depends on the p2p context.

- **Protocol.** Current p2p implementations rest on the packet protocol layer of TCP/IP, sometimes UDP/IP, overlaid with more sophisticated application and session protocols to create the virtual network that defines a particular implementation space. Ideally, the implementation should be fairly agnostic about this layering process and be able to transparently translate across different protocols as required.

This list of components is used in the later implementation chapters in Part II to provide a baseline table for a summary comparison between the different implementation architectures.

Although neither exhaustive nor the only way to examine functionality, these items are a useful way to highlight significant differences between implementations. Maintaining a focus on these primary characteristics helps a user evaluate critical features and discount non-essentials in a given implementation's feature list.

The relative importance of each characteristic is largely dependent on intended purpose and scope of the application, but some general conclusions are still possible. One is the overall importance of *identity*. This might seem trivial—surely you need some form of identity to communicate—yet some implementations totally lack any concept of user identity. In such cases, the implementation works because the purpose doesn't require any defined identity. Others allow arbitrary, even multiple, user-selectable names that are unique only within a particular context.

Even with a well-defined identity, the question remains as to what exactly that identity is tied to—message, person, role, digital signature, software, computer component—each has advantages in certain contexts, and clear limitations in others, particularly in the degree of addressability, security, or portability each offers.

Another conclusion is that some characteristics, such as *presence*, are often undervalued in p2p designs. This view applies even to basic online status, let alone to more advanced concepts of presence which might be applicable to a wider context involving autonomous agencies acting on the behalf of a user.

> **Bit 2.4   Presence is a crucial issue in human-usable p2p applications.**
> Qualitatively speaking, human users find a well-supported implementation of simple presence as *the single most valuable and useful feature* in a p2p client.

Autonomous *agency* remains very much in the realm of speculation and vision, but is an enticing goal in the face of the ever-mounting floods of unfiltered and unsorted information that confront a human user on the Internet or at work. Such prospects are dealt with in more detail in Part III.

We next examine the primary architecture models of p2p.

ARCHITECTURAL MODELS

The three architectural models for p2p considered here are

- Atomistic

- User-centric

- Data-centric

The last two are similar in that they usually rely on centralized servers to mediate connectivity based on directories of users or resources and data.

Each model is examined to show its main and distinctive characteristics.

ATOMISTIC P2P

In the atomistic model (AP2P), all nodes are equally server and client. There is no central administration or connection arbiter, although such might be implemented as distributed services within the network. For purists, this model is the original and only "true" p2p architecture.

Each node in the atomistic model is autonomous and fully manages its own resources and connectivity. Figure 2.2 shows the schematic connectivity model.

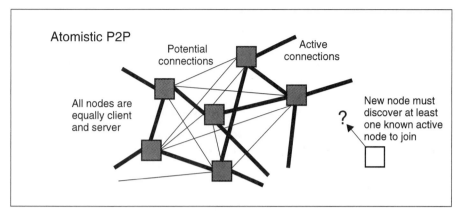

FIGURE 2.2   *An atomistic p2p network is constructed from an arbitrary number of nodes. Each typically maintains contact with several others, although virtual direct connectivity can be established between any two.*

The atomistic model contains a fundamental bootstrap problem: *how to join.* The prospective member must somehow first determine which other nodes in the network it can establish connections with. Without a central server, no easy way of determining resource or user availability is apparent in advance.

Two traditional answers are seen to this peer-discovery situation:

• Use a broadcast protocol to send a query to join and await a response.

• Attempt to connect to suitable "known" node addresses that will either accept new nodes or provide further node addresses to try.

When the client has physical connectivity to the p2p network infrastructure, for example in a LAN, it's feasible to use the broadcast method, effectively calling into the dark, "Hello, I'm here. Who's available out there?" The implemented protocol determines how this message is framed to be detected by other client nodes and how these nodes should respond. The query can be a request to join a designated *group.*

Multiplayer games often use this method to establish gaming sessions over a local network. *Ad hoc* sessions are created when several clients detect each other on the basis of broadcast messages plus a matching selection of game, scenario, and other criteria. In these cases, one system becomes the host server for the session.

While broadcast methods can sometimes be used on a larger, general network such as the Internet, the likelihood of successfully reaching active p2p nodes is then much smaller. More practical is to probe known addresses or address blocks for responding clients. The new client can attempt to connect directly to known addresses and through one such node create a response list of other nodes. Alternatively, it can first connect to a published "service provider" node that maintains dynamic lists of active nodes within their horizon. The client downloads this list and proceeds to work through it, attempting to establish a predetermined number of connections.

> **Bit 2.5   Up-to-date nodelists are a valuable resource in AP2P.**
> Considerable effort can be invested in atomistic networks to compile and distribute suitable and updated "seed" lists for new nodes, even using external channels.

Once a successful connection is established to at least one node, a client (or other software) can listen to messages passing through the network and build its own list of active nodes for later connection attempts. Furthermore, if the client is configured to accept incoming connections, the user might find that much of the subsequent connectivity is maintained by "incoming" requests from other nodes.

While the formal lack of central administration in AP2P can cause a significant and frustrating threshold to joining the network, it also means that the network is essentially self-maintaining and resilient within the bounds of its capacity. AP2P is therefore the preferred architecture for systems that wish to ensure maximum availability and persistence of distributed data, despite the acknowledged vulnerability in the common practice of distributing nodelists externally.

One or more trusted nodes (or Web sites, or IRC channels) with guaranteed access might in some networks be effectively declared a service provider, mainly to alleviate peer discovery. A fixed address, perhaps of last resort, is then often part of the client distribution and available at first start-up. The fundamental all-nodes-are-equal paradigm is essentially unchanged, except with regard to node discovery.

Lately, some Internet p2p networks are for various reasons moving towards an extension of the service provider concept: a formal two-tier variation of the atomistic model. Particular nodes are then elevated to "super-peer" status because of their proven capacity, connectivity, and reliability. This process is made easier by automatic history and reputation tracking. Reliable or trusted super-nodes can act as list repositories, primary connection nodes, and sometimes search hubs. They provide a sort of backbone network in much the same way that backbone servers came to do for the Internet in general.

Later implementation chapters detail some of the discovery strategies in relation to the specific design goals and security concerns in each case.

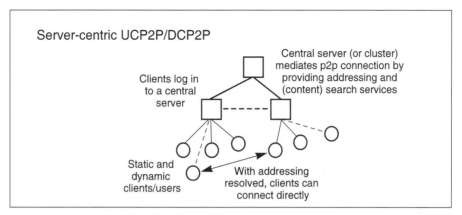

FIGURE 2.3   *Simple illustration of either user-centric or data-centric p2p. Even though clients usually connect using the traditional infrastructure, the user sees a different, peer-oriented namespace with new services unavailable in the underlying physical network.*

USER-CENTRIC P2P

The user-centric p2p (UCP2P) model adds to the basic atomistic one a form of central server mediation. In its simplest form, the server component adds a *directory* based on (usually permanent) unique user identity to simplify how nodes can find each other. Identities tied to client or other entities are also possible, if sometimes less intuitive. Strictly speaking, one should probably refer to "*directory-centric*" for proper scope, but the term "user-centric" is the one most commonly used.

The directory provides persistent logical links that uniquely (and possibly within a specific context) identify each node, and a translation mechanism to enable direct connection by the user over the underlying network infrastructure. In an Internet context, this translates to the current IP numbers corresponding to the registered and available active nodes. Figure 2.3 shows a simple geometry of this model. In reality, the ongoing direct connections between individual clients would be a much richer web-like structure than this figure suggests.

Clients register with the directory service to announce their availability to the network. Some form of periodic update to this status is tracked so that the server knows when a node is no longer available—either "pings" sent from the client at regular intervals, which is sometimes referred to as its "heartbeat", or responses to service queries. Users might select a specific *transponder* status such as "busy" or "extended away" that will be reported to the server, thereby distinguishing between simple node availability and a more nuanced user-selected availability.

A user can scan/search the directory for other users who meet particular criteria, and from the listing they can determine the current connection address. With a known address, the user can then establish a direct client-to-client connection. The target node registered itself as active and known to be online, so it usually responds right away. Depending on the scope of the server mediation, the connection with the directory server might remain, either to exchange supplementary information or to track current p2p transfer status.

User-centric p2p has proven to be the most popular architecture. The most publicized implementation is surely Napster file sharing. This popularity is despite the fact that the UCP2P model has a far greater deployment in the older instant messaging technologies: Miribilis ICQ ("I seek you", now owned by AOL), AOL Instant Messaging (AIM), and MSN Messenger, to name the best known. Napster as a public representative of UCP2P is doubly ironic, because the primary interest of the users in the system is not to find users, but to find particular *content* on some remote computer. One would therefore have expected an explicitly data-centric focus, where the MP3-tracks constitute the permanent index of content—after all, to all practical intents, users are mutually anonymous in the system, often away, and their identities (which are arbitrarily user-chosen at sign-up) need not be tracked at all. On the other hand, UCP2P makes the current transition attempts from a free service to a registered subscriber service much easier from the technical point of view.

One issue of concern with UCP2P networks is this reliance on central directories, which introduces specific vulnerabilities and raises privacy issues. A user directory can track user behavior and generate personal profiles. Such profiles can be worth considerable sums of money to the compiler if sold to advertisers. They also invoke the specter of user monitoring by various overt or covert agencies.

If we take the example of instant messaging, these solutions also illustrate another downside of centralized server solutions: closed, proprietary standards deliberately kept incompatible by the companies that control them. Independent services like Jabber attempt to work around the barriers by providing modular support for the different standards and so allow users access from a single client. It remains to be seen whether this strategy will become more than just experimental.

Ownership and control of directory services is perceived as increasingly important in the business community the larger the aggregate UCP2P user base grows. This conjecture is proven by how Napster clones were bought up by commercial interests even as they were being closed down for alleged music piracy.

All these issues are discussed later in more detail in both the general (Chapter 4) and the application-particular (Chapter 6) contexts.

Data-Centric P2P

Data-centric p2p (DCP2P) is very similar to the user-centric model, and it can thus be illustrated by the same figure used earlier (Figure 2.3). The distinction made in DCP2P is that the central server maintains an index over available resources, not individual users. The index is a collection of logical links that map the resources to registered nodes in the same way that UCP2P maps identified users.

Again, the term should really be "index-centric" or "resource-centric", but prevailing usage prefers "data-centric". However, just as a UCP2P directory can indirectly access content (think Napster), it's possible to indirectly access individuals from a properly structured DCP2P resource index. In this respect at least, UCP2P and DCP2P can be seen as interchangeable and the choice somewhat arbitrary.

When clients register with the DCP2P server, they mainly provide a list of currently available resources on that node. Although this is usually assumed to be data content of one kind or another—that is, files or documents—nothing requires it must be. Resources can include more abstract entities, such as client-managed services, storage, gateway interfaces, and other intangibles.

Users can in DCP2P architecture search for and access data (or content) held on other nodes. With data in primary focus, it's understandable that different forms of content management solutions turn mainly to DCP2P. It is the area of greatest excitement and promise for p2p in business, as opposed to private use.

Access in DCP2P tends to be more governed by rules than in UCP2P, especially in corporate contexts. Not everyone is allowed to access everything, at any time. Exclusion/admittance policy requires more "intelligence" in server index and client management, so this kind of architecture is still very much under development, targeting enterprise solutions. Furthermore, security issues are paramount because of the deep access into registered nodes—both in terms of data and functionality, and the often sensitive nature of the content.

Leveraged P2P

When dealing with the last two entries in Table 2.1, computation-centric and next-generation Web models, I would like to use the term "leveraged p2p" (LP2P), insofar as such implementations are to be considered in purely peer-to-peer contexts. Each can be combined with the other, and also with elements from the previous three p2p architectures. They might also be fully incorporated into these respective p2p contexts to achieve synergies that can dramatically improve network performance. However, it didn't feel appropriate to include deeper discussions of these models in this book.

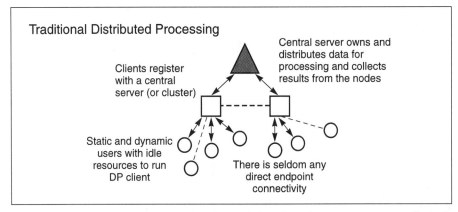

FIGURE 2.4 *Simple illustration of traditional distributed processing. Typically little or no communication occurs between nodes. Data is owned by the central server(s), and tasks are sent out to nodes that sent back results.*

Take for example distributed processing. Traditional DP implementations tend to be highly server-centric, as shown in Figure 2.4, because the primary interest has been for a single owner of large amounts of raw data to process it using distributed and otherwise idle resources. Owners of idle capacity, say a PC on a network, install client software and register with the server. They then let the client autonomously request and process data for the server owner, but generally have no insight or control of the process, or the data. The best known example is the SETI@home Project, which tries to analyze the vast reams of data available from radio telescopes in order to detect evidence of intelligent life in the universe.

The thorny issue of data ownership and potential rights to processed results in a public DP setting arose with a comparable distributed effort to identify genes in human DNA. Ostentatiously hosted by a university for cancer research, any results gleaned turned out to be patentable and exclusively owned by a private company. When this fact was made public, many users left that DP network in disgust.

Using DP in a proper p2p context is comparatively rare as yet. In fact, the usual definition of "large processing tasks segmented into component blocks, delivered to a number of machines where these blocks are processed, and reassembled by a central machine" is pretty clear about the strict hierarchy model.

One potential network-specific application of DP based on p2p is distributed indexing, where nodes in a DCP2P network assume responsibility for a portion of the total indexing task and work together in fulfilling search requests. Various distributed search schemes are possible, index-based or instance-compiled on varying scope.

A combination of DP and the new Web, sometimes called "Web Mk2", offers other prospects. In the p2p context, one can envision autonomous, roaming Web agents opportunistically using p2p nodes as temporary hosts as they go about their assigned information-gathering tasks—a kind of benign Internet "worm". These and other visions of future potential are dealt with in Part III.

SPECIFIC ARCHITECTURES

This section describes how some common p2p-capable implementations, especially those built into operating systems, have applied one or another of the general architectural models. We examine how closely each implementation adheres to a given model, and of particular interest is to note how each has tried to solve issues relating to user convenience, reliability, scale, and so on.

These examples are intended as illustrative of concept, not as exhaustive analysis, and they mainly provide a general backdrop to the detailed analysis of more recent technologies in Part II. Although capable of creating legitimate and often perfectly adequate p2p solutions in the LAN context, they aren't in themselves necessarily practical solutions for deploying peer networks today. Modern p2p solutions are based on **open source** applications that create virtual networks and can run on any network-aware system, which gives numerous advantages compared to proprietary solutions that depend on particular operating systems.

Before looking at the p2p solutions that can build on any operating system, the following section takes up native networking abilities in the main operating systems encountered by individual users today. I discuss "OS-bundled" networking in this limited way, because it falls somewhat outside the intended scope of this book.

NATIVE NETWORKING

By "native networking" we understand the inherent ability to connect to a network (of peers) using only those components already present in the respective operating system, possibly with further installation of some non-default ones.

Such networking ability enables "instant" peer networking on the machine level, at least for messaging and resource sharing across the network. In today's systems, this native capability almost always means Internet connectivity, in addition to transport support for local networks. Native networking is distinguished from the application-level p2p networking that is the main focus of this book, and it is often neglected in discussions of p2p technologies.

Application-level solutions communicate on top of the established machine-level networking, but can be independent of the latter's addressing and peer or non-peer ability, and are therefore seen as complementary enhancements.

Unix to Unix

As mentioned in Chapter 1, the first computer networking was between mainframes. It quickly evolved to communication between Unix machines, which early had a basic peer protocol called UUCP (Unix to Unix Copy Protocol).

Because UUCP is a standard copy process between all Unix machines that can be applied to any content, it was also used to transport messages. Many newsgroup servers still rely on UUCP to transport messages to and from other systems. Although ancient and not especially efficient, its main merit is that it's always available, whatever the Unix system. Early chat, e-mail and the newsgroups (on **Usenet**) were built on top of this protocol. Unix defined the interoperable standards for all e-mail support, mailbox format, and applications—and were inherited by Linux.

Reference to Unix characteristics common to a variety of implementations of either Unix or derivatives like Linux is commonly denoted by writing " *nix".

Peer Networking in MS Windows

One of the better design decisions in 32-bit MS Windows was the integration of generic networking components. Once the hardware, protocol, and workgroup configurations are properly set up, basic peer networking is essentially plug-and-play, whatever the mix of Windows platforms—95, 98, ME, NT, 2000, or XP.

Network components however are not default in Windows (prior to XP) but are installed and configured whenever hardware or software that requires them are added to the system. Installing for example a network interface card or a modem not only requests the appropriate device driver, but also sets up the corresponding client and protocol layers to handle network abstraction. Figure 2.5 illustrates the model used, with reference to the OSI protocol layers.

The supported network protocols are not just Microsoft's enhanced version of network BIOS, NetBEUI, for Microsoft Networking, but also for Novell NetWare (IPX/ISX) and Internet-compatible networking (TCP/IP). Others can be added. Network support is largely transparent to the user.

The default configuration prior to Windows XP relies on the proprietary NetBEUI protocol, although it is relatively painless to reconfigure it to TCP/IP from the Network Properties dialogs—XP defaults to TCP/IP. The advantage of NetBEUI

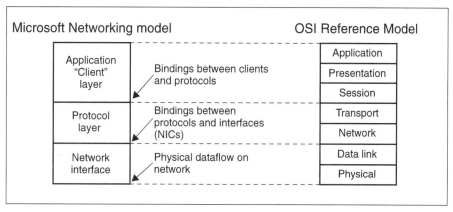

FIGURE 2.5 *Microsoft Networking models the network as three layers and two bindings, here compared to the OSI model. The user must configure one or more appropriate binding paths Client-Protocol-NIC for each application and network used.*

in the small local network is that it doesn't require any setup apart from uniquely naming each machine and assigning it to a common workgroup. Once connected, machines will "see" each other using the integrated network browser. The integrated network browser makes access of remote files and resources transparent, and to the user as easy as accessing local files and resources.

> **Bit 2.6   Workgroup networking in Windows is an atomistic p2p architecture.**
> The primary focus of Windows native networking is resource and file sharing, with shares managed by the individual machine's administrator/user.

As each machine's resources (such as hard disk partitions or printers) are locally declared shared, they can be accessed by other machines in the workgroup. There is no built-in central administration. Resources and access are controlled locally for each machine by the respective user (in Windows NT, by the local Administrator account). In the corporate or home LAN case, all the machines tend to be physically administered from external notes and lists managed by one person.

It's straightforward to use machines running some flavor of 32-bit Windows as p2p nodes in a NetBEUI-type LAN with up to perhaps 10 or 15 PC workstations. Beyond that scale, the complexities of consistently administering names, shares, and permissions easily get unmanageable.

Microsoft later implemented a scalable server-centric model for Windows Networking based on NT Server, where resource and access control is handled by a designated Primary Domain Controller (PDC) in the LAN. Users must then first log in to the PDC using their local client before gaining access to the network. Using Microsoft domains adds considerable complexity, but also the kind of power and centralized control that larger corporate networks usually need. This kind of domain-centric network scales tolerably well to thousands of nodes.

The default NetBEUI protocol is furthermore constrained to a small physical LAN, because it only handles network data frames with explicit hardware addressing. The price NetBEUI pays for its simplicity is the inability to cross network boundaries. To route across virtual networks, you need support for software addressing, such as in TCP/IP's packet addressing. Hence, for maximum flexibility, Windows's systems should be configured for TCP/IP. Given the continued Internet focus of Microsoft, TCP/IP might become the only networking option in future versions of Windows.

With TCP/IP as the protocol, it's possible and often desirable to install support for point-to-point tunneling protocol (PPTP), which is an **encryption**-protected virtual private network (VPN) connection between NT servers, or between a Windows client and a server. This protocol is primarily intended to provide secure access to corporate networks from external, dial-up users. It however could also be used to construct a virtual, distributed, and private p2p LAN of up to 256 connections per node.

Home LANs have become more common in later years: several machines in a p2p network sharing an Internet connection, possibly through a cable router. A better understanding of p2p principles even in Windows can greatly enhance the utility of such home clusters by allowing different approaches to how data and resources are deployed, and perhaps shared from outside the home as well.

For the purposes of this book, it's assumed that most readers have Internet connectivity with either some flavor of Windows or Linux, or a Mac, on which system they intend to install application-level p2p solutions.

Peer Networking in Apple Macintosh

Apple's Macintosh early included peer network capability in their operating system. Native support for ubiquitous 10/100 Base-T Ethernet makes physical network connection easy.

The Mac supports either proprietary AppleTalk or open TCP/IP protocols, and can natively build peer networks. Stringing together some Macs with AppleTalk is the easiest route, but easy comes at the price of the power and sophistication that more complex protocols give. AppleTalk is in addition known as a "chatty" broadcast protocol that doesn't scale very well to larger networks.

The early dominance of Mac systems in corporate and educational environments has waned over the years, although they are still fairly common in the latter. The proprietary architecture, solutions, and protocols have always been an impediment to broad interoperability with other platforms, networked or not.

A number of solutions exist to interconnect Macs and PCs to the respective proprietary protocol networks, but TCP/IP is usually the protocol of choice. As with Windows, Mac p2p applications install on top of the current transport. The newer OS X is a Unix derivative, so it supports many *nix tools and applications—with broader support for p2p than older Macs.

OS/2 Peer Networks

IBM's OS/2 is no longer a current operating system for the average user, although not so many years ago, OS/2 Warp was billed as the next dominant desktop OS. It might have taken a significant share of the market too, if IBM hadn't so abruptly dropped support for it and instead begun to bundle Windows.

OS/2 is worth mentioning because it lives on in some corporate networks and among a core group of enthusiasts. Even today, some still maintain its suitability for office use, with words much like this:

> *If you want a consistent, friendly interface that has the power to run the office, run your old DOS/Windows programs, and connect to the outside world (all simultaneously), then OS/2 Warp Connect is worth a look.*

The last OS/2 Warp versions, Connect and v4, were true 32-bit, multitasking and network-aware operating systems roughly comparable to Windows NT or Linux. Warp consumes less resources than NT, more like Windows 95, and can run most Windows programs intended for the early 32-bit extensions. For our purposes, the question is how well OS/2 supports peer networking.

Network software setup for OS2/Warp is similar to the Mac in its ease of use. Finding a working NIC driver can sometimes be problematic, given the lack of vendor OS/2 support for newer hardware, but the rest is an easy walk. Other platforms may match up to Warp in any one area, yet IBM covered its bases much better overall.

IBM's proprietary networking protocol, OS/2 Peer, is limited to sharing resources among machines running Warp Connect. However, TCP/IP is also supported, albeit an older version that's less easy to configure. Protocols are session

TABLE **2.2** *Main OS/2 Peer Networking components*

Component	Function
Sharing and Connecting	A program that enables you to connect to the resources of other users, and declare which of your resources are available to other users, and to what degree.
Network Messaging	OS/2 Peer's internal e-mail system.
Peer Workstation Logon / Logoff	Logon and logoff service for network access.

specific, so you can log on to OS/2 Peer, IBM LAN Server, Novell NetWare, Microsoft LAN Manager, Windows for Workgroups, and TCP/IP networks simultaneously.

The OS/2 desktop has three network-related folders: OS/2 Peer, Network, and UPM Services (the latter for user and password maintenance). The OS/2 Peer folder contains all of the good stuff, the most important being Sharing and Connecting, Network Messaging, Clipboard and DDE, Information, and Peer Workstation Logon/ Logoff—as explained in Table 2.2.

Linux Networking

A Linux installation is inherently a full-featured server in the Internet networking model, natively supports TCP/IP, and also includes all the associated client software. Linux is based on Unix, which to all intents and purposes *is* the Internet.

Linux exists in a variety of branches and distributions, all similar and generally interoperable, but with different configurations and purposes. Full-scale Linux installations are admittedly not easy to master, but they do have all the power and options for networking you could possibly want. A network of machines running Linux can therefore easily function as both client-server and p2p node using the full array of software developed for the Internet.

This kind of system, partly due to the more "experimentally involved" attitude of the typical Linux user, readily participates in many p2p contexts, locally and over the Internet. One such common context is to return e-mail to the p2p model, because Linux machines can, and often do, each run the server software for sending and receiving e-mail in a variety of protocols, messaging, and sharing files or other content. That way Linux users easily turn their machines into p2p endpoints for a broad range of services. Similar functionality is available in Windows and other systems by adding comparable third-party software, but Linux support is native.

QNX Networking

QNX is a mature distributed *nix-like operating system, generally found in but by no means restricted to embedded real-time systems. For several decades, QNX development has sort of paralleled Linux, and can on a PC generally emulate or run much Linux software.

QNX has native networking at several levels, including support for distributed processes and modules, and it of course supports the ubiquitous TCP/IP. It's however rare to find QNX on a desktop PC outside of special developer contexts.

OTHER APPLICATION GROUPS

This chapter ends with a brief tour of application-level solutions that might or might not be strictly p2p, but are related in concept at some level.

Peer Servers

As a kind of catch-all, the term "peer servers" can be used to designate various forms of Internet or LAN servers that maintain p2p connectivity with each other, while serving a host of clients in a traditional client-server role.

Most of the discussions about p2p networking are equally applicable to the server-to-server p2p role, even though little is said about this role in this book. This is in part because the main focus is on the end-user perspective, and not so much on software such as traditional servers that are not administered by the user.

Nevertheless, it's also true that the node application in p2p technologies is quite clearly a "peer server" because all the nodes participate in this role. The server role becomes more explicit in cases like Mojo Nation and Freenet (see Chapters 8 and 9, respectively), where the node software does have a clear client-server role towards separate client software (at the user endpoint) running on the same machine.

Internet Relay Chat gets a brief mention here only because its relay servers function p2p with each other. The IRC client-to-client chat transactions almost exclusively go through the servers, so these relationships are not p2p. Nevertheless, IRC one-to-one chat and many-to-many (or chatroom) discussions can be a method to discover potential peers for other direct p2p connectivity. IRC support is therefore a common extra component in many atomistic p2p technologies. A multi-transport chat client such as Jabber (see Chapter 6) is especially useful in such contexts because it supports several other p2p messaging and file transfer protocols in addition to IRC chat and its own open client and services protocol.

HailStorm

At the time of writing, Microsoft's new and controversial p2p entry, dubbed HailStorm, is barely past prototype status. Although details will surely change over time, Hailstorm and its associated services appear clear enough in principle that mention of this implementation should be made.

Launched as the first real .NET (pronounced and sometimes written as "dot-NET") initiative in March 2001, it is described as a set of user-centric *Web services* that will "turn the Web inside out". The concept assumes some aspects of the traditional client-server relationship. HailStorm defines a basic network framework around which third-party developers are invited to write applications that rely on user identification. The approach has been described by Microsoft in this way:

> Instead of having an application be your gateway to the data, in HailStorm, the user is the gateway to the data.

Unusually for Microsoft, the framework rests on a set of open standards, XML and Simple Object Access Protocol (SOAP), rather than proprietary protocols. It remains to be seen, however, whether these assimilated open standards will in future be extended in proprietary ways. HailStorm's security protocol, based on Kerberos, has already been extended by Microsoft, with unclear consequences for continuing its open and interoperable characteristics.

While officially described as an open p2p system, closer inspection shows that HailStorm sits in an uneasy balance between the centralized closed server and the open p2p models. Depending on how the final implementation designs play, Hailstorm could turn out to be the largest client-server architecture ever devised, with rather minimal peer focus overall.

The core concept depends on a user-centric, or strictly speaking an *authentication-centric* server model. This has the audacious goal of centrally validating any and all Internet user identities in the world! It would (by way of the Passport service) mediate and authorize valid user access not only to all distributed Web services, but also to *locally installed software*. The thought is that software registration management will be yet another service sold by Microsoft.

It should be noted that the concept of "personal identity" that HailStorm deals with is not just a simple *who am I*, but is at minimum a three-tier structure that uniquely specifies the *individual*, the *application* that the individual is running, and the *location* where that software is running. This information is encrypted into Kerberos application requests sent to a Passport server for **authentication** checks.

Passport defines identity, security and description models common to all services. As currently deployed, Passport identity is keyed to the user's e-mail address, whether existing or created on the Passport server just for authentication purposes. The official motivation for this massive central control is that all the proposed .NET services, especially commercial and banking, are defined as tied to a unique user identity that has to be administered globally. Microsoft is promoting Passport as a one-stop service for identifying people at online outlets.

An example of large-scale, public use of the Passport service for user authentication is the multi-user game *Asheron's Call*, a Microsoft Zone gaming site that in December 2001 began using the new identity verification system. Users that log in are shunted to a Passport server to verify their identity before being allowed into the game. It's not clear whether continued participation depends on Passport tracking user presence, but that feature is mentioned in other Passport contexts. Windows Messenger (WM) relies on presence tracking with Passport authentication.

Central Authentication

Crucial to the Passport concept, as its name implies, is that the distributed services and software honor the identification protocol. Significant is the list of standard functions, such as myAddress (electronic and geographic address), myProfile (personal information), myBuddies (contacts roster), myInbox (e-mail), myCalendar (agenda), and myWallet (e-cash), to name the first offering.

Needless to say, not everyone is comfortable with the idea of one company (with a less-than-reassuring track record for online reliability and interoperability) totally in control of individual and corporate public identity at this global level. One worry is that all identity credential transactions, and hence by extension most commercial transactions, would require participation of central Passport server(s).

Early criticism of the system can be summed up in the sentence:

HailStorm is the business idea of getting you to give up your identity to Microsoft, who will then rent it back to you for a small monthly fee.

Undeniably, there is at least one obvious ulterior motive for implementation of Passport: central identity validation for the new pay-by-use, personal-rental model for software-as-service that the company is adopting to replace the previous user licensing model of software-as-product. Deploying the infrastructure for a single global identity for each individual makes it much easier to manage registration and payment.

Significantly, the HailStorm infrastructure moves the revenue model from selling or licensing proprietary products on a proprietary platform, to pay-per-use fees culled from anyone running anything on any Internet-connected platform. HailStorm is a very "egalitarian" commercial venture in this respect—it asks both developers and users to pay for access, though the nature and size of these fees are far from worked out. Assume some form of periodic subscription or pay-by-use.

Privacy groups and others have meanwhile complained the service lacks adequate safety measures for securing sensitive consumer information, charges that Microsoft denied, despite the discovery in October 2001 of a security flaw in the Wallet part of the Passport system that could have exposed confidential user financial data to intruders. Glitches in the transition of the Gaming Zone site in December 2001 reawakened public skepticism.

Nevertheless, momentum is growing for Passport as more companies sign on and switch to a Passport-mediated log-in, use the MS bCentral portal service, or build new applications that lean on Passport services. Needless to say, Microsoft's applications for Internet communication, for example, Exchange Server or the IM client Windows Messaging, all tie into the Passport authentication scheme—sometimes as an option, sometimes as a necessary component.

Open Access

The distributed aspect of HailStorm is described as "open access", meaning that in principle any minimally connected device that is compliant with the XML Web SOAP framework can access applicable HailStorm services. No Microsoft runtime or tool is required to call them.

This concept seems clear enough at the client level, but less so at the server level. There, Microsoft has only vaguely stated that servers running on non-Microsoft operating systems like Linux or Solaris will be able to "participate" in HailStorm; the degree of actual integration has not been specified any further. In September 2001, Microsoft opened the gates by announcing that .NET will allow third-party identity providers to compete with Passport. This move is promising, albeit surprising at this early stage of deployment because the detailed strategy of the company can only be the subject of speculation. It however is strengthening the utility of HailStorm (which, by the way, has been renamed ".NET MyServices").

A good place to start if looking for more overview material on the many aspects of .NET and HailStorm is a Belgian site at I.T. Works (www.itworks.be/webservices/info.html). Another, more technical resource is DevX (www.devx.com).

In the next chapter, we leave the overview for more practical matters.

Internet-based Peer Network Applications

A fter the previous overview of the architecture models for p2p, the logical next step is to provide an introduction to a selection of practical peer network applications, their aims, and some of the issues they address. The deployment and general use of any p2p technology entails common practical issues that need to be discussed before examining the details of individual implementations.

The Internet has become a largely unified whole reachable with a single multiprotocol Web browser client, despite a legacy of different access protocols and specialized clients (mainly for e-mail, Web browsing, file transfer, and newsgroups). The Web browser has therefore become a standard interface to Internet resources. The user can "surf" to any resource without needing to know which application or protocol to use. At most, some sites and content require plug-in applets or updates, but their retrieval and installation is relatively transparent.

By contrast, the current crop of p2p application solutions form mostly insular webs floating on the underlying Internet infrastructure. The respective client/server applications rarely communicate with any other than their own kind, which makes selecting a particular solution difficult. Commitment ties one to a specific application suite.

This chapter primarily discusses the technical issues related to how the different implementations work—issues that underlie the respective strengths or unique characteristics, and sometimes weaknesses of each solution. The comparative approach used here is intended to complement the deeper individual analysis in the Part II chapters, which has a much narrower focus.

CHAPTER 3 AT A GLANCE

This chapter discusses technical issues as a basis for how the different technologies examined later in Part II might resolve them, or not, as the case may be.

Implementation Overview introduces the chosen implementations with a comparative table before discussing the issues further.

- *Particular Focus* looks at the different focus approaches that p2p technologies might adopt, and how each approach can determine the scope and usefulness of the implementations for particular contexts.

Searching the Network looks at functionality critical for many p2p applications.

- The section mainly takes up the two different methods of *Atomistic Search* and *Distributed Search*, contrasting these approaches to finding and retrieving content.

Content Management looks at another critical functionality.

- The text examines the different methods of *Storage and Retrieval*, followed by a section on *Improving Retrieval Performance*.

IMPLEMENTATION OVERVIEW

For a detailed look at practical p2p technology, let's turn the focus to a selection of implementations that are in development or currently available for networks.

These are selected not only as practical solutions for different peer-suitable situations but also as illustrations of significantly different approaches and feature sets. The headings of the chapters in Part II indicate what could be called the main aspect of each implementation type, although application areas overlap considerably. The aspects chosen are messaging, file sharing, resource and content management, secure distributed storage, and collaborative frameworks.

Table 3.1 lists the different implementations examined in detail in this book, with brief mention of the characteristics particular to each. Many more implementations exist—in fact, each time I researched something in the course of writing these chapters, mention of yet another "new p2p" technology turned up. Trying to include them all (or even just a representative mention) seemed doomed to become a Sisyphean labor of endless rewrites chasing implementations and versions. It was bad enough as it was.

The practical course therefore was to focus on a selection of distinctive peer traits for different contexts, and good implementation examples to discuss them in, and thus provide a deeper understanding of common p2p characteristics that we can find time and again in many different implementations.

Particular Focus

Seen from an abstract perspective, a technology can approach the whole concept of peer-to-peer in various ways. The chosen approach or focus area determines the solutions used and the overall potential of the technology.

Application Software or Infrastructure

As the examples in Part II show, a p2p technology can focus on specific applications (or clients) for particular purposes or on an entire network infrastructure to support arbitrary applications.

It's in the nature of things that the client focus, where the network arises *ad hoc* from the chosen client-to-client protocol, was both the earliest form and often the most limited. On the other hand, such applications have proven remarkably useful, even robust, in contexts much larger or different than the original intent.

TABLE **3.1**   *Major p2p implementations examined in detail in this book*

Name and domain	Chapter	Type of technology	Comments
ICQ (and AIM) icq.com (aol.com)	6	Proprietary IM protocol.	Instant messaging.
Jabber jabber.org	6	XML generic protocol. Messaging, IRC, file transfer, and more.	Server-mediated user-centric directory. Any client application.
Napster napster.com	7	Proprietary file sharing.	Historic example.
Gnutella gnutelliums.com gnutellanews.com	7	HTTP-based protocol. Usually implemented as file search and transfer.	Fully atomistic, any client application. Each peer is responsible for its own shared files.
Mojo Nation (version discontinued in 2002)	8	Encrypted over TCP/IP. Distributed file sharing.	Atomistic. Demand-driven micropayment services, distributed swarm storage.
Swarmcast swarmcast.com	8	Distributed swarm file broadcast on demand.	Server mediated swarm broadcasting of requested content.
Freenet freenetproject.org	9	Distributed secure document publishing and retrieval.	Atomistic. Encrypted, anonymized, distributed storage.
Groove groove.net	10	Shared workspace collaboration.	Server-mediated.
JXTA jxta.org	10	Distributed computing in general, protocol development.	Services and applications for peer groups, collaboration.

Some have cast the evolution of the Internet in discrete phases—for example, "Internet 1.0", "Internet 2.0", and "Internet 3.0", similar to the way software versions are numbered. In this view, v1.0 was the original server-to-server p2p model, while v2.0 stands for the client-server model of the Web today. Thus, Internet 3.0 stands for the new infrastructure based on p2p networks and ubiquitous connectivity for both devices and persons. This version is the Internet that the infrastructure solutions are trying to build, by making peer connectivity not only natural and easy, but inevitable and an essential part of the functionality.

Identity, Content, or Resources

The issue of primary focus or of the actual target of the implementation raises some questions. Is the focus on individual user identity, important in messaging? Does it instead identify specific content, perhaps even making the user anonymous in favor of file identity? Or does it mainly concern the distributed network and its aggregate resources, so that individual users and clients are interchangeable?

Each of these options results in different types of p2p technologies with different feature sets, different strengths, and different weaknesses. This is true no matter whether the focus is on application or infrastructure, even though the latter leaves greater latitude for application-specific focus to vary according to context.

Security

The focus might also be on security aspects. Early p2p solutions, like the early Internet solutions, were conceived in an inherently trusting environment. Any security was essentially external, so that anyone who was trusted with access to a computer, was also trusted to access content.

The modern e-world is far less trusting, and the threats to individuals and content far more serious and imminent. Over time, even the older solutions have often been retrofit with various measures to combat spoofing, denial of service, and malicious hacking. These measures may be adequate for individuals in non-critical messaging, just as plain-text e-mail is still widely accepted despite the wide-open e-postcard model. In closed environments, unsecured peer communication has not been seen as a problem either, even in enterprise, although this view is changing.

A side issue is that other network security measures, such as firewalls, can block p2p communications from outside the protection. Most peer technologies manage to work around this problem, as long as at least one end of a connection can receive.

However, the modern peer technologies implement far stronger security as a matter of integral design to safeguard both identity and content, usually based on variants of **hash** algorithms, strong encryption, public key signatures, and node trust systems. This level of security might well seem overkill for many users. It does make the solution adaptable to virtually any situation, however, from individual to enterprise, and it confers the ability to securely and consistently authenticate content sources—even anonymous ones.

It's no coincidence that the more advanced solutions discussed in later chapters rely on these stronger encryption methods, and that even the simpler, narrow focus messaging and file-sharing implementations are adopting similar strategies in later versions of their software and protocols.

In e-mail and Web contexts, it's sometimes a complaint that the use of strong encryption and digital signatures is both unwieldy and awkward. Implementations vary, and it's true that the security features are seldom convenient or transparent to the user. Nor are they necessarily interoperable between sites or contexts (secure **HTTPS** server connections are a notable exception). This sad state of affairs seems unlikely to be the case with future p2p platforms.

> **Bit 3.1   Strong encryption will be a ubiquitous feature of p2p systems.**
> This is inevitable because of the boost it gives to system robustness and utility.

The real issue with p2p security appears to be whether the authentication services will be tightly bound to central servers, as in .NET Passport, or whether they will be implemented as distributed trust systems, as in public key exchanges or other trust-based infrastructures.

Dynamic or Persistent

Some peer technologies are predominantly designed to allow great node freedom. In fact, the point is made earlier (in Chapter 1) that transient connectivity is a significant characteristic of the current p2p paradigm.

Many of the solutions described implement various strategies to deal with the issues that dynamic connectivity gives rise to: identity addressing, event **journalizing**, maintaining network cohesion, fault tolerance, and so on. They do so with varying degrees of success in terms of performance or convenience to the user—think search and retrieval in Gnutella, for example, as discussed later.

On the other hand, other solutions are not especially tolerant of transient-node connectivity, because their focus is on resolving other network issues, such as persistent storage or distributed resource management. To some extent, one can then see nodes in these systems in terms of coupled client-server applications on a single host machine, where the server component is expected to be more or less continuously connected to the network, with much more relaxed constraints on the client component that interfaces with the user as a result.

SEARCHING THE NETWORK

Leaving aside the communicative p2p implementations, probably the next most common reason for running a p2p network is distributing and sharing resources. A core functionality in the network is the ability to search for specific resources, distributed services, or for that matter, people.

For the purposes of this discussion of principles, it's convenient to restrict the focus to finding content, as in the common file-sharing applications. Although the related issues of storing and retrieving content is mentioned in this context, the *Content Management* section looks specifically at this aspect.

The seemingly trivial issue of finding content is actually quite complex in practical implementation. Different networks—and for that matter, different clients—have their own approaches to this issue. It depends on the architecture, and on the surprisingly seldom discussed philosophy behind how to search for something.

> **Bit 3.2   Atomistic networks can be characterized as "search and discovery".**
> How search is (or can be) implemented depends to a great extent on how the p2p client designers view content storage and its acquisition through simple queries.

ATOMISTIC SEARCH

We look first at implementations that use atomistic content storage. The simple image that most users have for an atomistic network (such as Gnutella, the implementation details of which are discussed in Chapter 7, although it is used as an example in the following) is that the search function simply looks through the file names in its database, reporting back anything that matches the text string in the query.

Because the atomistic model does not have a centralized content database like a Web search engine or say Napster, all nodes within query range must act individually. The query horizon means that any search is by necessity incomplete. Each responding node must search its own locally stored content (for example, in a list of files). And, because the search is not coordinated, the collected unfiltered result is likely to contain many duplicates when popular files are stored by many nodes.

Furthermore, the search is at the mercy of contributing users who can apply arbitrary name variants (and even misspellings) to the same file, or the same name to different files. It's also possible that a responding node disconnects after providing a hit result, making its files inaccessible for the duration of the session.

However, a number of hidden assumptions in the filename-search image aren't necessarily true, which is due to our preconceptions about how centralized or atomistic search is implemented and how content is stored and managed.

Question and Answer

Many p2p technologies only protocol-specify the query and result formats. Exactly how the search is implemented in a particular client is completely up to the developer of the software—so too is the content of the response.

The situation is much like asking a person a question. Spoken or written languages have public syntax rules to enable us to understand the communication, but the process of deriving an answer is completely internal and hidden from public inspection. It should therefore not be a surprise that the same question can return different responses depending on who you ask and in what context.

Search on atomistic content functions much the same. Different clients can process the query in different ways. Some look only at the superficial names of the local shared files, perhaps even requiring strict matches. Others might look at a larger context when determining a match—for instance, parent folder name, fuzzy-logic matches, associated descriptive texts, even a detailed inspection of file content.

Bit 3.3   Atomistic search returns arbitrary, *source-determined* relevancy.
Unfortunately, as a search instigator, you have little way of determining the quality or exhaustive nature of the different results that eventually return. The return can even be bogus, intentionally misleading to entice you to download malicious code.

Compare this inexactness with centralized search engines, where we can be fairly confident that our query will be processed the same way every time—no surprises and reproducible. But is this always desirable? Are we not then dependent on one search algorithm and its possible failings or unsuitability for our purposes? To be sure, the big search engines provide "advanced" syntax options to fine-tune our query, and we can move on to another engine (and another database) to try a different approach. Meta-search engines can even query a host of different machines, yet often the results are frustratingly dependent on our ability to frame the right match criteria—we have to guess sufficiently close to the format of the result we're looking for. And for the most part, we can deal effectively mainly only with text, with little intelligence in the way results are sorted, filtered and ranked.

Not Just Files

Interestingly, there is no requirement in p2p protocols such as Gnutella that queries must have anything to do with file names or any static content at all. Broadening our perspectives for a moment, it's sufficient that a query can be intelligently parsed in some client-relevant context to return a result.

Why not, for example, have a mix of many different kinds of clients on the same network? Some could implement Gnutella's original intent of collecting recipes. A query for "nutella spread" could then return actual recipes (or pointers to recipe files, or URIs to web resources with such recipes). On the other hand, a query formulated as a mathematical equation might find a client somewhere that can make sense of it and return a calculated answer. Another client might parse it differently and return a pointer to a list of applicable theorems. Some clients might be entirely image oriented. Yet others might provide dictionary entries, translation services, or encyclopedia-style articles based on the query words. Another valid response could be a list of people who have expressed an interest in subjects suggested by the query.

The client-based process works because of the way the query protocol is defined. Clients who can't parse a particular request do nothing, except pass it on.

> **Bit 3.4 Atomistic search entities only return responses to queries for which they can process and return a relevant "hit".**
>
> Again, *the responding software decides what constitutes a hit.* Client software can be designed any way at all as long as it understands and responds to protocol messages.

So, what might initially be seen as a grave fault in the p2p network, an imperfection in search, can in some situations turn out to be an unexpectedly powerful feature. New functionality can be deployed to respond to specific queries, with no change to the existing network protocol, even when these extensions are not anticipated in the original protocols and clients. Like HTML-rendering browsers, the clients that understand a new feature will respond, those that don't should ignore.

More Innovation Needed

So far, however, we see little of such innovations in the field. To a large extent, the majority of users are interested in swapping files, mostly music and video.

Most developers, and consequently clients, myopically focus on simple file searches and expect to go to download mode when the user requests this from a hit.

It's important to realize that file download is not the only response and that the end result could just as well be from a network-located *service*.

> **Bit 3.5   Peer networks can provide innovative services to simple queries.**
> Clients and users should be open to new kinds of queries and new types of responses to network "search", which may require sophisticated filtering of received results.

A prototype for nontraditional search responses was demonstrated in June 2000 by InfraSearch (www.infrasearch.com) by programmers Gene Kan, Yaroslav Faybishenko, Spencer Kimball, and Tracy Scott. The prototype was a Web-accessed search engine—in reality just a front-end server to a small local network of Gnutella-aware clients, each specialized for a particular context. The proof-of-concept experiment included an image database, stock quotes through a **proxy**, an archive of news headlines, and a simple calculator. Each responded to whatever query made sense according to its parsing rules. The front-end process received the node results and presented a compilation to the querying user.

One vision for the InfraSearch project was to redefine the paradigm of Web search, so that results would be based on actual site content at search time, instead of on an out-of-date database laboriously compiled by various Web-indexing robots. Some saw this innovation as heralding yet another shake-out (YASO) in the dot-com field, this time for the likes of Yahoo! and traditional search engine sites in general.

InfraSearch (the company) was subsequently acquired by Sun Microsystems in March 2001, clearly with an aim to strengthening relevant aspects of its Project JXTA p2p effort. JXTA is described fully in Chapter 10. Further information about its design and software (known as JXTA Search and presented as Distributed Search for Distributed Networks) is found at the search.jxta.org site. The design centers around an open XML protocol called Query Routing Protocol (QRP).

The need for new search methods has been highlighted by studies of the amount of data stored in distributed systems, of which the Web is but one example. Consider that "good" search engines index (and at that, incompletely) perhaps at most half of the openly accessible billion or so static Web pages. This indexed content forms a partial and out-of-date database for the search algorithms applied. Additionally, a large and unknown number of corresponding dynamic pages can't be indexed at all. Such pages are the so-called "deep content" from site databases, which is estimated to be another order of magnitude larger, ten billion or more pages.

Furthermore, it was estimated in a study in early 2001 by The Industry Standard (issue archive at www.thestandard.com) that distributed networks held over 550 billion content documents (not "pages"). This incredible mass of mostly unindexed data can safely be assumed to be growing rapidly with increased use of p2p networks in general, and distributed content management within business in particular.

It's also becoming generally recognized that a wider array of client devices need to access distributed content, not just the traditional PC-with-Web-browser. This range of devices includes roving laptops, handheld PDAs, mobile phones, public kiosk terminals, and likely also devices that we can't at the moment foresee. Such clients will not only be search consumers, but in all probability also increasingly function as content providers and local search agents. This capability can be realized only with some model of distributed network and a whole new range of so-called "deep search" methods with highly directed queries. It's likely, too, that we might need more search dimensions or structuring protocols to keep from being flooded by returns that are irrelevant to a particular purpose. For example, a small PDA should be able to frame the request or filter returns so only small-screen text results are shown.

File Storage Model Affects Search

Other p2p networks, atomistic but with distributed storage, provide a counterpoint to the fully atomistic model. Mojo Nation and Freenet, for instance, force a unified search approach. This is not because they represent a less atomistic p2p model as such, but because of the way their distributed storage is designed. The focus is squarely on files as content, published to the network, and inaccessible except through the unique identity code assigned by the publishing agents.

Searches are still spread among many nodes, but these nodes act as collective agents for a unified search algorithm that must produce a valid file identity. Client software must conform to more detailed specifications to function on the network. Although likely to be more efficient than the simplistic-but-open, protocol-based model discussed earlier, such networks are also more rigidly bound to some initial vision of purpose. They are also bound to a single method of searching and presenting hits, which might not be equally valid for all users or types of content.

> **Bit 3.6   Storage model decisions can restrict innovative functionality.**
>
> For example, an explicit reliance on externalized file metadata (for instance, user-supplied descriptions) can make context or functionality-based responses impossible, or at least hard to implement without redesigning the network.

A chosen search model invariably represents a trade-off between the open-ended approach on one hand and constraint issues on the other—requirements on efficient (or just fast) search, good content availability, secure (especially encrypted) and redundant storage, publishing as opposed to sharing, and possibly anonymity of source. The decision thus boils down to which philosophy influences the design and working model of the implementation. If the Gnutella focus can most easily be stated as sharing content, as files in a search-and-discovery kind of network, then other solutions are primarily about sharing bandwidth, storage, and services.

But content might be stored in a distributed manner. And more importantly, search might be implemented as a distributed service, shared among many nodes for content not necessarily stored on just the local system.

Distributed Search

While simple content-*sharing* systems are based on content stored locally, and thus also searched locally, more sophisticated content-*publishing* systems decouple content from the individual nodes, at least to some extent.

Publishing systems make sharing an explicit act of "uploading" a file to the network as a whole. The upload may be either a physical submission of the entire file and its description, or less commonly, a submission of only the descriptor metadata. The point is that the shared content list is kept separate from any particular node and is often managed by a distributed tracking system.

The content itself is usually split up and distributed/replicated across many nodes in some hash-determined way. Its availability is therefore vastly better and independent of the online status of individual nodes. Searching in these situations is quite different than in the fully atomistic model, because queries in distributed searches are directed to specific search services that can respond with pointers to current storage locations.

> **Bit 3.7   Distributed search and storage promote content availability.**
> Performance is usually better as well, although other design considerations might make a distributed storage network initially slower to respond.

The previous discussions refer to how the chosen storage model affects the search strategies and their performance, but in a general way. In the following, relevant storage models are examined and explained in more detail.

CONTENT MANAGEMENT

So far, the previous sections have discussed only search, storage and retrieval issues. Content management is a more systematic view, but it also implies the question of *ownership*, and hence *governance*—the control of who may use what, when they may use it, and in what manner. It's therefore understandable if momentary confusion can set in when studying peer technology solutions to content control issues.

It's true, p2p content management as applied to governance is filled with paradox and contradiction because of the mixed viewpoints encountered.

- On the one hand, p2p is said to empower users by allowing them to control their own resources. This is the case for simple, fully atomistic networks.

- On the other, some p2p solutions remove resource and content control from everyone, except for the functions of publishing and updating. No less atomistic, all control is distributed over network services that function automatically according to some rules set.

- Meanwhile, corporate or other environments wish to have all the benefits of p2p networking, yet still retain central control over content access and distribution.

- Not to mention all the in-between solutions that might have a bit of this and a bit of that.

So, it all depends....

But in fact, it turns out that we can implement functional governance even in the absence of clear-cut ownership in the traditional sense. Let's see how.

Governance requires the ability to describe and effect content activities, and to support their tendency to change over time. Simple governance may require nothing more than support for distributed authoring with remote document locking, access control and versioning. This support can be automated and integrates well into the basic p2p outlook, no matter how ownership as such is assigned.

More complicated governance often relies on notification services that bring changes or access attempts to the immediate attention of subscribing users/owners. Mobile task descriptions that anyone with authority and capability can fulfill might also be supported. Further along the scale, proposed or implemented functionality for the management of digital rights is yet another expression of the kind of detailed governance that could be implemented in p2p contexts.

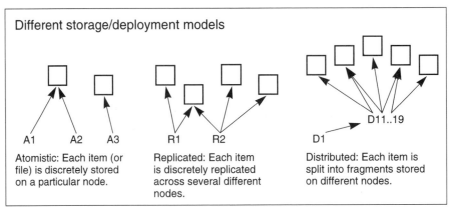

Different storage/deployment models

A1 A2 A3	R1 R2	D1 D11..19
Atomistic: Each item (or file) is discretely stored on a particular node.	Replicated: Each item is discretely replicated across several different nodes.	Distributed: Each item is split into fragments stored on different nodes.

FIGURE 3.1   *Storage models. In the distributed model, shown at right, one often calls the service-managed store a virtual distributed filesystem.*

STORAGE AND RETRIEVAL

Storage and retrieval of content are intimately interlinked, for obvious reasons. The focus may be heavily on "content" here, but to a large extent, the models are applicable to *any resource deployment,* for example, including network services.

The basic content storage models are illustrated in Figure 3.1:

- Atomistic (shared from local store)

- Replicated (shared from multiple sources)

- Distributed (shared from virtual store)

Practical content-sharing implementations commonly mix elements of two or more of these models. For example, atomistic implementations often show (at least implicit) replication due to the content duplication caused by locally determined sharing of popular and just-downloaded files. In more advanced (usually publishing) systems, replication is an intentional feature, often made adaptive to demand.

Distributed systems also commonly implement replication of the fragments to ensure availability or improve retrieval performance. Both replication and distribution are important enough in this context that they are often implemented for retrieval functionality even when the storage model is initially purely atomistic. Swarmcast, discussed in Chapter 8, is but one example.

IMPROVING RETRIEVAL PERFORMANCE

Client software can have great freedom in implementing the functionality based on the basic p2p protocol, or even in extending it in useful ways. Gnutella provides a good example of such developer freedom.

A common feature to enhance the download experience is to track multiple occurrences of the same file on different nodes and automatically try each node in turn until a download transfer is established. The user will usually see a status during the attempt—something like "trying host 1 (of 3)". Extended information for that file shows the individual host addresses and other characteristics, such as transfer rate and client type. The client can then retry the others on a lost connection.

A major improvement in download *performance*, on the other hand, is the ability to resume a transfer at a specified offset in the file, instead of just starting over. This must be implemented in the software at both ends of the connection.

Resuming transfer might seem trivial enough to implement when dealing with the same physical file on the same host. The downloading client specifies that the host should advance its pointer a certain number of bytes into the file, assuming that the protocol (or a client extension to it) provides a mechanism for such an instruction.

The file must have in this context a persistent, unique identity, on the client side coupled with the host identity, so that the file can be identified and the transfer resumed even after the connection is broken and established again later. Many file-sharing hosts can have dynamic network identities, and the file identity descriptor might therefore not reliably persist across connection sessions.

A feature that depends on mapping identical files on *different* hosts is the ability to skip from an established connection to an alternate host in mid-transfer, for example on a lost connection. One reason for forcing skip manually might be that the actual bandwidth allocated to the download by the first selected host is far less than the stated rate, making the initial transfer unacceptably slow. An example of both a lost connection and a skipped host for the same file is illustrated in Figure 3.2.

A third feature, relying on more advanced resume-transfer coding in the client, allows downloading different file fragments in parallel from multiple hosts. The ability to access multiple hosts for the same content, in sequence or in parallel, is a powerful way to work around the main disadvantage of discrete files in atomistic content storage, that of dependence on single nodes for retrieval.

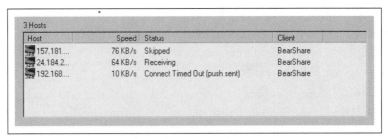

FIGURE 3.2   *File-sharing clients generally have the ability to identify identical files stored at several nodes, and try each in turn until a download connection is established. A host can also be substituted (skipped) in mid-transfer for performance reasons.*

There are few more frustrating experiences than interminably waiting for a large file in a slow download, only to lose the connection with only a few kilobytes left to completion. Strategies that automate reliable transfer are very valuable.

> **Bit 3.8   Transfer resume and multiple host sourcing must be considered almost essential features in content sharing and distribution.**
>
> Transfer resume is still not supported by many Internet file-repository servers, so in that respect, even the simplest p2p clients are more advanced.

Determining what constitutes identical content across multiple hosts is nontrivial, however, given the freedom in client design. The content descriptor (usually file properties information) sent by each host must be constructed and compared in a sensible way—a file's name, length, and **checksum** would be minimum data for a reasonably confident match. In atomistic sharing, the filename is arbitrarily assigned by each user, and not that good an identifier even for general searches.

This identification situation is easier to resolve in the network publishing implementations because they have built-in functionality for tracking content, which automatically provides persistent and unique identification on a network-wide basis. In this context, clients don't need to deal directly with the issue at all.

Encryption Helps Identification

These days, unique content identity is often based on hashed keys and checksums calculated on the entire content. These methods are often implemented hand-in-hand with public key encryption to safeguard the content.

The trend in all areas is for greater security and integrity of content, using public key encryption and digital signatures, and fortunately, this technology also provides reliable built-in mechanisms for uniquely identifying particular content in p2p contexts. If the hash is generated from the actual content, then two identical hashes by definition mean that the content is identical.

Hashed keys do have a problem in that the human-readable form of seemingly random characters in a long string is not especially convenient to handle directly for the user. In the simplest cases where access is through a hyperlink-aware interface, such as in a Web browser, the messy detail can easily be hidden behind a meaningful text anchor. This kind of solution is found in several technologies that use hashed keys as primary identifiers and retrieval handles.

As they become more common, many hash-key systems for resolving identity are fortunately evolving better client interfaces that make the key handling transparent to the user. While the easy solution of a Web interface through the system Web browser has a sort of instant gratification, it does impose a number of restrictions in how the keys can be handled, and lacks the potential for automation and agency that are natural extensions to most p2p usage situations.

A second issue is also resolved with the addition of encryption and hashes—namely, ensuring that the content is what one expects it to be, unaltered. As it stands, both users and client implementations show an amazing level of blind trust when retrieving content from essentially anonymous sources. Especially if the content is some form of executable file, it becomes crucial for the user to know that it has not been tampered with, infected with virus, or even replaced by a trojan that will wreak havoc with the user's system. Digital signatures and hashes based on content are currently the best way of ensuring the authenticity of content.

What's still lacking in this context is a widespread trust and authentication system, so that content hashes can be verified against secure sources to prove that the content does in fact originate with the purported creator. The extensive infrastructure solutions for the new Internet, some aspects of which are dealt with in Chapters 9 and 10, include components intended to create this kind of trust infrastructure. Other implementations might include smaller-scale or partial solutions to the problem. The discussions in Part III also return to issues of trust.

Security,
Vulnerability,
and the Legal
Issues of P2P

Security and vulnerability are issues rarely considered by most individuals using computers, and even less so in the specific contexts of p2p applications. Witness the recurring global rashes of virus-infested e-mail and server worms, many of which would never have occurred, or at least would have had marginal effects, if only users and administrators had exercised even a modicum of precaution and common sense.

In fact, it's a safe bet to assume that even those who consider their systems "secure" or "reasonably safe" from intrusion have given little thought to how the use of a p2p client might easily circumvent existing security measures. Such breaches of security can be a serious problem in environments where there is wide-spread complacency and implicit trust in for instance corporate firewalls and established policies. A first step towards addressing the problem is to be informed about the risks and to have a greater understanding of the technologies involved.

The implementations examined in detail in later chapters have sections that deal with these issues in the specific application context. This chapter serves as a more general background and provides a broader understanding of how p2p technologies introduce both new risks and new possibilities. In some situations and with the proper preparations, a deployed p2p technology might even prove more secure and robust than the traditional client-server network.

Security and legal issues are intimately related, even if we consider only the immediate risks of liabilities and litigation raised by inappropriate access or distribution of content by users. It therefore seems appropriate to end the chapter with some mention of common legal issues you should be aware of.

CHAPTER 4 AT A GLANCE

This chapter is meant to be an overview of security, integrity, and legal issues that are raised by p2p technologies, although the discussion roams fairly wide.

Security Issues deals with network security measures from a general perspective.

- *The Dimensions of Security* lists how differing p2p focus highlights or relaxes particular concerns.

- A section about *Firewalls and Tunnels* describes why p2p makes automatic reliance on these safeguards an illusion.

- *Subversive P2P* notes that some technologies are aggressively anti-control.

- *Redundancy and Persistence* outlines why p2p deployment can provide solutions to these particular issues of accessibility.

Legal Issues outlines a difficult area, which, to make things worse, is under hard-to-track and rapid change as new legislation is proposed and enacted.

- Issues particular to *Peer Communication* and *File Sharing* are considered in more detail.

- The discussion closes with a look at the changing face of *Intellectual Property Rights* and a discussion about *Anonymity* issues.

SECURITY ISSUES

We start with security issues, because a clear grasp of them and how a particular peer technology is secured is a prerequisite to analyzing legal ramifications.

Peer technologies must be considered "security porous" in the sense that they inherently provide great individual freedom for the user and are designed to easily establish direct connections between peers. In short, p2p clients have a (nasty for controlled IT policy) tendency to blithely ignore or actively circumvent traditional security measures such as corporate firewalls or filters. Information can thus cross otherwise established boundaries "without permission, assistance, or knowledge of any central authority or support groups", as one corporate vendor puts it.

THE DIMENSIONS OF SECURITY

Security in peer technologies has a number of dimensions, and should in this discussion also be extended to include techniques for ensuring availability and preventing illicit modification of content.

We can examine these issues in terms of the same list of characteristics defined in Chapter 2, which is used later to summarize characteristics of the examined implementations. This analysis looks slightly different, depending on the particular application focus of the p2p technology, as discussed in Chapter 3. Each focus might require a tighter security implementation for some characteristics, yet at the same time, it may allow very relaxed constraints on others.

Communication and Security

In communication contexts, most commonly messaging (see Chapter 6), the primary focus is on the personal identity of the user. Table 4.1 summarizes some of the specific security issues raised, along with possible solutions.

When selecting an IM technology, it seems reasonable to examine it for the kind of identity security it can provide, yet this issue often appears to be neglected even in enterprise IM environments. With few or no safeguards, the risk is great that identity misrepresentation can occur with potentially grave consequences.

Many established IM systems paradoxically don't really care *who* you are, only that you provide a unique identifier or "handle" to which other users can consistently refer. Your real "identity" is then implied in the social context of the people you have conversations with—a more or less trusted identity depending on how well they know you and can determine that you are who you claim to be.

TABLE 4.1   *Summary of security issues in p2p communication contexts*

Issue	Problem	Possible solution
Identity	Authentication, as many p2p clients don't care or just assume you are who you say you are.	External mechanisms (machine, client, intranet, service login). Selection of client that cares. Identity token, digital signature.
Presence	Not always valid for user; indicates online client. Personal integrity issues.	Better user selection, automatic inactivity-detection by client. User-selectable invisibility, etc.
Roster	Integrity issues.	Ability to ensure roster privacy, exclusion from others' lists.
Agency	Proper delegation of authority.	Stronger authentication measures.
Browsing	Exposure of local data, risk for intrusion.	User consent, authentication, and filters required.
Architecture	Vulnerabilities, unintentional exposure of local systems.	Open source, rigorous testing, external safeguards such as firewalls, clear usage policies.
Protocol	Vulnerabilities, lack of interoperability.	Open source, clear intent for interoperable platforms.

In some cases, the identity handle is one or more permanently server-registered identities or tokens tied to a particular client or client configuration. In others, it's an informal, per-session or per-peergroup-defined uniqueness, adequate for the closed group but of little value elsewhere.

> **Bit 4.1   Popular IM systems "track personal identity" but don't actually care about a user's real identity or authentication proof-of-use.**
>
> Users concerned with such matters must use external means and tools to accredit themselves with recipients, such as trusted public keys and digital signatures.

Casual anonymity is then easy in IM, if perhaps a dangerous illusion in the face of someone determined to track you down. This last issue is explored in detail in the context of distributed technologies that attempt to provide a secure anonymity for its users—for example Freenet, discussed in Chapter 9.

As agency in various forms becomes more widespread, autonomous agents deployed by a user client will more often be found acting on behalf of the user, and thus the issue of proper authentication and delegation must drive a demand for more secure identification to be implemented. E-commerce also requires authentication.

> **Bit 4.2   Both agency and e-commerce require secure authentication.**
>
> To be resolved is whether the authentication mechanism will be tightly centralized (like .NET Passport) or distributed trust systems (such as proposed by JXTA).

Authentication of identity in p2p contexts can be any one of the following, in increasing degrees of formal security:

1. Nonexistent (the system accepts whatever you say at face value).
2. Implicit (you can run an identifiable instance of the client software).
3. Based on local machine, client, or LAN log-in (local password access).
4. Login to a p2p server/service (p2p network authenticated access).
5. External secure authentication mediated by the p2p service (a central authentication service with encrypted signature, such as Passport).

While still rare, network or external "public" authentication based on public key digital signatures is being deployed in newer solutions with increasing frequency. The solution that might tip the balance to the requirement to always use such strong authentication, even in casual IM, is Windows Messenger (see Chapter 2) with its reliance on centralized .NET Passport server authentication.

> **Bit 4.3   Full-featured IM clients expose far more than the user assumes.**
>
> It's important to be familiar with all the configuration options of an IM client—also with what the extra features might mean for the different security and integrity issues.

A second major problem with casual deployment of IM clients is the degree of "**exposure**" they entail. This exposure can be on different levels; a threat to personal integrity, data integrity, or corporate integrity. Through the client, a particular IM system might expose the individual's personal detail, behavior, and private roster.

Some implementations or retrofits to automated presence can be used to monitor employee work and Internet habits. The client might gratuitously expose sensitive data from the client system or details of the client-side LAN to any external party that cares to look. The client software and its features might offer an unsuspected route through an otherwise adequate firewall for malicious intrusion.

The measures that can be taken to limit such client-mediated exposure depend on external policies and careful selection, and above all on sensible configuration of client software. In a general sense, while proprietary solutions might seem adequately safe, they are seldom described in sufficient detail for an informed risk evaluation. They can often include undesirable **spyware** components for advertising, and at the very least, they introduce unwanted dependencies on third-party servers.

Sharing and Security

In the sharing context, the focus is less on who you are; the primary interest is the (usually static) content that can be retrieved through the network. This doesn't mean that all p2p sharing-networks consider identity issues such as authentication irrelevant, but it's dictated more by external factors and the kind of network.

> **Bit 4.4   Common p2p file sharing systems tend to ignore user identity.**
> This is not necessarily a disadvantage or failing but depends entirely on context. In some cases, you might even wish for deliberate and secure user anonymity.

Table 4.2 summarizes some of the issues for content sharing, which are different if only because the sharing context is rarely concerned with personal presence. The issue of authenticated data identity, discussed in Chapter 3, is a more serious issue that can safeguard against downloading malicious code disguised as content.

Individual identity, or authentication of individuals, becomes important in contexts where the sharing community is closed in some way, or when sharing requires explicit person-to-person consent. Otherwise, the focus is on the client/host role and possibly on implementing a trust system based on node identity to deal with unreliable, disruptive, or malicious nodes.

As a rule, in sharing, one assumes that the client software is in the active role, ideally an autonomous participant in the network no matter what the user is doing. Content access is then an anonymous and automatic process, where the client fulfills requests from all comers silently in the background.

TABLE 4.2 *Summary of security issues in p2p sharing contexts*

Issue	Problem	Possible solution
Identity (user or data)	Authority to share, but many clients don't care.	External mechanisms (as with IM), digital certificates.
	Malicious nodes.	Trust systems for node identity.
Presence	Online node status only.	Not really relevant unless retrieval consent is required.
Roster	Associating specific content with nodes.	Specific sharing policies.
Agency	Little or no control of how content is shared or resources used.	Closed p2p networks, node IP block filtering, clear sharing policies, consent dialog.
Browsing	Open, autoscan for files.	As before, configuration issue.
Architecture	Vulnerabilities, unintentional exposure of local systems.	Open source, rigorous testing, external safeguards such as firewalls, clear usage policies.
Protocol	Vulnerabilities, lack of interoperability.	Open source, clear intent for interoperable platforms.

This process is natural enough if the focus is solely on stored content, without any special concerns for who can access it. The casual approach to identity can cause problems if the context for the deployed p2p network requires user authentication, although this vetting can usually be left to other general security mechanisms already in place, such as machine or intranet login.

It's common corporate practice that anyone trusted enough to have normal access to the physical local network is by default trusted to access its resources and content, and thus presumably trusted enough to access content stored in a p2p virtual network deployed on it. The situation becomes more complex when "outside" access is allowed, for instance from remote machines across the Internet. Were the p2p layer just accessed through the existing LAN, the usual authentication mechanisms that allow the remote user to access the physical intranet would be adequate to authenticate access to the peer network as well.

On the other hand, the p2p technologies discussed here deploy their own virtual connectivity layer, an independent network. Outside clients can directly contact inside ones, blithely ignoring the intranet authentication mechanisms, and typically crossing the firewall barrier with impunity. This last issue deserves special attention.

FIREWALLS AND TUNNELS

When a corporate intranet connects to the Internet—and this applies to many other local and even home LANs, for that matter—it's almost a certainty these days that a firewall shields the internal network from intrusions. This is in addition to the usual network address translation that multiplexes a single external Internet IP address to many LAN identities.

Most p2p clients and protocols have evolved ways to work even behind firewalls, so the existence of a secure firewall does not by itself prohibit the virtual p2p network from spanning across this barrier. It's usually easy to set up a client inside the secure zone that will happily join a p2p network on the general Internet. The user often won't even realize that his deployment of the client provides a tunnel into the secure zone and constitutes a serious transgression of firewall policy.

> **Bit 4.5 P2P deployment can easily mean a breach of firewall security.**
> For example, most instant messaging technologies work around firewalls to provide virtual direct access to the client system, these days even allowing unregulated background file transfers that would otherwise not be possible.

In the absence of specific p2p policy and means of enforcement, sensitive content considered secure behind a firewall can unwittingly become easily accessible to external, unauthorized individuals who are on the common p2p network. In many cases, the security breach is bidirectional through this tunnel effect.

> **Bit 4.6 "Clever" clients can unwittingly subvert proxy/firewall protection.**
> This means that some software is coded with hidden "optimizing" features, some of which can compromise explicit security settings.

Illustrative of proxy subversion is the ubiquitous MS IE (v5+) Web client, not p2p to be sure. It has at least one little-known quirk concerning its (rather convoluted) settings for proxy use. IE will blatantly ignore these settings if it can determine that a direct (as it sees it, "optimal") connection is possible. Thus, it's possible for a home-firewall user to be firewall/filter protected only on the first outgoing connection attempt of a session—IE bypasses the proxy on all subsequent connections.

Convenience Lapses

One **convenience feature** to be careful of is the automatic scan of the hard disk for files to share, along with the setting to recursively scan folders. It's easy to share too much. Optional scan (default off), clear settings and indications, and the ability to specify "safe" file types and exclude categories are some of the desired control options.

A feature in some client implementations that's a potential security risk is the automatic client upgrade, where the software can detect when newer versions or new components are available on the network (or from an internally specified server) and automatically initiate a user-transparent fetch and upgrade process. An unattended p2p client can thus continually "evolve" and automatically restart itself as the latest release version without any user interaction. This is not exclusive to p2p because many other types of Windows software have similar auto-upgrade functionality.

This feature is undeniably a valuable convenience when client software is rapidly evolving, ensuring that everyone quickly gets the latest versions without reinstalling. However, the process also restarts the client so that the new version can be executed in its place, which disrupts connectivity. In many cases, it means an entirely new network topology is seen by the peer application after it rejoins the network. A related risk, especially on an untended system, is when an upgrade turns out to be unstable. It's little consolation to the user of a crashed unattended system, that on occasions when this happens, an emergency upgrade is quickly released.

You should note that the setting for detect and upgrade is typically enabled by default. A related setting, sometimes invisible, is how often the client checks for new versions. At best, both can be user configured, though often hard to find.

More seriously, the upgrade process could be subverted so that a client is tricked into fetching and executing a rogue program instead of the usual upgrader. The rogue program can do all manner of malicious activities from the machine it's running on, having bypassed virus and permission checks because it's a child process to the client.

This kind of piecemeal application-internalized updating and its associated risks are made unnecessary when the update mechanism is integrated with the operating system, such as in FreeBSD Unix. Similar schemes are being developed in Linux. With Debian GNU/Linux, for example, the user can upgrade all installed software with the latest versions by entering a single command ("apt-get upgrade"), or optionally upgrade just specified applications or groups. The packages are fetched from trusted **FTP** servers all over the world, according to the stability criteria set by the user: stable (well-tested), testing, or unstable (bleeding-edge). Nothing like this is available for Windows (yet), despite Windows Update and third party auto-upgraders.

SUBVERSIVE P2P

Some p2p solutions are intentionally designed with more than a little bit of "subversion" in mind. Although such a design might seem attractive for other reasons (for example, encrypted content storage or protection against content manipulation), it's an aspect of the solution that carries some risks.

Above all, adoption of such a technology in the wrong setting, such as in enterprise, can prove both ill-advised and embarrassing if management demands central control of content and clear audit trails.

Some p2p developers believe that once information is digitized, it is free for everyone and must never be censored. Therefore, they make their p2p designs profoundly reflect that view. Such a technology solution can make it *impossible* to apply any serious content management to make the deployment compliant with overall corporate network policy.

Other technologies go to great lengths to ensure anonymity of both ends of a node conversation. But anonymity might be inappropriate for contexts where clear sender-receiver trails are necessary for external reasons. Anonymity is discussed later in this chapter, while implementation examples are found in Chapter 9.

REDUNDANCY AND PERSISTENCE

We tend to assume that stored content remains available forever, despite experiences to the contrary when personal PCs crash or corporate servers go down. Backups can restore lost content—usually—and more often in the latter case. But that's with centralized content management (by user or IT department).

What of p2p content? That depends on the technology and network. In simple atomistic p2p, like Gnutella, random duplication of content covers most of the slack in backup through sheer **redundancy**—the more critical issue is finding nodes online with the desired content and the free capacity to transfer it.

Distributed storage generally has built-in replication and error-correction functionality, which also compensates for a lack of formal backups. Some storage solutions provide automatic replication based on demand, which not only improves performance, but also ensures greater redundant availability.

Explicit content management is usually not an option, however. Systems like Freenet even automate purging of content by dropping content that isn't requested often enough. This kind of management is totally agnostic of content, based solely on demand, and clearly not suitable for general-purpose archival purposes.

Other systems might prioritize total persistence but show unacceptable retrieval response for everyday use. An analogue would be to compare online storage (on hard disk) with offline storage (such as on tape or CD/DVD). The former is comparatively fast but somewhat risky, and often-used data is given priority in the constrained capacity. The latter is slower and must be manually mounted to access, but storage capacity is essentially unlimited. In addition, offline-stored information is far more secure in terms of persistence. Offline storage media are therefore suitable for permanent archival purposes. (We ignore for the moment that no storage media is *guaranteed* persistent. Even CD data can be eaten to oblivion by bacteria.)

As with every other technology, p2p is fraught with compromise and trade-off. It's well worth the extra effort to explore these issues before committing large amounts of content to a particular technology.

> **Bit 4.7   When considering p2p, think of leveraging existing resources and storage more than migrating to an entirely new infrastructure.**
>
> P2P is more about the process of communicating and moving data, notwithstanding that it offers interesting innovations for distributed, adaptive storage.

Perhaps the most attractive solution in most contexts is one that can leverage existing storage, giving an edge to some of the simpler implementations that focus only on making the content accessible. Building on existing infrastructure allows great flexibility in deployment without necessitating major restructuring.

LEGAL ISSUES

First, realize that no book can even begin to replace professional advice from lawyers who are accustomed to dealing with individual or corporate legal issues relevant to your particular situation and location. This section can only attempt to raise your awareness of what issues might be at stake, so that you can intelligently pose the appropriate questions to such professionals.

In fact, even the professionals can get it "wrong" according to after-the-fact court rulings, especially in such complex and changing areas as intellectual property rights, digital rights, and jurisdiction applicability to the Internet.

See this section as an overview of a partially explored land, describing some of the landmarks that have become visible and indicating some of the hazards that will need to be navigated or landscaped away at some future time.

PEER COMMUNICATION

The root of most of the potential legal problems lies in the fundamental fact that p2p is decentralized by design, at times aggressively so. Because they actively promote the notion of user control of local resources, p2p applications inherently tend to conflict with centralized control, authentication, and traditional corporate security measures. This may or may not be a problem depending on the situation. Unconsidered, it is.

It may seem innocent enough, for example, that a user installs a messaging client in order to converse with other people on the Internet. But as noted earlier, such an action opens an external, uncontrolled access point to that user's computer through the client software. By extension, it might also open external access (with user permissions) to other resources on the corporate network through the user's computer. The client might allow any number of other services, such as file sharing, in ways that ignore firewalls and are perhaps unknown to the user, which introduces the risk that legal liabilities arise through actions by the local user or other peer users.

> **Bit 4.8   Peer clients invariably open unconsidered security holes.**
> If only because of their "uncontrollable" nature, p2p technology must be examined as a potential loose cannon in security-conscious environments and be deployed only after careful consideration of potential effects and applicable precautions.

The worst thing is not knowing what the situation is. A particular IM client might be designed just for messaging, equivalent to a phone call, but then again it might allow much, much more. With some understanding of what a given client might be capable of, and how it does this, informed precautions can at least ensure that inappropriate services are not activated by default, or that the connectivity scope is limited to the LAN or proxy. A clear policy of which client implementations are acceptable or not also helps; some implementations carry greater risks than others or may even include spyware components that the average user is unaware of.

This is nothing specific to p2p technology. It's been highlighted that much commercial software can pose similar risks. For example, the automated diagnostic reporting in MS Office XP not only "phones home" and sends details of software and hardware status after crashes, but might also include sensitive documents being worked on when the application crashed. Other products might compile profiles of usage or storage that could prove a serious liability in some contexts.

Even "enterprise-approved" solutions, such as Windows Messenger, can mandate the redesign or upgrade of existing firewall products in order to work at all and still allow reasonable intranet security. We may note that the adoption of the Universal Plug and Play (UPnP) standard by Microsoft enables applications to reconfigure external equipment on-the-fly. Newer firewall products will comply with UPnP, and the stated intent is that, for example, the WM client will be able to open firewall ports on demand, *automatically and remotely!* (Is it just me, or did I future-sense some especially security-conscious readers fainting at this point?) This is one reason why the recent Windows XP UPnP vulnerability exploit got such immediate attention by security experts.

FILE SHARING

The legal and ethical issues raised by file-sharing technology can be complex even within supposedly well-controlled, corporate LAN environments. On a public, distributed peer network, the issue of control becomes an illusion—or a nightmare, depending on your perspective. In fact, in some p2p implementations, it's by design "impossible" to police or censor content, save by shutting down all connectivity.

Deploying a peer network to share content invariably opens at least the potential risk that users will exchange content they legally shouldn't. The practical point here isn't whether or not the people involved might have done so by other means anyway, or the legality of such sharing, it's that the peer technology makes the process immediate, easy, transparent, and hard to detect. In addition, it might involve access by an anonymous external party without the knowledge of the hosting user.

The legal exposure of a company hosting a file-sharing network is unclear, and probably depends both on what the content is and what external policies and control structures are in place—ultimately how public the access is.

> **Bit 4.9 Even a "closed" p2p network might inadvertently become public.**
> Careless configurations, user-initiated connection to external networks, and dependencies on third-party servers all conspire to make external access possible.

This kind of exposure issue is not however a totally new consideration, because it has been applied to the situation of faxes and individual e-mail content sent (or sent wrongly) through a corporate network. The inherently automatic peer-sharing of content in most p2p clients does aggravate the situation because users can end up disseminating proprietary or sensitive content without realizing it. Just think of how often an e-mail response intended as a private reply is instead broadcast to an entire mailing list, only because the default return address used by mail clients is the usually hidden Reply-to address (to a list relay server), not the visible From address. Worse, it might carry the bulk of the thread, auto-appended as quotes to the bottom.

A further complication is the current shifting of the entire foundations for copyright protection and enforcement, which seriously puts into question even the accepted traditions of fair use. The ultimate results of this have yet to be determined, especially with regard to content sharing, but it must be realized that much of p2p technology is specifically designed to ensure "free information" even in the face of hostile content ownership regulation, censorship, and inspection. The bias, intentional or not, is therefore to facilitate exchange of any content.

Digital content has become the battleground that defines an emerging new economy based on unlimited replication at infinitesimal cost. No matter which views one has about one or the other side in the arguments about content ownership, it's undeniable that unregulated digital content is a serious threat to those who have investments in traditional commercial content distribution systems. This issue is discussed at length in Chapter 11, where we also look at the social implications.

Exchange Liability

Part of the liability issue was highlighted by Napster's rapid rise to popularity, mainly because of the focus on MP3 music files and the fact that users wanted to swap and collect any music files. Superficially, the case was simple:

1. Users allowed others to download MP3 files on their system.

2. Users could freely download MP3 files from millions of other users.

3. Most MP3 files were recordings made from somebody's CD (in other words, a copy of a commercial song).

From the perspective of the record labels that own the distribution rights to most of the music on commercial CDs, p2p file sharing represented content piracy on an outrageous scale. In moments of candor, current rights owners also admit to the legal interpretation that *any* act of copying, even for personal use, must be stopped. This restriction goes far beyond what the majority of consumers are prepared to agree to.

So, predictably, the labels did their utmost to close down Napster, along with any other service that allowed the transfer of music files over the Internet. This included sites like mp3.com, which tried to profile their services merely as a way for legitimate owners of CDs to listen to the musical content from other locations, not exchange promiscuously with others. In legal terms, this may matter little, because as mentioned, any act of copying is now (probably) seen as illegal.

> **Bit 4.10 Any p2p deployment must consider what the users are likely to use it for, especially when the focus is content sharing.**
>
> Taking the stance that it is the responsibility of the individual user is clearly not a viable defence, or at least not an easy one, in the current litigious climate.

Napster and other services were immediately held liable and possible to shut down, if only due to their centralized directory services. Without the directory services, there is no search and exchange service and thus no functional network. The ultimatum was that either the directory owners implemented effective filters for commercial content or be shut down. The former proved impossible in the allowed time frame, so the fate for Napster-like p2p was a given. The services are instead being retooled into commercial outlets for the labels, although it's still unclear whether the stated tight filtering of subsequent user content swapping will prove successful.

The second round of litigation centers on applying pressure to those who develop or provide software for the distributed networks that lack a central server. Several interesting client implementations being developed have already been abandoned in response to such threats.

A possible third round might involve any owners of the systems that in any way host p2p technologies capable of unlawful file exchanges. This last is where a possible, albeit not too likely, crunch can come for those who deploy sharing systems for other purposes. This is probably as good a reason as any to not completely rebuild your infrastructure into the p2p sharing model, but instead "overlay" existing functionality in a way that makes a fast retreat possible.

As broadband connectivity becomes more common, the issue of copies of movies from DVD is approaching a similar situation, with the added dimension of how such exchanges saturate Internet bandwidth with files larger by several orders of magnitude than the music tracks at issue previously. These exchanges are made over decentralized sharing networks as well, and they therefore bring additional litigious pressure to the p2p arena from the studios that own the rights to the movies.

INTELLECTUAL PROPERTY RIGHTS

The legal dimension of content sharing is not limited to music or video, but includes commercial software, images, books, and pretty much anything. Anytime a claim to intellectual property ownership (such as copyright) is made on digital content, there is likely to be contention about what one can or cannot do with it.

Trying to manage intellectual property rights (IPR) in an electronic context presents several problems. Distribution contracts, legislation, and judicial practicalities all provide contradictory interpretations and rulings. We can deal only with the "obvious" cases to gain a minimum of insight.

Public Licensing

The simplest situation is when content explicitly states that it may be copied and freely distributed. In a more legally binding (and mind numbing) form, we have numerous "public licenses" based on the open source and open content movements. There is little problem in such cases: it's free, it's fair, it's legal. One must still be mindful of the license stipulations, however, in details such as whether the material can be distributed, modified, or used in commercial contexts.

Though not always well understood, material where the rights have expired are in the "public domain" and may also be freely copied and modified. The difficulty with supposed public domain is that additional rights might remain or might have been renewed past an expected expiry date, and different countries have different rules about this sort of thing. The copyright owner can also place material in the public domain at any time prior to expiration—such an action, at least, is an *explicit* declaration. Unfortunately, the aggressive threats by the commercial interests sometimes extend to what are formally public domain or fair use areas.

> *A practical example (and by no means unique) is the story of the not-for-profit OnLine Guitar Archive Sites (OLGA) that collected tablature notations for early guitar works. It legitimately provided a valuable cultural resource for music that was unavailable in any format. The Harry Fox Agency (representing the National Music Publishers' Association) essentially forced the site to close down because it was impossible for the owners to prove that, among the many thousands of tablatures, there was not a single one that might be under copyright protection. Note that HFA itself made no distinction between original music and third-party notations or derivative arrangements.*

A problem is that it's often unrealistic for individuals or even companies to pursue the matter further. Under the threat of immediate closure by Internet service or presence provider (ISP/IPP) of Web site and e-mail services to an established domain, many site owners take the prudent but unfortunate route of quickly acquiescing to even outrageous demands rather than contesting the legal interpretations.

A vast range of confusion does exist with regard to content on the Internet. Whenever an explicit statement of ownership or copyright is involved, it should be honored, along with any instructions as to fair use. Most people however have a pretty casual attitude to anything published on public sites or available as download, and the attitude extends to much material within corporate networks in the absence of clear rules by management. Because of the ease of digital copying and sending copies, the step in effort and reflection from private copies for home to free copies for friends is infinitesimal. Thus it's vital not just to clearly mark sensitive material, but also to ensure protection from casual, sight-unseen sharing by p2p clients.

Created or Owned Content

Equally simple, it would seem, is the situation with content you have created yourself or that you or your corporation own outright. Turns out it might not be that simple because ownership and distributive rights are being decoupled in new and unforeseen ways, and sometimes usage and distribution are blindly enforced by third parties.

Recall the view that all copying is illegal? This view is already being extended into the world of physical devices. For example, it's impossible to copy minidisc MP3 recordings to a second disc, the hardware/firmware won't let you do it—no matter if the recording is one you created yourself. In a similar vein, you might soon find that videocam recordings archived on digital media can't be replicated on your VCR. Some new music CDs incorporate strong copy prevention, at times compromising playability on older CD-players or computers. In this case, however, Philips inserted a wrench (or spanner, in UK parlance) by contesting the right to call such a product a "CD", a registered name that implies a certain minimum quality/playability.

Interesting times....

Media-embedded copy prevention, or "digital content management" (DCM), could spell the end of p2p content-sharing technologies, along with a number of other things we take for granted. Many media player products are already DCM-compliant. A new and different infrastructure of hardware, firmware, and legislation is growing, which full blown and fully deployed could mean that any distribution or usage of digital content would require registration of creative ownership with a central content-tracking server, along with usage and distribution terms, then approval from the same server whenever it is accessed or copied—probably for a per-use fee. Unregistered content would simply be unstorable on legislation-compliant media.

For many, this scenario is a nightmare vision that negates the very idea of personal ownership and media use. Some commercial interests, on the other hand, see it as a highly desirable cornerstone for generic pay-per-use, rent-everything applicable to software, content access, and eternal revenue flow.

> *If this seems far-fetched or draconian, consider that it has for many years been illegal in most modern countries to play or perform music in "public" places, including background music in shops, without paying a pro rata monthly fee to the RIAA-equivalent national body that collects performance royalties for the music labels, even if the music happens to be original and the rights "owned" by the one playing, or in the public domain. The fees are totally unrelated to what is played, and are distributed centrally according to quotas set by whatever is played most often, as a rule based on radio playlists.*

A curious ramification of this one-sided arrangement is that even "obvious" rights to one's own creative efforts are eroding, the very rights that "copyright" were supposed to safeguard. I surely must own the music, art, photography, writing that I create; yet what good is that right if I can't store any of it electronically, freely perform it in public, or distribute copies to others at my own discretion? Small wonder that creative people everywhere who realize this fact are beginning to react.

What is the current legal and social state of digital ownership anyway?

Digital Ownership and Fair Use

In the public mind, "ownership" usually has a different meaning than the strict legal sense. With material things, this discrepancy has little consequence. You buy something; you own it. Proof of ownership is pragmatically that you possess the thing—*possession is nine-tenths of the law* is after all the old Anglo-Saxon adage.

When I buy something, I usually feel that I can do what I wish with it. I can sell it, give it away, lend it to a friend, whatever. I can use it as many times as I wish, until it "breaks" or I no longer possess it. This practical state of affairs has applied to copyrighted material as well—think of physical books or CDs. The commercial transactions were tied to an identifiable original item, never mind that it was mass produced—it could be replicated only by expending resources beyond the means of the ordinary individual. This situation shifted dramatically in just decades.

Enter cheap, fast, ubiquitous photocopying technology. With some transitional problems, a concept of "fair use" emerged. To begin with, it was highly unlikely that anyone would mistake the copy for the original. Copying entire books was possible, but something few were likely to do and hardly for profit. Despite the undisputed legal problem, many would consider photocopying an out of print or otherwise unavailable volume a legitimate, if cumbersome, fair-use action. People did so all the time, notwithstanding compelling reasons why this might be a form of theft.

Enter electronic storage. Now an endless supply of identical copies could be produced at virtually no cost at all. Or put another way: *All copies are originals*. Although this lossless replication is invaluable in many ways, it caused serious disruption to the traditional interpretations of ownership.

> **Bit 4.11 Digital items are critically different from physical items, yet the public perception of ownership remains relatively unchanged.**
>
> It's unclear at present whether a different view of ownership, as proposed by new DCM legislation, would be generally acceptable to the broad public.

The public paradigm is that possession equates to ownership. The application of this interpretation is simple to see. To own two copies of a book stored electronically, or a CD with favorite music, I no longer need to buy another. I just copy the file, or duplicate the CD, or alternatively make a collection of MP3 files from it. Convenient and practical, copying content for personal use is to most people perfectly OK, and it used to be considered fair use. People do it all the time without a qualm. I can have a "working copy" or several in different locations, yet keep my "original" safe. Digital technology has thus *empowered* ownership.

Working copies have long been standard procedure with software, even recommended, though many vendors have tried to make the practice difficult or impossible—legally, through restrictive contract licensing, as well as with various copy-prevention tricks. Buyers get upset when their perceived ownership rights are thwarted by such measures. On their part, vendors have tried to redefine the commercial transaction as first a licensing agreement, later a limited pay-for-use agreement, saying you can't purchase ownership of the product, only a limited usage right. Digital technology is a powerful influence even here because it also makes it possible to monitor, record and *restrict* what people look at, listen to, read, or use.

The registered license, pay-per-use and time-limited consumption models devised to limit the unauthorized distribution of software are all rapidly entering the arena of digital content management. At the same time, the corporate holders of IPR are actively working to enlarge their rights at the expense of users.

The shift can impact deployment of p2p solutions and security in various ways.

- What has traditionally been seen as legitimate limited copying, in the fair-use sense, and distribution of copyright-protected content can now often be successfully prosecuted as infringement of IPR.

- New media display and storage technologies (for hardware as well as software) can incorporate both "report-home/register" and "blocking" functionality that can seriously compromise network security or seriously impair the reliable function of local machines.

- Some IPR holders have been accused of using the questionable tactic of infiltrating public p2p networks with bogus clients that are capable of automatic denial-of-service (**DoS**) attacks on nodes and subnets that appear to store copyright-protected content.

The conclusion must be that as long as these free versus protected issues are being debated, deployment of p2p solutions that can be accessed from the Internet can imply significant but largely unquantifiable security and legal risks.

In most cases, individuals, organizations, and businesses tend to "wing it" and just hope the legal issue never comes to a head. Unfortunately, this behavior is based on a perception of a simpler time, when rights to fair use were easier to defend and when the formal rights owners weren't quite as aggressive about asserting control. In some contexts, notably educational, attempts made to formalize fair-use guidelines for faculty note with some resignation that defence strategy rests on case law as a rule, but as yet no suitable cases exist to refer to that directly address educational, nonprofit fair use in the new and narrower interpretation.

For most, the projected costs of trying to contest the accusation of illegal use is such that the mere threat of litigation forces closure of the contested activity.

The Legislative Mess

In the space of only a few years, and largely as a result of the Digital Millennium Copyright Act (DMCA) legislation, the United States currently suffers restrictions on fair use of copyrighted material unknown elsewhere in the world, seriously affecting the traditional fair-use areas of criticism, comment, news reporting, teaching, scholarship, and research.

The pending Consumer Broadband and Digital Television Promotion Act (CBDTPA), formerly called the Security Systems Standards and Certification Act (SSSCA), if passed in U.S. Congress, would make that situation far more critical. In the opinion of some, it would make even the Internet as a whole essentially illegal the way it works now—see the Electronic Frontier Foundation site (www.eff.org). The criteria set out in the Act don't require the preservation or protection of fair use, first sale, the public domain, or any of the other rights reserved for the public by copyright law. The Act would furthermore require digital-rights management mechanisms to be embedded in any "interactive digital device" to enforce compliance with the legislated ban on handling unlicensed content. This is the recording block mentioned earlier extended to all content and all devices—past, present, and future.

One might reasonably object that U.S. legislation should not apply to a borderless global medium such as the Internet. However, the rest of the world, led by Europe, is rapidly catching up with equally draconian legislation. The DCMA was after all an implementation of the 1996 WIPO World Copyright Treaty, although the WCT largely reflects American IPR interests. Besides, international compliance to U.S. laws would be automatic if DCM technology is unilaterally embedded in the hardware, firmware, and software used to access content. Analysis and circumvention of DCM would be illegal, with noncompliant foreign interests harshly penalized or prosecuted. What remains to be seen is whether this kind of legislation can be enforced, and whether it can be applied to the globally mobile user of the Internet, even assuming he or she can be reliably identified with any given content transaction.

As a side note, under U.S. law, a claim of copyright violation merits prior restraint of publication—one of the rare exceptions to the First Amendment's general prohibition on prior restraint. Thus, even media reporting about copyright-related (or IPO) infringement could be muzzled if the climate became that extreme. There have already been tendencies in that direction in the much-publicized case after a then16-year-old Norwegian student posted on the Internet in 2000 a program (DeCSS) that defeats the security software on DVD-formatted movies, with the intent of making DVD movies playable on **platforms** such as Linux that lack official support for DVD players. Detained and prosecuted by the Norwegian authorities, and sued by the DVD Copy Control Association in December 2000, the boy and his father suffered what many feel is unjust persecution, yet much of the fuss stemmed from the largely unsuccessful attempts to ban both publication of and hyperlink reference to the source code and its documentation. This case led to closure of Web sites and attempts to prosecute others who objected that they were only reporting on the situation. A comprehensive (and in parts, ironic) compilation of material specific to DeCSS and the legal convolutions around the controversy can be found at the university site www-2.cs.cmu.edu/~dst/DeCSS/Gallery/. While the DeCSS controversy is specific to the decoding of DVD recordings, it nonetheless indicates the borderline-absurd interpretational maelstrom that arises around half-baked interpretations of the new copyright laws (such as the DCMA).

Anyone interested in this arcane field of digital rights legislation can do worse than looking up the book *Digital Copyright*, by Jessica Litman (Prometheus Books, 2001). A part of the material can be read online at www.digital-copyright.com.

ANONYMITY

A legal issue seldom probed, but made relevant by the way some p2p solutions offer authenticated anonymity to both content publishers and retrievers, is that of secure personal anonymity. Is this a right, or a threat? The interesting thing about this "new" anonymity is how, when combined with the power of digital signatures based on public key encryption, it allows anyone to be both anonymous and trusted (or authenticated) at the same time. In other words, it's possible to remain fully anonymous, yet be able to publicly prove that you are unrefutably the originator of particular messages or published content.

Some find this new anonymity concept absolutely fabulous, putting a new meaning to the term "trusted but unnamed source". We meet it again in the contexts of encrypted solutions, examined in Chapter 9, and of p2p journalism, which is discussed in Chapter 12. The concept of anonymity has several dimensions, an analysis of which was developed in detail for a Web context in *Anonymous Web Transactions with Crowds* by M.K. Reiter and A.D. Rubin (Communications of the ACM 42, 1999). They specified three degrees to any analysis of anonymity.

- **Type,** which specifies sender or receiver anonymity.

- **Adversary,** or who is trying to break the anonymity.

- **Degree,** which may range from *absolute privacy* (imperceptible presence), through *beyond suspicion, probable innocence, possible innocence, exposed* (to the adversary), to *provably exposed* (to others).

Different technical solutions to anonymity plot differently in this T-A-D volume, to which we must in fairness add a fourth dimension of *authenticity* or trust—it's not enough to just say an implementation allows anonymous access. An analysis must also factor in what parts of anonymity have priority, so that for example, some "adversaries" might be allowed limited insight, or it might be enough to shelter behind "probable innocence" in most circumstances.

Peer to Peer Solutions

Deploying P2P Solutions

Before getting lost in the technical detail of the different implementations, fascinating as that may be, let's take a moment to consider the practicalities of choosing and deploying a p2p solution in the first place. In other words, we should try to relate the deployment context and the goals with a general evaluation of the potential benefits and problems that peer technologies might bring.

The individual user usually has great freedom to install any desired peer technology and usually demonstrates a casual attitude to connecting p2p to an external and essentially untrusted network such as the Internet. Therefore, the deployment discussion has a marked bias towards business contexts, where multiple clients and a particular technology are to be deployed into a specific context and an existing community. The corporate decision process is more involved and is often determined by factors other than simple functionality requirements, and it's some of these factors that are considered in this chapter.

However, deployers in both individual and business contexts do well to consider the general issues. Even the casual individual user should look for the nonobvious requirements and constraints that are built into particular solutions, any one of which could easily turn into a "gotcha" after deployment. Such an awareness, sensitized by asking the right questions and examining the solutions from a perspective nearer the corporate one, can promote the realization that some client software might be unacceptably limited or intrusive for virtually any context.

CHAPTER 5 AT A GLANCE

This chapter examines many of the questions that should be considered in advance of installation and potential deployment of peer technologies.

Practical Considerations takes up general deployment issues seen in particular contexts, pros and cons, with a special focus on business environments.

- *Why Deploy P2P?* is a question to ponder because it might not always make sense to do so in a given context.

- *Business Considerations* examines the pros and cons from the perspective of making business sense.

- *The Benefits* goes into more detail, contrasted by the following section on *The Problems*.

Selecting and Deploying the Technology provides a rough deployment guide.

- Examples are given of the kinds of practical checklists and considerations, grouped by general categories, that should be examined.

- *Dynamic or Static* notes critical differences in peer networks compared to server-client ones.

- Specific groups of questions are in *Determining Purpose and Scope* as a guide to planning and in *Select an Implementation* as a guide to selection.

Scalability Barriers examines the growth constraints of particular solutions.

- This section addresses network growth in terms of *Connectivity and Scale*, and *Addressability and Scale*.

- Different architectural models scale differently, as discussed in *Scalability in the Atomistic Model*, *Scalability in the User-Centric Model*, and *Scalability in the Data-Centric Model*.

- Finally, *An Adaptive Large-Scale Solution* looks at hot-off-the-sourceforge protocol for massive concurrent network connectivity that could solve the scalability problem for peer networks in some contexts.

PRACTICAL CONSIDERATIONS

It's easy to become beguiled by the promise and potential of the feature sets that p2p implementations claim, especially when looking at the promotional claims coming from both the free and commercial camps in the field.

While a peer technology can be ideal for some applications of information access, it will assuredly fail miserably in others. The first requirement of any intelligent choice is at least being able to identify the general areas where a particular application might be spectacularly inappropriate.

Take for example a simple file-sharing system with files individually managed at every node. Files are probably duplicated across many nodes, which is fine for content that is unchanging. Random duplication can even help retrieval and download performance, needing nothing more sophisticated than broadcast query search.

However, such a simple system would be unsuitable for another environment where content is constantly being changed, say documentation for a project team. The overriding issue for retrieval in such a system would be: *Where is the most up-to-date copy?* Simple query results can't answer that question, because the dynamic-content situation requires some form of versioning or managed metadata tracking. A better solution in this case would be a publish-oriented distributed storage. The best answer might be an ordinary server-based versioning system and to focus the p2p aspect on providing peer communication and collaboration—an IM system.

Define the goals, ask if they are appropriate or reasonable, and match the software solutions. Then check if the proposed solutions actually can deliver on the real questions in the user context, as indicated by the previous thought example.

Why Deploy P2P?

The first question about p2p deployment that should arise is "Why am I considering p2p solutions?" Other formulations with a more specific focus can also come to mind: What are the benefits? What are the risks? *Is it worth it?*

To adequately answer these and similar questions requires an understanding of your specific requirements in relation to what p2p in general can and can't do, along with a feeling for the capabilities of a considered implementation.

Equally important is some kind of *guiding vision* of what you are embarking on. Because p2p is often as much about attitude and community as it is about technology, your users may need an articulated vision in order to understand and effectively use the new capabilities that a deployed peer system provides. In fact, you may need to actively evangelize the vision to promote usage.

We'll recap some of the fundamental p2p principles in this analytic context.

Bit 5.1   Peer computers respond independently to requests from other peers.
This is fundamental. However, the scope of requests and responses, their execution, and the degree of user involvement are all application specific.

The functionality of peer technology is built on endpoint messaging and shared resources. Direct exchanges between peer members of the p2p network manage access and the use of these resources. In other words, a peer can directly initiate messaging with other peers; request information about content stored on other peers; have content read, copied, or stored; request transfer of this content to others; request processing of information and have results sent back—all without any central control, or even awareness of the exchanges, and often without the immediate knowledge of the local users.

Bit 5.2   Peer computers normally act and respond without central control.
Peer technology makes sense only if such autonomous behavior is allowed within the context of the deployed p2p network.

So one major question becomes: Do you *want* this kind of free exchange between individual computers in your network? Or more to the point for business deployment: Is this kind of exchange allowed within the context of current network or corporate policy? Might there be contexts where it is, and others where it isn't?

Clearly, there are vast differences in this respect between a p2p network limited to a local intranet, a p2p deployment that allows authenticated remote access over public lines, and a solution that is open to peer clients on the Internet at large. The selection of an appropriate technology critically depends on such scope decisions.

As for the issue of context, not everything lends itself easily to decentralization and hence to redesign as a p2p system. For enterprise, service-oriented architectures are considered the most adaptable to structural change. Therefore, services are the first likely candidates for migration to peer architecture.

But all services might not be suitable. Many mission-critical services need to be carefully managed—quality-of-service (QoS) monitored for high availability, performance, and data integrity. It's possible that a p2p technology can be successfully deployed in such a critical environment, but it will assuredly take hard work and careful design to achieve the same goals. The more immediate objection can be that there's little margin for experiment in mission-critical contexts.

As a group, process-oriented systems aren't normally good candidates for p2p. They tend to be too formalized and tied to all manner of centralized decision, control, and quality assurance mechanisms. However, a loosely coupled business process, controlled overall by a workflow or business process management system, could be restructured to be delivered by autonomous p2p systems without too great an effort. Newer Web services often fall into this category.

Redesign is a nontrivial task in either case, so it must be sufficiently motivated. Avoid the critical systems unless there's adequate margin and redundancy until the new system is verifiably functional. Instead of redesign, perhaps set a first goal to implement new services that don't exist yet because they are really possible only in a peer environment. With a successful deployment, the experience is bound to make a proposed redesign more manageable and perhaps more acceptable to all affected.

When in doubt, let this adage be your guide: *If it ain't broke, don't fix it!* And from the pragmatic business point of view: *Don't build what you can't manage.* An even more pragmatic approach might be to apply these criteria to adoption:

1. Ease of use
2. Utility of use
3. Cost of use
4. Necessity of use

The last is sometimes the only one that matters, although the necessity might not be obvious from the start.

Decentralized collaboration tools are the kind of deployments that users and managers end up finding a necessity only after adopting and learning to use them over a period of time—initial reactions from the old working methodology viewpoint are frequently expressed as "What's the point?"

Business Considerations

An overall business analysis of the "new Internet", in which distributed processing and peer networking seems destined to be an integral part, can be found in a special report, *Internet Infrastructure & Services* by Chris Kwak and Robert Fagin (Bear Sternes and Equity Research Technology, May 2001)—Appendix B for sources.

The 178-page report is well worth perusal, although like everything else in this field, the underlying situation changes so rapidly and sometimes so unexpectedly that any published material risks being outdated. The report is perhaps most interesting for the insight it gives to a number of business ventures in 1999 and 2000 that were based on distributed processing and peer technologies. Several of the visible projects based on these solutions give little or no surface indication that they are built on distributed or peer technologies, so the investigative effort published in reports like this give a better indication of what's going on.

The advocate point is often made that *p2p is less costly for enterprise* than traditional centralized client-server (cC-S) solutions. The previously mentioned report makes this astute observation about probable cost savings:

> *cC-S systems are also high-maintenance. Servicing cC-S systems can be prohibitively expensive, much more costly than equipment and software. For example Oracle derives over 70% of its revenues from services, not its database software and applications. Microsoft derives over 30% of revenues from services; this would likely be much higher if Microsoft did not sell Windows to consumers. According to IDC, the cost of managing storage is four times the cost of storage hardware.*

Aside from direct service cost, companies also feel indirect costs caused by server vulnerabilities and the costs for backup systems. Significant bottom-line pressure is therefore exerted on business to find more cost-effective solutions, and this reality explains much of the drive to try p2p in the face of cautionary factors that would otherwise be deemed prohibitive.

On the other hand, and only indirectly alluded to in the report, is the simple math that the aggregate equipment and operating cost for the entire p2p network and its resources can be much, much larger than the centralized server solution, even allowing for its greater capacity. This cost is usually not an issue because, on the one hand, most of these distributed resources already exist and are paid for, and on the other, the procurement and operating costs are equally distributed and thus relatively small for each cost accounting entity.

THE BENEFITS

Both technical advantages and "social" benefits to using p2p technology can be identified, albeit their perceived and relative importance can vary considerably between different settings.

One bottom line seems clear for business: *Networks create value.* The natural extension of this is that any enhancement of digital networks will have profound economic consequences for any business operation. The enhancements can be to the pervasiveness, reach, value, or flexibility of the network; all possible with p2p.

The special feature of p2p in a business environment is a direct function of peer communication: the ability to form *ad hoc* groupings or peer groups based on common interests and goals. Numerous situations exist where informal groupings can be leveraged by peer technologies to make collaboration more effective. Incidentally, when considering groupings, don't forget to include the entirely new collaboration possibilities that a peer application might provide.

Business Benefits

The business viewpoint is largely congruent with economy, but it also considers such things as QoS, adaptability, and security. Nevertheless, we can make the case that the most significant factor to determine adoption is the perceived size of the opportunity.

Some of the more specific issues that can benefit from distributed peer architectures are

- **Geographic locality.** Traditional server centralization has problems adapting to mobility and access from all parts of a far-flung company. Peer solutions are distributed and can thus provide data, resources, and services where they are needed.

- **Server downtime.** An offline server can paralyze many corporate activities across the board because of server dependencies. E-mail service is just one example. Peer solutions distribute the risks, and the network can remain functional despite a large number of nonresponsive nodes.

- **Central administration bottlenecks.** Not everyone can make themselves heard or have their needs fulfilled in a heavily centralized scheme. The peer approach is that users manage their own resources to fulfill their own needs, or they contact directly other nodes that can. Initial setup of peer workgroups by the participants is also easy—project groups can form and change quickly.

- **Granularity issues.** Solutions or services in centralized systems don't always avail themselves to individual users at their own convenience. Peer granularity, by definition, is at the user level.

- **Intermediated workflow.** Critical client-server conduits must pass through centralized services. In peer systems, contact is direct, which is often better.

- **Fragmentation of network.** It becomes difficult for users in one area to contact resources and users in another, tied to another server. Again, peer connectivity is direct, dynamically forming virtually connected interest groups as users gravitate towards some common purpose.

- **Resource bottlenecks.** Network delays and service unavailability are a side effect of the fact that everyone in a centralized system must communicate through the central server instead of directly. Peer resources are distributed, and they are often replicated and made adaptive to demand.

The common factor for a lot of these issues is the way server-bound networking introduces extraneous links and components to what should be more direct connectivity, and therefore ends up being constraining and resource wasteful.

What about cost? The advantage of p2p is that existing capacity can be interconnected and used in ways impossible before. The actual cost of the processing assets (that is, procurement and operation) might be considerable, but it too is distributed and absorbed by many users. The per-unit cost is usually relatively small, and it's covered by the normal purpose of the equipment. The assumption is that most of the time, each unit has ample idle capacity to contribute to the network.

Most PCs typically sit idle most of the time, perhaps as much as 90 percent of the potential processing capacity—its single most expensive component—unused. Large companies like Intel have successfully increased in-house distributed processing to the point where it routinely can save time and hundreds of millions of dollars on design validation projects.

Similar calculations for potential savings could be made for unused storage, bandwidth, and the ability to effect parallel distribution and processes. For example, storage on disk is significantly cheaper than the cost of using bandwidth to repeatedly transfer the data from a central server. Informal estimates suggest that enterprise PC hard disks on average use only about an eighth of their storage capacity, a figure probably decreasing as the drive capacity steadily increases year by year. This is what makes network local caching and peer distributed replication so attractive from the purely economic perspective, not to mention the boost in performance.

Technical Benefits

From a technical and performance view, a p2p solution frees users from the traditional dependence on central servers and from the associated bottlenecks—both human and machine. This is especially true in areas like content publishing.

That's not to say bottlenecks disappear; central dependencies remain in server-mediated solutions, albeit loads on servers are light. The critical bottlenecks instead depend more on bandwidth and other constraints at each node but don't usually affect more than the nodes currently conversing. The same goes for failure-points.

Users gain control over the services that they utilize. In addition, content and implemented services can be distributed and made automatically load-balancing. Multiple computers can share files seamlessly, no matter where they are located in the network. This can greatly erase the distinctions between home and office networks, in that, for example, an office worker telecommuting from home might transparently access files and information that reside within the "office" network—peer technology extending the office network to any number of home workers and partners. In fact, the employee can become fully roaming, able to access (and be accessed by) the network and all its resources from any workstation location, even from wireless LAN devices such as PDAs and newer cellular phones.

The distributed nature of otherwise largely idle resources confers many benefits to network members. Benefits include freely available content storage and processing power, and optimized performance. As a rule, the resulting distributed system exhibits good performance, has fault tolerance and scalability, requires little maintenance, adapts well to change, and is cost-efficient to deploy.

For enterprise, costly data center functions can sometimes be replaced by distributed services between clients. The added advantage is that content can be managed locally and updated by the people who are directly responsible for it. Similar considerations apply to distributed remote maintenance of resources through an infrastructure capable of direct access. In particular, geographically distributed parts of a far flung corporation could automatically cross-index and update inventory, project files, resource lists, personal agendas, and so on. Team members can always have the latest data at hand at any location and reach other members and staff through a wide variety of channels.

Not all content is equally suited to distribution, but the potentials make it worth investigating. In some cases, a mix of central store, distributed publishing of updates, and local access by users might be a better solution than a fully decentralized peer topology. Automatic network agents might fulfill a number of roles here.

Social Benefits

From the social point of view, p2p users can dynamically form a broad range of *ad hoc* "communities" (known as "peer groups") to efficiently and securely fulfill their own needs—albeit this scenario assumes they will actually work together in this way. Community members can form the primary web for communication, requests, collaboration, and resource sharing.

No less important are the psychological benefits gained from establishing what are sometimes expressed as *edge services*. Despite the term "edge" suggesting remote users at the periphery of an organization, the actual location of the users involved is immaterial. That is to say, users collectively maintain and control their own services in a local setting, independently from the central parts of an organization. Users thereby feel "in control", free from centralized bureaucracy. Based on p2p technology, both user community and services can readily adapt to changes in the local environment.

The organization center in a network with edge services no longer needs to anticipate, investigate, or manage user needs in detail throughout the organization. Freed from such time-consuming tasks, it can instead focus on overall matters of policy and guidance, which is supposedly its main purpose anyway.

The Problems

Given these advantages and benefits, what then are the problems?

The Control Thing

Well, yes, of course: loss of control can be a serious problem.

The "autonomous edge" and "free agent" functionality might simply not be acceptable in some organization settings, as a matter of principle. This policy may be the stance of management as a whole, or IT management in particular; either way, such lack of acceptance can easily kill any attempts to deploy alternative structures of any kind, including p2p.

Notwithstanding unfavorable policy, one can still find some p2p solutions in "hostile" environments, albeit then introduced under the radar, limited in scope, and camouflage-described in "management acceptable" ways.

Security

Related to control is security. In addition, it is generally assumed that you can't have security without control.

Peer technologies, because of the way they circumvent central control, often also circumvent various security measures. This issue is complex and is described in detail in connection with specific situations and implementations in following chapters.

Suffice it to say here that p2p deployment in most settings, not just business ones, raises significant security concerns, which must be adequately addressed with respect to the particular technical solution chosen. Ideally, security issues should guide the selection process, rather than come in as an afterthought requiring fixes.

Inappropriate Setting

Peer technologies emphasize informal cooperation and de-emphasize hierarchies. This characteristic can make p2p inappropriate from some settings that require a more formal work process or workflow model.

With an awareness of the informal aspect inherent in p2p technologies, a solution may often be deployed as a successful complement to the formal process—as organizational aid, brainstorming facilitator, team communication channel, discussion medium, preparatory collaboration tool ahead of formal meetings, background resource manager, and so on. Informal and direct-contact aspects of p2p are why people on their own initiative install messaging clients such as ICQ.

Indifferent Users

Just because a suitable technology is deployed doesn't mean that users automatically will use it (or use it as intended). If they don't see the point or resist changing their way of working, deployment might be a futile effort—even counterproductive.

The problem of involving users arises any time a workplace infrastructure is changed, and it can literally take years to have workflow regain normal efficiency, even without significant user resistance to the innovations. When introducing new ways of working, it's crucial to have the users involved and open for change.

User resistance to new technologies expresses itself in two ways:

- **Overt resistance**, where people simply protest and refuse to use the new tools and methods, or actively sabotage the intended changes.

- **Covert resistance**, where people might avow, and sometimes themselves believe, that they are using the tools and methods, but where independent investigation shows that they in fact do things quite differently.

The latter effect has been documented only recently in studies of how people (especially teams) apply the formalized methodologies mandated in their work. It's very interesting to see how the verbalized reality-views of management and teams diverge so markedly from the actuality of how people do work and get project deliverable code out the door. See, for example, *Agile Software Development* by Alistair Cockburn (Addison-Wesley, December 2001) for a detailed discussion relating to programming teams and collaborative methodologies.

Messaging (mainly IM and e-mail) and file-sharing applications tend to be relatively simple to deploy and have people use—typical client usage meshes well with the way people intuitively go about dealing with messages or searching for and retrieving content. These activities are often asynchronous and single-user activated, and content retrieval is highly autonomous and anonymous.

The technologies with a strong collaborative focus are the difficult ones to deploy effectively because they are inherently more invasive in the way that people are used to working. User will need to adapt to a different way of working, just like they need to learn to work in project teams or use specific methodologies. The collaborative conventions need to be explored and refined for the situation, and sometimes spelled out or supported by explicit scaffolding for newcomers.

Which Software?

The buzz popularity of p2p is, paradoxically, also a problem. By early 2001, perhaps some 200 companies were depicting themselves as p2p-solution providers. Research projects targeted business-to-business (b2b), business-to-customer (b2c), customer-care (c2 or cc, meaning support), and e-commerce applications. Some also targeted consumer-to-consumer (c2c) space—for instance, auctions (as in Firstpeer).

Some of these companies were simply exploiting the trendy p2p word from the previous year, perhaps fearing to be perceived as not with it, and on closer inspection, their solutions had little to do with any useful p2p technology. By late 2001, many of these companies had vanished from the Web, or they had p2p-related Web pages that hadn't been updated since sometime in 2000. The situation is partly due to the general downturn and shakeout in the IT sector, where even seemingly viable p2p solutions appeared stricken. In some cases, the simple answer might be that the initial seed money ran out, and no investors were willing to provide more funding.

Anyway, the problem is not just to identify a viable implementation of p2p technology suitable for practical deployment but to identify—actually, *guess*—which technologies will remain viable and supported later, when your deployment is a fact and your users are dependent on the new distributed services. Many solutions available now, although interesting and workable, are proprietary, single-source offerings, which disqualifies them for many corporate settings.

Other solutions are "beta" quality or under such rapid and unpredictable development that their deployment must be seen as highly experimental. Open source implementations at least have the virtue of being maintainable in-house if someone can assume the responsibility for the deployed code.

In this book, both proprietary and open solutions are explored, so this issue is one to be mindful of with respect to the implementations discussed.

SELECTING AND DEPLOYING THE TECHNOLOGY

As a rough guide to the issues encountered, this section outlines some of the steps in the process of selecting and deploying a p2p technology.

While there is a great difference between installing a p2p solution for personal use or home LAN and deploying a solution for enterprise and thousands of users, most of the same questions should be considered even if the consequences have very different impact. All too seldom are the benefits, problems, and consequences examined in light of one's intended purpose with the deployment.

DYNAMIC OR STATIC

Something to get used to when using p2p technology, as defined in the modern sense of virtual networks overlaid on the fixed Internet or LAN infrastructure, is the intensely dynamic nature of the network so created. This is an application-level network, defined by client-to-client protocol connections that are invisibly translated at some lower protocol layer to the arbitrary physical network addresses needed to route the data packets.

Many p2p clients even eschew making the traditional Internet addressing visible to the user, mainly because it's not considered interesting or relevant to the primary objective of sharing and searching. Those clients that do show such underlying detail can provide practical insight into how connectivity constantly changes as the p2p network ceaselessly reforms into new topologies, like eddying conversations at a vast, endless cocktail party.

To be sure, a p2p network established on a corporate LAN has a relative permanence and persistence vastly more static than a public network, yet availability of individual nodes will still vary. With roving laptops and users connecting to virtual groupings from different locations, the seemingly static network suddenly appears far more dynamic than expected. It is emphatically not the same as your average Windows workgroup.

However, this dynamic indeterminism is of little consequence to the p2p clients because they are programmed not only to work with it, but even to turn it into an advantage. A potential administrative nightmare for centralized resource brokering is handled with ease. Network access usually depends only on making an initial connection to a single node—any node already a member. Even if this node refuses the connection, it can provide information about other potential nodes to try.

Determining Purpose and Scope

Peer technologies can be seen as valuable in many ways. Depending on context and setting, it may be enough or desirable to tightly focus on only one practical application. In other situations, an overall vision of p2p community might be preferable, with a high degree of user involvement in an ongoing deployment process and an openness to new uses as yet unthought of.

Some examples of purpose and scope are given in the following, by no means exhaustive, list. It's no accident that many functioning examples of these or similar applications can be found thriving on the Internet, whether they are supported by basic Internet infrastructure, public p2p technologies, proprietary solutions, or a free-wheeling mix of all of these.

- **Shared content storage and distributed accessibility.** These applications are often the ones that come first to mind, in part due to the public popularity of file-sharing p2p networks such as Napster and Gnutella. A number of good implementations that define a valid (albeit limited) application area for p2p technology are readily available for this purpose, easily adaptable to local networks as well as Internet use.

- **Secure content storage.** Situations that require reliable and redundant storage, encrypted and distributed storage, or just optimized utilization of distributed available storage capacity on a network are all possible with p2p technologies. Included in the requirements can be issues such as tracking trusted sites and reputation management.

- **Messaging networks.** Again, the wide popularity of ICQ, AIM, and other (often proprietary) messaging solutions makes messaging a natural reason for deploying p2p technology, even though you might reasonably ask why deploy another when so many users already have popular messaging clients installed. However, the use of these existing Internet messaging services raises numerous security concerns not easily addressed. For several reasons, open solutions are likely to be more attractive, yet perhaps still be compatible with the same public network protocols as the closed clients.

- **Collaborative efforts, content creation, and community web.** In a deployed p2p context providing suitable functionality, this kind of creative community can be formed *ad hoc* and dynamically around shared interests, without presupposing any form of prior organization or central control. Shared interests can include collaborative and distributed forms of virus detection, eradication, and protection.

- **Software development and support functionality.** The advantage of a p2p solution for this application area is mainly that users nearest the problems and users nearest the solutions may interact directly with each other. Users might also access and update a distributed knowledge database.

- **Actual e-business ventures firmly based in p2p.** Deployment of a suitable technology can add new capabilities for both supplier and customer chains. Applications might distribute information, content, software, or support services more effectively from locally maintained nodes.

- **Distributed content search.** In many settings, it makes sense to distribute search functionality to local nodes that store or generate the required content. Performance penalties are offset by up-to-date search results and distributed loading capability.

- **Distributed content delivery.** Suitable p2p technology can both simplify and optimize ways to provide complex and bandwidth-demanding content on demand from "nearby" storage locations, often utilizing parallel channels to improve the user experience.

- **Decentralized spaces.** Virtual marketplaces, distributed knowledge exchanges, and network-based social spaces are some examples.

- **Gaming contexts.** A peer infrastructure is a natural foundation for the inherently decentralized development and production of online community games. Developers collaborate from arbitrary locations.

Practical work might entail a mix of traditional hierarchical functionality and decentralized p2p technology. The wise deployer of the latter will invest time and effort in coaching users towards the mindset that will enable them to choose the tool and mode of working that is most appropriate to the situation. Virtual deployment is flexible deployment—and rest assured, deployment will change over time.

Decisions

A number of critical decisions are required in this selection stage in the process of deploying a p2p technology. Representative decisions are summarized as follows.

- Identify the issues that determine which particular architecture and server/ client setup is needed or is suitable. Such issues involve primary purpose and scope specifications. Is the purpose distributed file storage, file transfer, user communication or conferencing, content collaboration, or...?

- Determine which existing p2p technologies and already functional networks might provide desired functionality in the intended context. Purpose, scope, and security issues may well disqualify particular implementations.

- Decide the degree of user involvement in initial deployment, self-determination of usage, and in later evolution of functionality. It can be helpful to inventory existing p2p client software in place and user knowledge of the technology options.

- Identify other needs or issues that might require further technology, reconfigurations, constraint measures, policy clarifications, and user rules.

Be prepared to iterate several times over the decision points, in discussion with appropriate issues-responsible people, for instance, if it involves a corporate setting. This is the time to get management on board for the "vision" suggested earlier.

Further decision points are more administrative in nature, and they are perhaps not fully resolvable prior to actual deployment. Some example questions follow:

- What are the requirements on content creation and upkeep? Is simple file sharing adequate, or does the context require a formal publishing model possibly with versioning?

- Who decides what? The peer model of everybody managing their own resources is perhaps too idealistic for current needs. Central management can be replaced by other nonindividual forms of control instead, such as consensus rules or voluntary adherence to guidelines.

- How do we promote community growth? Community aspects in a peer network deserve attention at all stages, from involving users in planning and deployment to supporting early use and collaboration efforts. Neglecting community issues in p2p can cause serious usage problems later.

SELECT AN IMPLEMENTATION

Before selecting a particular implementation, it helps to list the main characteristics of comparative solutions, looking for potential deployment or usage gotchas. The following sections discuss a number of common problem areas.

Platform Dependencies

That a particular implementation is exclusively for MS Windows might not be a problem in some environments. Other settings require that Mac or Linux clients are also supported. In yet others, there might be a long-term goal that arbitrary devices can act as peer agents as far as their respective capabilities allow.

Be advised that some proprietary Windows clients can consume an inordinate amount of system resources and are therefore hardly the lightweight background applications you might expect. The naive view is that Windows applications *always* consume space and resources. This myth is easily debunked by studying some of the excellent software (often German in origin) available with small footprints and high performance, and with no visible penalty on functionality. For instance, IM client size can range from the tens of megabytes to the tens of kilobytes. Avoid the extreme bloatware, which is usually wasteful of resources and tends to be less reliable.

Several peer solutions assume that a Java runtime environment is installed, which often is when the system is running a Java-enabled Web browser. While in some contexts a disadvantage, the approach does lend a broad device portability and interoperability to client software that's hard to match with other coding. Java applications also tend to run small, relying on the install-once Java runtime library. Java software runs interpretatively, so this unfortunately makes the applications run slower than traditional compiled software. Do check the version compatibility for the client software, as there are a number of different runtime implementations.

Performance

Comparing pure-peer and server-mediated performance can be difficult, but general application requirements can indicate which type of implementation is more suited to the task at hand.

The needs to consider are usually related to providing discovery/directory services and to tracking presence status. An additional requirement of corporate environments may be the ability to centrally manage content and resources. Different implementations are more or less amenable to allowing centralized management, with commercial or enterprise solutions tending to have built-in hooks for it.

Application Capabilities

The merged client/server capabilities in p2p applications can often be derived from a summary of the feature list, combined with any noted limitations or inherent constraints imposed by the technology itself, perhaps by the protocol. For example, an implementation might require that all peer messages go through the mediating directory server, and this requirement can be a critical deployment constraint that's not at all obvious from the initial feature list.

Other questions to ask include whether the application supports the kind of namespace that you would desire (or require), if it has unique user identities at all, and what if any authentication model it supports. Depending on context, the answers to these and related questions might immediately disqualify some applications.

When considering content systems, special attention should be given to the storage model and whether the technology implements directory, publishing, replication, and encryption services. You need to evaluate the required kind of storage and sharing model, and from this determine how advanced a solution is adequate.

Platform Extensibility

The question of extensibility is usually answered by noting whether the implementation has a tight application focus (such as a file-sharing client), or is a more comprehensive infrastructure approach with a focus on protocol, interoperability, and a wide variety of possible client types.

Deploying the former application type of p2p network solution commonly allows you to be up and running in no time but leaves little flexibility for extended features to be added over time. Deploying an infrastructure-focus style of client software might take longer and seem more experimental, easily risking a lack of application focus, but the result is very open ended and extensible.

Network Issues

Different network topologies and transport technologies pose different constraints on client operability. Note especially any hidden requirements for clients to be always online or for constant connectivity to an external server. Interoperability with other peer networks or the Internet in general might also be relevant.

How the deployed network will interact with any firewall or other barrier to free connectivity is one issue. Some solutions are unable to cross a firewall or NAT, or might require specific ports to be open. Others pass such barriers with impunity, which means special attention must be given to this breach of security.

SCALABILITY BARRIERS

A fundamental problem when deploying any system is the issue of scalability. Something that works well in the small prototype scale might later behave differently, become unstable, or even stop working when fully deployed and taken past a particular size. A subtly different usage pattern than envisioned can also cause unexpected difficulties that relate to local scaling effects.

Understanding both the limits of a design and the reasons for these constraints is important. Examining practical networks illustrates both something of such limits and how the original models can be adapted for better performance. While some of this material could have been presented together with the particular implementation, it would easily have disappeared in the other technical detail. Besides, the scalability analysis really has more relevance to the deployment discussion because it lends a practical view to the abstract issues discussed so far.

CONNECTIVITY AND SCALE

The historical overview already mentioned physical connectivity as a general constraint of any network when scaling up the number of nodes. The mathematical relation of $(n^2-n)/2$ connections for n nodes, for large n approximately just n^2, very quickly makes applying other physical network topologies than direct one-to-one physical ones essential.

In both LAN and Internet contexts, larger networks are subdivided into smaller local groups with single connection points in each acting as gateways. Although the abstract addressing model makes connections in a virtual p2p network look like point-to-point, the actual message routing instead follows a more hierarchical model. The relatively few main data conduits are then dimensioned to handle the resulting greater flow. This makes both logistic and economic sense, even though it introduces a number of dependencies and vulnerabilities into the network. Figure 5.1 illustrates this relationship between abstract and physical connectivity for two nodes establishing a p2p connection.

The details of physical network design fall outside the scope of this book, and in any case, an extensive body of study of the topic is available. It's instead assumed that the available network connectivity is adequate for the purposes of any virtual p2p architecture dealt with here. Like that of telephony, the growth of the Internet has provided a background infrastructure as a sort of public utility, so this assumption is a reasonable one. When relevant, however, constraints imposed on p2p networks by typical user connectivity are examined in their proper context.

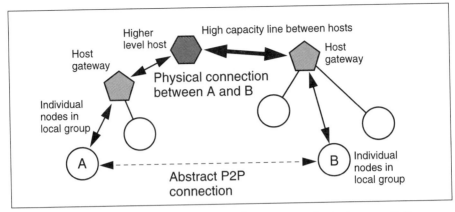

FIGURE 5.1   *In practical networks such as the Internet, physical connectivity between individual nodes is limited to higher-level "hosts" that are in turn connected to high-capacity "backbones" between hosts.*

ADDRESSABILITY AND SCALE

In addition to connectivity, each participating node in a p2p network needs a unique address. The nature of the addressing model depends on many factors, and its constraints in turn determine how well the network scales.

Atomistic p2p networks are dependent on the addressing model of the underlying network. As a rule, they are also dependent on fixed addresses.

Internet connectivity is based on the IP numbering model, which originally assumed that any connected machine was at a fixed location with a permanent IP number. However, a certain measure of portability emerged with the domain namespace abstraction, in that DNS translation could map a particular domain to its currently assigned IP number. Domains can be moved freely as long as the authoritative DNS entry is always updated to point to the correct host. Any user has the choice of specifying a known IP number to a particular connection or specifying a domain and letting DNS ensure that the correct connection is established.

The main problem stemming from the current IP numbering implementation (IPv4) is that the scheme has a theoretical limit of something over 4.2 billion unique addresses. When IPv4 was defined in 1984, this limit seemed vastly overdimensioned. However, the way these addresses were originally assigned in large blocks and the subsequent explosion of Internet users meant that the demand soon outstripped the availability of unique IP numbers. Connectivity suppliers began to reuse their IP numbers as dynamic assignments from the static block they controlled, and virtual hosting suppliers began to assign multiple domains to the same static IP.

IP constraints are not directly a problem for p2p. Instead, innovative solutions to manage translation between user namespace and IP address allowed a remarkable growth curve for some of the most popular IM technologies. It took 16 years for the number of registered Internet domains to reach 25 million. It took only 4 years for the number of p2p user addresses to reach a conservative estimate of some 200 million.

Server-mediated p2p networks can manage alternative addressing models and better cope with issues such as transient or roaming connectivity. An early example of network independent addressing is the ICQ chat user directory service (discussed in Chapter 6). Introduced in 1996, ICQ was the first large-scale system to provide p2p connectivity for intermittently connected PC users. ICQ maintained its own user directory and mapped these "addresses" to currently online users.

Each registered ICQ client is assigned a unique user ID in the form of a number. For one user to chat with another, the ICQ directory server must track each online client and translate user ID to Internet IP-address. The user client updates the central directory by reporting its presence to an available directory server whenever connectivity is established or user status changes.

> **Bit 5.3** **Offline, a peer user's real network address is unknown.**
> This characteristic of p2p networks is why presence information is needed.

Unlike in a telephone system, a messaging user can't "dial up" a user who isn't already online. A particular user's client is accessible for incoming requests only when that client registers its current IP identity with the directory server. Because the user ID is fixed and tied to the client as the basis for the user directory, handling transient users with varying network identity is a transparent process.

To structure the following discussion, we examine situations in each of the common p2p architectures discussed in Chapter 2, starting with the "pure" atomistic one. However, note that most implementations probably can and do function in several modes depending on context. For example, Microsoft's NetMeeting can adhere to the atomistic model when conferencing with other clients at known IP addresses. On the other hand, it's common to connect to a central server to first determine user availability in a user-centric directory maintained there.

SCALABILITY IN THE ATOMISTIC MODEL

Traditionally, atomistic p2p networks have been considered limited to on the order of hundreds of nodes, say 200. In early LAN and for example Workgroups networking, where one deals with generally fixed and known identities, the administration of many distributed PC resources, permissions, and availability tends to become unmanageable far sooner. Perhaps 10 to 20 nodes was considered the practical limit, beyond which one turned to server-controlled solutions, such as the Windows NT domain model that was developed for this reason.

Some might argue that these LAN networks were not pure atomistic p2p models because they effectively relied on an external administrative "server" (and bottleneck, the network administrator) to manage the resources! It was stated earlier that one of the characteristics of p2p is that the resources are managed by the nodes—traditional centralized management of LAN resources goes against that.

In the more fluid atomistic p2p networks that form over the Internet, there is no comparable central administration, only a standardized protocol and the software implementations that adhere to it. The simplest and so far very common approach is to implement a broadcast-route protocol.

> **Bit 5.4 Broadcast-route in p2p refers to request propagation.**
> Each request message received by a host is broadcast to every open connection but not back to the connection the request arrived on. The host also typically performs filtering of "bad", duplicate, and "expired" requests (as determined by protocol rules), updating any relevant data fields and counters in request headers as it does so. Responses are routed back along the path the originating request came from.

Those who have applied theoretical analysis of tree graphs to broadcast-route peer networks have tended to make some rather broad, even simplistic assumptions, and they have derived upper bounds on practical network size that have proven unfounded in real p2p webs—an example analysis is given later in this section. The user-relevant behavioral constraints of the dynamic network depend on considerably more factors than such analysis examines. The Internet's exponential growth has consistently confounded expectations for this very reason.

Let's now examine the dynamic performance issues that are the subject of such analysis attempts, and start with the fundamental issue of bandwidth limits.

Basic Bandwidth Constraints

Theoretically, there's no question that the major performance issue in atomistic p2p networks is the bandwidth constraints exhibited by individual nodes. The relationship is just a simple application of the law of the weakest link.

> **Bit 5.5   Amdahl's Law: System speed is determined by the slowest component in the data path.**
>
> While simple in concept, the applicability of this law to variable p2p webs is not always straightforward because actual performance also depends on architecture and protocol details, storage model, and other, nonobvious factors.

In simple atomistic architecture solutions, network traffic is passed along between nodes without any regard to the capabilities of the individual nodes. The implicit assumption is that all nodes are equal and consequently all possible routes through the network are equal. This assumption is valid only insofar as the nodes can adequately and transparently handle requests and throughput.

Individual node constraints are particularly relevant to common Internet p2p networks where many nodes participate in a transient way and over low-bandwidth dial-up. As a rule, p2p messages are passed using TCP, which as a reliable protocol entails handshaking and a specific cut-off point when the data path's lowest bandwidth limit becomes saturated. At that point, the node software can do one of three things, any of which increases latency (delays), disrupts connectivity, or both:

- Drop (or refuse) the actual connection, losing many requests during downtime, and especially responses due to lost return path. Lost responses tend to cause repeat broadcasts of unfulfilled requests, further exacerbating and spreading the bandwidth congestion. This is a bad thing.

- Drop the data (usually a request or response), which is like breaking the connection but only affects this particular request or response. However, dropped data also shrinks the effective user reach of search or discovery.

- Try to buffer the data in hope that it will be able to send it later. At best, the action only introduces latency, but it can still trigger a repeat request broadcast. Buffering costs memory at the node.

While latency may seem the lesser evil, its consequences can be bad enough. Most obviously, it means you have to wait longer for requests to propagate and responses to return—seconds turn to long minutes. Less obviously, increased latency means, for example, that the finite stack space (allocated in the node applications for those ID and return path stores, providing the routing table) fills up or overflows. When that happens, return paths are lost, compromising the discovery and search functionality, ultimately to the point where users find the network useless.

The data-buffering option in the TCP connection context is largely out of the control of the p2p application programmer; it happens deep in the networking code as a way of ensuring data transfer reliability at the expense of latency, until criticality is reached. This behavior is optimized for transient data burst situations, and the application layer remains unaware of the accrued delays until the deeper layer runs out of TCP buffers. At this point, it's too late to do anything about the situation because the system's connectivity response has just been hosed. Besides, by then, network timeouts are likely to have occurred elsewhere along the data path.

As overall loading rises above some threshold value in enough nodes with less capacity margins, this kind of network tends to show sudden unstable behavior. It will as a rule not scale very well, unless the client software or network protocols can implement more intelligent strategies or be more forgiving of data transfer latencies.

> **Bit 5.6   At any loading, there will always be some nodes in the network that drop or delay requests due to local bandwidth saturation.**
>
> This is another major source of broken connectivity and discarded messages, but is not critical to the network as a whole until enough nodes reach their maximum capacity.

In the simple atomistic model, Amdahl's Law is therefore an absolute.

The Gnutella Bottleneck

Gnutella (see Chapter 7) provided a practical example of this vulnerability in July 2000, when it started to very rapidly receive more members. This influx came at a time when it first became apparent that Napster might be shut down.

Users of Gnutella reported increasing difficulties and markedly poorer performance during this period when the average query rate in the network doubled. A later and sustained usage surge resulted in widespread speculation that the Gnutella network was collapsing and would ultimately disappear.

In September 2000, the development company Clip2 Distributed Search Solutions published a report on p2p scalability with a particular focus on the observed degradation of the Gnutella network. Titled *Bandwidth Barriers to Gnutella Network Scalability*, the report is found at www.clip2.com/dss_barrier.html.

> *As passing testimony to the general volatility of the p2p and dot-com arena, Clip2 DSS discontinued its p2p network tracking, reflector and host-cache services, and development as of sometime around July-August 2001. A Web-visit in 2002 shows only the short text that Clip2 has ceased operations, yet the deep link to the report document is still valid. I therefore remind readers that although the Internet addresses given in the book are repeatedly verified during writing and production, some might become invalid by the time you read this.*

The report provides more than just speculation and is interesting reading whether or not one accepts all the conclusions. An attempt to quantify performance constraints in Gnutella's broadcast-route design suggested that the network, as implemented then, had a critical threshold of some 10 queries per second. When the average query rate increased further (for example due to a larger membership base), overall performance invariably plummeted. Queries are a broadcast-type message passed on from node to node, and they affect all nodes in broadcast networks equally within their range of time to live (TTL). As such, they constitute a reasonable measurement of loading.

This loading metric was derived mainly from how increased queries resulted in fewer nodes responding to internode pings. The report theorized that this bottleneck reflected the saturation point for the slower dial-up nodes in the network, whose bandwidth ceiling of 56**Kbps** (57.6 **kbps**, ISO) make them not up to the peer demands of the larger network. A large enough number of Gnutella nodes were modem-based to have their limitations determine overall network performance.

Based on visual inspections of Napster client lists of online users, from where many of the new Gnutella users came at the time, I might even conjecture that modem dial-up at 56Kbps or less then dominated the user base. Undeniable is that Gnutella's atomistic model and egalitarian view of all nodes being equal resulted in a clearly definable "scalability barrier" as far as further growth was concerned. We can examine the technical side in more detail to understand why.

The analysis of Gnutella traffic showed that it comprised five common message types at any node. Apart from the broadcast queries already mentioned, there was a regular exchange of "pings" with typically three other nodes. These pings alone at 10 queries per second would consume on the order of 17 kbps for the sending node. Nodes respond to pings with their "pongs", adding to the load. In addition, hit results are sent back up the query path. Finally, older Gnutella software contributed measurably to the flow with *broadcast* **push** requests passed along by other nodes.

Even assuming lower bounds, the aggregate volume of this traffic at 10 queries per second translated to in excess of 67 kbps, which is clearly enough to saturate the ability of any modem-connected node, even single-channel ISDN, to respond to further queries. As each node reaches saturation, it no longer responds to new messages and thus effectively disappears from the network, compromising network cohesiveness. If enough nodes drop out under load, a point comes when the p2p network fragments, or even collapses from the perspective of later queries.

The report concludes by making the plausible assumption that for any (or at least any atomistic) p2p network, the specific saturation point is determined by the lowest common bandwidth among the nodes. Were 33Kbps and 56Kbps modem connectivity replaced generally by better bandwidth, for example, the saturation query rate would merely be raised correspondingly, not eliminated.

Bandwidth Bottleneck Solutions

Still, it's valid to ask how serious a practical problem this least-common-bandwidth issue really is. Gilder's Law, introduced in Chapter 1, implies that the average bandwidth capacity doubles every six months. That rate would automatically make the bandwidth bottleneck problem a consistently receding one, would it not?

In fact, this problem and its possible solutions are already well known from other network contexts that have seen rapid and large growth: the telephone system and the Internet. There, too, ever-increasing bandwidth has often come to the rescue. From the user's point of view: Just wait a few months and somebody, somewhere, will throw enough bandwidth at the congestion points to make the problem go away.

Increasing bandwidth is by no means a panacea, but thanks to Gilder's Law, it's one easy solution; as network (and dial-up) components are replaced with newer ones over time, the bandwidth increase is automatically deployed throughout the network. Conscious and directed upgrades merely amplify the effect and make it quicker.

Although bandwidth loading tends to rapidly increase to take advantage of increased resources, a perceived performance improvement is almost always noted. It can be interesting to revisit the Gnutella situation as it was only a year later. The average number of connected nodes seemed to be higher, 5 to 7, and a subjective impression suggested that more users had moved from 56Kbps modem to higher bandwidth connectivity such as cable, ISDN, or DSL. This would seem to bear out Gilder's Law (factor 2 to 4 in this time frame) and imply that the network now had on average a richer interconnectivity (from average 3 to average 6 connections). We might then expect oscillation between congested and improved states, as bandwidth and loading take turns in playing catch-up to the latest increase of the other.

Another solution deals with deploying more intelligent routing of messages through the network. The older broadcast-push method was replaced by a more efficient and less bandwidth-costly routed-push solution, for example. Various other changes to improve network stability also improved effective bandwidth.

One can encourage "trunk lines" and "backbones" as main conduits between major traffic centers, based on nodes and connections that have especially high reliability and throughput. Over time, the network will then become redesigned to reflect and strengthen this multitier hierarchy, simply because most of the upgrade resources will be directed to these critical paths and super-servers. The current Internet, and now Internet2, exemplifies the practical result of such a drift away from the original flat p2p design of ARPANET and the early Internet.

Similar avenues of development in the Gnutella network include

- Moving from simple broadcast to more optimized query routing. Several more sophisticated p2p solutions examined later provide successful examples of this approach.

- Relaxing the reliable-TCP constraint on broadcast queries and so lowering overhead by accepting **unreliable transport** forwarding. Using UDP (User Datagram Protocol) instead is an example.

- Considering ways of introducing a two-tier system. Some form of "super-peer" nodes with proven bandwidth, capability, and reliability to handle the bulk of node communication can act as a high-performance backbone.

Proof-of-concept experiments of this last solution were tried with a Clip2 Reflector, whereby messages could be routed through predetermined and robust paths. This routing solution does lead to a stratified network and has certain disadvantages.

As implied by the Internet example, introducing preferred nodes moves the network away from the original p2p design towards an implied hierarchy that introduces identifiable, localized vulnerabilities. If a connection goes down in a flat-design p2p system, it's doubtful that anyone would notice; there is no dependency on one single path. If a backbone connection goes down, on the other hand, many users experience severe slowdowns or even outages of service, even when the rest of the network tries to route around the problem.

While bandwidth, routing, and tier strategies might all have relevance to your p2p deployment, some of the implementations discussed in later chapters provide examples of other, less obvious strategies for conserving bandwidth and routing traffic, strategies that don't compromise the essential p2p design philosophy.

One proposed general solution to the bandwidth/latency meltdown in the Gnutella context is a special routing algorithm, worth mentioning here if only to indulge in some techno-nerd analysis. It's called the Flow Control Algorithm for distributed broadcast-route networks with reliable (usually TCP) transport links.

The Flow Control Algorithm

The Flow Control Algorithm (FCA) is designed for Gnutella-type networks that use reliable transport links (such as TCP). Usefulness of the algorithm is not limited to only TCP-based networks, however, but is also applicable to "unreliable" transport protocols like UDP because applications using this frequently utilize reliable protocols (for example, Internet Point-to-Point Protocol, PPP) at some other level.

The FCA approach tries to apply a form of intelligent flow control to how a node forwards request and response messages and a sensible priority scheme to how it drops messages that won't fit into the connections. In addition, a predictive algorithm guesses statistical request-response traffic to winnow excessive requests. The intent is to satisfy the following conditions:

- Allow an infinitely scalable broadcast search network by avoiding the saturation effect of unlimited request/response forwarding.

- Keep broadcast search delay to a technically reasonable minimum, to avoid excessive request/response buffering.

- Allow tolerant connectivity between servents with varying link capacities, so that high-capacity nodes don't saturate low-bandwidth connections.

- Make a best-effort attempt to share connections irrespective of bandwidth and thus also be reasonably resistant to DoS attacks that try to swamp node capacity over a particular connection.

- Be backward compatible with an existing server/client code base.

The functionality is realized by coding three control components into the client software that handles node connectivity and message forwarding: outgoing flow, Q-algorithm dispatcher, and fairness arbiter, as illustrated in Figure 5.2.

The outgoing FCA component uses the simplest "zig-zag" data receipt confirmation possible between the clients on the application level of the protocol. In Gnutella, ping messages with a TTL value of 1 are inserted into the outgoing data stream at regular intervals (every 512 bytes). The only expected replies to this are pong messages from the immediate connection neighbor, where the ping expires. Any

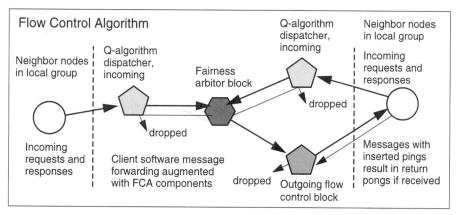

FIGURE 5.2 *Principle functionality blocks of the flow control algorithm solution. The aggregate flow control performs a simple receipt check on receiving nodes, prevents overloading, and arbitrates fair connection usage.*

received pong thus confirms that at least the preceding data segment (of 512 bytes) was received by the neighbor node and that it's safe to send the next segment.

The bandwidth overhead for this receipt mechanism is a tolerable 10 percent, and the maximum network layer buffering never exceeds the chosen segment size plus the corresponding ping/pong pair. The gain lies in never saturating the connection.

A number of refinements to the basic principle ensure low latency even when faced with ping loss or incorrect ping forwarding by noncompliant client software.

The direct cost to client performance is a lower maximum transfer rate over the connection due to that receipt overhead, although the effective rate is usually throttled by client settings anyway. The outgoing flow control must also manage queued requests and responses that are to be forwarded to the connection, or dropped if there is no pong response for a longer time. This is done in concert with the Q block, with priority given to low-hop response forwarding—it's deemed more important to reliably service nearer destinations and shorter routes.

The Q-algorithm block acts as a dispatcher and is implemented on the receiving end of a connection. Its job is to analyze the incoming requests and to determine which of them should be broadcast over other connections (that is, passed to the respective outgoing flow control block) and which should just be dropped. It tries to arbitrate the available forwarding capacity between requests and responses, favoring responses because these represent a greater investment of network resources.

Because responses to incoming requests will be routed back along the same connection, it also tries to limit forwarded requests to minimize the risk that later responses will overflow the backlink channel. The theory gets a bit obtuse at this point, as we're dealing with statistical expectations, but the guiding principle is that it's far less damaging to the network to drop requests than to drop responses. Broadcast requests are likely to propagate anyway through alternative routes.

The fairness arbiter block is a logical extension to the outgoing flow control block, and its purpose is to ensure that the available outgoing connection bandwidth (as regulated by the outgoing component) is "fairly distributed" between the back-traffic (defined by responses) intended for that connection and the forward-traffic (or requests) from the other connections—the latter being the total output of their Q-algorithms. In addition, it tries to distribute the forward capacity fairly between these connections. The guiding principle is that no stream or a group of streams should be able to monopolize the bandwidth of any connection.

The main constraint to the applicability of FCA is that the requests and responses should not be cast larger than some reasonable size (typically, on the order of 3KB). This practical limit is usually satisfied, although it must be noted that the Gnutella protocol allows these message types to be up to 64KB in size. More detail on FCA can be found at one of several Gnutella development sites.

Presence Transience and Event Horizon Constraints

Characteristic of most p2p networks, and broadcast-route ones in particular, is the "event-horizon" limit. In more general terms: How many of the other connected nodes in the network can you "see" from any one node at any given time?

The constraint is simply, that if you can't discover a node through response analysis in an atomistic p2p network, you have no way of knowing that it exists (as a current address), or whether it is connected and available (as a presence state). Some networks with different request-routing strategies, such as Freenet, deliberately obfuscate visibility in the interests of security. In these cases, you really don't "see" past the immediate neighbor nodes, but then don't need to either.

When peer clients are desktop applications for sharing, common behavior by some users is to log in to the network only when looking for or downloading a file. A guesstimate of average session duration for a typical dial-up Gnutella user is therefore on the order of only an hour or so, with perhaps a couple of sessions per day—that roughly translates to a daily 1 in 10 chance of detecting this user based on presence alone! Overly pessimistic perhaps, but indicative. We might note that some recent clients (designed for 24/7 connectivity) are rather difficult to shut down or disconnect completely. Instead, they default to a hidden or background state, where they continue to relay network packets while the user works with other things.

The event-horizon effect further limits visible nodes to at best a few tens of thousands, but in conjunction with widely varying node branching is usually more like a few hundred to a few thousand. So, on the face of it, your typical Internet p2p network suddenly seems very limited, no matter how many potential members or installed clients it has in absolute numbers. The network appears badly fragmented into an unknown number of much smaller disconnected subwebs, each of which seems to manifest some fundamental scalability limit of the network.

Fortunately, matters aren't that grim at all. In fact, some advocates claim that even simple broadcast-route p2p networks can be made "infinitely" scalable given the right set of conditions and node behavior. We've neglected a few things in this quick look at these apparent limitations.

First, detection at a given time is only part of the story. Assume that you are connected and see a particular subweb based on your connections to immediate hosts. Both your connections, and those of the nodes further out, are constantly changing. Over time, your event horizon encompasses different subsets of all potential members—a full day's session might therefore easily detect *ten or twenty times* the total visible at any given moment, just not all at once.

Knowing a node address, your chances of contacting this node increase significantly because you're no longer limited to the times when that node is inside your current topology's horizon, only to the times when it's available anywhere at all on the network. This is particularly applicable to messaging or content search, because if a detected host address is retained, you can probably still reach that node even when a later discovery or search would fail to find it.

Scalability in the User-Centric Model

The addition of a central server component to manage a user directory allows for a much improved scalability and, at least in theory, the visibility of all present nodes. Network performance is limited mainly by the nature of the directory, the capacity of the servers and connectivity. There is no need to fill bandwidth with general broadcast messages or relayed queries. Ah, the digital silence....

The load experienced by the central server is in principle minimal because any data transfers initiated between nodes occur in a direct p2p connection. Traffic with the server is mainly due to clients registering with the directory service to announce their availability and to client requests for information supplied by the server. The other major server load occurs when a user performs a search in the directory for other users who meet particular criteria.

Various implementations can keep client connections alive for the duration of the user session to exchange supplementary information or track p2p status. Some automatically offer to transfer new client versions when they detect that the current one is old. Such additional features consume more server resources and can limit how large a network can effectively be supported.

Napster's Compromises

It's interesting to review the public understanding of p2p as popularized by Napster, which was not an atomistic model as most assumed, nor did it allow access to all the content available from peers connected at any given time. This perspective gives a more realistic view of network statistics for other, similar sharing technologies.

Instead, Napster was a simplified, and in some ways incomplete implementation of the user-centric model of p2p. Content was indexed indirectly. The strong point, and a major contributor to Napster's popularity, was user convenience and relatively rapid response times to queries. As its phenomenal growth showed, the Napster model also scaled well—in fact far beyond expectations. Implemented optimization strategies were aimed at giving reasonable results for the majority of users, insensitivity to transient connectivity, and perceived fast response.

The basic connection model for the original Napster is shown in Figure 5.3, and it indicates a few of the hidden optimization characteristics. First of all, the Napster client software automatically connected not to a specific server, but to a special *connection host*. The connection host received information about the availability and relative loading of Napster servers within a particular group—apparently five to each site cluster. It then assigned (at random) a lightly loaded server in a local cluster to the connecting client. The client proceeded to register with the assigned server, providing information about user identity, connection type and speed, and shared files.

The directory service provided a list of users and their shared files. Selecting one initiated a server-mediated connection attempt between the endpoint clients. Once established, further communication and file transfer occurred in "direct" mode. Server loading was restricted to data needed to administer clients and the list.

The list of available users and shared files was initially restricted to those users registered with the same server. Most people assumed, in part because of the global users and shared files statistics shown in the client window, that all online users and files were always available. This assumption was simply not true, and the search mechanism was further restricted by how the directory service was implemented.

When the user submitted a search query, the search had two basic criteria for completion: either 100 hits found or 15 seconds elapsed. The underlying search

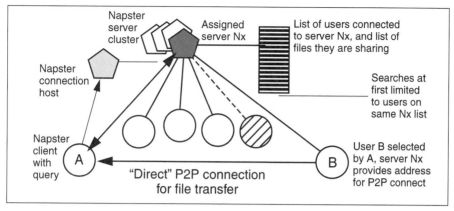

FIGURE 5.3   *Napster's server-mediated p2p model. User A connects to the "first available" server assigned by a connection host. The initial user/file list is based on the users recently connected to the same server.*

database was initially restricted to only recently connected users on the same server. If the search completed with less than 100 hits found and elapsed time allowed, the query was passed on to a (randomly chosen?) neighbor server and another segment of the total database. Bandwidth and server requirements were thus kept to a minimum, and scalability was very good as long as the number of servers and their performance/connectivity was adequate to the active user base.

Although this solution clearly gives a "snappy" response for impatient users compared to the usual search waits in an atomistic p2p network such as Gnutella, it presents certain disadvantages. One is that the search response of "no hits" is misleading. The negative response means only that no hit was found in the current (and local subset) database within the mandated 15 seconds. Repeated searches might well respond differently. Furthermore, the database is dynamic because users log in or drop out all the time. Finally, because a client connects to a randomly selected server, it will see a different subset of the total database for each session.

Admittedly, this analysis is fairly specific to Napster's former architecture, but it is a reasonably clear and well-documented illustration of the kind of trade-off that might be hidden behind the scenes in any directory-based search that caters to user convenience—commonly expressed as minimizing user wait.

SCALABILITY IN THE DATA-CENTRIC MODEL

The data-centric p2p model is similar to the user-centric one, but instead of server mediation providing a directory service to identify nodes (that is, users), it uses an index service to directly track data or resource location. In practical implementations, server mediation often adds both directory and index services in some form, possibly deriving one from the other, so it can be difficult to assign a particular p2p implementation to exclusively one or the other model.

Scalability considerations are similar to the user directory model, but a purely resource-centric implementation might easily be a significantly more static situation, in that resources as a whole are likely to be significantly less transient than human users dropping in and out of the network to chat or swap files. Machines and software are, as yet, less mobile than people in terms of connectivity change, making directory management and server loading less demanding, and useful network size larger.

While networks such as Napster obfuscated the issue of "reach" (that is to say, what and how much was available to a search query), it is perhaps a reasonable design objective not to cater to the human trait of wanting to reach *everything* all at once. Dealing with distributed resources in general, often replicated, it should be sufficient to find the first available instance that meets the request requirements. Therefore, searches need not be comprehensive. Dealing with human connectivity is more difficult because the desired match to a search request can be a single target instance (usually a person) at a single location, which does rather presume a comprehensive search of the entire network, ideally without too long a wait.

We could distill out of this discussion the realization that if search is a significant functionality in the directory or index model, then it is the one component in the implementation that will require the most thought, work, and optimization to be useful. Otherwise decent p2p implementations can be seriously crippled by deficient or incomplete search functionality, and it's an area that is under constant development. Witness the different strategies taken by the implementations covered. Different situations require different solutions.

As the "content" in the network increases, the importance of a good search component will increase even faster. Anyone who doubts this need only look as far as the Internet, where it's estimated that the relative importance of good search engines has increased far faster than the growth of content. I won't bother to try and correlate this estimate with the power curves for relationships and value, tempting as that might seem. Personally, I invariably start looking for information on the Web with a proven search engine such as Google (www.google.com) and rarely go to the traditional hierarchical directories that were the mainstay of finding content in earlier years. It's faster, and in most cases, it's more than good enough.

An Adaptive Large-Scale Solution

In discussing bandwidth constraints, the focus so far has been on the problems with broadcast queries and managing traffic flow over TCP connections with known neighboring nodes. This focus is natural, considering that "secure" connectivity is desired—that is to say, we require protocol-based acknowledgement that packets are received and messages passed on. Other strategies are possible.

One such innovative alternative is represented by the Alpine (Adaptive Large-scale Peer2peer Networking) protocol. Rather than describe it in the file-sharing implementation section (for example, in Chapter 7), I chose to examine it here in the scalability section because the applicability is not only specific to file sharing, but might have far-reaching implications for peer networking in general. In any case, the current software stands at only version beta-01 (source and *nix binaries).

Alpine (www.cubicmetercrystal.com/alpine) is a messenging protocol intended for massive concurrent peer connectivity. It is defined in open source software released under the GNU Lesser General Public License. Both a peer-based application (as a client+server pair) and a network infrastructure, it is designed for decentralized information location and discovery. It is not designed for large-scale data transport between peers, which is instead normally handed off to some other transfer protocol, such as Swarmcast, Freenet, **HTTP**, or FTP.

The short feature summary runs as follows:

- High concurrent connection support (over 10,000 nodes)
- Adaptive configuration for enhanced accuracy and quality of responses
- True flat peer network, with no hierarchy or central servers
- Low communication overhead (small UDP packets, no forwarding)
- Module support to allow extensions to query and transport operations

How does it do this? Normal TCP connections demand far too much overhead for large numbers of concurrent connections (which might also be constrained by hard-coded limits, as in Windows 2000 patched to update SP2).

Alpine allows the transparent multiplexing of a vast number of connections on a single UDP connection, what its author Martin Peck ("coderman") calls an adaptive social discovery mechanism suitable for use in large peer-based networks. Distributed TCP (DTCP) is used for simple query and control type messages, and the process is akin to how addressed packet broadcasting at the lower network level multiplexes multiple higher-level connections over a single physical line.

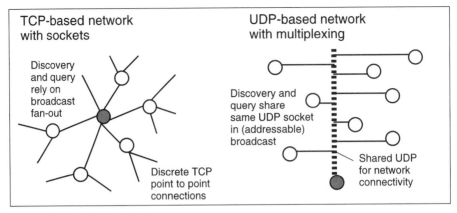

FIGURE 5.4 *Conceptual difference between traditional TCP-connected nodes and the multiplexed UDP scheme implemented by the Alpine protocol. The addressable broadcast in the latter can provide an unreliable endpoint connection for simple control and query messages.*

Just as network devices can "sniff out" destination information from headers, Alpine applications share the same UDP connection, yet still use individual routing when relevant. To the host system, these many connections look like normal UDP traffic going over a single UDP port—the overhead associated with each connection is therefore very minimal. This is implied by the bus-like schematic in Figure 5.4. The 4-byte addressing allows for a theoretical 4 billion unique endpoints, but other constraint factors such as host memory, activities and bandwidth limits suggest practical network sizes of tens to hundreds of thousands of nodes.

The essential characteristic for this kind of connectivity is that neither timeout nor completion status is associated with individual messages. Any query that is broadcast is completely unreliable. If you get a response back from a peer, great. If not, then no big loss, the next peer may have the response you are looking for.

A Social Discovery Analogue

The social discovery aspect is based on an analogue with how people find out things—experience. You know who to ask and where to turn when looking for specific answers, because in the past, you have learned about the particular interests and proficiencies of each person you can contact. Over time you develop a detailed map of people and resources that are proficient at certain things. In this view, broadcast queries, such as in the original Gnutella, are like standing in the local mall's parking lot on a busy shopping day, shouting out your questions to the wind in the hope that random passersby might have the answers you seek.

Alpine clients continually discover new peers on the network to communicate with and determine which proficiencies each may have, based on the messages that flow on the common UDP connection that defines the network. With every query or operation performed, a client also determines how proficient a given peer is for certain tasks. Peers who are very proficient and helpful become important members of a peer group, which are then utilized in preference to lesser-known peers. This combines a local services directory with a form of reputation system, which includes resistance to spamming and malicious node behavior.

Protocol Overview

DTCP is a lightweight and compact datagram protocol that allows

- Connection multiplexing for large numbers of concurrent connections
- Connection persistence despite changes in IP address or port for endpoints
- Support for NAT discovery and dual NAT communication
- Both reliable and unreliable packet transfer

Although not very final at this point, the groundwork has been laid for the bare minimum protocol required for basic operation. Refinements and extensions are still in the works, so this description is more functional than precise.

Connection setup consists of each peer selecting an available ID for the other, unique in the local space, and handshaking on this selection to inform the other which identity should be used in further messages. Thereafter, messages sent from either endpoint are recognized on reception by referencing this identity, which remains constant irrespective of variable IP/port until this virtual connection is terminated. An important reason for having identity set by the other side is to prevent casual spoofing, although it should be noted that this common strategy is like many adequate precautions ultimately vulnerable to packet sniffing at the endpoint.

Two kinds of data packet transfers are supported:

- **Unreliable** packet transfer, which is identical in functionality to the UDP datagram transfer. This is a best effort, unreliable packet transfer, and the normal mode of messages between peers.

- **Reliable** packet transfer, which incorporates timers and retransmission to guarantee delivery. An **exponential backoff algorithm** is required to avoid collisions when retransmitting unacknowledged packets, and only a single packet is allowed in route for a given endpoint at any time.

NAT discovery allows an address-translated peer to learn its outside address equivalent (as requesting endpoint) for use in further operations that need an explicit endpoint address. Poll and Ack packets correspond to ping and pong to test endpoint connectivity established from the values received.

Queries and responses provide the basic discovery mechanism. A query is sent in to the peers in a particular affinity group (or the default one). This progresses in a linear fashion until a sufficient number of resources are located, or until the user terminates the query process. Optimization is achieved by ordering the query sequence according to associated quality values in peer profiles maintained locally and trying to identify the peers that perform best within different query categories.

Peer profiles and ratings are implemented as protocol values pertaining to bandwidth, quality, and affinity. Using these, Alpine avoids congestion by keeping the connection pool tuned to the appropriate size with the correct types of DTCP peers to minimize query request loading. Each client can halt, slow, alter, or resume any peer query at will to optimize use of limited bandwidth. You can set precisely how much bandwidth you want the DTCP stack to use for reception and broadcast, and it can be set on a peer or peer-group basis, along with a cap on number of concurrent peers.

This strategy has higher-level implications and interactions with the reputation system, because you control exactly how often or how much response you provide to incoming queries. If you are getting swamped, for example, you will respond to less and less queries—your quality in the eyes of those peers will drop. As a consequence of their preference logic, you will then receive less queries: self-regulating loading.

Neither congestion control nor performance tuning is implemented at the DTCP layer. Instead, such refinements are specifically intended for the protocol implemented atop DTCP, a clever strategy which provides the flexibility required to support specific types of traffic. The protocol stack is a complete and functional component in its own right. If desired, you could use it directly for any type of low-bandwidth, disperse messaging type of data transfer.

Peer Affinity

Alpine maintains two main categories of information for every peer in the connection pool. The first is the peer's quality and affinity to the queries performed. The second tracks peer resource impact, including but not limited to bandwidth usage.

If a peer responds to a query, its affinity value increases. Otherwise unchanged, the value can be decreased—for example, for responses with worthless content. Relative affinity value subsequently affects the order in which peers are queried, using a weighted, fuzzy algorithm designed to preserve some dynamic behavior, so that untested or low-affinity peers always get a fair chance to prove their worth. Server behavior defaults towards reliable by remaining online in the background (as a daemon process) even if the client and visible interface is shut down.

Logical connectivity between peers can actually span separate online sessions at either endpoint because the messages are tied by locally assigned identity and UDP connectivity, not any specific TCP socket with defined timeout. This promotes history building and peer profiling in the reputation system.

A similar set of values tracks the bandwidth that a peer uses when sending packets to you. Peers that use large amounts of bandwidth in relation to the other peers in your pool will be the first to be dropped if bandwidth exceeds the allocation threshold of the server. This mechanism provides a relief valve should traffic start to increase towards congestion.

The discovery protocol allows a client to gradually build local lists based on affinity groups maintained by other peers with high affinity. In this way, your perceived network can reliably scale with consistent quality to an arbitrary, but user-controlled size, no matter how large the total network is.

Search and delivery protocols are both implemented as core components in the basic server. Search functionality can be modified and extended using modules, and hit returns can be configured based on among other things the affinity values. An interesting application of this fine tuning is that trusted peers can be sent more or better information than untrusted ones. Standard HTTP and FTP protocols are considered the default for transfers. Additional protocols and transports can be added using a component interface to define extra modules.

Client and server communicate through a CORBA (Common Object Request Broker Architecture) interface, and can be disassociated so that on a local LAN, only one machine runs the full server, while the others only have the client half. It's envisioned that flexible support for alternative interfaces, such as **RPC** (Remote Procedure Call), XML-RPC, SOAP (Simple Object Access Protocol), or DCOM (Distributed Common Object Model), could easily be added.

When Traditional Solutions Are Better

Interestingly, some considerations are presented in the Alpine overview about when existing mechanisms might be preferable to Alpine in search contexts.

- When the target has a very specific name. Then a search engine like Google, or a hashed-index system like Freenet, is probably more efficient in large networks with indexed material.

- Keyword-based or fuzzy-logic search are also well-implemented on Web search engines, though it's noted that Alpine might excel when dealing with dynamic content that can't be pre-indexed. However, if a centralized server search technology can be used, this alternative should still be considered.

- If correlation between peer-stored content and peer group category is weak, other search mechanisms might be better. In other words, because Alpine is adaptive and preferential in which peers are contacted, weakly associated content on other peers is easily overlooked.

- Performing searches many times per second consumes a fair amount of bandwidth to query a large set of peers. The protocol uses an iterative unicast operation to send query packets directly to peers, and this process could saturate uplink connectivity if used excessively.

- Reliable queries are unsuited to Alpine, based as it is on unreliable UDP. In other words, applications that, for example, need a query receipt mechanism must rely on some other protocol to implement it.

Instant Messaging

Theoretical considerations aside, after selection and installation comes the time to actually use the technology. Then we must address such issues as usability, performance, reliability, availability, and of course security.

Part of this practicality must be determined by the selection of software and network model. However, the whole is always more (or less) than the parts, and when the dynamics of a practical network come into play, nothing is quite as it seemed on paper. Time after time, a seemingly decent design is committed to use only to reveal interesting and unexpected flaws determined by its context of usage.

In this part of the book, we therefore examine some of these issues from the perspective of real implementations, sorted by chapter into application groups, and provide in-depth analysis of how some common, and sometimes not-so-common technologies work. In this and the following chapters, the presented solutions may not always be the recommended ones for every deployment situation but are sometimes selected simply for the complementary light they shed on the others.

This chapter introduces a number of popular technologies for instant messaging (IM), most of which turn out to be rather different in their internal workings than one would suspect based on their common "p2p" moniker. This analysis of messaging technologies starts off with some of the older, often proprietary, but still widely used p2p solutions, and this relative age shows in their implementation details.

The later solutions are newer, usually more open, and should prove more interesting for many readers in terms of future deployment potential. Taken together, all solutions should give considerable insight into messaging technology.

CHAPTER 6 AT A GLANCE

This chapter provides an in-depth exploration of IM technologies, shows how they work, and discusses the inherent risks and limitations in the current popular implementations.

Beyond E-Mail introduces messaging with a familiar application.

- The section explains how and why e-mail stopped being p2p for the majority of users, instead replaced by other forms of p2p with more immediacy—*Net-Babble*, or instant messaging.

Messaging Technologies provides a technology background to IM.

- *Some IM Concepts* are defined and explained, the terms of which are central to later analysis throughout the book. *ICQ—IM for the Masses* provides some historical background to popular IM.

ICQ and AIM provides a core examination of ICQ technology.

- *ICQ Protocol* provides a fairly detailed look inside. The concluding section *Using ICQ* makes a few observations about this popular application. AOL's own *AIM* client is described and differences from ICQ noted.

Jabber presents a general networking technology, first presented as an IM application.

- The background to the open source Jabber project and its other application areas is followed by the detailed IM-client technical information in the *Infrastructure* and *Jabber Protocol* sections.

Brief Mentions takes up a few other IM client options to illustrate the broad range of different implementations that are available for IM.

- *Psst* is a short section introducing a simple but fully encrypted atomistic messaging client. *Trillian* describes an elegant multiprotocol IM client. *P2PQ* looks a peer client designed specifically to query the virtual knowledge base of aggregate users. Finally, *Windows Messenger* examines the latest Microsoft IM client, discussing some technical detail and issues that might delay widespread acceptance of WM.

BEYOND E-MAIL

E-mail was inherently peer to peer in its original implementation—a message from a user at a terminal on one machine to a user on another, something that underlies the basic syntax of the "user@machine" address invented thirty years ago by Ray Tomlinson to streamline a feature that was already then some six years old.

Over time, however, this direct user-to-user communication became more indirect. The user model of terminals directly connected to respective mainframe computers evolved into a situation where most had individual transient connections from local PCs to the network and could not support the protocol requirements.

E-mail transport presupposes a constant connectivity on the part of the recipient service, so it's not practical in the dial-up situation for each user system to incorporate its own mailbox server. Instead, host systems provide both **mailbox services** and **sendmail services** for large groups of users, each of whom access the services with local client software. The e-mail addressing model (now based on repointable domain rather than a specific machine) ensures that the sendmail service finds the host mailbox service of the addressee. This indirection has become the prevailing e-mail paradigm, and the concept is illustrated in Figure 6.1.

Note that nothing in the network architecture prevents using local machine implementations to send and receive e-mail directly, for those who can and wish to do so. The practical requirement is merely that the user's e-mail address properly translates to a machine running mailbox software that is online regularly. This ability to receive e-mail correctly is also a prerequisite to compliant sending, because the sending system must be able to receive e-mail response messages in case of problems.

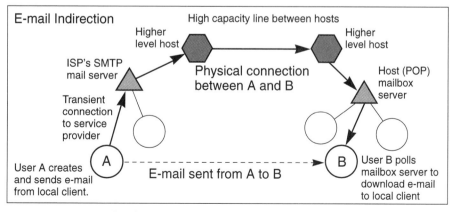

FIGURE **6.1** *Typical indirection in modern Internet-transported e-mail.*

Despite the sometimes problematic extensions of e-mail formats (rich text, html, forms, attachments, media content, etc.), an ongoing evolution, the underlying e-mail protocol is an *open* and *uniform* one, not dependent on platform. This means that anyone with an e-mail address and an e-mail client (or a web browser and access to a **webmail service**) can in principle communicate with anyone else. Anyone can implement compliant software.

> **Bit 6.1   E-mail is an open, uniform and extensible, albeit asynchronous and low-priority p2p (server) protocol.**
>
> Easily the most popular application of the Internet, e-mail early became its killer application for the general user base, but evolved away from user p2p.

Unfortunately, e-mail got the short end of the stick with regard to network priority, so network congestion and other problems can quickly stall e-mail transfer. In addition, some mail "vanishes" in the system; undeliverable without error responses reaching the sender. The built-in ability to request delivery and read receipts can't compensate for this uncertainty, because the problem of unsolicited e-mail abusing these requests to confirm valid addresses, along with issues of corporate security, have led to the default mail server and client behavior of ignoring such requests. Lack of receipt responses therefore tells the sender nothing.

E-mail however is not a real-time conversation; it's a ping-pong of message and reply separated by arbitrary time delays. And this is perhaps, at the same time, both the greatest feature and failing of e-mail.

- Feature, because it allows recipients to deal with messages *at their own convenience*, without interrupting the tasks at hand. (Notwithstanding the fact that in practice many users with constant connectivity still allow themselves to be interrupted by incoming mail; stressed to formulate an immediate reply, as if they were answering a phone call.)

- Failing, because people prefer real-time conversations, as in telephony. In the text-based message context, this translates to *immediate* end-user delivery, which e-mail is not guaranteed (or, guaranteed *not*) to be.

This latter preference for real-time communication paved the way for both chat and instant messaging as strong contenders for the title "killer application of the Internet" (at least for people who frequently sit in front of a computer).

In passing, server-relayed chat over the Internet broadcast to connected members is not considered user p2p, although the many IRC servers are themselves peer connected. IRC however can often serve as a valuable precursor to user p2p by allowing presumptive peers to discover each other and initiate direct contact using other client technologies, sometimes built into the chat client itself. Some p2p client software therefore includes IRC chat as an extra component or use a special automated IRC channel as an "**out-of-band**" means to distribute node lists or other information. General p2p development discussions are also often held over chat.

Somewhat confusing is the way the term "chat" is sometimes used both for broadcast relay to multiple users and for private messaging over a true end-to-end connection. A separate group of applications became dedicated to the latter, and IM rapidly emerged—IM is the term used here for the peer-connectivity version of chat, which is considered in detail in the next section.

Net-Babble

This flip heading refers to instant communication over p2p networks. Conversing with social or professional peers always seems to be the primary interest of users, irrespective of medium or other pursuits.

Early in the book, telephony was called the earliest p2p technology—not because of the technology's inherent characteristics, but simply because that was the way people came to use it. The implementations adapted. As we've seen, this insatiable desire for personal communication has driven the evolution of telephony to the ubiquitous personal cell phone. Never mind that this mobile mode of phoning is significantly more expensive than using the older fixed-location phones, people prefer to use it even for the most trivial connections.

Along the way, other direct modes for conversation developed. IM provided a text-based analogue to a phone conversation, over LAN or over Internet; useful for those who often sat by their PCs. IM is faster and more convenient than e-mail because it's usually a real-time conversation, just like a phone call. It's not as fast or convenient as a real face-to-face conversation, but then neither is a phone call—both lack important nonverbal cues. On the other hand, both IM and e-mail have as written text a form of **persistency** and can be archived.

A special convenience of IM is that it transparently supports an intermediate form of delayed response that's socially less demanding than a real-time conversation. Thus, the first impression of an IM conversation—that user A connects with user B, they exchange typed messages, and then they disconnect—is not representative.

In practice, the IM situation is more commonly that user A is doing something and needs an answer to a question. A knows that B on his "buddy list" probably knows the answer. Now, user A could phone B, but A is busy and knows that phoning often leads to longer conversations. Phoning just to ask a short question risks seeming rude, and there's the risk of interrupting B—user A doesn't know what B is doing beforehand. E-mail would risk being too slow if B doesn't check his inbox that often.

> **Bit 6.2   That IM implements the notion of user presence is its greatest asset.**
> IM needs presence because its primary focus is on immediate end-user delivery. Neither phone nor e-mail has this feature. (Cellular phones might get it.)

Extensive presence information was readily available on early Internet-connected systems because users had open sessions to well-known multiuser systems, and friends and colleagues could easily tell who was connected where and whether they were actively online. This kind of user information, still commonly available in the Unix and Linux environment, became obscured by the increasingly distributed computing infrastructure and the lack of a standard way to make presence information known to other peers. Different (p2p) technologies have tried to remedy this lack, though often in proprietary and nonstandard ways.

An IM system can, even with fairly simple presence information, in advance let A know if B is available for a quick question by simply indicating the online and presence status B currently has. If so, A can send a one-liner IM message to B and get back to other work, confident that B will respond immediately if it's convenient, or later if not. A flurry of follow-ups might result, or the single answer might be adequate. There's greater immediacy to an IM message than e-mail, because the client is on-screen to show notification, but it's not as intrusive as a ringing phone.

However, one major failing of the current generation of IM technologies is their lack of security—increasingly seen as a serious problem. Current popular IM clients usually communicate without encryption or proper authentication. In addition, they tend to pass through other security measures such as corporate firewalls without being subject to their restraints or filters.

Another serious failing is that unlike e-mail, the current dominant IM technologies implement both proprietary and intentionally incompatible networks. Members of one network can't communicate with members of another. It's therefore not unusual that a user must install several incompatible clients to reach important contacts. This issue is examined in the next section.

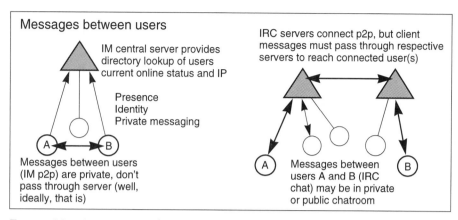

FIGURE 6.2 *A comparison between IM and IRC chat architectures*

MESSAGING TECHNOLOGIES

At the time of writing, the IM market is in the grip of what we could well call the "IM Wars", akin to the intense "browser wars" that characterized the last decade before Internet Explorer became the dominant Web browser.

The similarities to the browser wars are striking in that intentional incompatibilities are incorporated to prevent interoperability between rival clients, and that the rival companies are fiercely competing for users by offering ever more features and extensions to the basic messaging service. A series of buyouts have restructured part of the market, so that for example Miribilis ICQ, dominating the IM field, was acquired and incorporated into AOL with unclear aims for the future. Microsoft as usual went its own way and completely changed the way it was involved in the IM market, retiring established services in favor of new variations.

Some IM Concepts

Before getting into the implementation specifics, it can be useful to overview the concepts and issues that IM technologies should address. Some were introduced earlier, but they are summarized here more systematically.

IM is at bottom a peer extension of chat and exists in that respect parallel to IRC as a form of person-to-person communication. Figure 6.2 depicts the difference between the two messaging technologies in the form of simple connectivity diagrams, highlighting the fact that IM clients establish p2p connections to exchange messages. In IRC, even private messages must always pass through the central servers that clients connect to. At least that's the theory, some IM (notably AIM) clients do in fact server-relay in a manner similar to IRC private chat, but they are then tightly bound to a single service, unlike the IRC peer server network.

IM implements two core functionality concepts:

- **Individual presence,** as a means of finding, retrieving, and subscribing to changes in for example "online" or "offline" information of other users.

- **Instant messaging,** which is a means of sending small, simple, private messages that are delivered immediately to identified online users.

The latter immediacy is the major reason why presence information is so important. Taken together, these two explain why IM achieved its popularity. ICQ and AIM alone registered some 50 million users in just two years.

But IM also requires a third concept, not present at all in IRC:

- **Unique and persistent global identity,** which allows users to find each other and exchange messages, and the IM service to track user presence.

Strictly speaking, IM fudges identity a bit, because the implementations track only registered clients or user-supplied nicknames. Importantly, however, IM systems use their own directory services to bind unique numbering, user nickname, and current IP address into a workable addressing scheme that, when seen from the user perspective, is independent of the underlying Internet infrastructure's IP and DNS addressing.

Enhancing the Experience

With the effective disappearance of Napster, several IM clients began to offer the ability to exchange music (or other media) files, albeit usually with some restrictions on which files, transfer features, and performance.

The offerings could include the purchase of commercial MP3 tracks. For example, Sony set up Pressplay, an online-digital-music joint venture with Vivendi Universal. Rival AOL invested in another music service, Musicnet. However, it dropped a similar feature from its messaging service in 2000 that allowed users to search for music files due to concerns about possible illegal copying.

Another, less contentious enhancement is the addition of various "**push** *channels*" to promote various forms of broadcast content, and the availability of public chatrooms similar in flavor to what IRC provides.

Recent clients, such as ICQ's latest, described later, are really tending towards becoming full-featured personal information managers (PIM). They offer management of address books, to-do lists, e-mail services, reminders, notes, special interest group tracking, banner exchange programs, and so on. Other p2p services include various games, Web phone connectivity, send SMS, pager—the list just seems to grow all the time, along with the size of the client downloads.

Standardizing Basic Concepts

Like many Internet technologies, IM is defined in a "memo", here known as RFC 2779 "Instant Messaging / Presence Protocol Requirements", which sets out some of the fundamental terms and minimum functionality descriptions that IM implementations should adhere to.

RFCs do not as such constitute a formal set of standards, but they should be seen as precursors to standard proposals. They are therefore often used by developers in lieu of formal standards in the interests of promoting interoperability. The abstract in RFC 2779 describes the current IM situation succinctly:

> *Presence and Instant Messaging have recently emerged as a new medium of communications over the Internet. ... Applications of presence and instant messaging currently use independent, non-standard and non-interoperable protocols developed by various vendors. The goal of the Instant Messaging and Presence Protocol (IMPP) Working Group is to define a standard protocol so that independently developed applications of instant messaging and/or presence can interoperate across the Internet. This document defines a minimal set of requirements that IMPP must meet.*

This work (www.imppwg.org), under the overall supervision of the Internet Engineering Task Force (IETF, www.ietf.org), is expected to result in a consensus adoption of a truly open standard protocol for future IMPP implementations. The importance of this for coming mobile Internet is stressed later in the document:

> *It is expected that Presence and Instant Messaging services will be particularly valuable to users over mobile IP wireless access devices. Indeed the number of devices connected to the Internet via wireless means is expected to grow substantially in the coming years. It is not reasonable to assume that separate protocols will be available for the wireless portions of the Internet.*

Based on this expectation, the RFC recommends that the protocol implementations be especially designed for typical mobile contexts, tolerating high latency, low bandwidth, and intermittent connectivity. In addition, they should make modest requirements on computing power, device battery life, and screen size.

Minimum Functionality

Based on experience and the RFC, one can formulate some basic requirements that all IM technologies must implement, at least in future.

The protocols must allow a presence service to be available independent of whether an instant message service is available, and vice versa. These functionalities are seen as independent. It's also a practical requirement that message inbox and presence entity (termed *presentity*) be decoupled and fully independent of each other, even if they share the same identifier (in the supported namespace).

Interoperability is a core requirement, according to the RFC, which contrasts with the current fragmented deployment of IM. Support must include a minimum set of protocol features and a common message format.

User control is specified to span such things as instant and subscriber visibility, and the kind of information that others may see. IM (and chat) clients almost always implement some way for users to set different levels of presence, including "invisible" or DND (Do Not Disturb). There should also be adequate control over access to inbox services and who can send messages to the inbox. As a rule, this control is implemented as some form of filtering—for example, an ignore list. Both forms of control are required by the RFC to be implemented at least in part as autonomous agencies, capable of responding even when the user is not available, or perhaps even offline (in which case, it must be mediated by an IM server). These requirements apply especially to the functionality of subscribing to presence notifications.

What the RFC specifically calls for is a common presence format that includes adequate identification information along the lines of the vCard "visiting card" exchange format now broadly supported by e-mail clients and PIMs.

Areas that the RFC extends compared to current implementations are authentication and encryption. In general terms, the technology must ensure authenticated endpoints, noncorruption, nonplayback, and privacy. Current popular implementations lack most or all of these characteristics, which are otherwise commonly realized using public key encryption and digital signatures.

A Common Standard?

On 25 July 2000, a new industry standards organization, IM Unified (IMU), was created with the stated goal "to rapidly enable users of all members' instant messaging services to communicate in a seamless, convenient, private and secure manner" (see www.imunified.org).

The founding members of this coalition were AT&T, Excite@Home, iCAST, the MSN network of Internet services, Odigo, Phone.com, Prodigy, Tribal Voice, and Yahoo. In August 2000, the organization made public a first set of technical specifications for an open, standards-based, interoperable instant messaging protocol to achieve this goal. Implementation was scheduled for the end of that year, but at the latest check (late 2001), only Excite@Home had actually made use of the IMU protocol in their Excite Messenger client.

It's significant that AOL, the dominant IM player since acquiring ICQ, is not a member and evidently does not wish such interoperability unless it's based on AOL's own "internal" solutions. Partly for this reason, the IMU was seen by some merely as a marketing posture against AOL, rather than any serious attempt at an open interoperability standard. It also appears significant that the IMU Web site appears not to have been updated in over a year, since that announcement in August. The suspicion is that IMU was a blip, despite the claims made in mid-2001 by various IMU-member spokespersons that the technology is ready to go, only awaiting the working out of certain legal and logistical agreements between members.

However, both the IMU, and IM developers independent of IMU (such as Jabber) state an intention to adhere to the fully open IETF protocol specifications for IMPP, a work that was described earlier, when these become available. A successful early test of IMU interoperability with Excite@Home was nonetheless documented by Jabber (see www.jabber.org/?oid=1592).

True to form, Microsoft dropped out of IMU when it made MSN Messenger obsolete and opted for its own bundled all-in-one solution to beat everyone else. Thus, Windows Messenger is a brand-new instant messaging service that is exclusively tied into the Windows XP operating system, which features IM, video, telephony, file sharing, multimedia, and more, as part of the basic package.

By virtue of its inclusion in the operating system, the Microsoft solution could easily prove to become the dominant technology within a year or two—the next killer application—unless its own incompatibility with other Windows versions, or with NetMeeting H.323 and other established protocols, proves too bothersome.

There are things to both like and dislike about that scenario, including the way WM requires connectivity to the .NET Passport service (see Chapter 2) for authentication and to manage presence information. It's therefore not surprising to find question and answer on the Web about how to remove WM from Windows XP.

A brief look at WM is provided at the end of this chapter.

ICQ AND AIM

AOL's AIM and acquired ICQ technologies currently purport to include nine of ten IM clients, the remainder a mix primarily of Yahoo and MSN users. This dominance is to a large extent due to the already "captive" user base of AOL ISP subscribers and to the acquirement in 1998 of the main IM player, Miribilis ICQ.

> **Bit 6.3   Registered identities invariably overstates the number of users.**
>
> Many (most?) users in public IM directories have several registered identities.

Determining the real number of individual users for any IM system is difficult because people (intentionally or inadvertently) tend to have more than one identity with the system. Furthermore, because of the current lack of interoperability, the same user is typically registered with several different IM systems. Therefore, AIM's 40 million and ICQ's 150 million registered identities (at time of writing) must overlap and translate to less—perhaps significantly less—actual users.

Nevertheless, while AOL may have the dominant share of IM, it is under significant pressure to allow interoperability and thus a unified IM access independent of client system. So far, AOL has actively resisted such interoperability whenever any of the other IM systems have deployed the means to contact AIM users. It remains to be seen if this vision of "anyone contacting anyone" by instant messaging will ever be realized without AOL as a player.

Because ICQ technology was so trend setting, and still greatly dominates in relative share of users, this chapter mainly focuses on the ICQ implementation. Current ICQ software and support is provided at the main site, www.icq.com.

ICQ—IM FOR THE MASSES

Four Israelis, Yair Goldfinger, Arik Vardi, Sefi Vigiser, and Amnon Amir, founded the Miribilis company in July 1996 in order to introduce a new communication tool for the Internet. Their product ICQ (a mnemonic abbreviation for "I Seek You") was released in November that same year. It introduced a for the time startling sidestep for the user in terms of achieving public networking access.

There was suddenly no need to ask the local IT department about IP addresses, domain name servers, or hosting facilities. ICQ simply ignored the idea that anyone else had any say over how you used your computer. Instead, users just installed the client software, which could communicate with a central server administering its own namespace over member clients. After that, a user's computer could talk to any other machine with an address in the ICQ namespace. And it would do so from virtually anywhere with Internet access, even from behind firewalls.

ICQ bypassed Internet's DNS system of addressing in favor of creating its own directory of protocol-specific addresses, translated into real network IP addresses by a central server member directory on the fly. This meant that it could update IP addresses in real time, thus coping with intermittently connected PCs and dynamic IPs, a feature later also implemented in a similar way by technologies like Groove, Napster, and NetMeeting.

The other ways of dealing with identity and intermittent connectivity, also bypassing DNS, either rely on current IP directly, without server-mediated directories, or on using scheduled connections. The latter solution is common with distributed processing systems, such as SETI@Home.

The main focus of ICQ (like that of Napster years later) was ease of use—install, click and go—and a small, resident application always at hand. The ease explains part of the enormous appeal of the system, adopted by hundreds of millions of users, because the vast majority of users detest anything they must configure and tweak. Any really useful mass-appeal tool must allow an essentially transparent functionality as default behavior; anything else will necessarily have limited adoption.

Table 6.1 shows the component summary for ICQ.

Installing ICQ

While Miribilis ICQ originally was just for Windows systems running Miribilis clients, ports to other platforms do exist—both official versions and third-party clones. The ICQ protocol has been hacked repeatedly and is therefore fairly well documented on several unofficial ICQP sites. After going AOL, however, both server behavior and protocol shifts are making ICQ interoperability difficult for the clones.

Searching the Web for the conjunction of "ICQ" and "Linux", for example, turns up several sites that link to client software compatible with ICQ. Some Linux X-Window clients worth mentioning are LICQ (licq.wibble.net), GICQ for GTK (www.korsoft.com/gicq/), and KiCQ for KDE (www.cn.ua/~denis/kde/kicq.html). A number of text-based console clients are also available.

The original small Windows ICQ clients have evolved in the usual bloatware manner, so a full official ICQ installation package now runs about 5MB (ICQ2000); online help is another 600KB for a self-installing plug-in.

TABLE **6.1** *ICQ component summary, common to many IM implementations*

Component	Specific forms	Comments
Identity	Unique ICQ number tied to server directory with current online IP identity	Client IP identity tracked in real time by server and hence also presence status.
Presence	Usually online, offline, or one of a number of preset or custom states	Presence setting is customized by user.
Roster	Client-managed lists	Server can automatically notify of changed online status of specified users.
Agency	Automation settings in client plus server push	Functionality set in preferences and by subscription, and by inclusion of various plug-ins.
Browsing	Of server-presented content	Client minibrowser, or activation of system default Web browser.
Architecture	User-centric server mediated	Clients make p2p connections by default, with fallback channel through mediating server.
Protocol	Proprietary	Extensions and plug-ins.

Installation is still essentially click-and-go, but it takes a few extra clicks to deal with nag alerts, a welcome page, and some basic settings before reaching the running interface seen in Figure 6.3. The client is free, but as such it is also a conduit for paid banner advertising in the messaging windows, piped down from the ICQ server.

Figure 6.4 shows the advanced mode version of the interface, which makes more of the current ICQ functionality available up front. This hints at the extra features offered to entice users to join and remain with a particular vendor—and as hooks to potential revenue-generating services. The marketing push is comparatively low key, but it's not insignificant. The animated banners become very distracting if you have a couple of message windows open. The licensing agreement has a lower age-limit in —perhaps a good thing, because after registration, even with unspecified personal characteristics and a low profile, I immediately received unsolicited "invitations" from a number of unknown users. Ignoring future contact attempts is at least possible using a clearly visible button on the message dialog.

User "convenience" and automation comes at a price, however, and is an issue we meet again with other implementations. The price for preprogrammed and

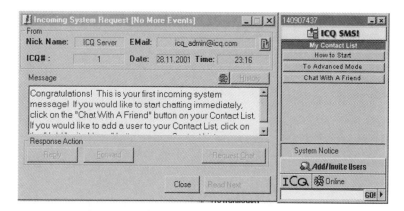

FIGURE 6.3   *Installing ICQ requires passing a number of registration dialogs first, but eventually you're online and are welcomed with a first, system message. Shown is the simple, default interface.*

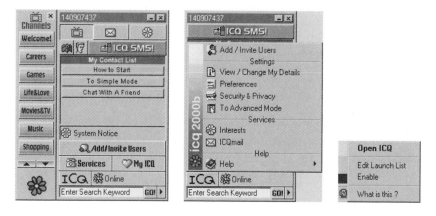

FIGURE 6.4   *Selecting Advanced Mode (left capture in this composite) provides more functionality up front, and the ICQ button gives a popup (middle capture) with access to Preferences among other things. An icon popup on the taskbar (far right) lets you disable or enable ICQ as a whole.*

automated convenience in ICQ is a distinct loss of control. For example, in a dial-up setting, the client by default is automatically live when a connection exists and asleep when it doesn't. One immediate consequence is that you must be online to access and change settings, because the client—and its automatic welcome window—go up and down like a yo-yo if you connect intermittently, for example during e-mail check.

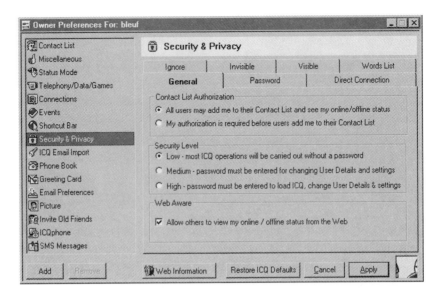

FIGURE 6.5 *Opening Owner Preferences provides access to a plethora of settings, thankfully also details of ICQ behavior and initial activity, along with security, proxy settings, and just plain visual tweaks. This is the Advanced Mode view; Simple Mode has far fewer settings.*

Furthermore, the client status overrides the normal connection control, so that if your e-mail client previously automatically closed the connection when its poll was complete, ICQ keeps it alive indefinitely once up. A number of such user issues need to be resolved after initial installation, unless you happen to like the default settings, and it's not always clear how to find the relevant setting.

Luckily, it's possible to disable ICQ in one click from the taskbar menu, for those situations when you don't want the client to react to connection status on its own. Not everyone thinks to look there, and you might easily look in vain elsewhere.

You can make more selective and detailed customization from the Preferences dialog, accessed through the ICQ popup, when you have the time and inclination to peruse the very many settings indicated by full feature set in Figure 6.5.

The user should note in this context that there are two *independent* profiles here; a less detailed one accessed from Simple Mode, plus the detailed dialog for Advanced Mode as shown in the previous figure. If you only tweak the one, changing to the other mode will use the default settings this still has—something that confused me the first time it happened.

ICQ PROTOCOL

The protocol used by ICQ is proprietary, and it has passed through several version iterations, each of them quite different from the preceding. Each version has been reverse-engineered from the current Windows clients in order to allow development of interoperable clients on other platforms.

The oldest version fully deployed and reportedly still in use by some (Java-based) clients is v2. What later came to be called v3/4 is a curious mix, where the server used an earlier v3 format packets (never fully deployed on the client side) to communicate with the clients, while clients instead used a later v4 format. Both v3 and v4 were in response to severe criticism of the security vulnerabilities in the v2 protocol, and they introduced anti-spoofing measures and client-side encryption, respectively.

The current ICQ protocol is v5, which should be seen as an attempt to clean up the patchwork result of the v3/4 security retrofits. It's worth noting that v5 clients have a setting to refuse communication with clients using older protocol versions. There are signs that AOL is considering a significant protocol change (a v6?) to make AIM and ICQ interoperable, and possibly try to close out clone clients (for a while).

> **Bit 6.4 Proprietary protocols tend to be haphazard constructions.**
> It appears significant that although closed protocols (such as ICQ or Napster) are often innovative, they tend to show inconsistent and incomplete design with numerous flaws. A general view is that open review in protocol design adds robustness.

Data Packets

The basis for all ICQ connectivity is a connection to the central ICQ server. Clients send packets to the server using the non-handshaking Internet protocol UDP. As of v4, these packets are encrypted before they are sent, unlike the packets sent from the server to a client, which are not—a legacy from v3/4 protocol.

(As an aside, tracing UDP packets to analyze the protocol did actually comply with the original Miribilis License agreement and was therefore not illegal.)

The header fields in an ICQ v5 packet are summarized in Table 6.2. ICQ packets must not exceed 450 bytes total length, so longer content requires multiple packets. For example, user lists are limited to about 120 names per packet.

Session ID might seem superfluous, given a unique client ID, but it's used by the server to prevent spoofing. Every packet the client sends must have this same number;

TABLE **6.2** *Header fields present in ICQ v5 protocol*

Header field	Description
Version	Fixed; protocol version (0x50 0x00 for v5)
Zero	4 null bytes, purpose unknown
UIN (32 bit)	Client identification number, assigned at registration
Session_ID (32 bit)	Random identification, assigned at each server login
Command	A 2-byte command
Seq_Num1	A 16-bit random number
Seq_Num2	A 16-bit number that starts off as 1
Checkcode	A 32-bit checksum value
Parameters	A variable length field for command parameters

the server ignores any packets that don't. This Session ID is also sent back with every packet from the server, so the client also ignores any packets that don't match.

Sequence numbers are used to ensure that all packets really arrive at the recipient and only do so once. Later packets with duplicate sequence numbers are ignored. Both numbers (random-set and 1-set) are incremented for each packet sent, except that the second is kept at value zero for certain commands.

UDP doesn't use handshaking to implement a reliable connection like TCP, but the ICQ server does explicitly acknowledge (with SRV_ACK) each packet received. If the client doesn't receive this ACK for any packet sent, it should resend the packet.

The server expects the client to send an acknowledgment for every packet received except for SRV_ACK. The ICQ client will actually resend only six times with an interval of ten seconds—the interval chosen so as not to unduly consume bandwidth. After six resends it then sends CMD_SEND_TEXT_CODE with a B_MESSAGE_ACK (see the following section about command sets), seemingly as a fallback measure.

Command Sets

There are two separate sets of commands; one for client-server messages (Table 6.3), the other for server-client messages (Table 6.4). These lists are not complete, but they are provided here for reference and as examples of the kinds of commands an IM system must implement for minimum functionality. The reverse-engineering process means that the names are descriptive, not official.

TABLE 6.3 *Client-to-server commands current in ICQ v5 protocol, packets sent encrypted*

Command	Description
CMD_REG_NEW_USER CMD_NEW_USER_INFO CMD_NEW_USER_1	Is sent in order to register a new user and request UIN. Only occurs prior to any session login. A subsequent login completes registration and sends entered information with new user info. Further users can be added to the same client with the last command.
CMD_LOGIN	Client request to start a session (contains UID, password, etc.).
CMD_ACK	Acknowledge a packet received from server.
CMD_ACK_MESSAGES	Remove old (offline) messages from server.
CMD_KEEP_ALIVE	Client sends this every two minutes to maintain online status with server (server provides a suggested value with login response).
CMD_STATUS_CHANGE	Updates user online presence status.
CMD_ADD_TO_LIST	Add a user to contact list (receive status changes).
CMD_CONTACT_LIST	Informs the server for which users you wish to receive online/offline events. May require multiple packets to send longer lists.
CMD_AUTH_UPDATE	Set whether users require permission to add you to their contact lists (not implemented in all clones).
CMD_SEARCH_UIN CMD_SEARCH_USER CMD_SEARCH_RAND	Request search for a user based on UIN, on (4) text fields, or at random from a specified group.
CMD_INFO_REQ CMD_EXT_INFO_REQ	Request basic or extended information about a particular user (UIN).
CMD_SEND_MESSAGE	Send a message through the server to an offline or invisible user. Parameters include target user UIN, message type, and length.
CMD_MSG_TO_NEW_USER	Sends a message to a user who is not in client contact list.
CMD_UPDATE_INFO CMD_UPDATE_EXT_INFO	Update normal and extended user info, respectively.
CMD_META_USER	Replaces a number of older commands to set or get user information (in particular, used to change password).
CMD_QUERY_SERVERS CMD_QUERY_ADDONS	Used to query server about addresses to other servers, and about availability of global add-ons.
CMD_INVIS_LIST CMD_VIS_LIST CMD_UPDATE_LIST	Overrides visibility status to specified users, specify users to see when in invisible mode, informs server of changes in visible/invisible lists.
CMD_SEND_TEXT_CODE	Extension mechanism to send other commands as text strings.

TABLE 6.4 *Server-to-client commands current in ICQ v5 protocol, sent not encrypted*

Command	Description
SRV_ACK	Acknowledgment for a command sent to the server. Received packet is identified by its sequence number.
SRV_GO_AWAY	Error message from the server. Client must disconnect and reconnect in order to continue.
SRV_NEW_UIN	A new UIN, requested by CMD_REG_NEW_USER, has been reserved (passed in the UIN header field). CMD_LOGIN completes registration.
SRV_LOGIN_REPLY	Response to correctly received CMD_LOGIN.
SRV_BAD_PASS	Response to invalid password in the login packet.
SRV_RECV_MESSAGE	Response after login if (offline) messages are waiting.
SRV_USER_ONLINE SRV_USER_OFFLINE	Changes to status for users on a contact list are notified to the client using these commands.
SRV_QUERY	Response to CMD_QUERY_SERVES and CMD_QUERY_ADDONS.
SRV_USER_FOUND SRV_END_OF_SEARCH	Responses to CMD_SEARCH_USER or CMD_SEARCH_UIN when user is found, one per packet. End for no more or too many.
SRV_RAND_USER	Response to CMD_SEARCH_RAND.
SRV_INFO_REPLY SRV_EXT_INFO_REPLY	Responses to respective request for information about a user.
SRV_NEW_USER SRV_UPDATE_EXT SRV_AUTH_UPDATE SRV_STATUS_UPDATE	Responses to corresponding client commands.
SRV_UPDATE_SUCCESS SRV_UPDATE_FAIL	Response to CMD_UPDATE_INFO, successfully changed user information, or not, respectively.
SRV_META_USER	Response to CMD_META_USER, update performed or data sent.
SRV_MULTI_PACKET	Several packets sent at once. Requires only a single CMD_ACK.
SRV_NOT_CONNECTED SRV_TRY_AGAIN SRV_SYS_DELIVERED_MESS SRV_SYSTEM_MESSAGE SRV_X1, SRV_X2	Identified commands not specified further in documentation.

The identified message types can be sorted into five main groups:

- Text
- **URL** (2 parts, description plus address)
- Authorization request to add user to contact list (five parts)
- Grant authorization request, user added (four parts)
- Send contacts (arbitrary number of parts)

Within each message, its component parts are in all cases delimited by a trailing byte value of 0xFE.

User presence status is defined by a single OR-able bit value, although some combinations are not allowed. The recognized component states are *online*, *away*, *do not disturb* (DND), *invisible*, *occupied*, *not available* (extended away), and *free for chat*. Optional components are *Web-aware* and *show current IP*. The state offline is defined by disconnecting from the server.

Client to Client

When ICQ clients are communicating p2p to each other (which they do for actual messaging, for instance), they use normal TCP protocol. Server relay is an automatic option for store-and-forward messaging when the recipient is offline.

Each type of client functionality (message, chat, file exchange, etc.) must set up its own listening TCP socket in order for client-initiated p2p communication to occur. Normally, however, only the Message listener is active by default; the others are created as the result of some event message received over the server UDP connection. Chat, file, and other transfers are in reverse TCP situations handled much the same as in the message case; the difference is that these are all initiated by a request message, so the receiving client always knows what to expect.

The normal TCP exchange needs to be "reversed" (that is to say, initiated by the target client) if, for some reason, it can't receive a TCP connection. In that case, it must be informed of the sender's IP address in a UDP packet sent by way of the server connection. The sequence of events for reverse TCP goes as follows, and it is similar in principle to any p2p exchange that needs to traverse a firewall (that is, use "push").

1. User A types in a message to send to user B.
2. Client A attempts to connect with client B but fails.
3. Client A builds a TCP_REQUEST packet and sends it to A's ICQ server.

4. Client B receives a `TCP_REQUEST` packet from its ICQ server containing IP:Port information for client A.

5. Client B attempts to connect to client A and succeeds.

6. Client B sends a `TCP_Init` packet to client A. (This is what client A would normally have sent if the connection attempt in step 2 had succeeded.)

7. Client A receives the `TCP_Init` packet and can then send the message typed by user A in step 1, with packet flow as if a normal TCP connection.

8. User B receives and reads the message.

In rare cases, neither client can receive a TCP connection, perhaps because both are behind firewalls. Then the fallback is to send messages as UDP packets, using the ICQ server as mediator. This process is automatic and transparent to the user.

Further details of the ICQ protocol can be found at the ICQ Protocol Site (at www.d.kth.se/~d95-mih/icq/), maintained by Magnus Ihse.

USING ICQ

Despite the increasing number of features that go beyond simple IM and the consequently larger client installation, the core of ICQ remains messaging.

On the basis of overall functionality and biggest user base, if the choice is between any of the popular proprietary IM systems, then ICQ seems the best bet and is supported by several third-party developers, notably with ICQ clients for Linux.

There are two main caveats to using ICQ, however. Since AOL owns ICQ, the protocol could easily change with little warning in a new version upgrade to promote a better internal interoperability, AIM-ICQ, leaving other clients in the cold. The other problem is the total dependence on the ICQ central server for connectivity, even though subsequent conversations between peers may be direct p2p. AOL servers are very unforgiving of even marginally noncompliant clients and summarily drop them.

AIM

For the sake of completeness, an overview of AIM is also in order. AOL's original IM system is a closed, proprietary technology based on a user-centric architecture. Clients are provided as free downloads but are exclusively tied to AOL servers that rarely acknowledge third-party clones for long. This made the AIM protocol harder to hack than ICQ when it was run by Miribilis. Table 6.5 lists the component summary.

TABLE **6.5**   *AIM component summary, very similar to ICQ*

Component	Specific forms	Comments
Identity	Unique screen name tied to server directory with current online IP identity	Client IP identity determined at login, presence status tracked by periodic advertising redirects.
Presence	Usually online, offline, or one of a number of preset or custom states	Presence setting is modified by user settings of permit/deny and visible/invisible.
Roster	Client-managed buddy lists	Server can automatically notify of changed online status of specified users.
Agency	Automation settings in client plus server push	Functionality set in preferences and by subscription, and by inclusion of various plug-ins.
Browsing	N/A	N/A
Architecture	User-centric server mediated, login server	Clients do IM entirely through message server relay.
Protocol	Proprietary	Locked to AOL's servers.

Connecting to AIM services is a two-step process. First, the client connects to a central authorization server (such as login.oscar.aol.com) for a login session. AIM clients use port 5190, but any will do. If this attempt succeeds, the server returns a success response message, plus a cookie that will automatically authorize the client to connect to any of the other messaging servers in the AIM service domain, or to the special-purpose servers used for advertisements, chat, etc. The authorizing server also recommends the client a "BOS" (Basic OSCAR Service) server to use for the primary services session. On receiving the authorization cookie, the client disconnects from the authorization server.

With cookie in hand, so to speak, the client then initiates a connection with a BOS server, as indicated by the address in the Authorization Response, and "signs on" for the service. Regular connections are automatically made during the session to designated Ad-servers that supply advertisement content to the client.

The periodic advertising redirects are how the AIM service tracks a user's online status, which is clearly why simply disconnecting from the service is sufficient to log off. Any clone client must, from the point of view of the BOS server, at least *appear* to support the advertisement component, or it will be disconnected.

User Roster

When signing on, the client sends a list of screen names (called the Buddy List) to the message server. Although the user sees the Buddy List organized into groups, this is a client-side feature; the server deals only with the individual names.

A full update of list member status occurs after signing on. The names on the list thereafter get watched server-side for login/logoff events, and notifications are sent back to the client when these events occur. Online status is also read and sent from the server as periodic updates to the client during the session, irrespective of any state changes—apparently, such updates ensure that no name is missed.

AIM users are classed in three groups: "AOL" for registered AOL members (using the AOL browser client), "free" for AIM-only users, and "trial" for anyone with an account less than a month old. What significance this classification might have for service level or access has never been disclosed.

You can access user information only for a user who is online. AIM servers don't store any information about users who aren't logged on. The basic information includes Member Class, Warning Level, Idle Time, Time of Sign-on, and the date when the member started the AOL/AIM account. This information is transported by the notification system for the oncoming buddy event.

Further information must be specifically requested as a personal profile. An "invalid user" response to this request usually means that the user isn't online. A user can also add names to permit/deny or visible/invisible lists. Users who have denied access to see them are effectively "offline" to the denied party.

Primary user search is by screen name (as in Buddy List), but the service also provides simple search by e-mail address. A search by real name was implemented originally, but it had an on/off kind of existence—sometimes it worked, sometimes it didn't. It seems to have been replaced by a "white pages" directory on the *AOL Anywhere* search site, the same as that accessed from the Web (at search.aol.com).

Messaging Functionality

Although the messaging functionality is formally p2p, AIM transport is in fact completely server mediated. All messages are sent to the message server, which relays them to the destination clients, much like IRC. This process is shown in Figure 6.6.

Bit 6.5   AIM peer messaging is entirely dependent on central server relay.
At no time does one client directly locate another client or even know its (IP) location.

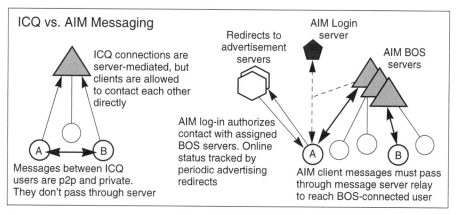

FIGURE 6.6 *AIM messaging is schematically like IRC, as messages must always be relayed by a message server. Clients have no location information about each other and can't connect directly p2p, unlike the case in ICQ.*

AOL MIME-types all message content as "text/x-aol-rtf", and the client wraps it in a rudimentary HTML wrapper. The HTML markup is evidently not necessary, and the AIM client supports only a subset of markup. Everything is sent in clear text, and the server relay is transparent to the content.

An e-mail gateway of sorts is provided for AIM's trivial "invite a friend" feature, which adds a short message to a server-generated e-mail inviting the recipient to join. AOL subscribers can check their e-mail account through AIM, and a form of POP account is possible for others. Notification of new mail is supported.

Protocol

The proprietary AIM protocol has been analyzed with the intent to provide interoperable clients for the AIM service. Unlike for ICQ, this work is made more difficult by countermeasures by AOL to keep AIM closed, as discussed later.

Adam Fritzler and Scott Werndorfer maintain an evolving overview of the AIM/ Oscar Protocol Specification (www.auk.cx/faim/protocol/ or www.zigamorph.net/ faim/protocol/) as a service to those who are trying to develop compatible clients, especially in the *nix world. There they motivate the work in this way:

> *AOL has provided very nice clients for the Windows and Macintosh platforms, but has left its UNIX(tm) users with a horrible (Java-based) "solution". Exposing this protocol will allow third-parties to develop nice, stable clients for other platforms, generally supporting the idea that "rewritten work is always better than the original".*

Everything has come from interpretation of AIM/Oscar packets coming straight off the wire. The pair state categorically that there's been no disassembly of any code.

Moving on to the protocol, we can note that it uses standard TCP packets. More than one command may be sent in a packet, as an abstraction layer above packets. Therefore, commands are in the data stream signaled by a six-byte header that begins with a byte value of 0x2a. The header also contains a byte-value for the channel ID, a two-byte sequence number, and a two-byte value for the variable length of the following data field. The data length offset would thus point to the next command header, if one is in the packet stream. Data is not terminated in any special way.

Sequence numbers are superfluous in TCP, but it seems they're used as a form of client validation. The seed origins are picked quite randomly, with no connection between server and client sequences. Sequence numbers are initialized for each opened TCP connection (or socket), are always incremented upward, and wrap.

AIM uses the concept of *channels* to multiplex information over the same connection, with somewhat the same functionality as TCP port numbers. Of the four observed channels, data is transmitted only over channel 2. New connections are set up using channel 1, error management uses channel 3, and "formal" termination uses channel 4. In practice, termination is commonly achieved by simply disconnecting— no server negotiation has been observed when using channel 4 notification.

The data field has its own structure, with a kind of subheader. This identifies Family ID for a group of services (of which there are very many) and subtype ID for the specific service or information provided in the data section. There are a couple of rarely used flags and a four-byte Request ID to identify nonatomic information. The last is vital to identify responses and associate them with the initiating queries.

Some identified command families are named in the analysis:

- Generic Service Controls

- Location Services (user information)

- Buddy List Management (and presence monitoring)

- Messaging

- Advertisement Management

- Administrative (information and account management)

- Popup Notices

- BOS-specific (services, group permissions)

- User Lookup

- Statistics (event reporting)

- Translate

- Chat Navigation

- Chat

- Notification List

Either as part of one command or directly in the first-level data field, a TLV triplet can occur (a 16-bit Type code, a 16-bit Length of the following Value field). They are commonly used for sending short strings and other values, for example {0x0011, 0x000d, "user@some.com"}, where this type identifies e-mail address.

Interoperability Problems

AOL has never been interested in opening its IM service to third-party software. The AIM client may be free, but it's theirs, and the intent seems to sign up and keep members for AOL more than just providing a generic IM service.

Observed AIM server behavior, especially in the context of analyzing the protocol, provides this list of entry barriers to clone clients.

- The OSCAR server will disconnect an offending client immediately if it receives a malformed command or command header.

- An out-of-order command, according to the header sequence numbering (not the actual order) causes the server to disconnect the client.

- Lost data is unacceptable in the AIM standard—for example, any client parsing errors in the command stream invariably results in disconnection by the server.

- Tracking of online status is indirect, intentionally tied to the redirects issued when the client periodically requests new advertising content.

The analysis of the server requirements on acceptable data from a client suggests a significant dependency on low-level timing constraints, such as when constructing headers. This might be why the *nix Java implementations for AIM connectivity work so poorly; they are simply too slow in this context.

Increasingly, similar hostile, xenophobic behavior is being noted by users and developers of the ICQ clone clients. Some AIM and ICQ clones perform better than others, but the situation tends to change without warning.

Covert Client Detection

It can be interesting to examine one method that AOL allegedly used to ensure that only its own clients can communicate with the AIM servers. The caveat here is that the analysis relies on anecdotal evidence, but the method is plausible and supported by trials that shows it to work across many client versions. It's also known that attempts to be interoperative have generally failed because AIM servers always manage to disconnect third-party clients that are otherwise protocol compliant.

At one time, Microsoft designed its MSN client with enough knowledge of the AIM protocol to be able to contact and exchange messages with AIM users. The assumption was that an AIM server at AOL should not care whether it's talking with the intended AIM client software (as written by AOL) or with the MSN client software (as written by Microsoft). This failed, just like the other attempts.

It was alleged that AOL exploited a software bug in its proprietary client code to covertly detect and disconnect non-AOL clients that attempted to be AIM/Oscar compliant. The described exploit is similar to that used by Internet virus and worm infiltration attempts that inject code using a buffer overrun. The AOL server can use the bug to make the user's machine execute a code fragment downloaded from the AIM server that will run with an expected response only in the AIM client.

It's been determined across several versions of the AIM client that all had the same long-standing vulnerability to overlong string data in a particular command context—a bug that was never publicized or fixed. Server packets have also been detected with data that will overrun the 256-byte buffer. A specially crafted 278-byte value can corrupt the running AIM client image, but in a carefully controlled way, so that execution resumes in the packet data.

A portion of the packet data is therefore prepared as executable code to do two things. One is to have the AIM client recover and seem to resume normal execution. The other is before this to form a return packet from some of the downloaded packet data and induce the AIM client to send this packet back to the AIM server.

What for all intents and purposes comes across as a retrospective protocol extension is used as a test of genuineness. No existing version of the AIM client was coded explicitly to respond to this contrived subcase, but the response is implicitly known by any old AIM client that has the "secret" buffer overflow bug.

This illustrates one of the disadvantages of closed source and proprietary solutions. No secret truly remains secret for long, but closed source and secret bugs pose serious risks by inviting exploits by others for purposes not as innocent as confirming genuineness.

JABBER

The stated focus of Jabber is to be a "conversational technology" for p2p in the most general sense, including not only person to person, but also person to application and especially application to application. Actually, Jabber more properly refers to a whole group of technologies that share common goals within an overall architecture.

Jabber (www.jabber.org) thus evolved as a project to bring together diverse applications, when a number of developers decided in 1998 to create a truly open, distributed p2p architecture as a basis for further specialized work. Jeremie Miller is credited as being behind that initiative. Public recognition came first in 1999.

The design began by choosing XML as a consistent way to encapsulate data, whatever the application, and yet allow arbitrary extension as the need arises. Application protocols are transparently implemented in XML and translated to native formats as required.

> **Bit 6.6   Jabber is an XML-based peer architecture, not any specific application.**
> Current Jabber clients focus on instant messaging and allow p2p file transfers between users. The protocol and architecture however is open to any number of other uses.

Some of the many projects developed within the Jabber framework are:

- Gateways to most existing IM services and their protocols
- Libraries for almost all current programming languages
- A modular open source server, plus client software for practically every platform
- A number of specialized services such as language translations

A particular emphasis is given to P-A communication (as introduced in Chapter 2) and to fostering a design approach that facilitates all p2p conversations (P-P, P-A and A-A), along with the access of dynamic data from many different services.

The first practical application of Jabber technology is as an instant messaging system focused on privacy, security, ease of use, access from anywhere using any device, and interoperability with IM, phone, and Web-based services.

Once again applying the generic list outlined in Chapter 2, Table 6.6 gives the component summary for Jabber IM.

TABLE 6.6 *Jabber component summary*

Component	Specific forms	Comments
Identity	user@server user@server/resource	Connectivity is server mediated. Direct p2p client connections natural.
Presence	Usually online, offline, or one of a number of preset or custom states	Jabber automatically manages presence for user and application.
Roster	List of users or resources with numerous management options	Adding, accessing, or removing through context-click, roster is server-stored and can follow user across different machines/clients.
Agency	Simple filters (blockers)	Management through single central identity.
Browsing	Similar to MS Nethood	User can make local paths and peers available for external browsing.
Architecture	Closely resembles e-mail with chain routing through servers	Clients can function in any client or server role. Provision for callback and other security features.
Protocol	XML, protocol agnostic transparent translation	Support for accessing major IM protocols, IRC, e-mail, A-A bridges, and so on.

Central to the open architecture is that all data transfer in any context occurs in XML format and protocol, which allows Jabber to function as both storage and exchange service for the applications. Metadata and structure are similarly defined in XML, and a number of working groups have set out standardized tag sets to describe useful namespaces for documents, music, and other content domains. Once defined, such tag sets allow meaningfully encoded data exchanges over other Jabber services, for instance in IM conversations that traditionally deal only with pure text.

> **Bit 6.7   Jabber serves as a conduit between peer applications.**
>
> Namespace support means that any XML data can be included in any namespace within a conversation. Applications and services can include, intercept, and modify their own XML data at any point.

So, although Jabber in theory can be many things, its most common implementation so far is to provide a general IM client, which is why Jabber is examined in this chapter. Using the service gateways, a Jabber client in principle allows a user to communicate with members of any of the major IM networks. The Jabber user must still obtain a valid user identity in each of these other IM systems, however, and must still "discover" which network a particular person might belong to (and which IM identity that person has).

Another development focus is the Jabber-as-Middleware (JAM) project, which has its goal to make the technology a vehicle for discovering services, authenticating sessions, reliably delivering XML packets containing service requests and responses, and notifying senders that their packets have been delivered. This **middleware** concept is similar to what for example HailStorm/Passport does (see Chapter 2), only Jabber can do it in a distributed manner without the extreme central server dependency.

INFRASTRUCTURE

Jabber infrastructure has some specific points worth expanding on, mainly because its focus is on generalized resources, rather than just IM identities. In particular, the Jabber IM system (not the general Jabber infrastructure) is distinguished from existing IM services, such as those discussed earlier, by several key features:

- XML foundation (structured, intelligent messaging; P-A, A-A)
- Distributed network (arbitrary number of servers/services)
- **Open protocol** and codebase (interoperability)
- Modular, extensible architecture

The underlying model that Jabber is based on is Internet e-mail—a distributed network of servers that use a common protocol, to which specialized clients connect to send and receive messages. In the case of Jabber, this also means other services. The main functional difference from e-mail is that Jabber incorporates presence and is close to real-time communication, unlike the store-and-forward e-mail model.

Servers are fully independent of each other and maintain their own user lists and services. They transfer messages and presence information among themselves in an atomistic p2p network, as in Figure 6.7. Any number of Jabber servers can form a network. A particular user is always associated with a specific server with an identity that looks like an e-mail address: bleuf@jabber.org. This identity is assigned in a registration process or during administrative setup of a server (enterprise).

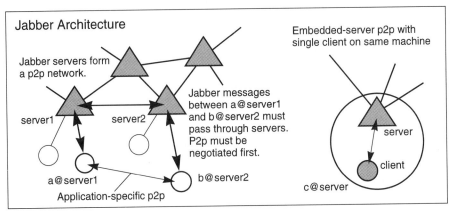

FIGURE 6.7 *Jabber architecture is client-server, but the server core is small enough that servers could be embedded on the client machines. Servers form the p2p network and exchange message and presence between connected clients. Servers also host extensible services (or transports).*

Identity

Choosing to format Jabber user identity in a format similar to an e-mail mailbox identity has immediate benefits. Partly, this is socially established and accepted, and it allows services and companies to resolve and manage user identities in ways that align with existing policies. It also defines a social (or chat) context for the user.

Based on the identity, a Jabber application can expose internal data to public access. A fully qualified external URI would thus take the form:

```
jabber://user@server/resource/data
```

This is a fully generic notation and translates directly to how Jabber clients manage peer access using XML.

Transport Agents

The theory is that the Jabber server(s) can implement functionality that can interface with other peer or messaging systems—Jabber calls these interservice interfaces *jabber transports*. Such server-side programs are easily added to the core server to provide arbitrary enhanced functionality to the **end user**.

For example, a user with a Jabber client connected to jabber.org can invoke its ICQ agent at icq.jabber.org. This server component then acts as a transport to the normal ICQ service, translating between Jabber XML and the other system's protocol. This currently assumes that the user already has an ICQ identity and that

jabber.org server status		
aim	down	5 months 2 weeks 5 days 7 hours 52 minutes 51 seconds
ccm	up	1 day 21 hours 17 minutes 32 seconds
conference	up	1 month 2 days 21 hours 31 minutes 31 seconds
icq	down	2 months 1 day 3 hours 5 minutes 16 seconds
jsm	up	1 month 2 days 21 hours 31 minutes 46 seconds
main	up	1 day 4 minutes 28 seconds
msn	up	17 hours 47 minutes 56 seconds
yahoo	down	2 weeks 41 minutes 2 seconds
Users Online: 696		Last Update: 17:49:29 (UTC -0600)

FIGURE 6.8 *A typical status page from jabber.org showing up- or down-times for the common transports being tested as they are developed. Note in particular the problem transports aim and recently icq, both to AOL.*

the other system will accept third-party connections. In a like manner, aim.jabber.org would do the same for a user registered with AIM, and irc.jabber.org acts as a feed for a selected IRC network.

There is no *a priori* constraint on what kind of gateway service a Jabber server can provide. Because Jabber is a prototype system, as yet only a few transports are deployed, and a user might often be unable to contact the agents. As noted earlier, AOL actively discourages such interoperability with AIM and ICQ servers, even by its own subscribers who wish to use another software, and Jabber transports are no less affected than other third-party clients in this respect. Figure 6.8 shows a recent server status page for jabber.org; the long AIM and ICQ transport downtimes highlight the AOL noninteroperability problem mentioned earlier. In addition, the requirement for an already registered identity for services like ICQ or AIM means even when it works, you can't (in Jabber) join as a new user through a gateway.

The following is from a recent update of the Jabber FAQ on the matter:

Unfortunately, for the last few months AOL has been actively working to block AIM subscribers who wish to connect to AIM through Jabber's AIM Transport. While jabber.org programmers have addressed these blockage

*attempts through various means (including updated versions of the AIM
Transport), at this time some public Jabber servers have not yet installed the
most recent versions of the AIM Transport (thus disabling communications
with AIM), and even those servers which have installed the most recent
versions may be experiencing intermittent communications to AIM. We
apologize for the inconvenience and sincerely hope that AOL, along with all
other providers of IM services, will work together for true interoperability.*

This is clearly a problem that's not going to go away anytime soon.

Clients and Servers

On the face of it, Jabber has a marked client-server architecture, in that clients log in
to a Jabber server prior to any p2p exchanges, and Jabber messages between clients
are relayed through the server. Each client session initializes an "XML Stream" to the
contacted server, and the stream lasts for the duration of the online session.

Direct peer connections (for example, file-sharing sessions between clients) are
defined as application-specific connections—perfectly possible, but they must first be
negotiated in the client-server context that at minimum conveys address and presence
information. This is similar to the ICQ and AIM model.

Part of the design philosophy for Jabber was to move much complexity (such as
transports) to the server component. This makes it easy for developers to create
clients, and easy for server administrators to add new functionality without requiring
massive client updates. The Jabber server core is relatively small, so that each machine
could in principle have its own embedded Jabber server, which would equate to
atomistic p2p from the user perspective.

The Jabber system is designed to support simple clients, imposing very few
restrictions. The client need only at minimum be able to

- Communicate with the Jabber server using TCP sockets

- Parse and interpret well-formed XML packets

- Understand message data types

The use of XML is an integral part of the architecture because this markup can
express almost any structured data. All Jabber components must speak XML within
the system, even transports that might use other protocols externally. At the same
time, Jabber doesn't care about the delivery medium. Thus, it places no inherent
restrictions on the delivery system and requires no built-in knowledge about it.

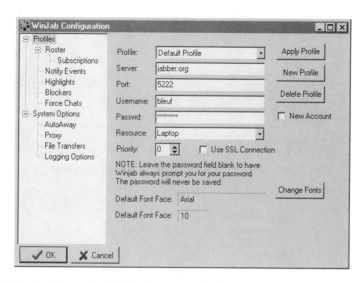

FIGURE **6.9** *Configuration dialog for WinJab, the popular Windows version of a Jabber client. Different profiles are possible for different purposes.*

Numerous client implementations are available, and the alternatives are described at www.jabbercentral.org. Most developers would tend to recommend WinJab for Windows, Jabbernaut for MacOS, and Gabber for Linux. Figure 6.9 shows the configuration dialog for the WinJab client, indicating the kind of profile the user sets up. The client normally uses HTTP port 5222, or 5223 if SSL (Secure Socket Layer, encryption based on digital signature exchange) is activated.

Running the client illustrates how available resources can be browsed in separate windows, as seen in Figure 6.10. The server informs the client which services are implemented and thus visible, while browsing them adds further information. This is in addition to the expected IM functionality localized to the main application window and its roster list: status notification, IM, chat, file sharing, and so on.

Anyone can download not just the Jabber client software; the server software is equally open and available, which lets anyone set up their own Jabber-based network. The corporate face of Jabber (jabber.com) is dedicated to deploying business solutions based on the technology.

Server software and source is distributed under the Jabber Open Source License (JOSL), an OSI-approved open source license similar to the Mozilla Public License (MPL). MPL-derived licenses narrow their definition of derivative works, focusing on the actual source code files. This enables developers to write additional modules without necessarily making those modules open-source, while at the same time

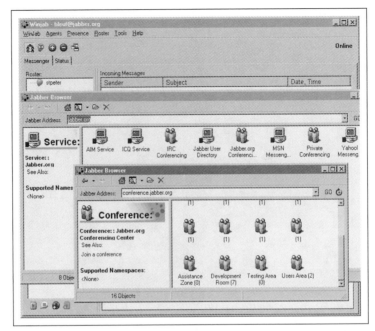

FIGURE **6.10** *Browsing Jabber services in WinJab, all of which are implemented as server components. At bottom left in the roster window pane, icon shortcuts activate common p2p functions for conversations with a selected user: send message, open chat, send URL, and send file.*

ensuring that any modifications to the original source code for the Jabber server are contributed back to the Jabber community for possible incorporation.

The core Jabber server includes components for

- Session management (login, presence tracking, and so on)
- User identity management (registration, authentication, profiles)
- Client-to-server communication (by extension, client-client messaging)
- Group chat management (many-to-many)
- DNS resolution (Internet domain names are used for server identity.)
- Server-to-server communication (also part of the messaging chain)
- Database lookups (for registered user list, etc.)
- Storing and retrieving offline messages, vCards, and other data
- Filtering messages based on user preferences

- Server-side application management (such as transports)
- System logging

Of particular interest is that the notification subscription service can pass on presence information to and from any entity that has a Jabber identity. This includes foreign entities that are connected over translating transports.

JABBER PROTOCOL

Messages in Jabber are wrapped in one of three top-level XML type containers: *message*, *presence*, and *info/query* (iq). The structure and syntax is otherwise very simple and human-readable, and "raw" messages can even be typed in over telnet—the simplest supported client. An example:

```
<message to='user@server' type='chat'>
 <body>The actual text of the message.</body>
</message>
```

A "from" attribute with sender identity is added by the sender's server. Clients might add, at their own discretion, an "id" attribute for internal tracking purposes.

The type specification is also optional; it defaults to a normal message type. Type "chat" assumes that the client displays this in a chat window, typically line-by-line. Other supported types are *group chat* (addressed to chatroom relay service), and *error* (its message held in an error container).

Other optional message element containers are:

- *html*, marks an alternate namespace for the message, like the multiple format convention for e-mail, based on XHTML 1.0 BASIC
- *subject*, user designated
- *thread*, client generated for reply tracking (usually formed from a hash of the sender's Jabber ID and the current time)
- *x*, which is an extension mechanism, or is used to send commands

The use of the "x" element requires that a separate namespace for it be declared, the range partially overlapping the info/query namespaces. Currently supported namespaces (basic functionality) are listed in Table 6.7, for both x and iq types.

TABLE **6.7** *Namespaces supported for the Jabber message "x" and "iq" element.*

Namespace	In element		Description
agent		iq	Obtain specific agent's properties.
(agents) see browse		iq	(Deprecated) List available agents (often transports) at server.
auth		iq	Simple client authentication. Authenticate and create a resource representing the connection to the server.
autoupdate	x	iq	Application version notification, or query about software updates that may be available.
browse		iq	Browse jid types to discover Jabber resources.
conference	x	iq	Invitations to conferences. Discovering and negotiating entrance to generic conferences.
delay	x		Marks object as delayed (timestamp offline storage).
encrypted	x		The message is (PGP/GPG) encrypted.
envelope	x		Allows for richer addressing, such as e-mail.
event	x		Tracks message status and allows for receipts.
expire	x		Allows for time-limited messages/delivery.
gateway		iq	Gateway user address negotiations (non-Jabber).
last		iq	Number of seconds since last use/connect/start.
oob	x	iq	Out-of-Band data, such as for file transfers (URI).
private		iq	Private data storage on the server (any XML data).
register		iq	Registration management for services.
roster	x	iq	Contains embedded roster items, list management.
search		iq	Handles database search in any service/transport.
signed	x		Encryption of presence information.
time		iq	A standard way of exchanging local client time.
(vCard-temp)	x		Implemented until vCard is XML standardized.
version		iq	Version information of another client.

Jabber identity (jid) types are a way to structure available resources, rather similar to how MIME can type content. Currently supported *jid* types include *application, conference, headline, keyword, render, service*, and *user*. These types are used extensively when browsing resources. The following example shows a browse query sent to a server, using iq type *get*.

```
<iq type="get" to="jabber.org">
 <query xmlns="jabber:iq:browse"/>
</iq>
```

The server would respond with a nested series of containers that describe the resources and services available. An abbreviated *result* example is shown.

```
<iq type="result" from="jabber.org">
 <service type="jabber" jid="jabber.org"
  xmlns="jabber:iq:browse">
  <service type="jud" jid="users.jabber.org"
   name="Jabber User Directory">
   <ns>jabber:iq:register</ns>
   <ns>jabber:iq:search</ns>
  </service>
 ...
  <conference type="private" jid="conference.jabber.org"
   name="Private Chatrooms">
  </service>
 </service>
</iq>
```

Similar browsing can be applied to each of the jid levels to find further detail relevant to each. In typical Jabber clients, this is abstracted in a browser window with clickable icons representing the various entries, much like browsing a filesystem hierarchy.

The iq type *set* is used to provide required information to the server, for example in order to join a discovered conference. More detail of such client-server conversations is given in the official Jabber Protocol Overview document, available as www.jabber.com/pdf/protocol.pdf, or in online readable HTML at docs.jabber.org/general/html/protocol.html.

BRIEF MENTIONS

To round off this chapter on arguably the most popular manifestation of peer technology, I decided to briefly cover a handful of implementations that are rather different from each other and from the previous clients. The last, Windows Messenger, might even become the dominant future IM technology, overtaking the current role of ICQ-AIM as the mediums of choice. This is because of it being bundled with all Windows XP systems, and the fact that it is as yet fairly clone friendly.

These clients, including to some extent WM, have in common that they are still very much under development and are all effectively in the v0.x stage. Nevertheless, they exist as public releases and are all eminently usable in their proper context. They range from the extremely light-weight but securely encrypted Psst, to the very broadly multiprotocol and versatile Trillian client, and all address at least some observed lack or deficiency in the established IM technologies.

If these clients stand the test of time, user acceptance and, perhaps critically, continued funding and development, a later edition of this book might examine them with the same level of detail as some of the other implementations. But until then, a quick overview is the least I can do to indicate the range of options that are open to anyone wanting to use IM tools, without opting for the standard and often less-than-optimal client that "everyone knows about" and is the default route to IM connectivity. I predict that the multiprotocol IM client solution will grow in importance faster than the prospects for full interoperability during 2002, because exchanging clients is a quick user decision. Interoperability is a slow process, even when all the major providers are committed to it—which they currently aren't.

Psst

Probably the smallest p2p IM implementation to feature strong session encryption is Psst, developed by David McNab from New Zealand. The Windows console binary weighs in at only 58kB, which seems incredible on the face of it, and the application is open source gcc-compilable under Linux.

Although still early in its development cycle, available at the time of writing were stable version 0.1.1 and test version 0.1.2 for Windows DOS, and v0.2 GUI binary versions for both Windows and Linux, plus sources (netforth.sourceforge.net/psst/download.html). Even the latter Windows GUI version is only a 152KB download, which is quite remarkable. These versions provided solid performance—despite the very rudimentary console (in DOS box) or GUI interfaces which are shown in Figure 6.11 and Figure 6.12 respectively.

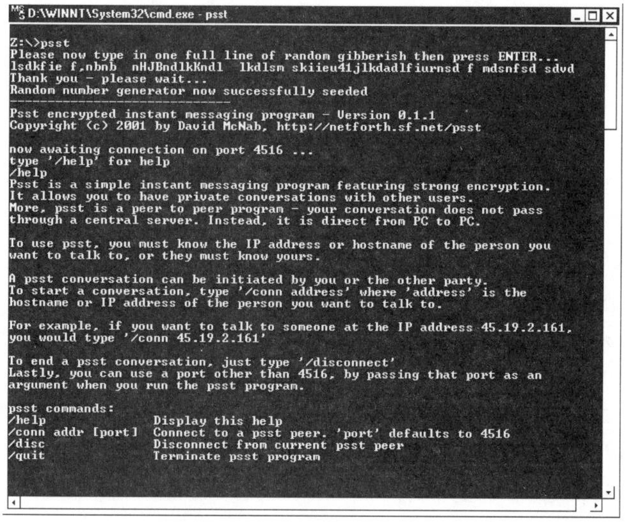

FIGURE **6.11** *Psst is a minimalistic p2p open source client for strongly encrypted IM sessions. Typing a row of gibberish in the console version seeds the key generation for the session, after which you just connect and type.*

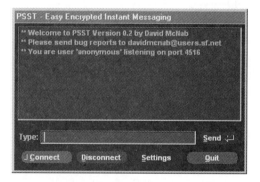

FIGURE **6.12** *Psst 0.2 provides a GUI version. On each session start, random mouse movements provide the seed used for subsequent encryption.*

Connectivity requires that the user initiating the conversation knows the Internet address of the other, whether domain or IP number, and that the other can receive incoming connections on the port used. *This is true p2p instant messaging!*—endpoint to endpoint, no server intermediaries, no arbitrary protocol changes by a service provider, and as secure as you're likely to get. Totally no-frills IM.

Note that the current implementations require same-version clients on both ends to communicate properly. Download your selection and pass a copy to your counterpart, determine your respective current IP addresses, and go. Later versions might well relax this same-version constraint as the codebase becomes more stable.

Psst fills a definite need in terms of simple support for securely private p2p conversations. The integral session encryption is transparent to the user, and the application leaves no overt traces of the session in the system. If you want to log something, that's up to you—manual copy and paste always works.

The overly paranoid Windows user can run the program from diskette or ramdisk, using command-line invocation, which ensures that later analysis won't show *any* system trace of the session or the conversation. It's of course up to the user to avoid any transcript copy or save operations that would allow potential recovery of conversation content from the hard disk. (You might note that other IM clients don't usually encrypt messages, and they frequently log sessions on disk by default.)

TRILLIAN

I ran across the Trillian client almost by accident at a late stage of review of this book and I liked it very much. Frankly, there's a lot to like here. Just the fact that it includes *now-working* native support for all the following major IM protocols, including Internet Relay Chat in one client is a major plus. The introduction on the client home page (www.trillian.cc) says it all:

> Communicate with Flexibility and Style. Trillian is everything you need for instant messaging. Connect to ICQ, AOL Instant Messenger, MSN Messenger, Yahoo! Messenger and IRC in a single, sleek and slim interface.

Yes, AIM and ICQ both actually worked in Trillian, most of the time, unlike in Jabber, the other most promising multiprotocol client discussed earlier. I attribute this to Trillian being based on a more recent (in other words, on-going) hack of the ever-shifting AIM and ICQ protocols, or to the client inherently being able to deal with the AOL servers in a better way. The client layout, which groups AIM and ICQ into the same connection manager dialog, indicates that the same AOL servers handle both. AOL is, as ever, emphatically opposed to any such interoperability.

During the technical review for the book, the Trillian client was in fact rapidly iterating through the minor version numbers in a tit-for-tat "AOL bug fix" process, evidently tracking an ongoing skirmish between Trillian and AOL programmers revising protocol and client's detailed behavior, respectively.

FIGURE **6.13** *Trillian is an effective and useful multiprotocol IM client that's very configurable for the user. Seen in this capture is the main, resizable status interface in its default skin, plus two concurrent session windows; one in ICQ and the other to the same user's Windows Messenger client.*

Trillian is **freeware** ("for free noncommercial use, forever")—currently a 2.2MB download in its Windows-only, most recent v0.72x incarnation. Behind Trillian, the client, is Cerulean Studios, the company (www.CeruleanStudios.com, although both domains go to the same Web site at present). Founded in May of 1998 by Kevin Kurtz and Scott Werndorfer, the company's only visible showing is Trillian.

And it's worth looking at. The client interface is shown in Figure 6.13, as it appears in its default skin and size. The capture shows two concurrent sessions over different mediums, here ICQ and MSN, to another user who needs multiple clients installed, the original for each service. Both the main status interface (with contacts list) and the session windows are resizable in a multitude of ways. (I blocked out contact names and any e-mail addresses in the sessions in the interest of privacy.)

Note the discrete row of icons on the bottom panel of the contacts list; each brings up a context menu relevant to the medium it represents—from left AIM, ICQ, IRC, MSN, and Yahoo. The online status for in the contact list is in the form of corresponding icons beside the name, visible on mouse-over or when online. Session windows show the same icon and current status on the top tab. The "is typing a message" presence information is more useful than one thinks.

(Personal reflection and aside) Have you noticed how many mainstream applications are "skinnable" these days? No longer just a matter of color themes, many applications (especially media players) have support for skins that sport a quasi-redesign of the user interface. Sometimes, this is good, but I often despair at limited selections of ready-to-use skins in spikey, odd-ball, psychedelic, and visually/usability-unfriendly themes. Rolling your own skin may be easy or hard, but takes more time than most are willing to spend.

P2PQ

Messaging doesn't have to be strict one-on-one, or even especially personal. What happens if you cross a search engine with a messaging client and remove the engine? Well, you might get a distributed user-driven knowledge-base, much like P2PQ.

P2PQ is a free service (www.p2pq.net) that works by recruiting people who volunteer to share their knowledge and provide their answer potential to others. It's a dynamic directory of live people, available to users from anywhere and any device. It promotes the concept *distributed aggregation* with the registered slogan "Put your mind online!" and a Web site with a form to enter an arbitrary question.

The small clients are installed and sit idle on the machines of the users until someone needs to "pick their brains" at the P2PQ Web site. A typed-in question (and a timeout for the query) is farmed out to distributed clients, where it's assumed that somebody will know the answer. Any client user can type and return a response to a received question. The collected results are displayed in a list of results, just like the results from a standard search engine query.

This solution is a kind of human-powered version of distributed processing, inspired it's said by the ancient story of *Kadikai*. It's not strictly p2p in the sense that this book uses the term, but it's still interesting in its possible implications for distributed social networks. The central server in this case sorts and sends queries to appropriate categories of client users who act as relevancy (and spam) filters. Approved queries are then passed on to the larger client community for a category.

Anyway, this service is clearly still in the early testing stage (there was only one category when I tried a query), and human responses require measurable time to compile. The advantage of a functional "peer" system of this kind rests on the adaptive nature of human response and the ability to correctly parse requests expressed in everyday language. It also encourages the "value" rated answers—useful personal qualifiers like "I think", "last I recall", "I recommend", "based on 10 years of experience with", and so on. Implicit is a trust that the people answering are sincere about their volunteer work. Worth keeping an eye on.

WINDOWS MESSENGER

Finally, an overview of Windows Messenger, what could quickly become a dominant IM player, if only by virtue of it being the IM technology bundled with Microsoft Windows XP and integrated into .NET. Some deeper detail is included because of this, but the focus remains on the broader issues.

WM effectively supplants the various IM and p2p technologies introduced in earlier versions of Windows. The new IM is further incompatible with earlier protocols such as MSN and NetMeeting H.323. Made specific to Windows XP, the client however can also be retrofit into some earlier versions of Windows, albeit then lacking a few features that only work with XP.

As far as can be determined at present, the MSN messaging network doesn't try to block compliant third-party client software—my experience with Trillian has shown no glitches—so we can expect to see numerous clones appear, especially for non-Windows platforms, as WM gains popularity. Trillian, described earlier, is one recent multiprotocol client under development that easily supports communicating with users who use the original WM client.

This kind of open interoperability should be the rule everywhere. The main requirement on any clone for full functionality with WM is that it can deal with the Passport authentication process when contacting the MSN servers.

Highly optimized for what it does, WM offers basic IM, telephony over Internet, video, file sharing, and a potentially long list of Microsoft and third-party extensions. I would expect WM, as a highly visible desktop client, to rapidly "infiltrate" the user experience in Windows at least as much as the Internet Explorer and Outlook combination (with their interrelated, hidden, GUI-extension components).

Although the new user wishing to get a registered WM identity is taken to a Microsoft Web registration site and given the default suggestion to sign up for a MSN or Hotmail e-mail account, another click allows the prospective user to register with Passport under any permanent e-mail address. The e-mail identity entered is the one that WM uses as its unique user identifier, but the user can freely choose any handle to be the default name shown in the contact lists of other users.

The application actually looks oddly similar to the AIM client at the default WM window—you can *add* a contact, *send* an instant message, or place a *call* (that is, establish a voice conversation). The same window also displays presence information about your contacts (that is to say, your roster). This all looks exceedingly simplistic at first, but the client hides most of the functionality controls from view until the context is relevant. You may or may not like this automation, but it *is* configurable.

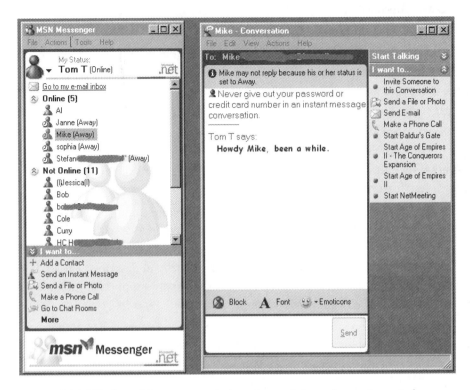

FIGURE **6.14** *Windows Messenger main interface to left, and a session window opened to right. Opening the latter has extended the options available in the interface. The client has a familiar "I want to" help system.*

Going to an IM window, for example, adds buttons to start video, send a file, invite others to start application sharing, start remote assistance, or start a whiteboard session, just to name a few—see Figure 6.14. The client can also be your gateway to multiplayer games. Except for IM sessions, which can optionally be one-to-many (*multicast*), all other WM features are implemented as one-to-one (*unicast*) only per session window.

The MSN panel shown at the bottom of the interface window is actually a fortuitous capture, because it normally shows (localized and profiled) animated banner advertising. This advertising is only slightly less annoying than that in the ICQ client which shows separate banners in each and every session window.

Voice quality is described as being as good as a clean phone connection. The fidelity is achieved using an impressive array of specialized codecs, dynamic jitter buffers, forward error correction for the streaming data, and acoustic echo cancellation. Video rates are up to 12 frames per second, depending on your available bandwidth—that's webcam-jerky but usable and surprisingly sharp from good sources.

Screen updates for application sharing are fast, and control of the application can be passed interactively between the users. Microsoft or in-house tech support can take complete control of a user's desktop using the Remote Assistance feature, walking users through difficult operations. This built-in remote control feature is a two-edged sword, of course, and not to everyone's liking. Time will also tell if the feature gets hacked and exploited for unauthorized purposes.

Usability Issues

Microsoft likes to embed various "convenience" features in its products, and WM functionality is no exception—in part this is coded into WM, in part it hinges on features inherent in the common Windows components used, and in part it is the entire design philosophy expressed in Microsoft-on-the-Internet and the Web components. The *inconvenient* aspect of automated convenience features is when their functionality doesn't match the needs or expectations of the user.

Let's take the matter of *locale*. Microsoft made Windows configurable for a wide variety of languages, keyboard layouts, international fonts, time zones, and location-specific settings. Localization is all good and well, and a welcome evolution from the extremely U.S.-centric applications we had before the 1990s. However, when extended (for example, to automatic redirects and update selections), things can get confusing, frustrating, and downright messy for the user who doesn't fit the form—especially when it's unclear what the automation is based on (keyboard layout, locale setting, system language version, originating IP-number block, and so on).

Consider this hypothetical scenario:

> *Susan is a user from the U.S. who is for a time working in Sweden. For practical reasons, she finds it convenient to set the laptop locale to correspond, and to sometimes also use a separate local-layout keyboard. One day, she needs to find the messaging identity of a co-worker in the U.S. Going to user search i MSN, she gets the response that there is no user by that name. She is even more mystified when a search of her own identity fails!*

Being bilingual, our example user didn't especially react to the fact that the MSN search site was serving localized pages (in Swedish). Many sites can today serve content in different languages—that is after all the purpose of the preferred languages setting in Web browsers. The MSN server, having queried the computer's locale setting, had transparently redirected the request to the country's local MSN site. The redirection would have been unnoticed and perfectly OK for the majority of users in that locale, but it trips up any user who doesn't fit all the assumptions.

To successfully find a registered MSN user, it would appear that you must search at the correct localized site where that user registered. In our example, the redirected site was msn.se, but both user and coworker were registered in msn.com site's database (international domain, but for users in the U.S.). For success, the ex-pat user must therefore either set locale appropriately or force connection and search to the U.S. site. This kind of hidden redirect can be even harder to detect when the language remains (more or less) the same while locale varies—for instance, English but U.S., Canada, U.K, or Australia. Try the default Web search feature in IE or Outlook with different locale settings and marvel at the wide range of page layout and functionality interfaces, not to mention different search rankings.

WM Protocol

The basic protocol underlying WM is Session Initiation Protocol (SIP), which is an open IETF standard (specified in RFC 2543). The choice indicates at least the potential for general interoperability with other technologies that support SIP on any platform. For example, a third-party SIP-to-PSTN gateway server would let you place a WM voice call to anyone who has a landline or cellular phone.

SIP is a generic application-layer control (or signaling) protocol for creating, modifying and terminating sessions with one or more participants. These sessions can include Internet multimedia conferences, Internet telephone calls, and multimedia distribution. Session communications can be multicast, unicast, or a combination—all depending on how the implementation supports these features. SIP transparently supports name-mapping and redirection services, a functionality that was seen as essential to the kind of user mobility that is rapidly becoming the norm.

The session management functionality in SIP includes support for

- Determining **user location**, which refers to the end system to be used for the communication

- Determining **user capabilities**, which selects the media and media parameters to be used

- Determining **user availability**, which also includes the *willingness* of the called party to engage in communications

- Managing **call setup**, which establishes call parameters at both ends of the connection, also known as "ringing"
- Managing **call handling**, which includes call transfer and termination

The similarities here with call management in ordinary telephony are no coincidence. These basic properties naturally tie in with the three basic Passport dimensions of user identity (that is, person, location and application).

SIP can also be used together with other call setup and signaling protocols. In that mode, an end system uses SIP exchanges with a protocol-independent address to determine the appropriate end system address and protocol. SIP can also be used to convey session-specific information to other protocols or application managers for specialized functionality that SIP itself doesn't support.

Plug and Wait

As yet, however, SIP is still a new protocol, and the applications that support it are relatively untested. Not that many products use SIP, and consequently, not many people are asking vendors about SIP support for their favorite products. It would seem, therefore, that increased SIP support will mainly come from vendors deciding to interoperate with Windows XP and WM.

More serious is probably the firewall situation. Current small office and home office (SOHO) gateways simply can't deal with the combination of secure NAT and how SIP uses dynamic port allocation. Anyone wondering what this issue is all about would do well to read up on similar concerns raised by the older H.323 protocol used by NetMeeting. One such source is the primer from the SANS Institute, which is found at www.sans.org/infosecFAQ/homeoffice/concerns.htm.

This document discusses the basic problems of trying to run a secure system behind routers, firewalls and proxies, in the context of applications that require many open communication ports to the outside world. Certainly it can be done, but the user (or administrator) must be aware of what the security trade-off is, especially with applications that don't require or enforce any kind of authentication mechanism.

Typical gateway and firewall vendors haven't yet come to grips with the new WM requirements, so plenty of user scenarios simply won't play. In general, all users who wish to use the real-time communication features supported by Windows XP are faced with this constraint for the simple reason that the new features all rely on SIP.

For example, it's highly unlikely that your average SOHO (Small Office Home Office) computer user behind a NAT-firewall/gateway will be able to WM-connect to a colleague behind the corporate firewall—even without any formal access restrictions on either firewall. It's been tried and it didn't work then, and probably won't until firewall software is patched or upgraded (as happened for H.323 support) or site-specific workaround is installed.

In that vein, the Universal Plug and Play (UPnP) Forum is working to establish PnP support between Windows XP and resident gateway products. XP and WM already support UPnP—or rather some subset/interpretation thereof. Future gateways will automatically configure themselves to support WM, or seen another way, the WM clients will reconfigure the firewall products on demand. The hairy security issues this raises are briefly noted in Chapter 4.

However, as recently as January 2002, only Ingate (www.ingate.com) had released what it claims to be the first SIP-compatible enterprise firewall product, thus providing the needed transparency to application functionality that relies on SIP: presence, instant messaging, internet telephony, and real-time video and audio conferencing, at least as it is implemented in the XP/WM model.

Still, the bottom line is that WM will be fully supported, eventually, as long as Microsoft is committed to their current vision of .NET and Windows XP—with a bundled, standard IM-and-more client with authentication features. Clearly, this is the path of least resistance for the corporate environment, with a firm commitment to a uniform application environment. Considering the poor security and authentication offered by the otherwise most popular IM implementations, that might not be such a bad thing in the corporate context.

There are, however, other interesting peer-based technologies to explore, especially if we look beyond simple IM and wish to eschew central servers.

Sharing Content

Sharing files is probably the most common and best known application of p2p technology, popularized by a number of early file-sharing networks the likes of Scour, Napster, Madster (formerly Aimster), and Gnutella. Popular misconceptions aside, this doesn't necessarily mean swapping "pirated" copies of music files or other protected content; never mind the contentious issue of what is or isn't illegal copying in any given situation. A cornucopia of explicitly free and legally distributable content is available to share, including many music and other multimedia files.

Because of its unprecedented popularity, the first example taken up is Napster. This is not because this particular implementation is especially suited for general file sharing—it isn't, for several reasons—but because a brief overview helps explain why the alternatives are better or more flexible. Understanding the differences between Napster and Gnutella, for instance, gives some practical insight into the discussions elsewhere about performance and scalability.

However, the main focus of this chapter is on Gnutella, as a good and analysis-friendly example of a baseline, "pure" atomistic architecture for file sharing, implemented in an open and fairly simple way. All it takes to set up a local Gnutella-style network is a selection of clients and a modicum of client configuration—no server needed. Because the technology is free and most clients are open source, it is easy to experiment with Gnutella and customize the network.

Explanations of the other, more complex implementations in later chapters build on many of the basic peer characteristics explained by example here for Gnutella.

CHAPTER 7 AT A GLANCE

This chapter discusses file-sharing technologies, and it uses a special focus on the atomistic Gnutella network to explore all the aspects of atomistic p2p.

Napster provides a detailed look at the sharing client that gave p2p broad public recognition. The new Napster has essentially the same architecture.

- *Napster Architecture* describes the server-mediated file-sharing model popularized by this client and discusses some of the reasoning behind this compromise away from "pure" p2p.

- *Alternatives Gain Users* briefly mentions some of the clones and other solutions that have emulated or replaced Napster before and after its closure.

Gnutella deals extensively with atomistic networks in general, using this popular, open source file-sharing implementation as a practical example.

- Gnutella is shown to be more an *Infrastructure* specification than any specific *Client Software* solution.

- The process of *Connecting to Others* without central server mediation is examined in detail. *Broadcast-Routing Strategy* is a technical discussion about the node horizon effect and what it means.

- The *Protocol* section explains Gnutella's open protocol in greater detail, while *Transfer Issues* looks at further aspects of the file-exchange process.

- The potential limits of the network are discussed in *Gnutella Scalability*, along with some client vulnerabilities.

Trust and Reputation Issues builds on the detailed Gnutella section.

- The section examines some of the vulnerabilities and general mechanisms for making atomistic p2p networks more stable and robust.

Madster is the new name for Aimster, and it deserved at least brief mention here.

- This short section describes what kind of p2p network this in-the-news technology is, what it might be becoming, and how it is different from the previously discussed examples.

NAPSTER

The free-for-all music-exchange fest at Napster (www.napster.com) finally ended in June 2001, marking the close of a remarkable era during which the service registered some 65 million users in just 20 months, with *billions* of client swaps a month. As with IM clients, the number of real, unique users was probably much lower.

After its earlier skin change when it became part of Bertelsmann multimedia publishing, Napster tried to profile itself more as a commercial music download service, but despite its attempts to prevent commercial CD music files from appearing in the server database, users could still find and download as before. Continued efforts to implement content management and filtering of the eventually million or so music titles specified by the music distribution companies marked the last months of free operation. Before Napster's servers shut down in July 2001, officially to upgrade its database software to support better file identification and stricter control as required by court order, membership was down from the 60 or 70 million claimed user peak to an estimated million or so, of whom perhaps 90 percent retained the client only to use it as a local MP3 player (or possibly connect to some alternative network set up with Napster-emulating servers).

Users who plan to remain as subscribers with Napster when it reopens need to upgrade to a new version of the client that actively supports content management—the new servers won't support older versions. The company explains that many legally free files will always be available at the discretion of the users, but commercial tracks won't unless purchased though its server-based download service. To protect this new system, Napster implements a filter that examines the digital structure of music files to verify their legality. In addition, in order to provide greater control over what is traded through its network, Napster developed a new, proprietary digital format (with the file extension .nap) to which MP3 music files will be converted.

This kind of central control (and client shutdown) is possible because the Napster architectural model is user-centric (UCP2P, introduced in Chapter 2). Clients go nowhere without the mediation of Napster's database servers, and it's reasonable to assume that this server dependency is strengthened in the new version.

After several delays and false starts, according to reports largely due to problems in achieving contractual agreements with the larger music distributors, the redesigned "clean" Napster network is scheduled to go back online in early 2002. Even so, a perceived monopoly situation due to the nature of the exclusive label contracts might still cause further delays and litigation threats. It remains to be seen how many users will accept this commercial model for music distribution, instead of permanently migrating to either Napster clone services or other free sharing networks.

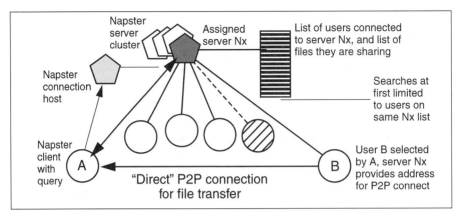

FIGURE 7.1 *Napster's server-mediated p2p model. User A connects to the "first available" server assigned by a connection host. Lists of users and files are based on the users recently connected to the same server.*

NAPSTER ARCHITECTURE

Figure 7.1 depicts the essentials of Napster's server-mediated architecture. Clients connect automatically to an internally designated "metaserver" that acts as common connection arbiter. This metaserver assigns at random an available, lightly loaded server from one of the clusters. Servers appeared to be clustered about five to a geographical site and Internet feed, and able to handle up to 15,000 users each.

The client then registers with the assigned server, providing identity and shared file information for the server's local database. In turn, the client receives information about connected users and available files from the server. Although formally organized around a user directory design, the Napster implementation is very data-centric. The primary UCP2P directory of users connected to a particular server is only used indirectly, to create file lists of content reported as shared by each node.

Users are almost always anonymous to each other; the user directory is never queried directly. The only interest is to search for content and determine a node from which to download. The directory therefore merely serves as a background translation service, from the host identity associated with particular content, to the currently registered IP address needed for a download connection to this client.

Network performance is tuned for quick server response to user queries, so searches are explicitly constrained in both scope (to a maximum of 100 hits) and time (15 seconds). Searches take place in the local files database maintained by the server but might (rarely) be passed on to neighboring servers in the same cluster.

ALTERNATIVES GAIN USERS

Characteristic for Napster was its exclusive focus on MP3-encoded music files. Although no other file types were supported, an intriguing subculture of client clones and tools soon arose, reverse-engineered from the Napster's closed-source clients. This is further proof of the Chapter 1 assertion that people tend to use new technology for what they want to do, not necessarily for what it's designed to do.

The intent behind the development was greater user control. For instance, a form of MP3 spoofing implemented by tools such as Wrapster could enclose an arbitrary file with a kind of wrapper that made it look like an MP3 file to the Napster servers. It would then appear in the server databases and be searchable by other clients wishing to download files other than music. An obstacle to this effort was that the artist-title description field allowed little information about the nonmusic file. This, the low ratio of nonmusic to music files, and the normal random distribution of connecting nodes conspired to make Napster's scope-limited searches highly unlikely to find special content. Tools such as Napigator were developed to allow users to connect to specific servers, bypassing metaserver arbitration. In this way, certain servers became known as Wrapster hangouts—primary sites for nonmusic content. Users looking for this kind of content were then more likely find it.

Nonmusic exchanges over Napster proper were never more than marginal, at least compared to alternative, content-agnostic systems such as Gnutella. Some alternative Napster servers, such as OpenNap (started as "safe-havens" for Napster users when Napster began filtering content), did for a while begin to fill the gap, tying together former Napster clients, clones and variations with a new kind of server that extended the original Napster protocol to all file types.

No matter how much the Napster model was reengineered, however, the fundamental requirement of a "Napster-compatible" central server remained a serious constraint for a network based on this technology or any of its clones. To transcend this limitation, other protocols and architecture models are needed—for example, serverless networks in the style of Gnutella.

GNUTELLA

Originally, Gnutella ("new-tella") was the name of a prototype client developed during just a few weeks in March 2000 by Justin Frankel and Tom Pepper, the same "Gnullsoft" team that created WinAmp, the first popular MP3 player.

In the release of the beta-test version, almost everyone saw a competitor to Napster designed to overcome its restrictions and limitations for swapping music files.

This was perhaps a natural if hasty conclusion based on the timing of the release. Tom Pepper solemnly maintains that their prototype client was actually developed to swap recipes—the name a play on the "Nutella" brandname of a hazelnut/chocolate sandwich spread used in desserts and baking.

The issue of original intent quickly became moot when America Online (AOL), which had just acquired Frankel's and Pepper's company Nullsoft, learned of the project. AOL immediately stopped further work on Gnutella software and pulled the prototype from the server just hours after its release. The story would have ended there, except for some covert assistance and inspired reverse-engineering by Bryan Mayland, an open-source developer. He quickly posted the deduced Gnutella protocol on the Web, which fired considerable interest in the developer community. Before long, the Open Source Gnutella project was cooking around the protocol.

Gnutella is now a generic term with several meanings: the protocol, the open source technology, and the deployed Internet network (Gnutella Net, or just gNET). The site www.gnutellanews.com, a primary resource, defines Gnutella this way:

> *Gnutella is a fully-distributed information-sharing technology.*
> *Loosely translated, it is what puts the power of information-sharing back into your hands.*

Another good resource is www.gnutella.co.uk, one of the first Gnutella Web sites.

The Gnutella manifesto—or less formally, *attitude*—is simply that atomistic peer architecture is how the Internet is supposed to be—no portals, no central authorities, no content control. Most open source p2p technologies manifest the same philosophy, more or less. Link, connect to, and share—*do*— anything with anyone. The decisions and details of when, how and what are left entirely up to the individual.

> **Bit 7.1   Gnutella is a common peer protocol, not any specific application.**
> While most implemented clients focus on file sharing and file search, it's possible to do much more than this using the Gnutella protocol or extensions to it.

INFRASTRUCTURE

Table 7.1 shows the component breakdown of Gnutella, with the caveat that it summarizes only popular current clients specialized for file sharing and does not indicate in any way any inherent limitations in the Gnutella architecture itself.

TABLE 7.1   *Gnutella component summary, as realized in current popular client implementations for file sharing.*

Component	Specific forms	Comments
Identity	Unique message descriptor ID derived from current IP number and port	The popular file-transfer clients don't actively support any direct naming scheme for active nodes but only track message ID.
Presence	Usually online, offline, or one of a number of preset or custom states	Presence is implemented in the client's IRC chat component.
Roster	Only indirectly through local host cache	Manual contacting of specific IP nodes is possible. The chat component has more options.
Agency	Simple filters (screen)	Search, throttle bandwidth usage.
Browsing	(Sometimes)	Some clients allow browsing shared file directory in another client node.
Architecture	Atomistic, mappable, possible evolution to two-tier	Reach bounded by TTL count, topology in constant change.
Protocol	Open, HTTP, ping/pong	Extensions possible.

As perceived today, Gnutella is primarily a file-sharing and exchange network that supports arbitrary file types. There are no central servers, and hence no central shutdown point. The private or public network is defined solely by whatever clients are currently in communication with each other. Collecting responses to client announcements to the network allows each connected user to build a local map of this network. There may be multiple networks, depending on how clients are configured to connect, or alternatively, a local network of Gnutella clients on a LAN.

To begin with, the specious gnutella.net, com, and org domains all merely pointed to a really simple status page with a count of active nodes (many thousands) and available file library (often in the ten millions of megabytes), as seen from that particular node in gNet. The gnutella.com domain appears lately to have changed into a growing portal site for the user and developer community. The associated gnutellameter.com site purports to show realtime network status in a variety of formats. The Gnutella Network Snapshot comprises a number of sorted query lists compiled from well-situated nodes to give an indication of network activity.

As a connected user, you have similar and more information directly available in many clients (for example, Gnucleus). The difference is that the connectivity is seen from your own position in the network—a more relevant view in any case.

Gnutella was often seen as a viable contender to Napster, not least because of this lack of a central shutdown point. Several Gnutella-protocol clients were in fact narrowly designed for MP3 file exchange only. Both the threats and actual closure of "free" Napster caused marked flows of users to Gnutella as a result.

The lack of central control points in Gnutella means that the legal responsibility for file transfers rests entirely with the users. Depending on your viewpoint, this is either a good thing or a bad thing—undeniable is that on gNET, you can find dubious content and illegal copies of pretty much anything at some time or another. Thus it boils down to the issues of whether, as a Gnutella node, you share inappropriate files, or search for and then decide to download files that might be considered illegal. Either way, it's a conscious decision and deliberate action by any user. Much like life :)

CLIENT SOFTWARE

There is no single, standard Gnutella client software. Instead one finds a diverse collection of clients that all support the basic Gnutella protocol. These clients can all communicate with each other, but developers are free to implement functionality and extensions as they see fit. This freedom of implementation and extension has some interesting consequences, discussed later.

Gnutella specifications and most clients are open source (as GnuGPL), but a few closed-source applications also exist. Clients are often rapidly evolving test versions; new ones appear, and others become "archived" (meaning orphaned software). A few have become established. They range from user-simple connect-search-download clients, to nerd-friendly applications with lots of node/packet statistics and logs.

The www.gnutelliums.com Web site maintains a comprehensive directory of Gnutella client downloads for the major platforms Windows, Linux/Unix, Java, and Macintosh. Table 7.2 shows the clients current at the time of writing, but the pace of development is rapid and changes are likely by the time you read this.

CONNECTING TO OTHERS

Logging on to the public Gnutella Network is likened to wading into a sea of people—faces in all directions, and a sort of horizon beyond which you see nothing. Each time you join the network, you wade into a different part of the virtual crowd and see a

TABLE 7.2 *Some current Gnutella-clone clients for different platforms*

Windows 32-bit	Linux/Unix	MacIntosh	Comments
Gnotella			Gnutella clone, graphic plots of dataflow, skins. (2.3MB)
		Mactella	Gnutella clone. (500KB)
Gnucleus			Nerd-friendly options and statistics, node mapping option. (1.8MB)
BearShare			Well-made and quite popular. (1.2MB) Unwary users will be subjected to alertbox advertising unless these components not installed.
LimeWire	LimeWire	LimeWire	Java-based. Very popular. Has many sophisticated control features. (3–10MB depending on platform).
Phex	Phex	Phex	Java-based development of (now unsupported) Furi (1.6MB, Java runtime files needed).
	Hagelslag		Dutch Gnutella implementation. (140KB)
	Qtella		Written in C++ / qt library. (150KB)
	Gnewtellium		MP3 files only (32KB), based on (now unsupported) Win32 Newtella.
	Gnut		Command-line client for any POSIX system. (280KB)

different selection of nodes. You talk to the nearest neighbors, and through them to others. Each session, it's a selection of different people and different information.

You can connect in principle with any of those you detect around you, but as in real life, many are too busy talking to others to pay much attention. Some will pointedly ignore you. Others just exchange a few words and move on. Eventually you find a suitable number to maintain longer contact with, who can reliably pass along queries and results. People come and go all the time, and the local configuration changes constantly, so over time you will be connecting with different ones.

Atomistic p2p networks such as Gnutella are highly dynamic and lack (or at least don't require) central address lists. Pragmatics, however, dictate that some form of bootstrap list is available for initial discovery, so clients do incorporate a few such options. The discovery process is discussed further in the protocol section.

This sea-of-people image is certainly apt on one level, but it obscures an essential feature: random physical location. Your nearest neighbors can be physically very remote indeed. Tracking node connectivity over time, and determining actual node location from the IP numbers, gives an appreciation of the global and dynamic reach of the Gnutella Network over the Internet. Some clients, such as BearShare seen in Figure 7.2, helpfully perform automatic DNS lookup and display little icons and country flags in the connectivity origin field.

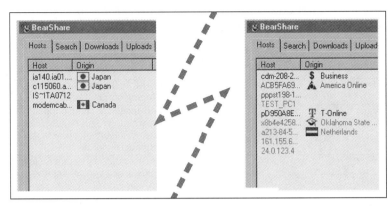

FIGURE 7.2 *Composite from Bearshare Gnutella client illustrating both the way your immediate connections change over time and the global cross section of nodes that make up a local web of "neighbor" nodes.*

BROADCAST-ROUTING STRATEGY

The horizon effect is a result of inherent (virtual) segmentation of the network, a design decision that (currently, with default client settings) limits the node count to about 15,000 on gNet as seen from any node—a client's *potential* reach. Older analysis suggested much more severe network segmentation with a reach of only a few thousand nodes or less, even in ideally balanced and equally distributed topologies, but this value is in practice very sensitive to many factors.

Nodes continually drift in and out of reach in an evolutionary process, in turn influencing which nodes you can reach through them. Over say a few hours, you might reach four times as many nodes as you see at any one time.

The main reason for the horizon effect is that messages have a time-to-live (TTL) counter. Typically, the TTL is set between 5 and 7, and the value is decremented by each node as it relays the message. Another counter tracks the number of hops. A simple example of the principle is illustrated in Figure 7.3. The critical values of TTL and number of node connections, together with each node's capacity and bandwidth, combine to determine network performance and stability. Some clients allow the user to manually adjust TTL and the number of keep-alive nodes, and thus to some extent extend the effective horizon.

Ideally, all messages live out their TTL, but sometimes a message is discarded by a node as a *bad packet*. The reason can be that the total number of hops exceeds a node's set limit, a duplicate is received, or the message is damaged or can't be parsed in some way. TTL-expired messages are often included in bad packet statistics.

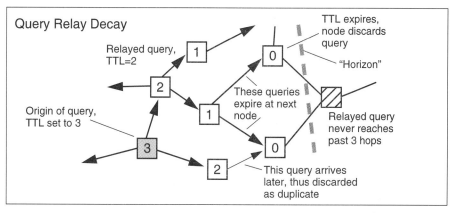

FIGURE 7.3   *How decrementing TTL (and discarding duplicates) ensures that a relayed message eventually stops spreading through the network.*

Table 7.3 gives a good idea of how potential (or ideal) reach varies geometrically as a function of two parameters, connectivity and TTL. The previous example with TTL=3 would thus have, according to the math, a maximum reach of 21 (assuming all nodes connected to three unique neighbors). The shaded region in the table is where most Gnutella clients operate, although usually not achieving these ideal reach values because actual node branching varies considerably from case to case.

Bit 7.2   TTL value is the only mechanism to expire descriptors on the network.

For this reason, each client examines TTL in passing messages and adjusts higher values down to its own TTL setting, which clamps TTL to a consensus maximum.

TABLE 7.3   *Ideal relationship of potential reach to the parameters connected nodes (N) and value of message TTL*

	TTL=2	TTL=3	TTL=4	TTL=5	TTL=6	TTL=7
N=2	4	6	8	10	12	14
N=3	9	21	45	93	189	381
N=4	16	52	160	484	1456	4372
N=5	25	105	425	1705	6825	27305
N=6	36	186	936	4686	23436	117186
N=7	49	301	1813	10885	65317	391909
N=8	64	456	3200	22408	156864	1098056

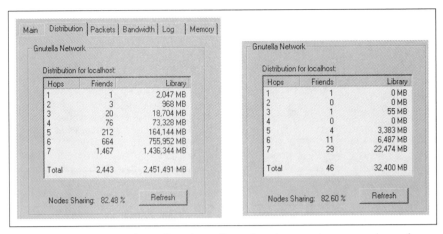

FIGURE 7.4   *Composite from Gnucleus client showing varying network reach as a function of how well each connected node branches to others.*

The value of TTL should probably never be set above 8 for risk of drowning the network in excessive query relaying. Client software tends to enforce upper limits here, ignoring and replacing higher settings in relayed messages. On the other hand, super-peer networks might operate with locally much higher values of N.

Network reach in practice is illustrated in Figure 7.4, where distribution mapping two connected nodes provide contrasting topologies. The first suggests an average N of over 4, a distribution and reach fairly close to ideal, and with potential access to a large library of files. The second, with a paltry 46 nodes after the same seven hops, shows several nodes with few friends. Poor path expansion severely limits searches, and impoverished node paths are good candidates for pruning. Reach may be understated, however, as newer clients no longer respond to multihop pings.

Looking at summed statistics for good client connectivity, Figure 7.5 shows that connectivity to five nodes provides access to something approximating the potential reach of N=4, TTL=7, despite lackluster statistics from a few of these node trees.

As noted earlier, there is inherent drift in the connection map, and over time the distribution map will look very different. But there's no need to wait passively; manual improvement and change is possible. The occasional, judicious culling of poorly performing nodes in the connection list allows new, probably better connections to form—a process not dissimilar to discarding poor cards in a poker hand and hoping for a better draw. This simple measure goes a long way to improving reach in the short term. Clients can also be set to automatically drop connections to nodes with less than a stated number of friends or those with no shared content.

Connected Nodes:

Node	Port	Friends	Library
24.181	6346	2,446	2,451,855 MB
63.180	Inbound	594	632,505 MB
64.228	Inbound	178	154,364 MB
66.65.	Inbound	1,262	1,103,900 MB
65.6.1	Inbound	427	413,106 MB
5 Connections		4,907	4,755,730 MB

FIGURE 7.5   *Summed statistics for client connectivity, where previously analyzed node trees converge. Identifying node numbers are masked in the capture for the purposes of this illustration.*

PROTOCOL

The Gnutella protocol is firmly anchored in the established HTTP protocol for the Internet. The defining point is that all nodes are "equal-rights", and the software acts as both server *and* client—a "servent". The functionality focus of the protocol is on distributed search for content.

Gnutella is open source and the protocol relatively simple, making it suitable as a kind of baseline comparison technology in this book. The full protocol details are published in various locations on the Web, but the essentials are explained in some detail in this section for the sake of later comparisons.

This basic protocol has been extended by some clients. For instance, Gnotella can include extra transfer statistics in the QueryHit message. BearShare as of v1.3.0 also extends the QueryHit result with more information about servent and transfer statistics, plus a field for proprietary data. Newer clients are extending the protocol to handle multiple download sources and other features. The insertion points seem reasonable, and the extra data should be ignored by clients without these extensions.

However, protocol extensions can be somewhat fragile in a mixed-client environment. For example, some (older) clients may misinterpret extended QueryHit messages and mangle them. Other nodes discard damaged QueryHits, so these can't be guaranteed to reach the original Query node in mixed-client networks.

The Gnutella protocol currently defines only five descriptors (for message types) to implement network functionality. They are listed in Table 7.4, along with explanatory comments relevant to nodes sending or receiving them.

Message examples are given later for different situations, showing just how servent message exchanges are structured for the common query-response pairs.

TABLE 7.4   *Gnutella Network Protocol v0.4 descriptors*

Descriptor	Sent	Received
Ping	Pings are sent to actively discover hosts on the network. A Ping has zero payload length, only header.	A servent receiving a Ping descriptor is expected to respond with one or more Pong descriptors.
Pong	Pongs are sent as response to pings. Includes the port and address of a connected Gnutella servent, plus information regarding the amount of data it is making available to the network.	Received Pongs can be used to map potential connections, count participating nodes, and compile node statistics.
Query	Queries are sent to search the distributed network.	A servent receiving a Query descriptor will respond with a QueryHit if a match is found against its local data set.
QueryHit	QueryHits are sent as positive response to Queries.	The QueryHit descriptor provides the recipient with enough information to acquire the data matching the corresponding Query.
Push	Push messages are sent to initiate file transfer from firewalled servents.	A firewalled servent receiving a Push is prompted to contribute file-based data to the network.

Each descriptor message is in turn defined by a message header, the components of which are given by Table 7.5. This header too is a fairly simple implementation with only five field types. The description in the table should be adequate to understand the context in which each is used.

Bit 7.3   Gnutella message headers have no special framing sequences.
Currently, the only way to reliably parse the network data stream of message descriptors is by examining each header's Payload Length to find the start of the next descriptor—the price paid for open-ended simplicity, perhaps?

This parsing constraint means that there is no built-in fault tolerance or recovery for descriptors that a node fails to parse—the messages are just discarded.

TABLE 7.5   *The header fields in any Gnutella v0.4 descriptor*

Header field	Description
Descriptor ID	A 16-byte (128-bit) string that uniquely identifies the descriptor on the network. As a rule, a function of the sending node's address, it is used in Pong and QueryHit as a destination (originator) identifier.
Payload Descriptor	Identifies the kind of descriptor. Currently used: 0x00 = Ping, 0x01 = Pong, 0x40 = Push 0x80 = Query, 0x81 = QueryHit
TTL	A counter specifying the number of times remaining for the descriptor to be forwarded before it is discarded. Each servent decrements TTL before passing it on to another node.
Hops	Hops value tracks the number of times the descriptor has been forwarded. The TTL and Hops fields of the header must satisfy (or be adjusted to) the following condition: $TTL(0) = TTL(i) + Hops(i)$ where $TTL(0)$ is usually the current servent's setting.
Payload Length	The length of the descriptor immediately following this header. The next descriptor header is located exactly this number of bytes from the end of this header (there are no gaps or pad bytes in the Gnutella data stream).

Because of the lack of framing sequences or other "eye-catchers" in the data stream, the protocol specification urges that servents rigorously validate the Payload Length field for each fixed length descriptor received. In the event a servent finds itself out of sync with an input stream, it should drop the connection associated with the stream—following the worst-case assumption that the upstream servent is either generating or forwarding invalid descriptors.

Connection and Discovery

Gnutella clients communicate by default on port 6346 (or 6347) using the normal Web protocol HTTP 1.0—each in effect functioning as a miniature browser/server application. Any port however can be specified. Some clients have built-in Web browser windows and can browse target server directories if it is allowed, while others hand off any Web page presentation to the system's default browser.

Establishing a connection to the network is a matter of making a TCP/IP connection to an existing node and sending the HTTP header message:

```
GNUTELLA CONNECT/<protocol version string>\n\n
```

A servent wishing to accept the connection must then respond with:

```
GNUTELLA OK\n\n
```

Any other response indicates unwillingness to accept the connection.

A servent may actively reject an incoming connection request for a variety of reasons. The user might have set the servent to not accept any incoming connections at all, preferring to maintain outgoing ones. Incoming connection slots are limited in any case by a client setting and may already be filled. A servent might not support the same version of the protocol and decline for this reason.

Nodes already connected in the network can map active node addresses through ping-pong responses from other nodes, but the Gnutella protocol doesn't specify any initial method to discover currently active nodes prior to joining. In the beginning, quasi-permanent node addresses were distributed through other, manual channels, and new users would enter them into a client until a connection could be established.

These days, node address acquisition for new nodes is usually handled automatically, through host cache services implemented on selected "permanent" network nodes with published addresses—for example the client home site, or from particular IRC channels with automatic response 'bots (short for virtual robots).

Clients preset in this way can automatically maintain local lists based on such downloads and later use recent node history from the local cache. Alternatively, the user can try manually entered node addresses. Independent Web sites, such as the zeropaid.com file-sharing portal, also provide updated Gnutella nodelists for download or manual entry.

Once connected to an active node, clients can map other nodes from received pongs, possibly after sending further ping descriptors up the network, and continue to establish connections with more nodes. A visualized example of such a network map constructed from node responses is shown in Figure 7.6, albeit limited to a hop depth of only four in order not to become too cluttered.

Ping-pong messages represent a significant portion of the total network traffic in a peer network of this kind, together as much as two-thirds or three-quarters of all messages through any connection, and the Gnutella protocol therefore strongly

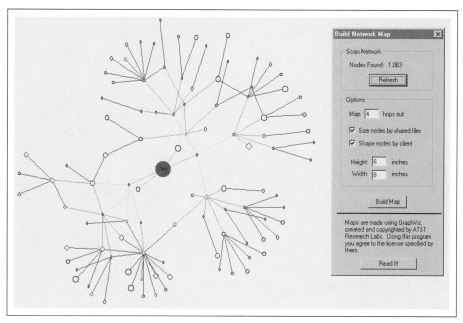

FIGURE 7.6 *Example of connection map created from node responses and visualized to depth 4 in Gnucleus using the GraphViz package.*

recommends minimizing the number and frequency of pings sent by any one client. The general discussion of scalability in Chapter 5, which used an analysis of a Gnutella network as an example, noted that just sending pings alone consumed a significant fraction of available client bandwidth, perhaps routinely fully a third for 56Kbps modem users. A recent trend is for clients not to respond to multihop pings.

The protocol further specifies a routing policy that a pong may only be sent back along the same path that the originating ping traversed. To comply, each servent maintains a cache of all the ping IDs it has seen in a kind of routing table, with information about which connection delivered it. Servents simply discard any received pong that doesn't match a seen ping. In addition, the ID cache allows a servent to discard duplicate descriptors, usually due to loops in the *ad hoc* network topology.

Bit 7.4   Pong data can refer to an arbitrary node.

The protocol doesn't require that an issued pong must refer to the same node that issues it. Usually it does, but it might in fact point to another host. A servent might send a series of pongs in response, including cached ones from other nodes.

Implementing Search

The core of a Gnutella network is the search, performed by sending a Query message. The normal broadcast-route method means each servent that receives the query—and determines that it is valid, not a duplicate, and still has time to live—caches the ID to its routing table (as for pings) and forwards the query to all its other connections. The software then performs a search on local content.

In addition to the query string, the descriptor payload starts with a field specifying a minimum supported transfer rate for response. A pragmatic way to conserve network bandwidth, the value tells servents with lower maximum rates to not bother responding. However, they will still forward the query as before.

Servents with a hit match to a query string respond with a QueryHit message, the body of which provides information needed to evaluate the host and contact it for transfer. QueryHit messages are sent back to the network, but the header contains the same descriptor ID as the Query. This allows the query client to correctly identify and associate QueryHit messages received from the data stream with the Query messages it initiated. Servents implement the same routing policy for QueryHit as for pongs.

> **Bit 7.5   Constantly changing topology means discarded descriptors.**
> Shifts in connection topology can destroy original paths. The local routing requirements mean that new nodes in a path initially discard all responses instead of passing them on—a major source of "bad" messages and failed discovery or search.

A typical transfer session is initiated by the Query client attempting to directly contact a QueryHit-identified servent. The fetch syntax used for the direct connection attempt is placed in the header directed to the target host. The end-of-line marker used throughout is the DOS-standard cr+lf, not as some might expect Unix/Web lf.

```
GET /get/<File Index>/<File Name>/ HTTP/1.0\r\n
Connection: Keep-Alive\r\n
Range: bytes=0-\r\n
User-Agent: <Agent Identifier>\r\n
\r\n
```

If all is well, the target servent responds by sending an acknowledgment header:

```
HTTP 200 OK\r\n
```

```
Server: <Agent Identifier>\r\n
Content-type: application/binary\r\n
Content-length: 4356789\r\n
\r\n
```

A successful handshake response allows the requesting servent to start the download. It's up to the user to determine whether bandwidth and reliability make the selected host worth continuing the download with. If the target servent is firewalled, such direct contacts from outside will fail. The backup method on failure is to try a "push" request passed up the node tree the same way that the original query was sent.

> **Bit 7.6 Gnutella transfer requires at least one servent with no firewall.**
> If both requesting and target servents are firewalled, then no transfer is possible. Other implementations sometimes get around this constraint. One possibility that can be implemented by Gnutella clients is to use a third, open node as a relay.

Push descriptors are routed like Pong or QueryHit responses, only according to the servent identifier field (from QueryHit), not the descriptor ID. The assumption is that since the target servent could read and process the query, it will also see the push. The servent acquires the IP address of the query client from the push descriptor. It can then from inside its firewall initiate direct contact and send a GIV transfer offer:

```
GIV <File Index>:<Servent Identifier>/<File Name>\n\n
```

The requesting site can from the offer extract the required file parameters and construct the same GET header as in the previous case to start receiving the file.

TRANSFER ISSUES

While file transfers occur directly between the two end nodes and therefore don't load the network, they do share the respective end-node bandwidth with normal network loading and other transfers in progress from either side. In addition, transfer bandwidth is often throttled in host clients so that "uploads" can never go faster than a preset rate, say perhaps 33Kbps, despite otherwise high bandwidth at the host.

It's not unusual to start a large download only to discover that the effective transfer rate falls to unacceptable values. At that point, the sensible user looks elsewhere, to other hosts. Clients such as Gnucleus can allow progression to the "next" host of several for a particular file.

Bit 7.7   A user can leave the network to improve download performance.
In some cases, a user might decide that an initiated transfer is important enough that all node bandwidth be dedicated to receiving it. Disconnecting from the network at this time can give marked transfer improvement. A shorter download time also increases the probability that the transfer completes successfully in a single session.

The Range parameter in the message implies the ability to resume interrupted transfers from a given offset, which most servents support. Resume is a valuable, perhaps even essential feature in transient networks where any sending host might disconnect at whim, disrupting an ongoing transfer.

Support for downloading different file segments from several alternate hosts simultaneously is successively being introduced in newer client versions (for example, LimeWire 1.9 and Gnucleus 1.6). Parallel downloads of offset data greatly improves both efficiency and reliability of transfers and is often a technique implemented in more advanced, distributed protocols (see Chapters 8 and 9).

In both resume and multihost cases, the issue is to correctly identify that the sources in fact are exact copies of the same file. A simple method is to offset fragments with a small overlap and test that this data always matches. When resuming a transfer at a later time, the receiving client must remember the addresses (often as IP numbers) of the hosts associated with that particular file. Otherwise, the user is forced to perform a new search. The risk then is that the shifting network topology no longer includes hosts with an "identical" copy—or it might not find that file at all.

Bit 7.8   The ability to resume transfer might be dependent on client state.
The list of transfer host addresses might be kept in a transient store, subject to loss.

Different client implementations might handle partial-transfer resumes differently, caching vital node and file data only temporarily. User interactions with the client software (for instance, closing result window, performing new search, or requesting re-search) can unexpectedly cause the loss of such information. Not all user manuals are especially forthcoming on this problem.

GNUTELLA SCALABILITY

Network scalability is discussed at length in the AP2P section of Chapter 5, using Gnutella as an example. A Gnutella network exemplifies well both the advantages and disadvantages of an atomistic peer architecture, especially in the context of what is sometimes called the Transient Web. Just as was experienced with the Internet, as the network grows, so too do the inherent scalability constraints in the basic architecture increasingly come into play.

A second-generation (Gnutella2) architecture is being deployed with a super-peer layer of clients to form a more reliable and persistent backbone. Probably this will also give the option of some permanent nodelist servers to make it easier for new users to connect to the network the first time. Super-peers are "elected" locally by virtue of their better bandwidth and capacity to form the mainstay of connectivity, thus retaining most of the atomistic and decentralized nature of the original AP2P model. The approach makes the network far less sensitive to the transient connectivity and limited bandwidth caused by the large number of dial-up users.

Predefined Networks

Installing and using Gnutella in a limited corporate intranet context is not difficult; recall that the network is defined by the topology of active nodes and a client list of nodes to try when joining. The administration involved is mainly deploying the most suitable clients with an approved nodelist. Some clients (such as Gnotella) even provide a settings dialog explicitly for forming a "subnet" for this very purpose—otherwise, the connection seed list must be edited by hand.

Forming a limited network is not the problem. The main risk in the limited network context is that if any one node should connect outside the prescribed list of nodes, that will instantly make the rest of the network and its effective nodelist available from outside. It only takes one client acting alone to subvert the closed network, unless explicit filtering or external measures can prevent connection casts outside the approved range of nodes. Rogue connectivity can also be caused by a virus (for example, Mandragore), unless client machine firewall software detects the ruse.

> **Bit 7.9   The Gnutella connectivity model is "allow" unless explicitly denied.**
> The default settings in most atomistic p2p clients currently allow arbitrary outbound connections. The same settings also allow anyone to initiate inbound connections to the client and freely download shared content from it.

The Risks

Granted that typical client software allows extensive filtering of which node connections it will accept and some restrictions on content sharing, but it must be explicitly configured in each. You therefore should preconfigure all participating clients in a closed network the same way to accept only nodes within, for instance, the same subnet. Correspondingly, they should also be preconfigured with only an approved nodelist to try when joining, removing any references to external sites.

Even so, if just one client bridges to an external network, then the private network becomes at least visible from outside due to the nature of the ping discovery process. Such external connectivity might occur because some user manually connects to the public Gnutella network to look for something while still a member of the local client network. This projected visibility increases the risk for directed probes or attacks on these now discovered nodes. If node filtering is insufficient in clients, then unauthorized sharing of content might also occur due to the default trust inherent in the basic Gnutella system.

> **Bit 7.10 Gnutella clients are natural gateway servers between networks.**
> Any Gnutella servent has this automatic ability to bridge between different virtual Gnutella-protocol networks by virtue of multiple node connections.

We can also note in passing that many recent client implementations, such as Gnucleus, support automatic detection of and upgrading to newer versions. Although convenient in that new versions of software can easily propagate through the network, this does pose something of a reliability and security issue. Lacking digital signature checks, for example, malicious software could conceivably be inserted from outside in this way. One reason for this risk is again the implicit trust built into the design and default configuration.

These issues were discussed from a general viewpoint in the Chapter 4 section on security. Ensuring adequate security in the current Gnutella implementations is to a large extent a matter of manual precautions and sensible defaults. The complete user control of the individual client does mean however that any one user might change settings or make connections that can be detrimental to the rest of the local network.

Solutions to better p2p security are coming as the technology matures—for example, in the form of more automated trust and reputation management. Some of the other architectures in this book deal with these issues already.

TRUST AND REPUTATION ISSUES

The basic p2p file-sharing implementations are usually open and blindly trusting. Any protocol-compliant computer that wishes to connect is accepted, assuming the accepting host's connectivity settings allow new incoming connections. This behavior is after all the original open paradigm of mutual trust that used to rule in networks.

Complete openness however also means that the network is open to disruptive intrusions by rogue software. Although the current implementations are fairly resilient and generally immune to message spoofing, computer and bandwidth resources are finite and can eventually be overwhelmed. Intruders can exploit various vulnerabilities to disrupt at least the immediate subweb for a time. Ping and request flooding, false hit messages, and directed denial-of-service attacks on discovered nodes are some disruptive methods seen.

In late 2001, for example, it seemed that concerted attempts to disrupt music-sharing networks by, it was said, agents acting on the behalf of the music copyright owners. Bogus clients would repeatedly join the network and proceed to DoS-flood selected nodes that responded to queries for commercial music tracks. As a rule, the attacks proved little more than an inconvenience—the disrupted nodes quickly reestablish connectivity as part of another subweb, and the dynamic network moved on pretty much as usual. After all, the whole point of atomistic p2p is that the network doesn't rely on any specific nodes to function.

Settings to filter or block connections based on user-specified criteria are generally available on all clients, but the default behavior has been not to filter. On the other hand, this initial openness is changing; more users begin to reconfigure the defaults, and more clients install with less permissive configurations. Typical filters will quickly drop nodes that aren't sharing any content or have fewer than a certain number of connections, in addition to blocking the usual lists of explicitly entered addresses or blocks of addresses that users lose patience with.

Lately, there is a growing trend to implement something more sophisticated, with features spearheaded by some of the more innovative implementations. The new forms of connectivity management for p2p applications include various forms of trust or reputation management, encryption and digital signatures. The desire is to make the network more reliable and robust without the extra security getting in the way of legitimate users. However, p2p developers also want to avoid the kind of central administration and filtering that are ever-more characteristic of the server-centric solutions. The latter rapidly become overly restrictive under litigious or governmental pressures that can be applied to any central node.

MADSTER

I'm sure some readers wondered: Madster? We'll briefly touch on this client, formerly and better known as Aimster, because it's been in the news from time to time. Some confusion exists concerning what kind of p2p model Madster is, or is becoming, and how "private" (in other words, secure) it is.

The Aimster name (and domain aimster.com) was legally contested by AOL as being too close to its AIM messaging client, and the court recently awarded both name and domain to AOL. The AbovePeer company's client and network were renamed Madster (madster.com). Only the name changed; Aimster clients still work.

Anyway, *nee* Aimster is a sharing system at root, essentially similar to Gnutella. In other words, it has no central servers. The company, however, obfuscated this and some of the earlier mentioned sharing and trust issues in its Guardian version client. The network is presented instead in terms of a "buddy" system, sort of like a messaging system roster, but defined by the user search results for common interests.

Actual file exchange in the client is downplayed, described merely as a simple browse and exchange using a private, shared session directory established after a direct message to a particular buddy. By implication, therefore, we are led to believe that any content sharing is only achieved through explicit personal consent between you and your buddy. Yet recall that searching is across the network and rosters are the temporary and transient result of a *content* ("special interest") search—you are unlikely to have encountered a particular listed "buddy" before. The fiction is perhaps viewed as helpful in fighting off the legal threats of music copyright violations that AbovePeer faces from the Recording Industry Association of America (RIAA) just like any other identifiable file-sharing public network instigator.

It was interesting to note in late 2001 that AbovePeer was evidently deploying a two-tier system, introducing Napster-like technology with a central server for its premium Club Madster subscriber service, which promises its paying members faster search and download. The nonpremium client remains atomistic, like Gnutella, with similar performance bottlenecks. This underlying difference is not mentioned in the presentations, which only coyly speak of "downloading a more powerful version of the Madster application".

The company has tried for a humorous spin on the loss of their established network and client name, with a nerdy rhyme on the new-domained home site.

Big companies are lamester / Now you can't call us A_ _ster
But if it still works the samester / What's in a namester

Distributed Content

An alternative to simply sharing existing content, where users access files made available by local decisions at each individual node of a p2p network, is to introduce network mechanisms to distribute shared storage across the nodes in the network. In other words, no longer is the aggregate content just the sum of the files that each node arbitrarily allows to be shared, but instead a common content *published* to the network at large.

This distinction can be important in some networks, especially because it decouples content from the requirement that the node that contributed it must be online for others to access it. Nodes contribute publishing, storage and retrieval resources, but they no longer have any explicit control over what is stored where. It is also possible to implement overall content management, without necessarily needing to assign central control over it.

Different methods of implementing distributed storage provide new and powerful ways to manage content and its availability. This chapter and the next together explore a few of the innovative solutions based on distributed storage, starting with a special focus on automatic resource management. It shows how "selfish" agents can maintain an optimized network through their interactions.

The technologies examined here focus on distribution or storage strategies that try to adapt to demand. Distributed peer technologies are especially suited for this kind of solution. The first examined, Mojo Nation, is a system that uses innovative micropayment technology to automatically manage network loading. For this reason, it can have important consequences for how the Internet could become economically viable. Both Mojo Nation and Swarmcast technologies are free, open source alternatives to similar, very expensive, commercial solutions developed for enterprise.

CHAPTER 8 AT A GLANCE

This chapter studies two solutions that approach distributed storage and distribution from different requirements.

Mojo Nation is the main section about the micropayment-based solution.

- *Infrastructure* outlines the basic architecture, and *Mojo Money and QoS* explains how the virtual micropayment system works to improve network performance.

- *Cooperative Content Storage* describes the storage strategy.

- A section on *Joining the Network* is followed by more detail about *Server and Broker*, the two main components.

- *Workable Micropayments* discusses how micropayment credit and token transactions occur between Brokers.

- This is followed by details about *File Management* on the network.

- Node conversations are examined in *Mojo Nation Protocol*, and later *Reputation Management* looks at strategies that deal with node trust.

- Finally, *Relay Services* takes up how computers behind firewalls can still participate as Mojo Nation nodes.

- A late addition, *MNnet* provides an update on the recent unclear status of the project.

Swarmcast is a technology mainly concerned with efficient content distribution.

- *How It Works* provides the architectural overview and some theory behind swarm distribution in general.

- As an example of a *Minimal Knowledge Solution*, Swarmcast provides a simple introduction to some key concepts encountered in the next chapter.

MOJO NATION

While networks such as Gnutella are "free" in all senses of the word, Mojo Nation takes the approach that network resources to support free distributed content should always be valued and traded, if only in a virtual sense. The rationale is that a demand-driven "market economy" can self-regulate a network and avoid issues such as overloading or the oft-cited "tragedy of the commons" freeloader problem that some claim will mean the end of free networks such as Gnutella.

Mojo Nation was free in that the public prototype network didn't require cash payments; the internal economy was virtual—on the other hand, some licensed commercial solutions could have technical support for business deployment. As the former (see the *MNnet* section) Web site described it: "The Mojo Nation technology enables licensees to distribute content using customer resources and bandwidth, realizing a significant savings in server, bandwidth, and administration costs. Strong cryptography provides security and trust management for enterprise applications of the technology and basic DRM tools for commercial content distribution."

In addition, a trusted third party on the network can ensure honesty between peer transactions. The technology can track usage and provide the accounting infrastructure for real-world payments for content royalties.

INFRASTRUCTURE

The component summary for Mojo Nation is in Table 8.1. Because the technology was deployed as a monoclient architecture with fairly specific requirements, the summary more closely corresponds to the actual network characteristics. There is little room for the kind of hack client extensions found in other, simpler systems.

To comment further on infrastructure, Mojo Nation is a *search-based* content system (like Gnutella). Storage however does not have any easily identifiable locality (content is assembled from swarms of nodes) nor readable identity (opaque keys). It does not go as far as networks such as Freenet that provide anonymity.

MOJO MONEY AND QOS

Participating in the simpler public Mojo Nation network demonstrated the use of an imaginary currency, Mojo, to efficiently arbitrate access to community resources without the need for central control. In Mojo Nation, every network transaction costs some Mojo. To acquire Mojo, users must contribute resources to the community—disk space, bandwidth, or processing cycles. Without Mojo, users must wait in line for

TABLE 8.1 *Mojo Nation component summary*

Component	Specific forms	Comments
Identity	Internal representation based on IP and Broker public key signature.	Connectivity is mediated through distributed metaservice.
Presence	Broker assumed online.	User conversations not supported in current design.
Roster	Internal reputation list of nodes maintained by business logic.	Transactions with trusted nodes favored, no direct user input.
Agency	Business logic rules.	Rules can be tweaked by user.
Browsing	Search in distributed content metaservice.	User browses in local result list. (User can't browse distributed files directly, only metadata).
Architecture	Distributed swarms of single kind of client software.	Clients buy and sell resources through automated transactions managed by background Broker.
Protocol	HTTP with public key encryption, Mojo microcredit system.	Essentially open protocol based on Mojo microcredit system.

contested resources. In this way, the Mojo micropayment system serves both as a distributed load balancer and as an incentive to contribute more resources.

When demand for content is low, the cost of providing it is close to zero. When there is contention for that resource, the payment system comes into play. Mojo Nation's distributed load balancing moves some clients to a less-occupied server. On the other hand, users with accumulated Mojo credit can use some of it to move to the head of line. You "buy" quality of service in a very direct way. Payment arbitration is handled with the **Broker** component.

Bit 8.1 Micropayment systems are resistant to DoS attacks and other abuse.
It's been argued that the main reason that spam and denial-of-service attacks are such a problem on the Internet is that there is no user accountability for resource usage. Excessive loading of a micropayment network would by contrast quickly exhaust user credit, thus automatically limiting abuse.

TABLE 8.2 *Distributed Mojo Nation services that manage the network and earn Mojo. In the aggregate, they implement the distributed network agents.*

Service	Function
Block server	A block server manages local storage of received pieces (blocks) of published Mojo Nation files. This is the mechanism behind offering storage space in return for Mojo.
Meta tracker	A meta tracker maps the network location of the Brokers which are online, along with their public ID keys and a list of the services they provide.
Content tracker	A content tracker stores file location maps, and provides methods to publish, query, and track file metadata (descriptions). These trackers form the network's search engine.
Publication tracker	A publication tracker provides methods to publish, retrieve, and track file data via the dinode blocklists.
Relay Server	A relay server works like a mailbox for peers behind firewalls which block incoming messages from reaching the Brokers. Relay servers on peers outside the firewall hold messages for firewalled Brokers. These Brokers can then go out and retrieve the messages for processing behind the firewall.

New users start with an account filled with one million Mojo. More is earned by running Mojo Nation "community services": block servers, meta trackers, content trackers, publication trackers, and relay servers—all explained in Table 8.2

A configuration dialog in the client sets these services up and allows the user to set prices for each of the offered services. It's a free market, but you would normally set low prices for resources you can afford to be generous with and high prices for those that you don't wish to be used constantly. You want a suitable balance between demand and supply, sort of like when playing a management simulation game. Services used during peak demand earn more Mojo credit.

Bit 8.2 Selling relay server services are a good 24/7 way to earn Mojo.
Brokers behind firewalls are continually asking relay servers about pending messages there and are therefore paying a steady toll in Mojo.

The Broker handles both micropayments for requested user actions and earnings from offered services. It also provides the interface to Mojo Nation content search. This agent component runs as a background process, and its function is dependent only on connectivity to the network. A user with flat-rate Internet connectivity can leave it running for as long as the system is running, and it will automatically offer services and administer resources the whole time—earning Mojo. Users therefore have an incentive to "lock in" resources and minimize peer downtime, which is beneficial to network stability and reliability.

It's the aggregate of these "selfish", profit-maximizing Brokers that implement the distributed agents that manage the network as a whole. Three distributed tracker agent services manage network content:

- **Meta trackers,** which note the network location of online Brokers, along with their public ID keys and a list of the services they provide.

- **Content trackers,** which store the maps that enable the retrieval agent to find the data blocks which make up a published file, and also act as Mojo Nation's distributed search engine.

- **Publication trackers,** which distribute published blocks and are responsible for injecting new data into the system.

The file-storage mechanism needs to be examined in detail to fully appreciate the strengths of the Mojo Nation architecture.

COOPERATIVE CONTENT STORAGE

Content is stored across peers using **swarm distribution,** which means that Mojo Nation breaks each uploaded file into small pieces (say 64KB), public-key encrypts them for privacy, then replicates each small piece in several places over the network.

File location on the network is tracked using a special *MojoID* that refers to a *sharemap* of blocks in a list called a *dinode* (distributed information node, the analogue of a Unix/Linux filesystem's i-node).

> **Bit 8.3   The MojoID is a human-readable URL designating a unique file.**
> Like all URLs, a MojoID can be posted, copied, and passed around as a convenient shortcut reference to stored data—an abstraction hiding the storage details.

Instead of contacting just one node for a requested file, the network (or rather its distributed services) can assemble it from a swarm of peers, each of which contributes a piece of the whole. The process is likened to a swarm of ants bringing fragments of food to an anthill.

The swarm distribution method is a clever workaround to the common problems of node availability, peer overload, and limited bandwidth. It's particularly suited to networks built from dial-up peers on limited bandwidth modems, providing speed and reliability. Contributing peers are lightly loaded, while the downloading peer can take advantage of many parallel transfers to speed retrieval.

Storage costs Mojo—it uses storage resources sold by other nodes. Publishing content therefore doesn't earn the contributor any Mojo. Quite the opposite, it costs, because uploading requires that the Broker buy the required storage space and publishing services from other peers. This fact evidently proves a bit counter-intuitive to new users to Mojo Nation, who tend to expect simple content *quid pro quo*; downloads for uploads.

Upload cost is logical, however, because contributions of data have no *intrinsic* value to the network. As far as the network sees, publishing just consumes resources that must be paid for by the publisher. The virtue of contributing content, despite the cost of publishing in this system, lies in the fact that more interesting and varied content should attract more users to the network, which does have value.

> **Bit 8.4   The network values new users who can provide more resources.**
> The network in this model doesn't care about content at all, except as a means to attract more users to join.

In other words, the operating rule is: It's worthwhile for users to pay for offering more content because it attracts more users and makes the network a better place to be. *More is better*—think Metcalfe's Law. More users provide greater resources, which improves performance, forms a better network, and also creates greater demand for the services the contributing peer is offering.

Something else that the pay-for-publishing model gives is a moment of reflection on the part of the publisher, which would be expected to reduce the number of duplicates and low-value files on the network. Wasteful use of free storage otherwise ends up being usual in other file-sharing systems, especially if user nodes are valued based simply on the raw storage space or number of files that are shared.

JOINING THE NETWORK

Peer discovery on first connection attempt is integrated into the client installation and is transparent to the user. It appears to have two parts:

- "Bootstrap" connection to a central server (was mojonation.net)
- Built-in "history" of established agents

See for example these extracts from a (verbose) startup log of a new installation:

```
...
(Broker) Checking for other Brokers running with the same config
file.
...
(mojobootpage) loading mojonation bootpage
(mojobootpage) bootpage url: http://www.mojonation.net:25000/
bootpage.txt
...
(counterparty) accounting with <YoxC>: requesting 10 credit from
her; total_spent with her = 150 [reason: list relay servers v2]
...
(counterparty) accounting with <ale9>: requesting 10 credit from
her; total_spent with her = 150 [reason: lookup contact info]
```

The last shows how the newly installed Broker thinks it has already done 150 credits worth of services purchasing from other agents—preinstalled transaction history.

> **Bit 8.5 Mojo Nation records all transactions in session logs.**
> The session log of a startup date/time is the place to look for information about what the Broker does and which agents it contacts.

Important recurring entries in the logs are the connections to meta tracker nodes, because this distributed service is how the Broker can locate active nodes for other services—find content, store content, publish content, find available storage space, find relay services, and so on. A meta tracker can be discovered from the bootpage information, whether downloaded or in the installation package.

```
2001-07-22_20:01:30 (mojobootpage) Found metatracker connection
info: TCP 64.71.128.167:25333
```

The following extract shows how the installation has autodetected that the client is running on a dynamic dial-up connection, which like firewall-protected clients requires the use of an external relay node.

```
(broker) You have a non-routable IP address.

(broker) SERVE_USING_A_RELAY has been enabled for you.

...

(MojoTransaction) start_listening()

(TCPCommsHandler) SERVE_USING_A_RELAY is set, not listening on a
socket.
```

The next sequence shows both a connection to the banker server to request withdrawal of a new Mojo token and a polling session with a relay server.

```
accounting with <0LWA>: requesting free transaction [reason:
'withdraw']

2001-07-22_20:10:40 (Conversation) MTM: msgId: <Atcz> :: 'are
there messages v2' with <rJTR>, completed after '4.42' seconds
for 45 mojo

2001-07-22_20:10:40 (Conversation) MTM: msgId: <nF1b> ::
'withdraw' with <0LWA>, completed after '1.39' seconds for 0 mojo

2001-07-22_20:10:41 (counterparty) accounting with <rJTR>:
performing free transaction [reason: 'message for you']

2001-07-22_20:10:41 (counterparty) accounting with <Ba1F>:
performing free transaction [reason: 'do you have blobs']
```

These different transactions are explained later in this chapter.

SERVER AND BROKER

Mojo Nation implements an atomistic peer model with decentralized cooperative services. Using opaque internal representations for nodes and content, the network deprecates aspects of identity. It relies on automated client agents communicating transparently with distributed lookup and search services composed of other agents.

The Mojo Nation client-server application, written in Python, can be seen as composed of two main parts: *Server* and *Broker*.

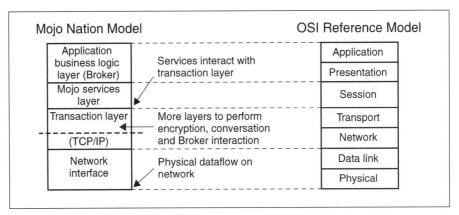

FIGURE 8.1 *A rough model of the different architectural layers in Mojo Nation (the Broker). Correspondence with OSI is approximate because the transaction layer uses TCP/IP for Broker interaction over the Internet.*

- The Server, *mojohttpd*, listens on a port (port 4004 by default) on the local network interface. It acts as a normal HTTP (or Web) server, handling requests from the user browser. It also formats the results of each command and displays the results to the user as a generated HTML page.

- The Broker performs all processing and computation, communicating with other Mojo Brokers over the network in order to satisfy each user request.

An approximate architecture model for the Mojo Broker is given in Figure 8.1.

Users can point their browsers directly at the mojohttpd, for example to the URL http://localhost:4004/broker. Certain URLs (such as http://localhost:4004/broker/ search_query?ctype=Audio) are interpreted as commands for the Broker. Normally, such addresses are not bared to the user, who instead sees the hyperlink as a much simpler text anchor to click on.

This tying of functionality to standard HTTP and using the Web browser as user interface makes the whole very flexible, especially when taking into consideration the fact that the open Python source allows, nay *encourages*, hack modifications.

A *Mojo Transaction* defines an interface between two Brokers in the network. Messages here can be in XML when dealing with content or metadata. Transactions are invoked from services and ultimately the application layer. Query, publish, retrieve, and exchange public key and other contact information—these are some of the operations performed as transactions.

On top of the Broker structure sits the business logic; pricing rules open to user modification. The concept is expressed in the user guide in this way:

> *Mojo Nation software comes with several business logic rules built in. There is a good chance you will want to tweak them. This is because you, the Mojo Nation user community, know your operations much better than we do. In the meantime, we have made it easy for you to create your own business logic, which you are encouraged to not only write but distribute to others.*

Most business decisions are made by the Broker on a per-request basis. It selects among potential service providers by applying the business logic rules. Each service provider is rated by adding user-created "handicaps" for high prices, unreliability, unfamiliarity, high latency, or other factors. The Broker then selects the provider that comes out lowest in the applied sum of squares evaluation.

Interestingly, a fairly sophisticated reputation system could be plugged in here. If you had information from friends of friends indicating that some service provider is unreliable, you could make a "handicapper", which returns such hearsay opinion, and it would be factored in along with the other considerations.

WORKABLE MICROPAYMENTS

Earlier, payment was qualified as *micropayment*. The digital *Mojo* defines a smallest currency "coin" as a digitally signed token. A Mojo Nation **token server**, which acts as a trusted bank, manages the currency. Actual payment between Brokers occurs when a token is sent from one to the other. However, payments (or more properly extended credit) can be specified to an arbitrarily small value.

Mojo payment/credit transactions are handled in the following way, wholly transparent to the user. In any transaction between two agents, an offer of Mojo is made, but the digital currency is not transferred at that time. Instead, an IOU for Mojo is sent from the initiating agent to the responding agent. One agent extends the other a bit of credit in order to complete the transaction. Agents track accumulated credit for all the other agents it does business with. A history function at both ends of the transactions also grades and records how the respective counterparts respond.

The creditor agent will call in its marker only if the debtor agent has reached a predetermined credit limit, or if the IOUs can be covered by a single coin. A creditor calling in a debt initiates a real token transfer from the debtor to normalize credit status with a debtor peer. The creditor then deposits the token with its account on the Mojo Nation token server.

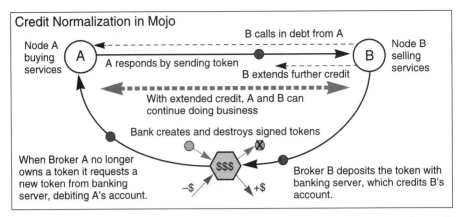

FIGURE **8.2** *Calling in a micropayment debt in Mojo Nation initiates a real transfer of a signed Mojo token to normalize credit status.*

The entire process of calling in a micropayment debt is illustrated in Figure 8.2 and the detailed step-by-step description follows:

1. The creditor requests payment, and the debtor's Broker responds by sending the creditor's Broker a signed Mojo token.

2. The creditor's Broker temporarily extends to the debtor an increase in credit equal to the token. This extra credit enables the two to continue doing business while the creditor is dealing with the token server.

3. The creditor's Broker completes the transfer by depositing the received token with the token server. The creditor then removes the temporary credit increase.

4. Meanwhile, the recipient withdraws a fresh token from the token server and is again prepared to respond to payment requests.

Each token is used just once and is digitally signed to prevent forgery. The token server keeps a list of current accounts and their balances. Accounts are not directly linked to user identities, however, only to Brokers.

The Broker's role in payment transactions is to keep track of how much Mojo one user owes another and effect real token transfers at some later time. Both microcredit and payment transactions are handled invisibly in the background, without direct user input or involvement.

By limiting the number of times a transfer of currency is actually made, the Mojo Nation system gains in fault tolerance and speed, expressed as

- **Faster transactions**. The microcredit IOUs have almost no overhead. IOU messages are integrated with the requests and responses that are already passing among peers. By contrast, each actual token payment requires communication with the token server,

- **Uninterrupted service**. The distributed economy continues to operate even if the token server is temporarily unavailable.

This agent delegation successfully addresses a serious criticism sometimes leveled at micropayment schemes in general, that micropayments are ultimately unrealistic because of the user overhead in making increasingly more difficult value judgements as item costs become smaller.

> **Bit 8.6   Realistic micropayment systems must be highly automated.**
> Users won't accept payment systems that demand constant attention to trivial sums. Even just a single extra click-through acceptance is often an unacceptable bother.

In the Mojo Nation economy, the detailed per-case decisions are invisible to the user, automated within a framework of general rules. The editable rules set defines overall strategy in terms of business logic, allowing meaningful user control at a level that's reasonable to handle manually.

FILE MANAGEMENT

Content distribution and online backup services are resource-expensive operations. Mojo Nation tries to harness and combine latent storage and bandwidth available on each peer. In a corporate context, a content distributor can thus realize significant cost savings from using existing hardware more efficiently.

A file is broken into fragments that are copied and distributed for storage and retrieval. This **swarm storage** allows many agents to work in parallel on each data transfer, thus providing greater availability and bandwidth than is possible for any single agent working alone. Each involved agent contributes incrementally to each task based upon available resources. A single download can therefore efficiently engage a mix of broadband and dial-up users to achieve very high transfer rates.

The Broker manages the process of publishing files. After fragmentation of the file into many pieces, each piece is broken into eight blocks, any four of which are enough to reconstruct the original piece. This method is an application of forward

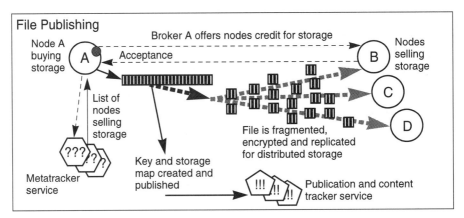

FIGURE 8.3 *Publishing a file in the Mojo Nation network. This schematic is a simplification that shows only major stages.*

error correction, a scheme discussed in Chapter 9. The data blocks are run through a cryptographic hash function that scrambles the blocks, generates a unique identity tag for each as a block ID, and assigns a bitmask to track them. Publishing these blocks to the network, as shown in Figure 8.3, then involves the following transactions:

1. The file is split into fragments and blocks, the blocks encrypted and assigned a unique ID, and copied. A bitmask is applied to define the block intervals.

2. A meta tracker service informs the Broker about available block servers on the network. Knowing their identity, the Broker can query some of them for current storage space and pricing information.

3. These block servers (or rather their respective Brokers) respond to the publishing Broker's queries with a list of storage prices and block ranges they will accept.

4. The Broker selects appropriate block servers to publish all the blocks, pays for their service, and distributes appropriate blocks to the selected storage nodes.

5. The Broker then informs a publication tracker that new blocks are available at the respective addresses.

6. A "sharemap" is created by the Broker, which explains how to reassemble the pieces of the file from the data blocks and then the file from the pieces. This is the dinode, the storage description of the file.

7. The sharemap is broken up, encrypted, and published by the Broker to responding content trackers, along with all other publisher and file descriptors—the file's metadata.

Published blocks are subsequently shared between peers, with more popular content automatically being replicated more widely among peer block servers.

> **Bit 8.7   More Mojo Nation content means more agents working together.**
>
> As the amount of data stored in the network increases, block servers generally must narrow the range of blocks they carry. Hence files become more distributed, which is mainly a function of available disk space in the respective peers.

Note that files are accessible only through storage agents working in concert across the network, because no single peer has all the blocks stored locally. And because of the encryption, less than a full complement of blocks keeps content unreadable and useless.

> **Bit 8.8   Private publication of content is possible in Mojo Nation.**
>
> The design allows users to publish highly secure private files on a public network. By not informing publication trackers, the encrypted file remains invisible and inaccessible unless the exact storage dinode is available to retrieve it.

Finding Files

File retrieval always begins with a content search. A user selects from a growing number of content types, each of which presents its own specific array of type fields to narrow the user's search. The "search" command invokes the Broker.

1. The Broker contacts the meta tracker service to locate every content tracker available on the network.

2. Content trackers are sorted, first by the lookup price each asks, then by the tracker's reputations.

3. The Broker then applies its business logic to pay one or more content trackers to hunt their respective databases for the user's search string.

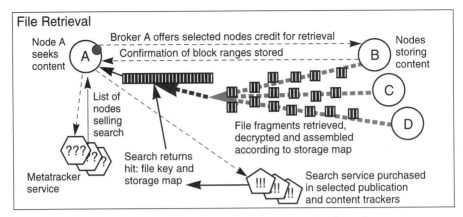

FIGURE 8.4 *Retrieving a file in the Mojo Nation network. This schematic is a simplification that shows only major stages.*

4. If the content tracker can match a stored filename or description to that string, it returns all available human-readable information about that file to the user, plus the critical dinode descriptor.

5. The user can then attempt to retrieve the file by requesting "download".

The process of searching and retrieving content is illustrated in Figure 8.4, and it is more or less the reverse of the publishing process. Search in the public Mojo Nation network has been described as lacking refinement and being surprisingly slow.

Retrieving Files

A Broker attempting a file retrieval first examines the list of block servers from which the user has purchased blocks before and the block ID ranges that they store. It tries to use these servers as a first option, partly because of their known reliability, partly in order to simplify micropayment accounting.

If the preferred servers don't store the needed blocks or aren't responding, the Broker queries the meta tracker service to find other block servers whose range of carried block IDs includes pieces of the fragments that make up the requested file. Fragments can be downloaded from different sources concurrently, minimizing total transfer time. Replication in the storage process means that any four of the eight distributed blocks for a fragment suffice to reconstruct it.

Assuming that all required blocks can be retrieved, and the fragments reconstructed and successfully reassembled according to the sharemap, the resulting complete file is passed to the user.

MOJO NATION PROTOCOL

The Mojo Nation protocol is message-based and asynchronous, and scopes four distinct layers:

1. *Mojo transaction layer*, which handles the microeconomy aspects. Every conversation between two agents in Mojo Nation involves an offer of Mojo, usually in return for an offered service.

2. *Conversation layer*, which supports two types of messages: initiating (for requests) and responding (request fulfillment). It matches responses to queries and administers filtering to stabilize network behavior. It also tracks which messages belong to which ongoing conversations.

3. *Encryption and authentication layer*, which provides secure and private communication between agents. It encrypts and decrypts each message using public-key RSA technology.

4. *Transport layer*, which moves secure (that is, encrypted) data between peers and tracks message length. Properly decoding encrypted messages requires length tracking. Transport can use any one of the available system protocols, such as the normal TCP/IP to achieve this.

The transport layer does not fully depend on any one transport layer but ensures reliable data transfers by being able to dynamically select among the available underlying protocols on a per-message basis at runtime.

Mojo Nation therefore doesn't depend on the underlying transport protocol to provide any guarantees with respect to reliability, ordering, bidirectionality, or quality of service. It instead implements a very flexible and secure communications abstraction that can be deployed atop a variety of communications systems.

Reliability, streaming, and other features are implemented by the higher-level code in Mojo Nation, using sophisticated techniques including swarming distribution and a special "self-healing" property for network.

The Mojo Nation protocol abstraction serves several important purposes:

- It insulates the application code from the underlying communication system so that the application can be ported to different communications systems. Dynamically taking advantage of the communications features available at runtime is a valuable feature from both security and performance perspectives.

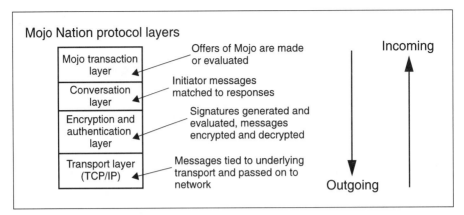

FIGURE 8.5 *Outgoing and incoming messages seen in terms of the Mojo Nation protocol layers. This is an expansion of the middle layers in the OSI comparison in the previous figure.*

- The "transaction" layer abstraction allows application code written on top of it to implement protocols in "query->response" terms without having to keep track of which response message goes with which query message.

- Encryption and integrity checks on each message prevent messages from being intercepted or altered in transit, either by accident or by malice, and protects against "active attacks" that could be used to illicitly manipulate the network.

The protocol is described (at Sourceforge) as EGTP (for Evil Geniuses Transport Protocol). While quite detailed, this textual description is neither fully specific nor necessarily totally accurate in all detail. Specific details must currently be validated and parsed from the well-documented reference source code written in Python.

Figure 8.5 shows message flow through the different layers of the protocol.

Messages

Messages are at the core of the functionality and are human-readable strings when decoded—simple and efficient to produce and to parse. They are described in the documentation as being as flexible and nearly as readable as XML.

Table 8.3 describes the message structure in terms of its components. Messages are further grouped according to the major system feature that they implement: network maintenance, block search and retrieval, message relay service, content tracking, and Mojo payments. These features are described in later sections.

TABLE 8.3   *Message structure in Mojo Nation*

Component	Function
Message Header	Contains the unique ID of the public key of the sender and recipient, and the type of message.
Transaction Header	Contains a unique nonce that can identify which transaction (query/response pair) includes the message.
Message Body	Arbitrary data determined by the specific message type. Supported messages are described in the installation's template file `OurMessages.py`.

Human-readable installation source files (`OurMessage.py`, `OurMessagesTokens.py`, and `OurMessagesPublicKey.py`) document the more detailed message specifications in the form of templates used to validate the message content.

The EGTP comms library maintains an in-memory "routing table" of the underlying communication protocol, along with a corresponding address within the context of that protocol. The pair is used to send messages to the Broker that holds the identified public key. This combination of communication protocol and an address is called a *comm strategy* in the EGTP specifications. It also supports making queries to the meta tracker service to determine the current comm strategy for that recipient in the event that the routing table doesn't have the required entry.

Message Management

Message authenticity is guaranteed by validating its digital signature. This signature can be generated only by the holder of the sender's private key. The signature itself is also encrypted by the RSA algorithm.

Messages are matched to each other using a random number (a "nonce") assigned to each initiating message. A matching response contains the same number in an encrypted hash (SHA-1), which is collision free. This check also confirms that the correct recipient received the initiating message because it is impossible to create such a cryptographic hash without first seeing the nonce. Having made note of the nonce, the initiator then won't repeat the query. It will also ignore any recurrent use of the hashed response. Such filtering protects the system from "replay vandalism" where intruders might resend intercepted messages.

The messages used for building and maintaining the network are listed and described in Table 8.4, along with expected responses. The ability to append contact information to other messages enables the network to adapt and heal during normal

TABLE 8.4 *Messages for building and maintaining the network*

Message Type	Response	Description
contact info (often appended to other messages, such as hello)	N/A	Contains an RSA public key, Broker version number, a list of one or more comm strategies, and a list services offered by the Broker. An incrementing counter allows newer contact info to be used in preference to older.
bootpage (retrieved from HTTP server)	N/A	A tiny text file used to bootstrap a broker into the system by providing contact info for meta trackers. Example Web URL: www.mojonation.net:25000/bootpage.txt
hello	success/failure	Broker contacts Meta Tracker.
goodbye	none	An advisory message that the Broker is going offline.
lookup contact info	contact info	Broker wishes to contact another Broker.
list block servers	list of: contact info	Broker wants to contact available block servers.
list relay servers	list of: contact info	Broker wants to contact available relay servers.

operation without sending separate messages. Success or failure responses are formatted in this simple way: 'result': 'success'.

Bootpage is simply the Mojo Nation implementation for node discovery and is (was) updated from the main Mojo nation Web site. With current contact information for one or more meta trackers, the newly started Broker can subsequently query for other services that are online.

Table 8.5 lists the messages used for content management: block search, retrieval and publication, along with content tracking. Data is a "magic-pattern" demarcated 64KB block prepended with the string "'data':".

Initiating messages include requests for service and a Mojo IOU, while responding messages include acceptance or rejection of that offer. Higher-level application logic uses these messages as input to its business logic.

A respondent can check its local price list for services at the Mojo transaction layer to see if the offer is acceptable. Then if the initiator's credit limit (or reputation) is deemed good, the initiator's Mojo offer is acceptable, and the transaction fits within

Table 8.5 *Block search, retrieval and publication, with content tracking*

Message type	Response	Description
do you have blocks	List of available block IDs	Contains a list of block IDs that the client wants to locate.
request block	Stored data	Specifies a single block ID that the client wants to download.
put block	Success/failure	Contains data contents of a single block for the block server to store.
content tracker submit	Success/failure	Contains XML-encoded metadata describing content, includes the MojoID (used as retrieval key on subsequent retrievals).
content tracker lookup	List of XML metadata and retrieval key	Contains an XML description of a database query on metadata. The expected result is a list of matches to the query.

the credit limit, the respondent accepts the IOU (by sending a message with the appropriate response) and provides the service.

Messages related to the use of relay servers are listed in Table 8.6. Earlier sections describe how relay servers assist clients that are behind firewalls and can't accept incoming connections. It only takes a few message types to implement this support. Note especially that the public key encryption used ensures that only the correct recipient can decode the messages passed along in this way.

Table 8.6 *Relay messages*

Message type	Response	Description
pass this along	Success/failure	Contains a recipient Broker ID and an encrypted message (only decodable by recipient).
are there messages	List of queued messages	Is sent empty to the relay server as a request to start relaying messages, including any queued.
message for you	Success/failure	Relay server sends this to Broker containing encrypted message (usually received with a pass this along message).

TABLE 8.7   *Payment messages*

Message type	Response	Description
payment	Success/failure	Contains a list of digitally signed tokens sent from Broker to Broker.
withdrawal	Digitally signed token, or failure	Contains a randomly generated token seed used by a token server to generate a token ID if there is adequate balance on the Broker's account.
deposit	Success/failure	Contains a digitally signed token to be deposited with a token server. If validated, server credits the Broker's account.

Finally, Table 8.7 details the messages used for payment management, including withdrawal and deposit of tokens with a token server. Again, only three simple messages are required for all aspects of token management.

REPUTATION MANAGEMENT

Aside from the integrated micropayment system to manage resources, a feature of Mojo Nation is a flexible "reputation" system that can be used in a variety of ways.

Each Broker maintains a local database of reputations for other Brokers. This includes a list of those with which it has done business, along with information about those transactions, such as

- Response times to queries
- Dependability for being online when queried
- Reliability for content and information delivery
- Extended credit limit

Credit rating is one practical example of a reputation value associated with each Broker. This value determines how much trust an agent will grant another at the start of their first conversation.

Integrating the payment system with a reputation system provides interesting alternative metrics for evaluating and seeking suitable levels of QoS. Especially interesting is how QoS issues can all be kept in the background by applying configurable rule sets. It enables users to make decisions to pay extra to retrieve data from block servers with reputations for low latency or to use a low-priority queue for background retrieval during times of low demand within the network.

But what happens for instance if one Broker tries to cheat another by not delivering promised information or services? With reputation management, neither fraud detection protocols nor third-party consultations are required for resolution of nondelivery situations. The requesting Broker just reduces the local reputation value of the other and instead completes the desired transaction with a different agent.

> **Bit 8.9   No single agent in Mojo Nation has a monopoly on anything.**
> The Mojo Nation network model ensures that there are always other agents with the same information or service.

RELAY SERVICES

So far, little has been said about relay services. They are a workaround to the common problem of potential peer users who are located behind firewalls and NAT services, or are otherwise blocked from accepting random incoming Internet connections (for instance, dial-up users with dynamic IP).

In Mojo Nation, Brokers must always be able to accept initiating queries from other agents. A relay service on another peer can cache incoming messages outside the firewall or NAT, acting as store-and-forward service, until the shielded or offline Broker makes an outgoing connection to retrieve them.

The relay server acts like a mailbox drop for Brokers that register with it. The situation is shown in Figure 8.6. This works because of the broadcast nature of messages on the network. The relay server simply listens for messages addressed to its registered clients and stores them locally.

A Broker that wants to use a relay service first asks a meta tracker for available agents that are providing relay services. It applies its business logic to the list to determine the "best buy" and contacts the node with a request for service and offer of Mojo. When an offer is accepted, the relay server registers the client, and the shielded Broker starts a regular polling of its message mailbox there.

Relay servers are a constant drain on the subscribing Broker's Mojo, providing a stronger motivation for it to sell some of its resources—typically offering block storage. Conversely, for Brokers that are in a position to offer relay services, providing the service becomes a regular source of Mojo revenue. The sums involved are never great, but do add up in the long run.

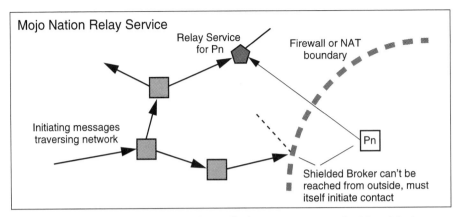

FIGURE 8.6   *A relay service allows firewalled participation in the Mojo Nation network by caching blocked initiating messages. The shielded Broker initiates periodic connections to fetch stored messages for processing.*

MNNET

As a last-minute postscript to the discussion of Mojo Nation, it should be noted that mojonation.net is no longer live in early 2002, and neither is the public network. The following message by CEO Jim McCoy was posted to the user list on 4 Feburary 2002 (archived as www.geocrawler.com/archives/3/5025/2002/2/0/7740786/):

> *After more than a year of testing the public prototype for the MojoNation technology platform we are shutting down the public network. The Mojo Nation technology will continue to be available via the soon to be announced MNnet project, of which more information will be made available at the CodeCon conference.*
>
> *It is expected that MNnet will remove several of the remaining centralized features of the Mojo Nation technology and result in a somewhat simplified version of the current system along with native Uis and other fun features.*

Subsequent postings discussed why MNnet is worth pursuing, one reason being the situation of nearly free storage but costly bandwidth for content-providing sites.

The development company Evil Genius for a Better Tomorrow, creator of the Mojo Nation protocol, is reportedly in hibernation after running out of funding, and all the developers were let go. EGBT also ran the mojonation.net and token servers, so there may be a connection with the stated intent of dropping centralized features. Commercial versions might also be on the horizon.

SWARMCAST

An implementation that has a more explicit focus on swarm distribution of content split into many different parts is Swarmcast (www.opencola.com, and developer site opencola.org since August 2001). It relies on central server mediation to administer content for a network of distributed clients.

Swarmcast is promoted as a high-speed content *distribution* system for large files, rather than a file-sharing system. Publishers of very large content files with expected great demand can efficiently and reliably distribute these files to many users with low bandwidth costs. Users experience that they can download large files faster and more reliably because the swarming technology adapts to demand both by scaling storage allocation and replicating content closer to the points of demand.

The Swarmcast solution has two key components:

- Swarmcast Gateway, which is a commercial piece of server software. It in effect publishes content as parts to swarms (or "meshes") of nodes, and later distributes each received user download request to the nodes available to serve up all the parts of the requested file.

- Swarmcast Client, which is the software that end users can download free of charge. They install it on their local machines to enable download of swarmcasted files.

The technology can be customized to work with other applications, such as download managers, software updaters and, as it happens, file-sharing applications.

It's implicit in much of the available documentation around Swarmcast that the primary market focus is on specific "content providers" who need to distribute information to many distributed users. This focus is evident in a number of design decisions, including the heavy reliance on a central gateway server.

This reliance clearly provides the commercial hook for the venture, although from the technology point of view, it also contributes a number of performance and control benefits—more properly seen as tradeoffs—as long as one is not overly concerned with the issue of a central point of failure, for example.

An open-access version of Swarmcast was run by the OpenCola company and offered a trial server gateway at no charge to demonstrate what it is like to swarmcast files. The intent was to show how much bandwidth (and money) the technology can save. The company is lately reported as moribund, but the Swarmcast software is available as open source from www.sourceforge.net/projects/swarmcast.

TABLE 8.8   *Swarmcast component summary*

Component	Specific forms	Comments
Identity	Internal representation based on IP.	Many-to-many peer connectivity is mediated through central gateway server.
Presence	Not applicable, although gateway tracks online nodes, their requests, and stage of download.	Users go online only to download content and their clients, then form informal meshes based on common content download.
Roster	Internal, maintained by gateway based on current content request.	Gateway directs online nodes with applicable packets to send them to other requesting peers.
Agency	Gateway, client.	Functionality can be tweaked by supplier.
Browsing	Central content list based on content provider publishing to central server.	There is no permanent distributed peer storage as such. Sharing occurs at packet level during download.
Architecture	Distributed, transient swarms of single kind of client software.	Content-centric. Clients request server-published content using unique hashed keys.
Protocol	HTTP, transport-layer agnostic.	Similar to streaming media, little negotiation between nodes.

The component summary for Swarmcast is in Table 8.8. Like Mojo Nation, Swarmcast is essentially a monoclient architecture because of the gateway server, and the summary closely corresponds to the actual network characteristics. Client extensions and customizations are possible for different environments.

How It Works

Swarmcast is based on how Web clients normally request files from HTTP Web servers. It provides a content-centric architecture, where content originally is published and resides on a central server. Each file is assigned a unique hashed key (SHA-1), which ensures data integrity and name independence, and allows authentication and privacy functionality. The chosen key system incidentally also allows integration with other key-based distributed networks such as Freenet.

The requirement for fast and reliable data transfer to many users is addressed in two main ways: providing multiple p2p paths to reduce bandwidth demand on each, and an advanced redundancy encoding of the parts being transferred. The intent is to aggressively push demanded content out into a local network of interested peers, freeing central bandwidth and minimizing the data path for most nodes.

In its basic implementation, Swarmcast technology doesn't really maintain a persistent p2p network at all. It instead assumes a normal, central server as the ultimate source for all content. This central source is all that users are aware of, and it can be in a remote location, or perhaps mirrored in traditional ways.

Users browse and request particular files through their respective clients, which then connect to the server through the gateway to download. Initially then, it's the central content server that provides the download. The file is split into identifiable encoded packets by the gateway and sent to the clients. Single requests to a particular file are therefore not much different from normal client-server downloads.

Leveraged Bandwidth

Things get more interesting when many users request the same file. The gateway then cycles through the file's packets, distributing them randomly among the requesting clients. Each node thus receives only a portion of the original packets, but the client software is also made aware of some of the other nodes receiving packets from the same file. As these nodes receive packets, they also rebroadcast them to each other. File packets are rapidly swapped back and forth between nodes in the mesh, at full LAN and client capacity, unconstrained by server bandwidth.

> **Bit 8.10 Swarmcast forms transient networks (meshes) based on demand.**
> As users connect to the gateway server for their own downloads, their clients are drafted into temporary p2p meshes to serve received parts of the same content to other users who want to download this data at the same time.

Recall that the distribution was made random by the gateway. Nodes check received packets to see if they are useful in reconstructing the requested file. The gateway's distribution makes it very likely that swapped packets help complete the download. The packet-encoding scheme ensures that packets can be received in any order, and when enough useful packets have been received, the file is decoded.

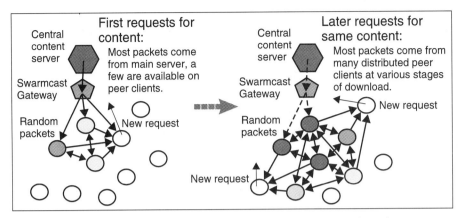

FIGURE 8.7   *Requesting clients form informal swarms or meshes based on common content. Within each mesh, clients rebroadcast packets to other peers requesting the same information, thus offloading the main server.*

Once a node has reassembled its requested file, it may leave the mesh. This is optional, however, and users can keep their computers as part of the mesh for some time after they've finished downloading. By staying in the mesh, these users make it easier for others to download the same content, because their complete copies of downloaded file packets are all available for immediate rebroadcast.

This file-swapping behavior between nodes progressively offloads the central server as demand increases and moves the bulk of transfer loading out into the mesh of clients interested in the same content. What the gateway server does, therefore, is leverage the bandwidth of other clients that are still downloading or have just finished downloading content.

In cases of high demand for the same files, and thus many nodes forming the download mesh, the growing availability of other nodes that can supply parts of the same content will eventually saturate any single client's download capacity. At this point, once it has served a complete copy of the content, the central server no longer needs to answer any requests because they are fulfilled by the mesh. The network's evolution towards peer serving is indicated by Figure 8.7.

Load Adaptation

Dynamic meshing is the basis for the scalability and load adaptation in Swarmcast. As demand increases, so too does the distributed availability of this content. Given enough clients, they eventually all download from parallel sources at their respective peak throughput. Meanwhile the server is free to handle requests for other content.

New meshes automatically form around nodes that download other content, again progressively offloading the server. Fallback behavior occurs as the mesh contracts with a decreasing number of connected clients, until they can no longer fill the demand, after which the gateway once again passes requests to the central server.

A side effect of this solution is that the same content server can be used to fulfill requests from both Swarmcast users and non-Swarmcast ones at the same time. The former's clients connect to the gateway and reap the benefits this allows, while the latter use their traditional clients to connect directly to the main server as before.

> **Bit 8.11 Swarmcast is a plug-in solution.**
> The technology is implemented as a self-contained interaction between the two components—gateway and client—that provide an alternative, parallel data path.

In this respect, Swarmcast is a plug-in p2p technology that doesn't require retrofit measures to existing servers and clients. It simply adds another, more efficient distribution channel that offloads the central server. As a side effect, this makes content distribution more efficient even for the old-technology clients, because the new or migrated clients won't be competing for the same bandwidth.

Redundancy Encoding

The second important feature implemented in this technology is the use of **Forward Error Correction (FEC)** encoding to boost reliability in the transfer. The encoding has the additional feature of making Swarmcast largely independent of network protocol.

Many network applications use some form of FEC to provide fault tolerance. Figure 8.8 shows the block-encoding principle employed in Swarmcast, Redundant FEC (RFEC). Recovery is possible even when a large number of packets are lost during transfer. It doesn't matter *which* packets are received, only that a minimum number of correctly decodable ones arrive, in any order.

Although the redundancy introduced by such encoding, on the face of it, would increase bandwidth demand for the same content, it isn't so in practice. First, the method allows a more lax transfer protocol with less messages between nodes. Download can be treated almost like streaming media—declared complete as soon as the client has received enough verified correct data packets to reconstruct the file. For this reason, there is usually no need to send *all* the encoded data, only a sufficient subset—that is to say, until the client says "Enough!"

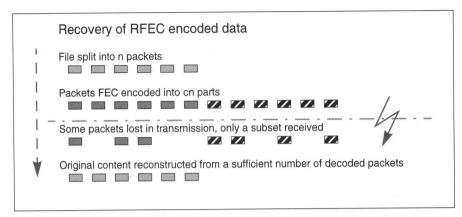

FIGURE 8.8 *Redundant forward error correction encoding works by allowing recovery of original data as long as a sufficient number of redundancy encoded packets are received and correctly decoded.*

Reliable transfer without redundancy and error correction otherwise normally means that packets need to be individually acknowledged, and all must be received correctly. If any packets are missed or damaged, the client must ask for them to be resent, perhaps many times if the network is heavily loaded. In this context, deteriorating network performance tends to rapidly spiral into even worse conditions as the number of resend requests escalate with falling performance.

An analysis or some textbook numbers based on a single-source multicast situation can illustrate the bandwidth gains from using FEC. Suppose that 10,000 users are receiving a multicast transmission and that the average rate of packet loss is 10 percent. In traditional reliable protocols (such as TCP), all of the packets are broadcast—sent and resent—until all recipients have acknowledged each and every one. Assuming an independent loss spread for the different users in this example, each packet ends up being transmitted on average approximately five times.

Compare this bandwidth-consuming situation with one where the transmission is arbitrarily partitioned into 100,000 packets and an FEC is used to add 25,000 redundant packets to the transmission (this is a configurable relationship). All packets are now sent just *once*. Then, it's a sufficient requirement that no user loses more than 25,000 packets (in other words, a maximum of at most about twice the average loss rate) for all users to receive enough of the encoding to reliably decode the message.

Let's restate the two fundamental facts about FEC transfer for emphasis:

- *Packet reception does not have to be acknowledged!*

- *No resends are necessary!*

Total bandwidth usage at the same loss rate as the original retransmission situation is here *factor four smaller*, without even considering the packet-handshaking overhead that can be saved using a much simpler protocol.

The simple multicast example was based on an ideal FEC encoding, which turns out to be too slow in practical implementation for larger files. A randomized, "irregular" FEC (IFEC) encoding scheme therefore was devised by Michael Luby and Michael Mitzenmacher to allow faster implementations.

IFEC allows encoding and decoding in a time proportional to the length of the encoding, multiplied by a small constant (typical value around 5), which is independent of the number of redundant packets. Encoding and decoding times of standard FEC codes by contrast are proportional to the length of the encoding multiplied by the number of redundant packets—clearly a much larger factor (by many orders of magnitude) for all but the smallest files.

In general, the irregular algorithm can be designed for any chosen trade-off between reliability margins and acceptable size/time overhead. Typical IFEC decoding times for multimegabyte-size files is less than a second with current processor speeds.

IFEC Applied to Swarmcast

The mesh of Swarmcast nodes available to send arbitrary subsets of received packets can be seen in one sense as a variably space/time-distributed multicast source. Hence, the IFEC solution is directly applicable to the situation. It doesn't matter from which nodes individual packets come, or in what order; the IFEC encoding ensures that correct reassembly is possible at the client, regardless.

In fact, no explicit interaction at all between the downloading users and the packet-sending node is even required—which is why FEC-based encoding is so frequently used for streaming media and true multicast situations. Variations also turn up in many p2p solutions to avoid loading bandwidth with heavy handshaking protocols that verify reception of each packet at each recipient.

The Swarmcast gateway can orchestrate a cyclic broadcast of constituent packets for any file from a server, and an arbitrary and changing mesh of receiving nodes until all requests for that file are satisfied.

Reliability in Swarmcast is actually improved as demand increases, because more nodes are available to send more parts of the file in parallel. Whenever possible, Swarmcast design avoids reliance on a single source for download—a design principle that goes well with transient, distributed networks.

MINIMAL KNOWLEDGE SOLUTION

Swarmcast is an example of the minimal knowledge agent approach. The gateway has minimal knowledge of the contents of the packets, of where they're going, or of the state of the network in general. This approach turns out to be good for efficiency, and some of the reasons why are explained in the following list:

- Randomization introduces deliberate chaos to combat the chaos of unstable, rapidly changing network conditions. An easier way of saying this is that if you're not attempting to enforce any particular order, then external changes often won't matter—disorder can be ignored.

- Minimal state-aware logic makes the technology workable in situations with rapidly changing state. Simple systems are often self-organizing—in other words, you don't need to explicitly care about the details.

- No feedback is required, which promotes stability. Out-of-sync feedback, caused by disorder and delays, worsens the conditions it's supposed to help. Hence, even high-latency networks are not a problem.

- Ignorance of global state means not trying to negotiate between hosts, thus saving sometimes considerable communications overhead and delay.

- Ignorance of state allows a small and fast implementation. There's less to worry about, so there's less code to worry about. Implementations focus on the primary task, moving data.

The bottom line then for Swarmcast technology: an aggressive "send-and-forget" attitude that proves surprisingly robust even in adverse conditions. In most cases, performance actually improves with loading conditions that would bring traditional distribution methods to a standstill.

What Swarmcast in particular doesn't try to address, however, is dependence on a central content server. This puts the technology slightly on the margins of this p2p survey, because the peer clients, from the user point of view, are merely recipients of centrally published content, and users really see only this server, not the peers. I chose to include it because of the way its simple-minded focus on distribution allows an undistracted analysis of distributed swarming technology. A similar swarmcasting strategy is in fact employed in a popular file-sharing client, e-Donkey2K.

In the next chapter, Freenet shows another, in some ways similar approach, this time designed for adaptive distribution of persistent content published by anyone, without any central server, with the added bonus of secure anonymity.

Persistent and Anonymous Solutions

Reasons to encrypt content stored on the Internet can be many, but a dominant theme is the persistence of published information, and the ability to successfully resist all attempts to either remove or change data. Practical solutions that ensure data persistency are found in a p2p context because one of the best safeguards is to not have any centralized storage or administration that could be compromised.

By many advocates seen as the original, now subverted purpose of the Internet as a whole, distributed and encrypted p2p solutions such as Freenet are viewed as the vanguard of a new Internet paradigm that will once again make information and its expression free—fundamental rights available to everyone.

This area is controversial, however, with strong and vocal fractions on either side. The kind of absolute freedom implied here is anathema to governments and corporations alike, no matter how open and liberal they profess to be. The fact that freedom of exchange in digital media has come to be on a collision course with commercial intellectual property rights protection (of text, music, images, and so on) has simply exacerbated the problem very quickly.

Nevertheless, the subject of encrypted and secure storage in a p2p context is an important one. In this chapter, we especially examine Freenet as a focus application to discuss the issues relevant to the subject. We showcase it as an ambitious technology to implement one possible solution to adaptive storage—one that's just begun to show promise as an enterprise solution as well.

CHAPTER 9 AT A GLANCE

This chapter looks at an interesting and evolving technology for totally secure, anonymous publishing of content and explains a form of distributive adaptive storage based on demand.

The public test and developer network of *Freenet* is used as an platform for discussing the advanced encryption and trust systems that make up a secure network.

- *Concept of Freedom* outlines the rationale behind Freenet and the main design goals.

- *How It Works* explains the overall functionality in simple terms, and in particular, the unusual and seemingly indirect way in which content is stored and retrieved. This includes how to publish content and a quick look at some of the client software available for Freenet.

- In *Trust and Content Veracity*, we examine a number of security issues and ask just how robust the network can be.

- *Protocol Details* presents the underlying protocol for how clients talk to nodes and nodes to each other to realize the functionality. The as-yet fluid issue of *Node Discovery* is explored with a summary of the current methods used by a node wishing to join.

- The *Malicious Nodes* section addresses a serious problem all p2p technologies must face. This leads to a general discussion on Freenet *Scalability and Stability*.

- *Practical Installation* comes late in this chapter, mainly because of Freenet's prototype status. Some of the other issues under development are taken up in the section on *Ongoing Work*.

- Finally, *Business Solutions* takes a quick look at how Freenet technology is recently emerging in commercial products aimed at business. *Related Work* adds a few last-minute references.

FREENET

Freenet (www.freenetproject.org) is defined as an open, democratic content storage-and-retrieval system that cannot be controlled by anyone, not even its creators. Called a "censorship-proof" network, by design no one can know the location of a specific piece of information. Consequently, no person or operator can be held accountable for storage of any particular piece of content.

Originally conceived by Ian Clarke as an information publication system similar to the World Wide Web, the Freenet Protocol (FNP) improves on the Web server model by its inherent characteristics of content being distributed, decentralized, and encrypted. Its self-organizing behavior automatically replicates and moves information nearer to points of high demand, thus distributing loading as well. FNP is open, allowing anyone to implement software for it.

Freenet is often called one of the "big threes" of p2p in name recognition (along with Gnutella and Napster), which is rather remarkable considering that it's still essentially a prototype network for debugging basic functionality issues.

While in many respects much of the public attention has been more about the *concept* than any real implementation, an evolving functional network has existed in the wild since March 2000. The open source (Java-based) model is rapidly being developed by a growing number of volunteers, and the code base was at version 0.4x in late 2001, with release 0.5 likely out by the time this book is published.

Freenet information, sources, compiled software, community and discussions are currently found at Sourceforge (freenet.sourceforge.net), where Ian Clarke is the project coordinator. Although Java implementations are preferred for cross-platform compatibility, any developmental language is accepted as long as the software remains compliant with the protocol. The basic Freenet software requires an installed recent (v1.1) Java runtime environment (a JRE such as Sun, IBM, Kaffe, etc.).

The summary component list is provided in Table 9.1.

CONCEPT OF FREEDOM

The concept of Freenet has to do with absolute freedom of speech, among other issues, because the technology is based on the idea that published content must be impossible to remove or censor, by anyone, ever.

Ian Clarke says that early thinking about the Freenet design, around 1998, working towards his thesis in 1999, was based on a kind of philosophical interest in addition to the technical interest. He says he felt concern about increasing moves to

TABLE 9.1   *Component summary for Freenet.*

Component	Specific forms	Comments
Identity	Unique message descriptor ID derived from current IP number and port, content keys from hashed descriptors.	No active support or direct naming scheme for active nodes, but only tracking of message ID and content keys. Users may be anonymous yet verifiable with digital signatures.
Presence	Not applicable for user, assumed 24/7 for nodes.	Client/server infrastructure, not tied to personal presence.
Roster	N/A	Nodes know only of their nearest connection neighbors.
Agency	Publishing and retrieval, other extended services.	Network nodes act on behalf of requesting user via client, who can't directly access distributed content or services.
Browsing	Optional, then usually of Web-type pages with hyperlinks.	Client-bundled plug-in allows browsing content with Web browser. Application gateway gives access from Web.
Architecture	Atomistic, unmapped, with persistent information identity.	Reach bounded by hop count. Topology and storage locations change with demand.
Protocol	Open, HTTP, encrypted.	Hashed key identification of content used for retrieval, public-key for signature.

impose censorship on the Internet, which were then nowhere near as serious threats to the free flow of information as he has seen in the past few years. He also found it curious that while nature's designs are invariably decentralized and damage resistant, humans almost always design highly centralized and very vulnerable systems.

Therefore, a core thrust to the effort to implement Freenet is an active decision to deploy technology that would withstand the increased efforts to both monitor and censor the Internet in dubious ways that simply wouldn't be tolerated if applied to more conventional means of communication, such as the postal service or the telephone networks. Hence also the decision to make encryption an integral part of the system, which has several benefits.

Besides safeguarding data from manipulation, encryption (and associated digital signatures) also allows a kind of trust system to evolve. Thus, anyone can prove from the signature that particular documents originate from particular, verifiable sources, even if these choose to remain anonymous or to use a (possibly collective) pseudonym.

The key issues that Freenet development addresses are summarized as follows:

- There is no centralized control or administration of the network. It's by design not even possible.

- Anyone can easily publish information, even if they lack permanent Internet connectivity or identity.

- Both publishing authors and readers may at their discretion remain anonymous. More accurately, they are anonymous until they explicitly move to divulge their real identity in some way.

- Despite full author anonymity, documents can be verified as originating from a particular source.

- In practice, it's impossible to forcibly remove information from a Freenet network. In fact, it is difficult to even localize particular information—even operators can't determine what content is stored on their local server.

- Availability of information should increase proportionately with demand, move closer to the demand, and decrease to release resources when it isn't.

Application of this technology can be varied. The obvious one is publishing information in a way that can't be censored. It's not feasible in Freenet to discover the true origin, storage locations, destination, or content of files passing through the network, and thus it's difficult for node operators to determine or be held accountable for the actual physical contents of their respective nodes.

Freenet additionally enables anyone to have a free Web site, without space restrictions or advertising banners, even without owning a computer. Needless to say, this kind of viewable content is protected in the same way as stored files.

Less obvious perhaps is how the adaptive caching and availability behavior in practical terms translates as increased bandwidth for high-demand content, making it easier to reliably distribute software updates for Linux, for example. Although not a dedicated distribution technology, as for example Swarmcast (discussed earlier, in Chapter 8), the two share some functional characteristics in their "swarm" adaptability to supply content demand.

How It Works

It can take a while to fully grasp how Freenet works and the power of the design. This is partly because Freenet is actually several different concepts tightly integrated into a synergetic whole that is more than just the sum of its parts.

The primary concept is to be a fully decentralized network, where each Freenet node acts freely and independently. The Freenet system operates at the application layer and requires an existing secure transport layer. It provides anonymity only for Freenet file transactions, not for general network usage.

Consider a request for information by some user. The information has a persistent identity in the network: the document key we use to retrieve it. The document must obviously be stored *somewhere*, and while storage is location-based after a fashion, we can't know in advance *which* location.

The request is initially made to a local node—or more specifically, to a node the user knows and trusts. In practice, this often means a copy of Freenet server software running on the user's own computer, but it could also be an arbitrary Freenet node contacted over the Internet. If this node already has the information, then the relevant document is retrieved, decoded, and presented to the user. End of story.

When the information is not available locally, the node forwards the request to another node that it considers more likely to have that particular piece of information. This determination of "most likely" hinges on a stack model that stores information about recently requested documents and the immediate address they came from.

> **Bit 9.1   Only the first contacted node knows the user's identity and location.**
> Subsequent forwarding of requests to other nodes does not pass on any user information, nor the identity of the node where the request originally came from.

To resolve request routing when a new node starts up, and therefore doesn't have any transfer history on which to base its request routing decision, dummy entries with random keys are put on the stack for each other node it knows about. Subsequent transfers allow the node to make better routing decisions later.

When each document is originally published, it is assigned a generated identity key, which in some meaningful, rather complex way, reflects a concept of "closeness" based on how its content relates to other "similar" documents that are then stored in close proximity in the network. In practical terms, the routing decision is made on the basis of the key numerically closest to the requested document's key, and the request is forwarded to its associated node address.

As documents pass through any node in the network, they leave behind on the stack this minimum trace: the document key and the address it just came from. For a transient time, the actual document content itself will also linger on the stack—this kind of "stickiness" is often called "lazy" replication. On the stack, it rises or sinks depending on weighted factors such as its size (that is, resource consumption), its request frequency, and its source (proven by trust-signature), until it is displaced by more recent documents. Keys and addresses, on the other hand, expire less rapidly and so have a greater "depth" and persistence in the stack. They then act as pointers to "previous" nodes where the content might still be stored.

> **Bit 9.2   Freenet's routing choices and performance improve over time.**
> This hypothesis is confirmed by actual network behavior. Successful requests align upstream pointers so that subsequent requests can find both related content quicker and the same content cached at closer locations.

The immediate stack-determined destination might not be where the document is stored, but it's likely to be "closer", and presumably that node in turn will be able to forward the request to a node even closer, and so on, until the request finally reaches a node that has a copy of the document. Requests are assigned unique identity numbers for tracking purposes and to allow suppression of copies in loops, and they leave stack traces in order to allow responses to be passed back along the chain.

If for any reason a node can't forward a request to its preferred downstream node, the node having the second-nearest key is tried, then the third-nearest, and so on. For practical reasons common to all query-forwarding systems, requests are assigned a hops-to-live (HTL) value, typically 20 to 30 hops. This value is always decremented for each try to ensure that the request eventually dies no matter what. This value may seem high, but unlike in the TTL discussion in Chapter 7, Freenet queries are routed. A node that runs out of paths to try reports failure back to its upstream neighbor, which will then try *its* second choice, etc. This is known as a *steepest-ascent hill-climbing search with backtracking*.

If the HTL limit is exceeded, no further nodes are tried at any level. Instead, a failure result is propagated back to the original requestor. Nodes may unilaterally clamp excessive HTL values to reduce network load. They may also time out pending requests to keep message memory free.

A document that fulfills a request is returned to the node from which the request came, and it is forwarded back along the chain until it reaches the request origin node. For each step, this document's key, previous node address, and content is copied onto the forwarding node's stack.

> **Bit 9.3   Freenet requests and hence users are in practical terms anonymous.**
> Because each node knows only the address of the previous forwarding node, it is very difficult (albeit not totally impossible) to identify the original requesting node. This proxy chaining suffices to guarantee the anonymity of Freenet users, even though it's really only a form of obscurity granted by an indeterminate number of proxies.

Successful requests for information thus automatically result in it being propagated across the network. In addition, it at least for a while moves nearer the requests. As noted, the request passes through a number of computers in order to reach a computer that stores a copy of the document, and when that is passed back, further copies are stored on all the computers that participated in the request.

> **Bit 9.4   Nearness to a node is totally unrelated to geographical proximity.**
> It's easy to forget at times that the notion of distance in a p2p network relates to the number of connection hops between computers essentially distributed at random across the globe, not any real geographical distance.

The overall result of demand propagation is that the more requests for a given piece of information, the more widely distributed it becomes for the duration of those requests. Conversely, as the frequency of requests goes down, then the content copies gradually expire and the distribution contracts, freeing network resources.

Another important result behind the scenes is that, as nodes process requests, they create new routing table entries for previously unknown nodes that supply files, increasing overall useful connectivity. This helps new nodes to discover more of the network through *direct links* to data sources, subsequently bypassing the intermediate nodes used on first requests.

The Storage Model

Somewhere, there must be an ultimate source cluster for each published document.
However, clustering is an automatic side-effect of the caching described earlier,
working in conjunction with the closeness algorithm for keys. Perhaps surprisingly to
some readers, there is no *a priori* assignment of content distribution.

In a newly started Freenet, the random seeding of each new node's stack,
described earlier, means that the initially stored documents will have a fairly random
distribution, because key routing will be random. As more documents are inserted,
stored information begin to cluster based on "nearness" to other keys, based on the
gradual alignment of node traces and caching of content—it becomes self-organizing.

Routine node interactions therefore spontaneously let certain nodes emerge as
what we could call authoritative sources for particular ranges of key values. This is
because they will simply be referenced most often for data with keys close to
documents they initially store and have fulfilled requests for. Requests for close
documents that aren't currently stored simply end up fetching copies from elsewhere.
Frequent requests subsequently maintain cached copies of the content in this closeness
range, or **keyspace**, while copies elsewhere just tend to expire sooner.

There is actually a balance in force between this clustering effect and the way a
frequently requested document is replicated across larger segments of the network.
The latter spread tends to break up tight clusters and promote the formation of
similar clusters in different parts of the network. Because the "closeness" relation that
defines a cluster is based on a hash with no real correlation to semantic meaning, and
hence user popularity, clustering is also unrelated to possible request demand for
semantically related data. This is one of the mechanisms that reduces the risk for
bottlenecks in the system, because it's highly unlikely that there will be demand peaks
for many documents from the same cluster at the same time.

This emerging keyspace specialization depends on random references held by
other nodes and is thus impossible to self-determine. It evolves from the overall
behavior of the network, might change over time, and is as noted earlier completely
decoupled from any notion of geographical location or clustering of nodes. Were that

not the case, then a given node could be subverted to specialize in a particular keyspace and subsequently manipulated to deny access to that content.

Hashing the namespace into numeric keys resolves the problem of namespace management, which otherwise would easily compromise the fully distributed model because administration implies some form of centralization. However, hashing does introduce a few problems of its own, as the current mechanism handles document names on a first-come-first-served basis. Human-readable document names have a strong tendency to cluster around particular ranges, which results in an unnecessarily high risk for key contention between different documents. A little bit of democracy is implemented in the hashing assignment to prevent what the developers call DNS-style abuse of the mechanism, but solutions for better implemented "management" are being discussed, and expected to be deployed in perhaps a 0.5x release.

Leveraged Retrieval

The routing concept of closeness also enhances retrieval functionality, because requests are handled more effectively than linear search (that is, visit all nodes) and much more efficiently than broadcast search (request in all directions). It's a node-directed, single-path search that's always improving as more requests get fulfilled.

In general, numerous studies of request propagation as routed in Freenet all confirm that in the average case, a request for information will require log(n) hops to retrieve information from a network of size n. This is reasonable efficiency even in very large networks—increasing size just means it gets better compared to other methods. Add to this the way Freenet storage adapts to successful request history.

The secret ingredient in closeness efficiency is the self-organizing structure of this kind of adaptive content storage. To begin with, content replicates closer to the nodes where it is requested, leaving a trace on intervening nodes, which both reduces retrieval latency and improves the efficiency of future searches. A second important effect is that insertion of new content occurs at nodes that are "closest" in terms of key comparison, which by itself optimizes future search and retrieval for even the very first attempt to find new content.

One beneficial consequence is that network message load remains relatively low and adaptively well balanced, and Freenet therefore scales better both for increased content and for more nodes. Such automatic load balancing incidentally makes the network as a whole quite resistant to common kinds of DoS or "flooding" attacks. The nodes act to concentrate request fulfilment to the nodes closest to such an attack, thereby localizing the damaging effects to just a few nodes.

Note that true search based on content or actual names as understood in other p2p storage models is not yet implemented in Freenet. Published content must be advertised or circulated outside the system, with potentially detrimental effects on user anonymity—e-mail lists, newsgroups, Web sites, special servers. Users have created external databases or lists that associate particular names, content keywords, or content extracts with assigned Freenet keys. Such compilations are assuredly searchable but often out of date. Retrieval in Freenet is strictly by known numeric key—a user must first obtain or calculate a file's hashed binary key, then send a request message to a trusted node specifying that key and suitable HTL value.

Granted, search capability to Freenet can easily be added just by running an ordinary hypertext spider like those used to search the Web—content is browsable. Although this solution might seem attractive, it conflicts with the design goal of avoiding centralization. Instead, users are encouraged to create their own special interest index compilations within Freenet, like the original indexing of the Web.

To preserve anonymity and security, Freenet's protocol recently defined In-Freenet Key Indices, a system that provides a way for data publishers to advertise inserted keys within the system so that other people can get to the data. There's a bootstrap problem here, however, which always returns in various guises in any fully decentralized system. In this case: *How do you find the index?*

The answer to that conundrum is yet to be implemented. For now, the developers can only recommend following the Freenet mailing lists, existing Web key lists, or Freenet Web sites to spot references to any node described there as an index server and to note down its associated Key Index Identifier. You can then use it with the normal Freenet tools to publish your keys to the list and search for others. Users are also encouraged to set up their own (probably special-interest) index keys, start collecting keys, and that way help build up the system.

A major and well-publicized source for off-Freenet index-related information is www.thalassocracy.org—in particular the section for keyindex. You can both browse and search for Freenet content and learn the keys associated with it.

Some clients try to incorporate their own indexing system. For example, the Windows client Frost (found at jtcfrost.sourceforge.net) maintains a compressed key-index that is shared among all online Frost clients. In contrast to the in-Freenet-indexes often used by other clients, Frost stores additional information: file size, date of last access, and checksum, along with a useful "key-score" to automatically delete "dead" keys. This last avoids creating huge indexes that might contain only a few valid keys. A sample search result in Frost is shown in Figure 9.1.

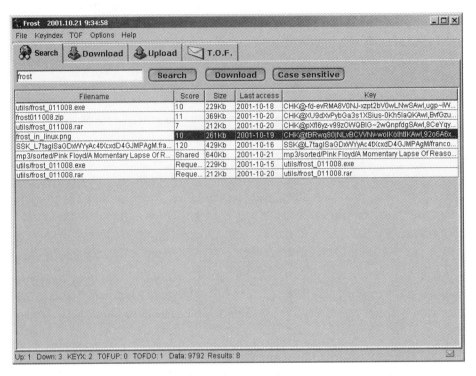

FIGURE **9.1** *Screenshot from the Freenet Frost client showing a list of files matching a search pattern, based on the built-in index shared among all active Frost clients. Note the hash key for each file, which is the identity needed to retrieve the file from the distributed storage.*

Besides key-retrieval, the user can also use FProxy, which is a Freenet plug-in included with the Freenet software and switched on by default. The plug-in allows the user to access Freenet through the host system's normal Web browser. In addition, gateways can allow access of Freenet content from anywhere on the Web, such as Freenet CGI Request Client (FCRC), which is included in the Freenet distribution.

Bit 9.6   Browsing and accessing content on Freenet is slow.

Compared to the Web, Freenet's usual latency—minutes rather than seconds—is the price paid for anonymity and encryption in the current implementation.

In practical terms, these solutions mean that one can surf Freenet in much the same way one might surf the Web, which is a convenient way to explore content that

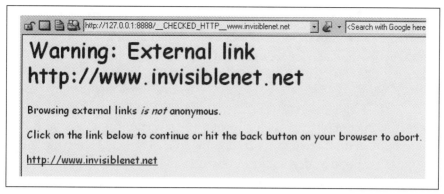

FIGURE 9.2 *Freenet links to the normal Web are formulated in a special way and invoke this click-through warning page, here seen from a local gateway.*

has been published as hyperlinked documents. Because of this visual similarity to normal Web browsing, links from Freenet pages to the normal Web are formatted in a special way to ensure that the user is made aware of the transition into "insecure" Web space. Following a link to an address located outside Freenet thus invokes a gateway-generated click-through page, as seen in the capture detail in Figure 9.2, reminding the user that Freenet anonymity ends here.

Can content ever be removed? No, and this is a core design issue. But it can "*expire*" and thus automatically disappear from the network.

Content Expiration

Content can—and will—in Freenet's design expire through lack of interest; when nobody wants to retrieve it over a period of time. If nobody wants it, then a reasonable question is: Why spend resources to store it?

A further constraint is due to the finite storage allocated by each node. When this allocated space is filled, further storage of more current content will displace least accessed content on the node's stack. This displacement is, of course, not fatal for a distributed document requested reasonably often, but it is a real source of attrition that becomes a factor in expiration for rarely requested content.

It's also inevitable with TTL and timeout constraints that some rarely requested content won't be found even when it exists somewhere. If some document is consistently not requested or found, Freenet's stack caching model ensures that sooner or later the last copy will automatically expire, no matter where it is.

Is this a bad thing? No, not necessarily.

> **Bit 9.7   Removal of expired documents is automatic, intrinsic node behavior.**
> Because removal depends on internal stack timers, maintained independently on individual nodes, the culling process cannot be controlled or manipulated based on file identity, and culled files are never identified when they are removed.

Freenet's stance is bluntly pragmatic in this context: As a network, it is not intended to be an eternal archive, nor is it going to try to assign content priorities. Instead, it just lets popular demand transparently and democratically determine what will remain available. As frequently requested content is replicated to optimize search, availability and bandwidth utilization, it also makes its retention almost certain.

Most storage systems implement some form of culling policy to remove "useless" data, either automatic or manual, based on various requirements and assessments. In many situations, it's a reasonable step to assume that content that is never requested is not (or no longer) relevant and should not continue to consume valuable finite network resources.

The distinction that Freenet very carefully preserves is to remove *unpopular* data, not *unwanted* data. If people aren't at all interested in some piece of information, that's one thing, but if people dislike it and actively remove it, that's a form of censorship even if the decision is based on a majority. This philosophical and political stance doesn't sit well with everyone, but it's valid nonetheless. And it leaves the choice of continued availability up to any single individual.

> **Bit 9.8   Fulfilled requests ensure continued document storage.**
> Anyone can easily and anonymously ensure that a particular document is not removed from storage by simply requesting it every so often. Failing that, the content can be reinserted by anyone who has a copy.

You might wonder if explicit removal is not an option, what about updates?

Trying to publish revised content under the same name generates the same key as the old version and is therefore denied due to the immutability of published content as the protocol was originally implemented. The denied attempt accesses the existing file in the same way as a normal request, delaying its expiration, and therefore actually serves to propagate the old version instead.

Later development modified this total immutability by allowing updates using the same digital signature as the original document. The application of this to publishing revised versions of content is discussed in detail in the later section about Freenet key types. An alternative or supplementary solution perhaps would be to implement some form of secure versioning system.

Publishing to Freenet

Publishing content to a Freenet network is somewhat involved at present, although a number of tools make the process more transparent to the user. However, it is not yet as easy for the user as Web-content publishing has become.

There is no requirement to be a member node of the network in order to publish. It is sufficient to be able to access an active node in some way; by client, gateway, or some other user interface to the Web.

One example of a publishing tool is the Frost client, mentioned earlier, which normally interfaces to a "localhost" instance of a Freenet server. The composite view in Figure 9.3 shows the tab views for both upload (or publish) and download (retrieve) sessions. The client enables a user to simply browse the local hard disk for a file to publish, then handles the details automatically. The index search facility, described earlier, makes selection for retrieval much easier than handling the long and opaque hashed keys that are the URI access mechanism for Freenet.

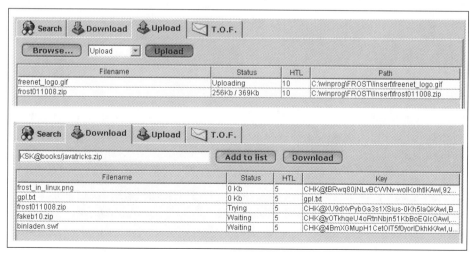

FIGURE 9.3   *Composite views from the Freenet Frost client showing both upload and download sessions. Note the hash key for each file, which is the identity needed to retrieve the file from the distributed storage.*

An increasingly popular Web-based publishing tool (only on Windows at present) is FreeWeb (found at freeweb.sourceforge.net), by David McNab—who also authored Psst, described in Chapter 6. Like many other Freenet applications, FreeWeb is strongly dependent on the current Freenet version.

Anyone can publish their own Web site content, for example, to the Freenet network—such sites are often called "freesites". This route avoids the usual problems associated with free Web hosts: content control, storage limits, and third-party advertising. Although freesites must have unique names, this naming scheme is internal to Freenet, unrelated to the usual domains or DNS services.

Unlike with traditional Web servers on the Web, a freesite originally had to be updated on a daily basis; otherwise, it would vanish. Newer client agents have eliminated this requirement, which was a consequence of the key-data immutability of cached storage model and of how the agent located and updated the published web. Changed freesite files are uploaded into different Freenet keys, as is a new "map" that defines the layout of the site.

Chances are, you wouldn't even notice when browsing the Web that you might have followed a hyperlink through a gateway system and were viewing published content stored as a freesite on Freenet. Only two things would be apparent on inspection: a marked and consistent latency in serving new page content and a URL that is somewhat more involved than your usual HTTP address. Neither characteristic is really that unusual even for normal Web sites, and server delays are far more common than users would like. Greater latency is a distinctive trait for Freenet content due to the overhead of encryption, however, and because of how content is stored and accessed. Mitigating this, popular content is served progressively faster as content gets automatically replicated nearer the requesting user.

Other Freenet Client Software

The documentation specifies a special subset of FNP for clients called Freenet Client Protocol (FCP), which is designed to abstract out the essentials of FNP so that client developers do not have to track the ever-evolving main protocol in all its gory details.

The intent is that FCP should embody the bare bones of FNP only—for example, metadata handling is not currently included in FCP. On the other hand, this subset protocol is never meant to go across a network but intended only for the loopback to a localhost server, so it doesn't need all the features of FNP. Server nodes therefore are designed to refuse FCP connections from hosts other than localhost by default.

This leads to some common characteristics of Freenet clients. They generally assume the existence of a local Freenet server and attempt to connect with it on a localhost port in the 8000 range. The clients may also assume the existence of a JRE, because it is a normal requirement of current server software.

FreeWeb author David McNab also provides FCPTools, a set of command-line tools that allow convenient insertion into Freenet of files (fcpput) or entire Web sites (fcpputsite). Also included in the set is FCPproxy, which is a small proxy that acts as a Freenet gateway for any URL starting with "http://free/" and will enable a normal Web browser to access known freesites. In addition, it performs useful filtering functions even when browsing the Web. As initially configured, the proxy attempts to connect with the local Freenet server on localhost port 8481; it listens on port 8000 for incoming messages. The configuration file explains other options.

Freesite publishers often want an anonymous way to allow feedback from readers. One of the most popular is Frost, a tool with a Usenet-like mechanism that operates anonymously over Freenet.

Freenet recently implemented a remote procedure call interface (XML-RPC) to a node, which is a simple and light protocol. Client software authors therefore no longer have to implement the complicated encryption and encoding needed to speak full FNP. The client doesn't even have to parse the protocol because it remotely accesses the node system's local API calls by way of a plug-in running on the node. Libraries to call methods using XML-RPC are already available from www.xmlrpc.com for many languages (such as Java, C, Python, Perl, PHP, Delphi, REBOL, Dylan, Tcl, ASP, COM, AppleScript, Ruby, Shell script, and C++).

Another area of application development for Freenet is collected under the Everything Over Freenet (EOF) project (at eof.sourceforge.net). The main headings found at this site include

- **Apt-get,** which is a Freenet version of the framework used for distributing Debian Linux packages over the Internet. An installed Debian system can thus automatically search and fetch updates from Freenet.

- **Mail,** which is a prototype of both the general e-mail transport using Freenet infrastructure and a server to provide the mailbox service. Not without some problems, but reported working. Stock e-mail clients communicate with a special gateway account.

- **News,** which is related to Mail, defines a prototype of the news infrastructure and a server for this purpose. Stock newsreaders are directed to a gateway port (as localhost:1119), if possible.

- **Chat,** which is a working prototype of a chat infrastructure. As yet no spiffy front-end interfaces, but only a test client. Freenet chat is said to be quite slow (painfully so) even for just two local users, with considerable startup lag. Consider this proof-of-concept only—the developers cheerfully admit to being insane to even try this application.

- **Gaming**, which is restricted to a generic gaming framework for turn-based games because of Freenet latency. It implements a secure, anonymous transport layer for asynchronous moves. Chess is the chosen prototype.

- **DNS**, which has the goal to implement Freenet Naming Service (FNS), an alternative method to map human-readable names to IP numbers. It restructures the hierarchical DNS or domain model into a peer model with arbitrary strings, removing the technical limitation in DNS that allows authoritarian control of namespace administration. The aim is that the FNS implementation can be a plug-in replacement for any network.

In other words, basically everything that today goes over the ordinary Internet is seen as potentially workable in a Freenet setting, conferring the privacy and persistence advantages of this network.

However, because of fundamental differences between the quasi-hierarchical Internet (which is very server-centric) and the server-agnostic Freenet, some of these services are implemented in significantly different ways. As indicated, some might not even be viable, while others, perhaps as yet unknown, will emerge.

TRUST AND CONTENT VERACITY

Freenet has the basic approach that *individual nodes are inherently untrusted*. The main issue at stake here is that a node must not be allowed to return false data.

Why is this so important? Look again at the caching process described earlier. Were a node able to pass on a bogus document, that false content would be cached by all nodes participating in the request fulfilment—it would spread "like a cancer". All content would by implication be suspect. Note that by "false content", we mean manipulated away from the content actually published; it's not a value judgement about the content as created by the original publisher of the document.

One kind of "falsehood" is allowed in Freenet, however. Because maintaining a table of data sources is a potential security concern, any node along the way may unilaterally decide to change reply message headers to claim itself or another arbitrarily chosen node as the data source. Such deliberate obfuscation of real sender identity strengthens proxy-chain obscurity.

Freenet Keys

Freenet keys provide the mechanism for ensuring true data and rejecting damaged or bogus data. A node can use the keys to validate that a document or message sent from another node is correct, and if it isn't, it will simply stop accepting traffic from that node—in principle forever if it's a signature failure. The request that generated the invalid response is then restarted to other nodes. State is signaled by control flags (usually CB_OK and CB_RESTARTED) in keys forwarded downstream.

The basic key types are supported by Freenet as URIs, with a format given as freenet:keytype@data. Keys can be chained through document metadata references to take advantage of several different key types.

> **Bit 9.9   Everything in Freenet is stored in terms of key-data pairs.**
> Ask Freenet for a key, and it will return any data mapped to that key. Provide a key and data to publish, and Freenet will store the data (any data) under that key.

The current key-exchange system is Diffie-Hellman. Interested readers are referred to sources dealing with cryptography, and the public key algorithms in particular. A short summary of the supported key types follows.

- **Content hash key (CHK)**, which is formed from a numeric hash (160-bit SHA 1) of the data. CHK is used to verify the integrity of the (document) data. A node would apply the same known hash algorithm to any data it transfers and compare the result with the CHK that follows the data.

- **Keyword signed key (KSK)**, which is derived from the descriptive text string. KSKs are similar to paths in a normal filesystem—subject/ subtheme/documentname. Despite this appearance, a KSK string is merely a human-readable identifier; it has nothing whatsoever to do with any hierarchical storage model in the network. The generated public/private key pair is used to hash a file key (public) or digitally sign the file (private).

- **Signature verification key (SVK)**, which (as type 0x0201) is similar to a KSK (type 0x0202), except that it is a purely numeric key to begin with. The purpose of a SVK is to generate a key pair, the private component of which remains with the originating client and provides a way for the publisher of a document to update it. Ownership (and trust assignment) resides with the bearer of a private SVK key.

Keys and File Management

CHKs are unique and tamper proof, and are the primary storage key used for Freenet data. A variant for validating large documents is Progressive CHK, which enables the document to be checked in stages, blocks of data at a time. Interestingly, the CHK also prevents the same document from being inserted into the network more than once, because this would generate identical keys and hence clash.

As for KSK strings, the client transforms them into a binary type using a one-way transformation process. It is therefore impractical to attempt recovery of the text string from an intercepted binary version of it. In order to regenerate a valid KSK document, you need to know the original KSK string, and this one step prevents a node from substituting other content for a binary KSK key.

In practical terms, knowing a KSK string, any user can have a node hash it and use the public key to retrieve the file. The KSK lock is the weakest of the keys used and has a number of issues that are being worked on in the ongoing Freenet development process. One issue is the globally flat namespace with risk for name clustering.

Namespace structure is partially addressed with the SVK subspace key (SSK), which is a client-side representation of SVK with a document name. SSKs allow the user to create a simple, personal-name subspace with some control over insertion. The trade-off due to this specific and controlled clustering is guessable keys. Using digital signatures and SSKs, published documents are clearly associated with the same source, and names won't collide with global ones.

Files are also encrypted by a randomly generated encryption key. To allow others to retrieve the file, the user publishes somewhere the CHK together with the decryption key. Note that the decryption key is never stored with the file, because to do so would provide a means for node operators to determine the content of stored files. The decryption key is instead only published with the file key.

Indirection and Updating Files

CHKs are most useful in an indirection mechanism together with SSKs. To store an updatable file, for instance, a user inserts it under its own CHK. An indirect file containing the relevant CHK is then inserted under an SSK. Other users are able to retrieve this content in two steps, using first the SSK, then the retrieved CHK.

Updating this content is also a two-step procedure. The owner first inserts a new version under a different CHK. The new indirect file pointing to the updated version is inserted under the original SSK, however. A key collision therefore occurs when this insert reaches a node that possesses the old version. If the signature on the new version is both valid and more recent, the node replaces the old indirection with the new. The SSK indirection therefore always leads to the most recent version of the file. Note that old versions can still be accessed directly by using the CHK—if not requested, these old versions eventually lapse from the network.

This same indirection method can be used to manage directories. Another use is to split large files into multiple parts, which can be desirable because of storage and bandwidth limitations. Splitting even medium-sized files into standard-sized parts also has advantages in combating traffic analysis. Each part is inserted separately under a CHK, with SSK indirection of one or more levels to point to the parts.

Keys figure prominently in the protocol analysis that follows.

Protocol Details

It's important to remember that FNP is under constant development, and the whole project remains at what is in effect early prototyping stage. Significant changes can occur between major versions, and several essentially different Freenets might be deployed concurrently, thus the importance of the common usage of specifying version in discussions—for example Freenet 0.3 or Freenet 0.4.

Bit 9.10 Freenet 0.3 and Freenet 0.4 are incompatible protocols.
Nodes running under one version can't communicate with nodes running under the other. Hence, content stored in one is not directly accessible in the other, except possibly through gateways or from the Web.

Freenet version distinctions are noted in the following only when relevant.

As mentioned earlier, clients generally use the subset FCP to communicate with a local server instance over the localhost loopback. Nodes then use FNP in their further communication with other nodes. A connection (that is, a session) is established and torn down for each transaction. FNP is packet oriented and doesn't care what underlying transport layer protocol is used for messages. Persistent protocols such as TCP allow multiple messages to be pipelined.

Each session is started with a four-byte identifier; two for session ID, two for presentation ID. Currently fixed at (0,0,0,2), these values may vary in the future depending on encryption status or alternate syntax formats. The identifier is followed by an initiating message, and the transaction is completed by the fulfilment response.

A timeout condition is implemented so that clients and nodes don't wait indefinitely. The timeout is a function of the HTL of the message, defined in seconds as *(mean * hops) + (1.28 * sd * sqrt (hops))*. Mean and sd are set to 12, which results in typical timeouts on the order of a few minutes at most.

Message Formats

A transaction message consists of a sequence of end-of-line delimited values (UTF-8 text) in either lf or crlf format. Messages are assumed passed over a "clean channel", which means that content must not be modified in any way. Implementations may simulate clean channels through encoding, such as the base64 scheme used to preserve keys, digital signatures, and binary file attachments to e-mail.

```
Header
[Field1=Value1]
. .
[FieldN=ValueN]
EndMessage
```

Header values define what kind of message. EndMessage does not appear in messages that end with a data field and trailing data. Table 9.2 shows the currently defined message types and their expected responses.

Looking in somewhat more detail at some of these message types, we can see that after a request, the client waits either for a terminating response (possibly an error condition) or for a success. A successful content request results in DataFound, here shown FCP simplified without some of the more esoteric fields for UniqueID, source, transport, hops, and so on that are used between nodes in the full FNP.

```
DataFound
DataLength=<number>
[MetadataLength=<number>]
EndMessage
```

The DataLength value is the total number of bytes for data and metadata together. The MetadataLength specifier is optional and defaults to zero. A sequence of DataChunk messages then follows to transfer the content to the client.

```
DataChunk
Length=<number>
Data
<Sequence of Length bytes of the data>
```

TABLE 9.2 *Summary of defined message header types and expected response types in client (FCP) and node (FNP) communication with a Freenet server node. Exact header names vary between different documentations.*

Message type	Possible responses	Comments

`ClientHello`
`RequestHandshake`
	`NodeHello`
	
	`ReplyHandshake`
	
	(terminates connection)
		Optional handshake, never forwarded (HTL=1).
		
		The response provides protocol and node (version) information.

`ClientGet`
`RequestData`
	`URIError,`
	`DataNotFound,`
	`RouteNotFound,`
	`Restarted,`
	`DataFound, DataChunk`
	
	`ReplyNotFound,`
	`ReplyRestart,`
	`RequestContinue,`
	`SendData,`
	`ReplyInsert`
		Frames a request for a particular document, as identified by its fully specified Freenet URI using its KSK.

`ClientPut`
`RequestInsert`
	`URIError, Restarted,`
	`RouteNotFound,`
	`KeyCollision,`
	`Success`
	
	`ReplyNotFound,`
	`ReplyRestart,`
	`RequestContinue,`
	`SendData,`
	`ReplyInsert`
		Frames a request to publish a particular document under a hashed key generated from its name.

`GenerateCHK`	`Success`	Requests node to generate the hashed key based on a text string.
`GenerateSVKPair`	`Success`	Requests node to generate a public signed key pair.
(any)	`Failed, TimedOut` (terminates session)	The transaction could not be completed because of a fault in the node. A descriptive text in the response can indicate why.
(any)	`FormatError` (terminates session)	The client message could not be parsed as a valid message type. A descriptive text in the response can provide diagnostic help.

DataChunk messages have a trailing data field of the length specified, and the node continues sending chunks until the transfer is done. There is no explicit EndMessage. The client already knows the total length of the transfer from the DataFound message and can therefore determine completion on its own. No special termination message is sent by the node; the connection simply dies after the last chunk.

Latency for longer messages (such as document transfers) is handled by tunneling between nodes, so that individual chunks are passed on downstream as soon as each is received, instead of waiting for the entire document to be received. Progressive CHKs and control flags, explained earlier, are implemented to allow rapid validation and containment of invalid data.

If chunk data fails at any time to verify at a node, it may send a Restarted message, indicating that the transfer will restart from the beginning (which implies that the client should simply discard all the previously received chunks). Alternatively, the error might be fatal in terms of this retrieval, in which case another suitable error message is sent to terminate the connection.

In the case of insertion, the message format is:

```
ClientPut
HopsToLive=<number>
URI=<string>
DataLength=<number>
[MetadataLength=<number>]
Data
<Sequence of DataLength number of bytes>
```

The URI is a fully specified Freenet KSK string, same as used for ClientGet. If the client is inserting a CHK or SVK, the URI may be abbreviated to just "CHK@" or "SVK@", respectively. In the former case, the node will calculate the CHK, and in the latter, the node will generate a new key pair.

Length specifiers are the same as for DataFound. However in this case, the specified data field must contain the entire content in one go; it can't be chunked. The node must get all of the trailing field before it can start the insert into Freenet.

In the case of a KeyCollision response, insertion was refused, and the message returns a URI field with the Freenet URI of the document that already occupied the requested key slot. Non-CHK key types have an upper limit of 32KB, which explains the SizeError response. There is no limit on content size.

On the other hand, successful insertion returns the Success message with the Freenet URI of the new document. If the inserted document was a SVK, it returns a private/public key pair. The format is

```
Success
URI=<string>
[PublicKey=<string: Public key>]
[PrivateKey=<string: Private key>]
EndMessage
```

The subject of key types and their generation was discussed earlier. The special key-generation requests affect only the immediate node, not the rest of the network, unlike when specifically inserted with the previous request options. To create a CHK from an arbitrary string uses this message format:

```
GenerateCHK
DataLength=<number>
[MetadataLength=<number>]
Data
<Sequence of DataLength number of bytes (data+metadata)>
```

Success simply returns the URI string. GenerateSVKPair has no extra fields, but is followed only by EndMessage. Success there returns the public and private keys as message fields in that order. They are constructed as Freenet-base64 encoded.

These key strings can subsequently be used to insert or request signed documents by including the appropriate one in the URI specification:

```
freenet:SSK@<PrivateKey>/docname -- (insertion)
freenet:SSK@<PublicKey>/docname -- (request)
```

Looking instead at messages between nodes, Table 9.3 summarizes the main message types encountered.

RequestData messages propagate downstream a routed chain, generating responses as might be expected. Successful requests result in some node responding with a SendData and the data. If HTL expires, a ReplyNotFound is passed back. On the other hand, if the last node in the chain runs out of paths to try and HTL is still valid, the response is instead RequestContinue with the remaining value of HTL. It is then the responsibility of the upstream node to try another, less-close key-path, and

TABLE 9.3 *Summary of defined message header types for (FNP) communications between Freenet server nodes. Exact header names vary between different documentations.*

Message type	Possible responses	Comments
RequestHandshake	ReplyHandshake (terminates connection)	Optional handshake, never forwarded (HTL=1). The response provides protocol and node (version) information.
RequestData	URIError, DataChunk ReplyNotFound, ReplyRestart, RequestContinue, SendData, ReplyInsert	Frames a request for a particular document, as identified by its fully specified Freenet URI using its KSK.
RequestInsert SendInsert	URIError, Success ReplyNotFound, ReplyRestart, RequestContinue, SendData, ReplyInsert	Frames a request to publish a particular document under a hashed key generated from its name.

send a ReplyRestart to its upstream node. This upstream process to try alternate paths iterates up the chain as necessary, until either the data is found along some other path or a RequestContinue comes back to the requestor. The latter, having exhausted all possible paths, may then conclude that the data is not available within the request horizon defined by current topology and HTL.

> **Bit 9.11 In Freenet, "not found" is not the same as "not stored anywhere".** Constrained searches are not exhaustive. While "found" responses are conclusive, "not found" depends on numerous variables, and are relative and indeterminate.

In practice, the success-reinforced "learning" behavior of the routing tables, and their inherent p2p adaptability, make search results for existing content converge towards successful retrieval for most requests at some typically small average path length. Connectivity in the tables is aligned towards found content, and successful retrieval replicates along request paths, further increasing chances of success.

Insertion attempts might generate a variety of responses. SendData implies a key collision with an existing file. ReplyNotFound also implies a collision, because routing table information was found, but a node with the content could not be contacted within allowed HTL and timeout constraints. A RequestContinue is also considered a failure in this context, because it is interpreted as meaning the request could not be extended to the required number of hops. However, if the insert request expires without encountering a collision, the last remote node in the chain replies with a ReplyInsert, indicating that the insert can proceed. As the inserted data is fed into the network using SendInsert, nodes store the data locally and pass it along downstream to the key-determined location.

> **Bit 9.12 Insertion occurs at locations where requests are likely to be routed.**
> The method of using CHK routing tables optimizes the match between initial storage location and subsequent request routing, without requiring that the data remain in any single location indefinitely.

Message Header

In the interests of completeness, Table 9.4 takes up the message header fields.

Freenet is a message-based protocol. Therefore, nodes are free in principle to close idle connections and connect back to the source later when responding. The Source header provides this reconnection information in the form of a return node address, the last immediate sender. This header is stacked at each hop, the forwarding node substituting its own address for the next hop.

Node addresses consist of a transport method plus a transport-specific identifier such as an IP address and port number (for example, tcp/192.168.10.1:9113). A node that changes IP addresses frequently may instead use a virtual address stored under an address-resolution key (ARK), which is an SSK regularly updated to contain the current real address.

The source field should be omitted for a node that doesn't wish to accept incoming connections of this nature—or can't because it's behind a firewall. The node should instead just keep the idle connection open for responses. The last return source address going back up a request chain is normally the address of the requesting node/client or possibly the address where this requestor wants the result delivered.

In the special case of a document being sent back to a requestor, it's allowed for a node to arbitrarily change the source pointer of these messages to any random address to obfuscate the real source of the content.

Because the transaction identifier UniqueID is just a random albeit large number, it's not guaranteed to be unique. On the other hand, the probability of a value

TABLE 9.4 *Summary of defined message header field types in Freenet messages. Numeric values are expressed in hexadecimal.*

Field name	Value	Comments
UniqueID	64-bit numeric transaction identifier	Identifies related messages. It is set to a random value by the originator of a message.
HopsToLive	Current hops to live (enforced <= 100)	Decremented at each hop (always) until it reaches 1, after which the message is discarded.
Depth	Number of hops made	Incremented each time the message is (successfully) forwarded.
KeepAlive	Boolean (default to True)	Informs node whether the connection should be kept alive or closed after forwarding.
Source	Transport protocol address (currently only tcp address and port)	Identifies the immediate sender of message. Is the basis for stacked return path.
Storable	String, free content (for example keys)	Nodes caching documents must also cache Storable fields and include them in any responses.

collision occurring during a transaction lifetime, among the limited set of nodes that it sees, is exceedingly low.

HTL is set by the originator of a message and is decremented at each hop to prevent messages being forwarded indefinitely. Actually, messages do not always terminate in Freenet after HTL reaches 1 but can sometimes be forwarded once again (with HTL still at 1). This ruse is simply to reduce the information that an attacker might gain from an intercepted message and HTL value.

HTL is also coupled to message timeout. A node sending or forwarding a message starts an associated local timer set for an expected maximum duration of time it should take for the message to be relayed through this number of nodes and return a response, after which it will assume failure. While the request is being processed, a remote node may periodically send back ReplyRestart messages indicating that a message is stalled, perhaps waiting on network timeouts. In this case, the sending node knows to extend its timer.

The purpose of hop-tracking Depth is to allow a replying node to set its response HTL just high enough to reach the requestor. Requestors on their part should initialize Depth to a small random value to obscure their location. Corresponding to the HTL value ruse, a depth of 1 is not always incremented, but with finite probability, it might be passed unchanged to the next node.

NODE DISCOVERY

Joining the network is simply a matter of connecting to a number of existing nodes in the network and starting to pass messages. Node discovery however is something that's tended to be glossed over in most descriptions of Freenet. How does any user client or local server find a Freenet node with which to connect? You'll recall this fundamental bootstrap problem from Gnutella (discussed in Chapter 7), and it's common to all atomistic p2p implementations.

As it turns out, the issue is glossed over in Freenet documentation as well; the discussions assume already functional nodes with content stacked and a message exchange history with other nodes. Although node discovery has been an often discussed subject on the Freenet developer mailing lists and the Freenet IRC channel, implementation of any solution has been decidedly *ad hoc*, described only as relying on "out-of-band" means—that is to say, on methods external to Freenet.

Actually, two different methods have been used so far.

- In Freenet 0.3 (the previous major version), a designated central server collects active node IP numbers. A newly started node therefore can request a list of active nodes from this server and try to connect to them. However, the existence of any centralized service exposes a vulnerable point in the network and is foreign, of course, to the basic design principles of Freenet.

- In Freenet 0.4 (current at time of writing), the Freenet developers prefer to use distributed reference files which contain the "seed" addresses to other nodes. While more flexible and less vulnerable, this alternative also presents problems similar to the issue of content index. How are these lists to be updated, distributed and accessed? How much of the address information will be outdated by the time a new node tries to use it?

At present, v0.4 nodes can be configured to use a mix of methods—manual entries as well as seed reference files. Like many other critical design points in this prototyping evolution, node discovery is very much an ongoing work.

Once connected, further node discovery is easier. Given at least one known address to an active node, the joining client begins to send messages. The request mechanism automatically enables the new nodes to learn about more of the network over time. However, because new nodes aren't normally in a position to successfully respond to requests and, in any case, will generally not be on a routing table to receive any, existing nodes won't discover the new nodes. Recall that Freenet nodes do not broadcast requests; they selectively route them.

New-Node Announcements

The solution for new nodes to gain recognition with other nodes is to somehow announce their presence. Such a solution unfortunately is complicated by two somewhat conflicting requirements.

On one hand, to promote efficient routing, all existing nodes should be consistent in deciding which keys to send a new node (and thus assign in their routing tables). On the other hand, it would cause a security problem if any one node could choose the routing key. This concern therefore rules out the most straightforward way of achieving consistency.

A cryptographic protocol was devised to satisfy both of these requirements. A new node chooses a random seed and sends an announcement message containing its address and the hash of that seed to some existing node. Whenever a node receives a new-node announcement, it generates a random seed, XORs that with the hash it received, and hashes the result again to create a "commitment". It then forwards the new hash to some node chosen randomly from its routing table.

This process continues until the HTL of the announcement runs out. The last node to receive the announcement just generates a seed. Next, all nodes in the resulting chain reveal their seeds. The key for the new node is assigned as the XOR of all the seeds. Checking the commitments enables each node to confirm that everyone revealed their seeds truthfully. This seemingly convoluted process yields a consistent random key that cannot be influenced by a malicious participant. Each node therefore can safely add an entry in its routing table under that key for the new node.

MALICIOUS NODES

The possibility of malicious nodes joining the network is the most difficult problem that a distributed network must face and has been addressed in various ways.

One solution attempt often seen in the networked gaming clients is to keep the protocol and software code proprietary and closed. This approach proves to provide only a short-term protection, and in any case, it doesn't usually address the issue of detecting malicious nodes that do manage to break through security measures.

Freenet philosophy is opposed to closed solutions, so it must seek answers elsewhere. The focus instead is on managing communication at the node level, so that requests are passed to a neighboring node (and data accepted from it) when it is providing evidence that it is functioning well, and routed away from it when it is not. The reasoning is that a malicious node can do little harm if other nodes refuse to communicate with it.

The practical full implementation of such a scheme still remains at the discussion level because various criteria must be evaluated to determine whether or not a particular node is "functioning well enough" to be accepted. These criteria include trust metric, reputation tracking, democratic node "votes", message index hashes to detect spoofing, and so on. The issue is an example of the ongoing work that the development teams regularly report on.

Modification of requested files by a malicious node in a request chain is an important threat and therefore a strong reason to devise methods against such threats. Only in part is this because of possible corruption of file content. Routing tables are based on replies to requests, so a node might attempt to steer traffic towards itself by returning fictitious data as bogus successful retrievals.

The use of both CHKs and SSKs addresses this threat, because other nodes can always detect invalid data unless a node successfully forges a cryptographic signature or finds a hash collision. Signatures based only on KSKs, on the other hand, can be created by anyone in possession of the original descriptive string, which fact renders KSK signatures vulnerable to dictionary attack due to the somewhat predictable nature of human-readable descriptor strings.

Existing files could potentially be displaced by inserting alternate versions under the same keys, but this is prevented by the immutability of storage unless an update is allowed by a valid CHK or SSK. File displacement using a KSK attack may result in both versions coexisting in the network. Normal node reaction to insert collisions is to return the original version, as described earlier, and this behavior is intended to make such attacks more difficult. Thus, the more corrupt copies an attacker attempts to circulate, the greater the chance that it results in key collision and a consequent increase in the number of genuine copies replicated across the network.

Finally, various DoS attack schemes might be devised as attempts to disrupt the network. The most significant DoS threat is probably that of trying to fill all of the network's storage capacity by inserting a large number of junk files. Various countermeasures have been suggested: "Hash Cash" to slow attacks by imposing a computational "payment" for insertion, dividing the data store into separate sections for new inserts (can be displaced) and proven requested files (can't be displaced), and others. The respective pros and cons of these measures are under constant developer review. Depending on the deployment environment for a Freenet type network, different approaches would be deemed appropriate

Security by Obscurity

The other aspect of malicious node management is to simply limit how much useful information they can collect by just being part of the network. As explained earlier, Freenet nodes work in a relatively isolated way and know little beyond the IP identities of their nearest neighbors.

The message and key analysis sections show how this relative obscurity is further enhanced by allowing nodes to arbitrarily provide false source identities and by not consistently updating the depth and HTL values. This makes it difficult to create reliable maps of the active network or determine where particular content is stored. While it's trivially true that a successful request will guarantee that the content is stored (for a time) in the neighbor node, there is no good way to localize where the "authoritative" node for that content is at any given time. (Unless of course you are in a position to continuously monitor and analyze traffic to and from all possible nodes—but then any form of anonymity and security becomes highly unlikely.)

The real identities of senders and requestors are similarly obscured. Freenet communication is not directed towards specific receivers, however, so receiver anonymity is more accurately viewed as key anonymity—hiding the key that is being requested or inserted. Strict key anonymity is not possible in the basic Freenet scheme, because routing depends on knowledge of the key, yet some measure of obscurity against casual eavesdropping is given by the use of hashes as keys. A residual vulnerability to a dictionary attack remains because their unhashed versions must be widely known in order to be useful. Sender anonymity is preserved against a collaboration of malicious nodes, because no node in a request path can determine whether its upstream neighbor initiated the request or merely forwarded it.

> **Bit 9.13 All security and anonymity measures make some assumptions.**
> Freenet assumes that nobody can monitor what is going on inside your computer, which is why the only truly "trusted" node for a client is one on your own machine.

The first node that a user client contacts is a weak link in that it can potentially act as a local eavesdropper, and no message protection is implemented against this. This vulnerability is why it's recommended that users connect only to server nodes running on their own machines, as a trusted first point of entry into the Freenet network. Messages between nodes are encrypted against local eavesdropping, although traffic analysis of these nodes might still determine probable point of origin.

Stronger sender and key anonymity in this context can be achieved by adding so-called "prerouting" of encrypted messages, where a succession of public key encryptions overrides the normal routing mechanism to determine the route that a message follows. Nodes along this route are unable to determine either message content, request key, or originator. When a message reaches the end of its prerouting path, it's injected into the normal Freenet network and subsequently behaves as though the preroute endpoint is the originator.

The fact that a node is listed as the data source for a particular key does not necessarily mean that it actually supplied that data or was even contacted in the course of the request. This is because the source field is occasionally changed by a node in the chain passing along the file. It's not possible to tell whether the downstream node provided the file or forwarded a reply sent by someone else.

In either case, a copy of the file remains on the downstream node, so a subsequent inspection of that node (for example, with a request probe with HTL=1) on suspicion reveals nothing about the prior state of affairs (an HTL=1 probe might be forwarded to another node regardless). This provides plausible legal ground that the data was not there until the act of investigation placed it there. The success of a large number of requests for related files, on the other hand, could conceivably provide grounds for suspicion that those files were being stored there previously.

SCALABILITY AND STABILITY

In the real world, scalability and stability are a matter of empirical study and not always well understood. Freenet is still experimental and changing. Nevertheless, some conclusions can be drawn both from theory and initial deployment.

Ian Clarke, Oskar Sandberg, Brandon Wiley, and Theodore W. Hong studied numerous aspects of theoretical, simulated and real network behavior to test some of the essential characteristics of the Freenet architecture. Their "Freenet: A Distributed Anonymous Information Storage and Retrieval System", published in June 2000 and revised in December, provides a rich source of information. It and Clake's original thesis are available from www.freenetproject.org/cgi-bin/twiki/view/Main/Papers.

The main simulations they performed were

- **Network convergence**, which tested the adaptivity of the network routing

- **Scalability,** which looked for any inherent constraints to growth
- **Fault tolerance,** which tested how resistant the network was to lost nodes

Convergence

Inserts of random keys were sent to random nodes in a simulated test network of 1,000 nodes, interspersed randomly with requests for randomly-chosen keys known to have been previously inserted, using a HTL of 20 for both. Every 100 time steps, a snapshot of the network was taken and its performance measured using a set of probe requests. Each probe consisted of 300 random requests for previously inserted keys, using a large HTL (500).

Initially, measured path lengths were very high. Most requests probably didn't succeed at all—failure by the test probes resulted in a measured value of the max HTL. However, path lengths decreased rapidly over time as the routing tables adapted to the actual distribution of keys. As the network converged, the median path length for requests dropped to a low value (6).

Scalability

The team started with a small network of 20 nodes and inserted more nodes over time, every five time steps. As before, they inserted new keys at random and measured the change in mean path length for random requests.

They found that the network scaled approximately logarithmically, which held up to a size limit of 40,000 nodes, probably determined by the size of the routing table (250 entries), after which path length increased more rapidly. Nevertheless, the network appeared to continue to scale reasonably to about a million nodes with the average path length reaching only 30, despite no pauses in growth to allow a steady state convergence process. Varying node bandwidth is ignored in this study. Real-world nodes could easily maintain routing tables with thousands of entries, with correspondingly greater potential scalability.

Fault Tolerance

The team grew a network to 1,000 nodes using the previous method, then removed randomly chosen nodes progressively from the network to simulate node failures.

The network proved surprisingly robust against quite large failures. The median path length in their examples remained below 20 even when up to a third of the nodes were removed. Such results bode well for full-scale performance of real networks. The team explained overall performance in terms of a "small-world" model, in which the majority of nodes have only relatively few, local connections to other nodes, while a small number of randomly dispersed nodes have large, wide-ranging sets of connections. Small-world networks permit efficient short paths between arbitrary points because of the shortcuts provided by the well-connected nodes.

The distribution of links within a Freenet network closely approximates a power law, which the team took as a sufficient property to qualify as a small-world model. Thus, random node failures are most likely to affect the majority that possess only a small number of connections. Losing poorly connected nodes will not affect routing very much in the network. Only when the number of random failures becomes high enough to disable a significant number of well-connected nodes does routing performance become significantly affected.

PRACTICAL INSTALLATION

Discussion of practical installation comes late in this chapter for several reasons. One is that in a prototype system like Freenet, much can change between time of writing and when you read this, easily making detailed installation information obsolete. Another is that much of the same user functionality can be realized through a gateway access from the Web without any particular user installations at all.

In Figure 9.4, we see the two main ways a user might access Freenet content—or for that matter, publish content to the network. Because access is always indirect, either by way of one's own "trusted" node on the local machine or by way of a remote gateway system, the degree of indirection matters little to the network, although the latter method can compromise the user's anonymity.

It should be noted in this context, that participation as a node in Freenet has a number of caveats, and it's recommended to have the intention of remaining online 24/7, or at least for long periods. Although the network has a proven ability to tolerate a certain fraction of transient nodes in the system, the design is such that overall performance and stability is better with more "permanent" nodes.

Pragmatically, continuous connectivity is a good thing for the user as well—it's simply in your own interest to stay connected. Recall from earlier discussions how the network adapts storage and routing. This particular kind of adaptive single-path routing puts new nodes at a distinct disadvantage when it comes to finding and retrieving content. It's not unusual for a user, who has just installed the node software, joined the network, and uncovered a number of content keys, to have great difficulty finding anything at all even with maximum HTL. The first key requests will be sent

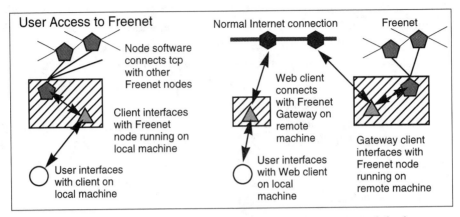

FIGURE 9.4   *Two ways to access (or publish) content on Freenet. At left, the user runs own trusted node with connections to other Freenet nodes and uses Freenet client software to access own node. The user to the right uses a normal Web browser to access a gateway on a remote machine.*

out in random directions, there being no stack history of successful requests on the local node to indicate a best routing. Therefore, they generally fail.

As the node remains online for a longer time, it eventually acquires a better routing table; in part from the successful requests that occasionally do occur, in part from participating in passing along results from other node searches that sometimes do take paths that include it. This routing improvement is clearly demonstrated when a new user successfully finds a freesite—associated content is suddenly also available, and finding related content is much more probable.

Node Installation

The first question for the user is which version of Freenet to join. Normally, you might be inclined to install the most recent node software, but in the case of Freenet 0.3 and 0.4, these versions define two separate and incompatible networks. If you are on the cusp of a new major version being deployed—v4 to v5 transition seems likely before this book ships—you might want to check on possible incompatibility between versions and perhaps set up the previous version instead. If the new version defines a new and incompatible network, then the previous one is where most of the content is initially. As the new version becomes established over time, it acquires more nodes and more available content. Then again, perhaps you prefer to be on the forefront and publish your content on the new network.

The other aspect to version choice depends on what kind of client software you wish to use. Much of this software has version dependencies or at least might require configuration tweaks to work on another version than originally intended for. This is admittedly a tough call before you've used any clients at all, but the developer sites often have feature lists and screenshots. The following is mainly about v0.4.

The first step for any Freenet node installation at present is to have a JRE installed on your system, whatever your operating system. A JRE can be obtained in many ways, from many sources. In some cases, it might already be present, installed by some other Java-enabled application—Web browsers such as Opera (www.opera.com) come in both plain and "j" versions; the latter will install a working v1.1 JRE that can also be used by Freenet software.

The second step is to decide whether you want to install a precompiled binary Freenet package or to compile your own from the sources. For Windows users, a self-installing binary is usually the best choice unless you're dedicated to keeping up with the bleeding-edge developer code daily snapshots. This decision is less of an issue for Linux users, because they normally have both the required compilation tools present and more experience in handling source-distributed software.

Installing the binary node software is rather undramatic. The main setting question encountered is type of connectivity, and it can be changed later. It's recommended to start with "transient" regardless, as it has no harmful effects, and move to permanent only when you're really sure you can reliably run 24/7. It seems that the 24/7 setting is crucial for some esoteric internals that might affect network stability or your own ability to reconnect if you are offline too much or too often.

The default install process makes some reasonable assumptions about storage allocations based on connectivity and current free space on your machine's hard disk. Such detail can be tweaked later, so don't worry about it.

> **Bit 9.14 Go with the defaults and recommendations for node installation and configuration, unless you really, really know what you're doing.**
> Many Advanced and Serious Geeks Only settings (yes, the dialog tab does say this!) are available in Configuration, most of which can seriously disrupt your Freenet connectivity if set incorrectly.

The other main user setting is mainly a "security" one: how to acquire "seed nodes" when starting. This is the bootstrap mechanism for node discovery, discussed earlier. The normal method is to go with the default, which makes the node go to a predefined Web address and retrieve a `seed.ref` file with a selection of known nodes.

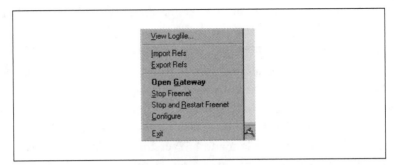

FIGURE 9.5   *The Freenet node popup menu from the taskbar icon in Windows.*

Someone more concerned about security can choose more circumspect methods of acquiring and selecting which nodes to initiate contact with. Because this network is still a prototype, there seems little reason to avoid the default method.

Assuming that your Internet connection is up and the node runs immediately, the Windows version stakes out a taskbar space for its status icon and retreats to the background. Right-click to reach the menu, shown in Figure 9.5, and from there select, for example, Configure to reach the configuration dialog. Other functionality options are to stop (and later start) or to stop-and-restart the node. Importing and exporting "refs" is a way of manually managing seed lists as local files, perhaps externally exchanging them encrypted through other channels with other users.

But essentially, once it's running, you can forget about the node software, as it manages node connectivity completely and unobtrusively in the background, with for the most part no measurable system loading.

OK, it's running. Now what? How do I reach Freenet content?

Through the local machine's Freenet node, of course.

Node Access

To communicate with the local node and, by extension, the rest of Freenet, you need a local client. Fortunately, the node is Web aware through a proxy component, so you can use your default Web browser.

Although you can manually type in the URL (localhost:port), where port number depends on version and configuration, it's more convenient to simply use the taskbar icon's popup menu. Select Open Gateway to automatically invoke your system Web browser with the proper URL.

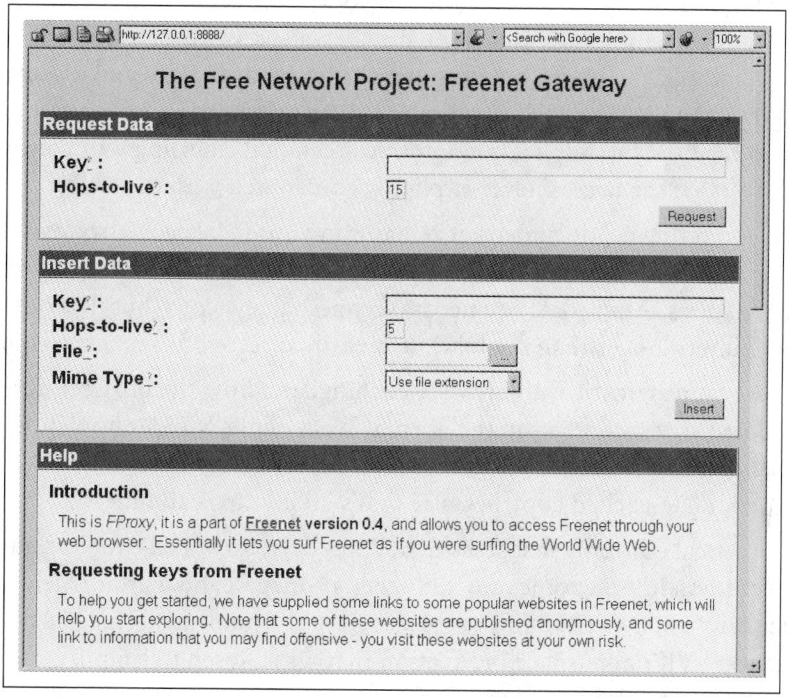

FIGURE 9.6   *The Freenet 0.4 node gateway's default page accessed with stock Web browser from the installation's localhost proxy. Note the forms for retrieval requests and browse-insertion of files from the local system.*

Figure 9.6 shows the Gateway-generated default page with forms for both document retrieval and file publishing (insertion). To request content from here, you must know the Freenet key for the document and either type it in manually (*No thanks!*) or paste it in from somewhere else. This page also provides useful tips on where to find lists of content keys.

Further down on the page, not visible in the screen capture, are some examples of normal-seeming Web page hyperlinks that in fact point to a number of Freenet resources, helpfully provided as examples to get the new user started without having to seek externally maintained content lists. The links hide URI addresses similar to the following (for a freesite):

```
http://127.0.0.1:8888/
SSK%40npfV5XQijFkF6sXZvuO0o%7EkG4wEPAgM/homepage//
```

This kind of key complexity can thankfully be hidden behind a plain text, descriptive anchor, which greatly simplifies publishing Freenet keys. Just click—and wait a goodly while since you've just joined the network—and with luck, the browser will suddenly display Freenet-published content when a successful retrieve reaches your local node. Like all Web interfaces, this one has both advantages and disadvantages compared to an application GUI. On the one hand, Web browsing is a familiar metaphor to the user, but application interfaces can make dealing with keys more transparent so that the user is never explicitly confronted with the hash.

Once you retrieve a document, it remains in your local cache (so revisits will load the page immediately) and on the stacks of the nodes that routed the result to you, until it expires. After that, you need to request a new copy, but the routing tables (retaining pointers longer than content) now easily direct your request to the source.

Readers familiar with Web browser caching, and how the browser detects and fetches updated server content on the normal Web, might wonder how it deals with Freenet caching. The short answer is that it doesn't. The browser can compare only with the local, node-cached copy because that's all it knows about.

The practical matter is that freesite updates currently "roll over" at midnight UTC (the common Internet time) and only then propagate, no matter when published. Before then, any updates remain invisible, even to the publisher. This has to do with the date-stamp SVK name-space indirection that was chosen to simplify keeping a freesite coherently available during selective updates. On the next midnight, therefore, your cached copy simply expires—in fact, *all* cached copies, everywhere, expire. A new read request by the browser after this will generate a new search for the content on the network. If the content publisher has updated during this time, you get back the new content; if not, you get another, "renewed" copy of the old, assuming the publisher (or publishing tool) is maintaining the site.

> **Bit 9.15 *Freesite content updates at midnight UTC—and only then.***
> Coordinated Universal Time (UTC) is the international time standard previously known as GMT and is used as the Freenet clock, as it is for the Internet as a whole.

However, don't be discouraged if you don't immediately find any of the example documents or freesites—remember, a new node has great difficulty finding anything until the routing tables evolve from their initial random values. This is why a broadcast request system like Gnutella performs better for transient nodes that have just connected, because search performance there depends only on the number of reachable nodes at any time.

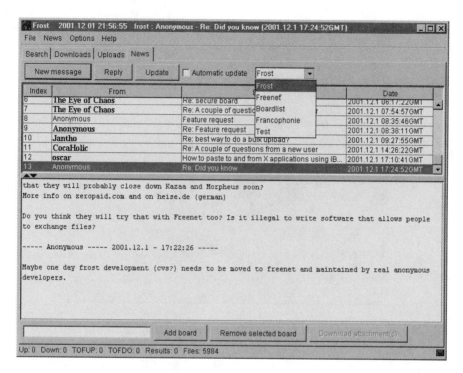

FIGURE 9.7   *Frost implements News Boards, which is an encrypted and anonymized form of newsgroup discussions internal to Freenet. The drop-down shown activated lists the current boards detected.*

Other Clients

A number of other clients that can communicate with a Freenet node are mentioned earlier in this chapter, Frost and FreeWeb to name two better known ones, not to mention the basic command-line clients bundled in the basic distribution.

The advantage of using some of the more developed clients comes from having a better interface (that is, a GUI), more features, and perhaps some optimization that the stock form requests can't provide. For example, Figure 9.7 shows one such extension: Frost's anonymous messaging system, the News Boards, which is a kind of newsgroup discussion securely passed between clients over Freenet.

Frost's basic functionality is discussed and shown in the earlier section on retrieving and publishing content on Freenet because it provides a convenient interface for download, upload, and messaging, plus an index-enhanced search. FreeWeb, also mentioned there as a popular publishing tool, is shown with its Site

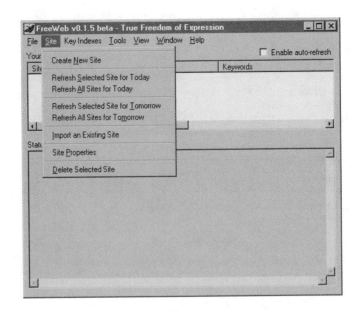

FIGURE 9.8 *FreeWeb client in Windows is for easy management of Freenet-published Web sites. The Site menu shows typical useful commands.*

menu visible in Figure 9.8, just to give an indication of how one can easily manage freesite content using it.

ONGOING WORK

Interested readers can track the ongoing development at the Freenet Wiki (at www.freenetproject.org/wiki/index.php)—anyone wondering what Wiki is should read *The Wiki Way: Collaboration on the Web* (Addison-Wesley, April 2001).

As noted earlier, a number of important Freenet issues are still being addressed, or sometimes they're still at the stage of being formulated. For example, there is a plan to implement a form of trusted nodes. Underlying mechanisms are partially in place, such as digital signatures, but it's unclear as yet how exactly such a trust system will work. Eventually, node-to-node communication will be fully encrypted, but the current prototype network still uses open messages in the interests of debugging.

True anonymity (that is, strong protection) would currently require connecting to a Freenet node by way of an external anonymizer that has full control of routing and encryption. Gateway solutions to this kind of strong privacy protection are under consideration.

Another issue that might be resolved in future versions of Freenet is that the current network is not especially tolerant of transient nodes; functionality deteriorates if too many (usually dial-up) nodes join only for shorter periods of time. This degradation relates to how stacked paths and cached content get disrupted and to the resulting increase in query traffic. Nodes with permanent connections are preferred, cable or DSL being deemed adequate. As long as these nodes form the majority, a smaller group of transient nodes doesn't impact performance too much.

Proposals for adding safe searching and indexing capabilities to Freenet are being discussed for the future—for instance, indexable hyperlinks, lists of keywords, or other readable metadata distributed through the network. As things stand, such extra data for searches must reside elsewhere and is vulnerable.

As mentioned earlier in the context of content expiration and removal, more flexible options for updating documents are being considered. In addition the current expiry model where a small document can displace a large without regard to this size difference is under review.

Because of the anonymous nature of the Freenet system, it is impossible to tell exactly how many users are in a deployed network, or how well the insert and request mechanisms are working. However, anecdotal evidence from the prototype and growing Freenet is so far very positive.

BUSINESS SOLUTIONS

A Freenet-derivative technology that's aimed at business users is KARMA (Key Accessed Redundant Memory Architecture), which is just another way of designating the Freenet storage and retrieval model.

KARMA technology is promoted by Uprizer (www.uprizer.com), a company cofounded by Rob Kramer and Freenet creator Ian Clarke in August 2000. They have developed a content distribution product line that addresses the problems of the traditional server-client architectures by aggregating unused and wireless network resources into a single, large, intelligent computer operating system.

With the stated goal of *building the next Internet*, often now referred to as *Internet 3.0*, Uprizer describes itself as a peer-to-peer technology company designed to create a new category of distributed computing software for enterprises, content providers, service providers, mobile operators, and application developers.

How KARMA Works

The system maintains secure control over a small portion of unused disk space on each node in a network. Nodes can be any network-aware device: PCs, mobile phones, and PDAs. The storage and bandwidth pool acts like distributed RAM, and the company refers to this pool as a *KARMA Drive*.

The idea is that applications can address this virtual resource like any other local storage device. In effect then, KARMA puts a common driver software interface on top of a Freenet-style network architecture. Looking at the more detailed descriptions, most of the component parts of Freenet, described earlier, are easily recognized— specifically, adaptive replication and key encryption.

The KARMA client (actually the node application) is very small and uses Freenet's heuristic routing method for requests, although here it's called a *Whispercast* process. One difference is that only dormant network resources are used to retrieve and replicate information, so client performance suffers no degradation. What implications this solution has for routing is unclear.

Like Freenet, KARMA assumes that all hardware nodes on the network and their communication links are potentially insecure. Public key encryption and digital signatures prevent unwanted content, such as viruses and worms, from being arbitrarily inserted into the network, and also ensures that received content has not been modified, either in transit or in storage.

Data is stored in encrypted chunks and retrieved using a specially designed self-correcting UDP protocol to minimize latency and network traffic. This technique seems to be a refinement of the original Freenet protocol but not radically different. Uprizer points to Freenet as the practical proof-of-concept for KARMA, further confirming that the differences between the two are minimal.

RELATED WORK

Espra (www.espra.net) deserves mention as a media file-sharing technology, like those discussed in Chapter 7, that uses Freenet as its network infrastructure. It has metadata and rating functionality, a system to reward content creators who publish to the system, and the inherent anonymity that Freenet provides. While nowhere close to mature, the underlying Freenet indexing concepts are interesting.

The Eternity Service project is an alternative server concept with aggressive encrypted distribution, where the goal is that published data is never lost. The defining paper is found at www.cl.cam.ac.uk/~rja14/eternity/eternity.html.

Collaborative P2P Spaces

Collaboration is for many what it's all about, whatever the technology. Many of the innovative aspects of the Internet as a whole evolved as a direct, or sometimes indirect result of people's desire to collaborate independently of location. Peer technologies are natural to informal collaborations in many ways, and encourage the forming of such coworking groups of people.

Granted that there is no real substitute yet for real physical presence—for example, one can rather easily determine this fact from models such as the "radiative heat" of information flow and how people communicate and work together. Yet people must often work together even in situations when they are physically remote or at variable locations, and then it becomes vital to lower any and all barriers to effective communication. Informal, p2p groupings are one way to go.

In fact, these informal groupings *are* the way people often do go, regardless of any formal structures that might be centrally mandated! This tendency is so pervasive, and so ingrained, that most people don't realize that this is what they're doing. When asked, they will sincerely maintain that they are working according to the hierarchical work methodology. However, study by outsiders can easily show otherwise—the actual work gets done in a rapid succession of p2p-like contacts.

This last implementation chapter covers those p2p technologies that, perhaps somewhat vaguely, address the context of maintaining "collaborative spaces" where people can meet, communicate, and work together. Some server-client solutions try to do this as well; WikiWiki webs, chat and conferencing tools are just a few examples. The following takes up some distributed p2p solutions.

CHAPTER 10 AT A GLANCE

As its focus, this chapter has two very different approaches to building a larger-scope platform for decentralized collaborative networks.

Groove is an example of application-space collaboration as middleware p2p.

- *The Architecture* examines the Groove peer product, which mainly targets corporate users, and goes on to explain its core concept of *Shared Workspaces*.

- The *Protocol* section describes what's known about the proprietary technical side.

- *Security Issues* and *Client Issues* take up both strong points and weak points in the current prototype.

JXTA presents an overview of an initiative also being developed commercially, but as open source, which targets the entire infrastructure of the Internet.

- *Jxta Architecture* looks at how the proposed platform is structured.

- *Peers and Groups* describes the JXTA way of defining these.

- *Firewalls* and *Security Model* deals with these aspects of the JXTA peer model.

- The section ends with a brief list of *Software Projects*.

GROOVE

Groove technology is mainly a vision of Ray Ozzie of Lotus Notes fame, who in 1997 formed a company, Groove Networks (GN, www.groove.net) around the concept of establishing collaborative spaces using a server-mediated p2p architecture.

At the time of writing, GN is moving from showcasing beta software to offering business solutions at all levels: individual, small business, government, and enterprise. This ambition somewhat adds "fuzziness" of the technological overview, because clearly the collaborative needs and deployment requirements of enterprise are vastly different than those of the individual. The company mission statement on its Web site is indicative of this dual intent, obviously striving to encompass both worlds with the stated goals to:

> *Help businesses achieve a greater "return on connection" from their relationships with customers, vendors and partners.*

> *Help individuals strengthen online connections with the people with whom they interact.*

In commercial terms, then, GN is offering Groove as middleware—that is to say, a third-party layer between applications and infrastructure. The company sees a number of commercial "scenarios" where its p2p solution fits.

- Distribution and marketing
- e-Commerce
- Financial services
- Negotiation, mergers and acquisitions
- Partner relationship management
- Pharmaceutical
- Product design
- Education

Testimonials from prerelease trials are cited to back these scenarios up.

Of perhaps more lasting interest to the general reader, the discussion forums hosted at www.groove.net/forums provide more immediate impressions of user experiences, along with current developmental issues.

THE ARCHITECTURE

The architecture is designed as a business tool, an applications platform, and as server-mediated p2p for simply connecting the peers. The design appears firmly on the road to the **fat client** model that individually includes much complex functionality, thus bucking the current **thin client** and distributed services paradigms.

Groove-based applications, or "tools" such as a calendar, notepad, contact manager, chat, and discussion forums, are already bundled. But the real business value lies in third-party products designed to leverage Groove's platform, created by the hundreds of partners who have signed on. Developers who plan to distribute their work for profit need to be licensed under the Groove Partner Program. This licensing is in clear distinction to most other p2p implementations that tend to be open source and focus mainly on a single application that defines the technology.

Users with Groove clients create **shared workspaces** on their local PCs, collaborating freely across corporate boundaries and firewalls. This collaboration occurs "without the permission, assistance, or knowledge" of any central authority or support groups. Although this *seems* very unsupervised and atomistic, the reader is cautioned against any uncritical assumption that because of its supposed unfettered nature, Groove is atomistic p2p, as in the manner of Gnutella. Instead, we must examine the actual implications of the architecture. Unfortunately, the protocol is closed and proprietary, but the general descriptions do provide sufficient firm evidence about how the Groove network works.

For starters, we may note the existence of "relay servers" and "enterprise servers" for management and integration. Another clue is in the fact that Groove clients are defined in two flavors: *basic* and *premium*. The latter is intended for business (up to enterprise level) and implements more centralized management and control. Premum clients can also communicate directly with back-office directories. This managed client enables administrators to define and implement specific policies, such as restricted sites and privileges, and management of shared spaces.

So much for autonomy....

Although the basic client lacks these built-in management features, it's been noted that third-party applications can easily retrofit such tools.

More conclusions about the real architectural model are drawn from the more detailed walk-through later. Already however, it can be stated that Groove is an example of a directory-based server-centric implementation of p2p—see the Table 10.1 summary of components.

TABLE 10.1 *Groove component summary*

Component	Specific forms	Comments
Identity	User-defined, arbitrary within a workspace, but also digital signatures	The relay server maintains a user directory, several identities (roles) for single user supported.
Presence	Server centric "awareness", optional subscription notification	User information continually updated by online clients.
Roster	Members of a workspace	Can be member of several shared workspaces.
Agency	Shared workspace tools	All activities and changes in a workspace are synchronized among members.
Browsing	Supported	Shared collaborative browsing possible, along with other.
Architecture	Server-centric directory, closed proprietary	Peer connectivity has relay server fallback.
Protocol	Closed proprietary, encrypted, signatures	Currently locked to Groove's central server.

SHARED WORKSPACES

The basic function implemented in Groove is *synchronizing two or more PCs across the Internet* in terms of activities that occur inside a defined *shared workspace*. This can mean anything from drawing on-screen, to moving tools or creating content.

All shared activities are encoded as XML representations of the changes in the space, compressed, and sent as encrypted **delta** (that is, change) messages to the connected peers. The other clients then interpret these state changes and move or modify their representations of shared data accordingly. This "minimalist" format serves to maximize interactivity and responsiveness.

The user interface, or *transceiver* as it's known in Groove terminology, tracks all of its content and activities locally in an XML object store. There's no requirement for any central, shared data store. The local content is passed to a local XML object-routing service, part of the Groove client, which in turn passes it to other endpoints over the Internet. This part of functionality is plainly p2p in its initial descriptions, as indicated in Figure 10.1, and performed in real time, at least in principle.

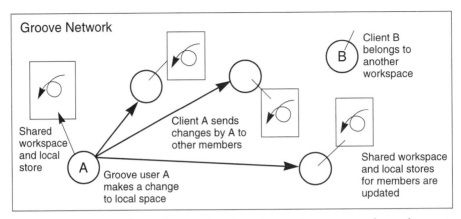

FIGURE 10.1 *Groove clients share a virtual workspace between members of a group, where all changes (such as user actions) in any client's representation are replicated by change messages sent to the other members. This schematic ignores the role of the transparent relay server.*

Users in the group can thus work interactively with the same tools, files, and other resources. Groove also supports shared, coordinated Web browsing and a number of other communication channels, such as instant messaging, live voice over Internet, text-based chat, and threaded discussions.

> **Tip 10.1 Groove is mostly about interactive collaboration efforts.**
> The technology has excellent support for some of the kinds of things that small groups of people might normally do if they were working together in the same room.

However, Groove's underlying architecture is *asynchronous*, which means that workspace sharing doesn't strictly require real-time connections. When all parties aren't connected at the same time, a store-and-forward "relay" service saves all deltas in a local queue and forwards them later to any absent member computers when they connect. Any changes made on disconnected clients are simultaneously propagated to the other group members at this time. This journalizing aspect also effectively and transparently bridges shorter connectivity glitches in workspace sessions, something that might prove especially valuable for networks that include mobile devices such as wireless LAN, handheld computers, and Internet-aware cell phones.

Note then that Groove's relay service introduces a centralized server-dependency for message passing as part of the package to allow this disconnectedness. Groove relay services are hosted and managed by Groove Networks at the company Web site, along with other centralized services, such as download of Groove software components. Although now available for free, the company plans to offer these and similar services for a fee, promising guaranteed service levels.

> **Tip 10.2 The relay server is a transparent facilitator for all p2p functionality.**
> Note that it is not possible in the current design to establish and maintain connectivity between Groove clients without connectivity to the proprietary Groove relay server.

Critically, the relay server also provides three other services, which because of client design, further lock in this server dependency. Figure 10.2 illustrates the basic connectivity through the relay and some of these other services schematically.

- **Awareness**, otherwise known as presence, which tracks which team members are online. It also tracks what they are doing—whether chatting, browsing (even to the extent of which URL!), using the notepad, or any number of other activities loosely associated with the workspace.

- **Fanout**, which is designed to minimize bandwidth consumption. If the transceiver detects network conditions that might cause significant delay to messages (for instance, high Internet latency), it just sends a single copy of a delta to the relay server for optimized distribution to the other members.

- **Transparency**, which confers the ability for clients to communicate with peers without knowing anything about possible firewalls or NAT devices. If clients can't communicate directly using TCP/IP (for instance due to firewalls or NATs), messages are automatically passed through the relay instead, perhaps encapsulated in HTTP as a tunneling proxy service.

Clients that go online publish local information to the relay server and continue to update this information for the duration of the session. Published information includes the client's IP address, firewall or NAT status, and as noted, current activities.

Hence, the relay server also acts as a common user directory service for locating team members at any given time, in fact any current workspace, and incidentally resolves the issue of node discovery for joining clients. Users may define one or more identities (such as user names, role names, multiple identities in same workspace), unless overall enterprise policy mandates that users import preexisting network identities. Third-party implementation of Lightweight Directory Access Protocol

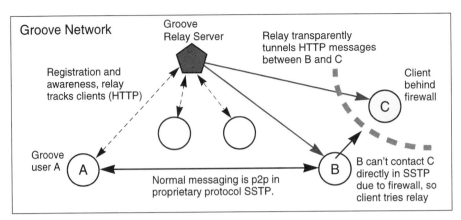

FIGURE 10.2 *All Groove connectivity is dependent on the central relay server in one way or another, even if peers normally communicate directly. The fallback for firewalled clients is to pass messages through the relay.*

(LDAP) might allow enforcement of unique names, but such naming functionality is unsupported as yet. In fact, the relative freedom of identity naming between different workspaces is promoted as a convenience.

The awareness service is implemented as a *subscriber notification* system, so users don't have to poll the server but are informed by selected events.

Server Bottleneck

As a security precaution, it's said, Groove proprietary client design is such that customers can't implement their own relay servers, and consequently, neither the services nor a Groove network on their own. The stated intent is to make it difficult for hackers to set up rogue relay services that could capture and attempt to decrypt Groove communications.

However, this restriction makes all Groove users totally dependent on Groove Networks, just like any other server-centric solution—and, yes, it includes the basic client, too. It's expected that Groove Networks may allow other trusted instances, such as ISPs, ASPs and telcos, to host and manage Groove relay services in the future.

The bottom line is that the Groove proxy and tunnel servers, which provide the essential relay, awareness, fanout, and transparency services, are potential performance bottlenecks. One might well expect that guaranteed service levels might become the offering that would make a fee-based premium service attractive.

PROTOCOL

Groove uses a proprietary protocol called Simple Symmetric Transfer Protocol (SSTP) to implement the message transport layer on top of TCP/IP or optionally HTTP. The company has declared an intention to sometime publish the SSTP specifications, but for now, it remains closed and unknown in its details.

The main requirement is that SSTP must handle rich-context, peer-to-peer interaction, including features such as compression, routing, security, real-time communication, and synchronous use. The company is also tracking emerging alternative protocols to see how they might be incorporated into SSTP—for example, Blocks eXtensible eXchange Protocol (BEEP or BXXP).

A firewall probably won't pass SSTP messages between Groove clients, however, and this is where the relay server's transparency comes in. It can try to "bridge" the clients. A client that can't reach a peer automatically sends its messages to the relay service, which then encapsulates them in HTTP and sends them to the intended but firewalled client. Because HTTP is such a fundamental Internet protocol, these messages will pass unhindered through a firewall as a rule. The Groove client on the other side can unwrap these encapsulated messages.

The HTTP mode is not totally firewall proof. An organization might restrict the locations from which HTTP can travel across the firewall. It's therefore possible for companies that value firewall rigor over user-initiated interaction to block such messages from the Groove relay service. In that case, Groove would be unusable behind the firewall unless the company acquired a license to run its own relay server.

As noted, XML is the representational protocol used to transfer encrypted data between clients. Groove also relies on SOAP, an object-oriented application protocol. Support thus exists for passing local and remote procedure calls over the Internet, which confers compatibility with future Internet security systems and Web services. Specifically, it gives the potential for interoperability with .NET services. This last feature could be an important aspect in gaining enterprise acceptance.

Internal API calls can be wrapped in Java, with multilevel remote access to client features, but it must be noted that Groove does not have native Java support.

In addition to this messaging layer, Groove also implements a proprietary Voice over Internet Protocol (VoIP), a technology area that's rapidly gaining popularity as complement to or replacement for traditional telephony—especially within the corporate context. VoIP allows voice chat between members with computers that support the necessary microphone and sound card hardware.

SECURITY ISSUES

The security issues with Groove can be seen from two different perspectives, largely because of the heavy emphasis on business and enterprise.

On the one hand, there is the common problem of being a target of malicious intrusion, whether to disrupt overall functionality, destroy or manipulate stored information, or steal data from the shared workspace. To this end, one generally designs a robust, independent system that cannot be controlled or manipulated.

On the other, there are legitimate corporate security concerns about the ability of Groove, or any p2p agent for that matter, being able to penetrate firewalls and ignore normal IT authority, policy, and control. It's a serious matter when individual users can arbitrarily share files with outside clients, perhaps inadvertently introduce virus software into the intranet, infringe intellectual property laws, or access sites normally banned from the workplace.

The different levels of protection afforded by Groove are

- **Privacy**, which is in the form of end-to-end public key encryption. Only the intended recipient can decrypt a message.

- **Authentication**, by transparently using public keys generated dynamically. Voice message attachments can convey a personal invitation to a shared space, also being an indirect (weak, but intuitive) authentication.

- **Nonrepudiation**, which just means that because all IM and shared space messages are digitally signed, a receiving client can automatically verify the signature using the sender's public key.

- **Data integrity**, which also relies on data encryption and digital signatures. This level ensures that recipients can verify that messages have not been modified or damaged, and that they come from the correct source. Additionally, all data stored locally is also encrypted.

The last two measures extend to tool downloads, mainly as virus protection. Groove automation means that users might download and execute tools without realizing that they are doing so. Without adequate protection, such a situation could rapidly spread virus-tainted software.

Keys are generated dynamically by the clients—as with PGP, there is currently no central key authority. Keys are generated for each identity when it is created, and in addition, for each workspace as it is opened. Users have no interaction with this

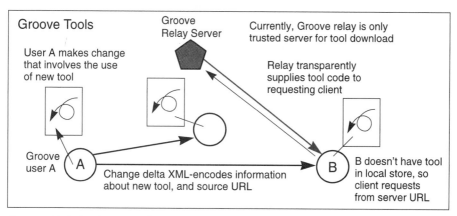

FIGURE 10.3 *Tools (as applications in the workspace) are handled transparently and downloaded from a trusted source when required by a change.*

Groove PKI layer because it works transparently. A downside to this deep design is that the PKI can't be integrated with external or existing corporate key systems.

Groove doesn't rely on signature verification alone, however, because tools are never downloaded from other clients directly. A request for a new tool comes encoded in XML with a URL to a central, trusted and approved Web site, currently only Groove Network's own servers, as shown in Figure 10.3. Although this might be extended to other sites in the future and is a measure motivated by security concerns, it does introduce vulnerability, trust, and performance issues of another kind.

The premium, managed client can be set up to further verify source and restrict from where tools can be downloaded. Alternatively, firewalls could be configured to deny even HTTP connectivity with all but particular sites or ranges of IP addresses.

CLIENT ISSUES

Clients implement four levels of sharing customization, some without requiring any programming experience on the part of the user.

- **Drag and drop**, where users can intuitively combine tools in a shared workspace to create a unique environment.

- **Scripting**, which uses JavaScript and VB Script to create communication links between tools—for example, one updating another of its changes. Groove tools are COM objects, so COM-based programs not designed as Groove tools can still integrate into the Groove environment.

- **Tools,** where programmers with C/C++ skills can build new Groove tools from scratch—that is to say, application objects that can be used in the shared workspace environment.

- **Connectors,** which are ways for C/C++ programmers to integrate connectivity with corporate back-end systems. These connectors can be either distributed connectors in terms of traditional channels or protocols, or *'bots* (here short for "knowbots"), software agents that act as a virtual member of the shared space.

So far, Groove is restricted to the simpler, unmanaged basic version, although the premium version is promised soon. The basic client should be seen as a "beta" version and functionality or features can change without warning.

The basic client might be adequate for individual use, but it does lack some features that could prove important in particular contexts. Some examples:

- Currently, Groove is a Windows-only product; a Linux port is but a indefinite promise as yet.

- Replication and synchronization issues are not addressed. Version control and conflict history features are lacking.

- File sharing at present means that Groove physically copies the file to each member's computer. Any subsequent changes to any copy means all member copies must be updated with deltas. Such change notification is inefficient and can consume much bandwidth and disk space for large files.

- Group membership confers full privileges, which means any member can do things such as destroy files without leaving an audit trail. Access control and role support is expected for the premium version.

- While management of group membership is admirably automatic and transparent, issuing new space keys for member changes, it does lack mechanisms for (especially role-based) invitation and membership control.

- A "whisper" mode has been promised for some time, to allow a member to converse, text or voice, with just one other member in the same group without resorting to other-channel tools.

Many of these issues are expected to be resolved with the commercial release of the premium version of the client, presumably some time in 2002.

Groove clients have the potential to grow libraries that could consist of hundreds of approved tools. The management of such a library across all client configurations in corporate environments seems likely to prove very difficult. Whether corporate management can be convinced that the benefits are worth this complexity remains to be seen.

Trade press expectations are that Groove's future viability lies with the technology eventually migrating in behind corporate firewalls, where a sustainable revenue model can ensure its continued development. To a large extent, this is true of all p2p technologies that are being commercialized in one form or another, either directly as products, or indirectly by way of consultancy and support.

Probably the biggest impediment to corporate acceptance of any technology is the single-source situation. For Groove, this is especially true with regard to the lack of licensing for relay servers that could operate behind corporate firewalls. As it stands now, deploying Groove means the need to communicate through the firewall with Groove Network's own servers and to rely totally on their uptime. It's been indicated that a limited licensing policy might become available in mid-2002.

Groove is best characterized as a tool most suited for informal and unstructured collaborations between smaller groups of so-called knowledge workers. It's been described as a "client-side portal" able to collect and concentrate information and communication at the PC for the end user. In this respect, it provides p2p networking with more focus than similar such efforts brought to the Windows desktop with MS Outlook or Windows XP. Like most p2p, on the other hand, it will probably not integrate well in more rigid process workflow environments, where more structured enterprise tools are available.

A major reason for including Groove in this detailed examination is that it has received considerable media coverage for what it promises, yet relatively little explanation about the actual implementation. Another is that Groove could easily become a *de facto* standard within business and enterprise if the company can calm corporate concerns about single-source and single-server. The reason for that is the extensive potential for back-office communication, management options, and security control that it appears to offer.

Interestingly enough, the Groove routing model is incorporated in its essentials into the Microsoft HailStorm technology (see the description at the end of Chapter 2), which strengthens the suggestion of a high degree of Groove interoperability with HailStorm Web services in the future.

JXTA

Project JXTA—the name ("*jux*-ta") is short for Juxtapose, as in side by side—is a Sun Microsystems initiative that seeks to integrate p2p technologies as complementary and distributed tools into a mainstream computing and Internet environment. The actual core platform is a fully decentralized network architecture. However, both centralized and decentralized services can be developed on top of the platform.

It started as a research project incubated at Sun under the guidance of Bill Joy and Mike Clary. The goal is to explore a vision of distributed computing using peer-to-peer topology and to develop basic building blocks and services that would enable innovative applications for peer groups. Recognizing this effort would benefit from outside expert programmers, the project posted a specification draft and some prototype code to a Web site (www.jxta.org), encouraging others to join the efforts under the Apache Software License.

Project JXTA is currently still prototype status—that is to say, the posted code (written in Java) and reference implementation this defines is deemed usable, but it's primarily intended as a jumping-off point for developers. It's a small footprint implementation, around 250KB, not counting the JRE.

The current implementations support local network peers which don't need to be connected to the Internet. The specifications additionally allow peer interaction over non-IP network protocols such as Bluetooth. Despite the early focus on Java, partly because of Sun's active promotion of it, but mainly to easily achieve platform independence, the specifications are intentionally language-independent. Alternate implementations are supported and encouraged.

Table 10.2 shows the JXTA component summary. On one level at least, JXTA targets the global Internet in much the same way as .NET, by offering the potential of a generic infrastructure that supports all manner of peer applications. Unlike .NET however, JXTA leaves server dependencies up to the individual applications. It also has a clearer focus on broad support for even comparatively simple (for the most part, appliance-embedded) clients in arbitrary contexts.

JXTA ARCHITECTURE

The intent of the JXTA architecture is that arbitrary network entities be able to find other network entities and collaborate with these in application-specified ways. It does not require any particular platform support by any of the participants but does specify the form and content of the discovery messages exchanged over the network.

TABLE 10.2 *JXTA component summary*

Component	Specific forms	Comments
Identity	User or application defined, arbitrary within a peer group	Defined by application and peer group context. Trust systems and digital signatures.
Presence	Application defined	Digital heartbeat minimum client requirement.
Roster	Application defined	Peer group, for example.
Agency	Application defined	Through services layer.
Browsing	Application defined	Application or services layer.
Architecture	Core layer networking, services layer and application layer	Modular based on common core for p2p networking.
Protocol	Open and fully specified, encryption support	Core protocols support all basic networking functions.

The architecture is described using three layers.

- **Application layer,** which supports the implementation of integrated applications, such as file sharing, resource sharing, monetary systems, and distributed storage.

- **Services layer,** which provides the API hooks for supported generic network services, commonly used by p2p applications. Typical examples include search functionality, sharing, and additional security features.

- **Core layer,** which implements the essential protocols and components for p2p networking. This layer includes node discovery, and a transport layer with firewall handling and some security. It also supports the creation of peers and peer groups.

The entire design is a very modular one, allowing developers to pick and choose the services and applications that suit their particular needs. The common core makes it easy for developed services to be interoperable and particular applications to mix and match desired features using existing and new modules, or add them later.

Defined core protocols are NetPeerGroup Protocol, Peer Discovery Protocol, PeerGroup Discovery Protocol, Peer Information and Management Protocol,

PeerGroup Membership Protocol, PeerGroup Resolver Protocol, and PeerGroup Sharing Protocol. All are fully open and specified.

PEERS AND GROUPS

Peers are defined in the JXTA context as any devices that support at least some of the Project JXTA protocols. A peer therefore can be anything with "a digital heartbeat" that supports the core layer. This definition can admit a whole range of devices, from servers, PCs, and PDAs, to cellular phones, and embedded manufacturing and medical equipment. The only requirement is that the peer needs to be connected to some kind of network, such as IP, Bluetooth, or Havi.

A *peer group* consists of any collection of peers that have agreed on a common set of rules to communicate between themselves, and to publish, share and access *codats*. Each peer group can establish its own membership policy, ranging from fully open to highly secure and protected.

> **Tip 10.3 Codats are the basic unit of information exchanged by JXTA peers.**
> A codat is a JXTA extension to Java objects that can hold both *code* and *data*.

FIREWALLS

Because JXTA peers rely on direct p2p communication, without a central server to mediate exchanges, it's fair to ask how it deals with firewalled clients. The answer is pretty much the standard "push" model familiar from other atomistic p2p.

Clients on either side of a firewall must be aware of each other at minimum, usually by the firewalled peer reaching out to open a connection with some peer outside the firewall. A client can be configured to use a proxy. Clients are identified with unique identities, not any particular IP, so address translation across NATs is not a problem. As long as the firewall allows normal HTTP communication, possibly with more than the default port 80, the peers will be able to exchange messages.

SECURITY MODEL

The heart of Project JXTA security is like so many other systems today based on the distributed public/private key signature and encryption scheme. Such a system provides strong and proven security, if set in a workable "trust" context.

The trust model, code-named a "P2P Web of Trust", is similar to the PGP "Web of Trust" used for secure e-mail, and it's implemented to exchange public keys among its members. Varying degrees of trust are assigned to different members, formally or informally, but keys that are signed by trusted members acquire a trusted status, at least in the eyes of those who accept the trust of the signing member. A peer group policy may give some members the authority to sign public keys for other members, in addition to routine tasks such as authentication, adding or removing members, and removing or revoking memberships.

Both the JXTA core and application layers can access the security module, so any service or application can have its own security component or protocol plug-in.

> **Tip 10.4 JXTA security is essentially up to the implementations.**
> The JXTA layers provide all the commonly required mechanisms as ready-to-use modules, but it is the responsibility of the application to implement the degree and scope of security measures or possibly to customize its own modules.

Security classes exist initially for the common algorithms (RSA key exchange, RC4 cipher, and SHA-1 hash). Combinations of security classes form security suites, and customized extended suites can be added as required.

A separate Pluggable Authentication Module (PAM) handles peer group authentication. There is authenticated login support, including anonymous or "guest" users. Peer group security policy determines whether a login session is in clear or cipher-text mode.

Software Projects

The JXTA portal site (platform.jxta.org) provides up-to-date information about the status of support on the various platforms, and access to the most recent builds of demo software. Core software, services, and usable applications are available.

To provide a hint of overview, the next section gives the development state of JXTA as it appeared in December 2001. The core projects define the peer software.

Core Projects

The core components of the JXTA system are developed in the framework of a number of separate projects, listed in Table 10.3.

TABLE 10.3 *JXTA core projects*

Name	Description	Comments
di	JXTA Distributed Indexing	Core search functionality.
jxme	JXTA for J2ME (CLDC/ MIDP)	Provide JXTA-compatible functionalities on small memory devices (such as cellular, PDA).
jxta-c	JXTA core C binding	C-language binding for JXTA core.
jxtaperl	JXTA core for Perl 5	An implementation of the core JXTA protocols in Perl 5.
jxtaruby	JXTA core for Ruby	Ruby implementation of the core JXTA protocols.
objc-jxta	JXTA core Objective C	An objective-c binding for the JXTA platform.
platform	JXTA platform	JXTA platform infrastructure and protocols for Java 2 SE.
pocketjxta	JXTA for PocketPC	Porting the JXTA platform to the PocketPC platform.
security	JXTA P2P Security Project	Core security and distributed trust mechanisms.
tini	JXTA platform TINI binding	Tiny Internet Interface, a Java virtual machine on SIMM-stick.

Services

This section specifies both core and optional JXTA p2p services. Required core services include Authentication, Discovery, and Codat management. Optional services include for example naming, routing, and codat indexing and searching. These services are used to build JXTA applications. Table 10.4 lists the projects, and the following text describes some of them in more detail.

For example, it's assumed that peers will both provide and receive certificates and digitally signed data, which makes it useful with an authority service that maintains common public root certificates and can validate certificate chains on behalf of peers. The *Caservice Project* is developing such a trust service.

TABLE 10.4 *JXTA services projects*

Name	Description	Comments
caservice	Certification	Peer service that can validate certificate chains.
cms	JXTA Content Management System	Early core service.
cpm	Compute Power Market resource management	Economics-driven computing platform and p2p marketplace.
edutella	Query, replication, mapping, and annotation services	RDF-based metadata infrastructure for p2p applications.
gisp	Global Information Sharing Protocol (GISP)	Distributed hash-selected query nodes for keywords.
ipeers	Artificial Intelligence in P2P Networks (AIPN)	Agent technology to create self-adaptive, intelligent networks.
jxrtl	Task distribution using XML and peer matching	Implements Active Networks in JXTA.
jxta-rmi	RMI API on top of JXTA	Java Remote Method Invocation extended to p2p context.
jxta-wire	Multiway communication	Provides a set of tools to allow many to many JXTA pipes.
jxta-xml-rpc	Remote procedure calls	JXTA transport binding implementation for XML-RPC.
jxtaspaces	Distributed Shared Memory Service (DSMS)	Programming distributed applications using a shared memory abstraction is less complex than explicitly using message passing.
jxtavfs	JXTA Virtual File System	Organizes JXTA network resources as virtual filesystem.
monitoring	Monitoring and Metering	Enhance and extend corresponding core functionality.
networkservices	JXTA Web Services	Integrates Web Services concepts and protocols into JXTA.
p2p-email	Peergroup E-mail	Peer e-mail group discussions using JXTA Peergroup technology.

TABLE 10.4 *JXTA services projects*

Name	Description	Comments
payment	Implements EPocketCash payment protocol	Anonymous and secure financial transactions on Internet.
replication	Replication/synch engine	Peer replication of files and data (Plasmid, SyncML).
rrs	Remote Rendezvous Service (RRS)	Local and remote administration of rendezvous peers.
rvmanager	RendezVous Manager (RVM)	Help nodes coordinate to discover other peers and groups.
search	JXTA Search	Distributed search service for JXTA and Web content and services.

JXTA implements a *Content Management Service*, with sharing across peers in a peer group. Simple searching is provided across all peers in a peer group. For example, the InstantP2P application uses the CMS service to implement the search, share, and unshare shell commands.

The *Compute Power Market* (CPM) Project implements an competitive market economics approach to managing computational resources similar to what was described for Mojo Nation, in Chapter 8. The idea is to transparently access computing power as a network commodity and allow providers to offer cost-effective service on demand. CPM defines one or more interoperable marketplaces to bring together resource providers and consumers.

CPM deploys a Resource Agent to provide a mechanism for defining resource access policy and requirements (and pricing) and a Resource Broker to lease resources in the network for executing applications in such a way that user QoS demands are met. Smart algorithms make resource discovery, selection, and scheduling decisions.

The *Edutella Project* has a first application focus on a p2p network for the exchange of educational resources between German universities (including Hannover, Braunschweig and Karlsruhe), Swedish universities (including Stockholm and Uppsala), Stanford University, and others. The vision is to provide the metadata services needed to enable interoperability between heterogeneous JXTA applications.

The *Global Information Sharing Protocol* (GISP) Project aims for worldwide information sharing using a distributed hashed-index service. GISP doesn't use broadcast query messages but takes information keywords and selects one peer to query for each keyword. The method is based on calculating the difference between the MD5 hash value of a keyword and MD5 hash values of different peer IDs, and selecting the peer with the smallest difference. A related core project is JXTA Distributed Indexing (di). The Jnushare Project, listed under applications, is an implementation of GISP.

The *Ipeers Project* is developing agents that automatically adapt to the network environment and that can bridge offline times for peers by continuing to act on their behalf on the network.

The *JxtaVFS Project* is about managing virtual files, which are dynamic files mapped to remote resources. It is a way to create a distributed, self-maintaining, yet hierarchical map of resources on the network. Each deployed instance of a JxtaVFS service is just one reflection of how a set of resources is organized in perspectives, knowledge of how these resources are categorized. Multiple instances of JxtaVFS can be aggregated together to form larger directory units that map the current availability of peer resources on the network.

The *P2P-E-mail Project* is an open standard framework to create and manage sustained group communication for spontaneous lightweight peer groups. It adheres to the implicit peer group organization as well as the transient, decentralized nature of p2p communications, with the intent to give an e-mail-like user experience. In later development, it must also provide security (encryption) and other-peer backup of messages for disaster recovery.

The goal of the *Payment Project* is to implement the EPocketCash payment protocol for financial transactions for JXTA, which allows anybody to be merchant or customer at the same time with the same account. This anonymous payment system will work on any device connected to the Internet—currently supported are Web, WAP, and I-Mode phones. Like other e-payment systems, its success hinges on how ubiquitous and transparent the infrastructure becomes for the average user.

The *JXTA Search Project* is an ambitious framework to have peers provide distributed network and Web content search functionality. It has its foundation in, among other things, the InfraSearch project mentioned in Chapter 3. Not only does JXTA Search intend to route and process queries but also to provide a notification service by indexing queries and tracking publication, leveraging the core *di* service.

Application Projects

These projects are to develop JXTA applications that enable interactive access to the JXTA P2P platform. Most are very lightweight; Java implementations with downloads in the 100Kb range. Table 10.5 lists the current ones.

TABLE 10.5 *JXTA application projects*

Name	Description	Comments
allhands	Event notification	Test JXTA use as a messaging and publishing KB framework.
brando	P2P Java source code sharing tool	Allow developers to work together without a central CVS source control system.
configurator	GUI configuration tool for the JXTA platform	Under development.
dfwbase	Peer network with a database at each peer	A distributed knowledge base application.
gnougat	Fully decentralized file caching	Distribution of static file content. Also allows file sharing.
jnushare	File sharing of GISP	File-sharing application using CMS.
juxtaprose	Text content sharing, using existing XML CMS	For Web and discussion. Also find, browse, and annotate JXTA resources in general.
jxauction	Auction software	Develop an auction software that can be used on any Internet-connected device (such as mobile).
jxta-httpd	JXTA Web publishing	Provides a set of JXTA services and tools for Web publishing.
myjxta (instantp2p)	JXTA Demonstration GUI (Group Chat, Chat, Search, Share)	MyJXTA replaces and enhances the functionality of the former InstantP2P GUI.
parlor	Collaborative p2p spaces (*tabletops*)	Application framework for creating collaborative spaces.
project2p	Share project documentation	Content p2p sharing in development contexts.
rosettachat	Messaging	Localized JXTA peer text messaging (real-time chat translation).
shell	JXTA Command Line Shell	For interactive access to JXTA platform (for developers).
www	Special "project" that collects information	HTML documents and information about JXTA.

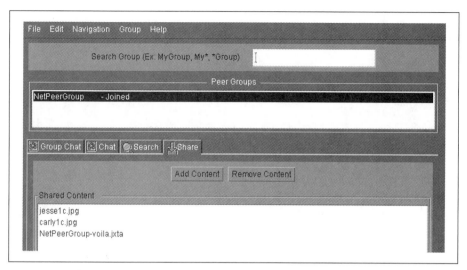

FIGURE 10.4 *A simple graphical interface in myJXTA allows a JXTA peer user to easily access chat, group chat, search, and share functionality.*

InstantP2P, now called *myJXTA* in its latest and enhanced implementation, is a Project JXTA demonstration application, designed to implement the most common p2p functionality sets of messaging, peer group chat, search, and file sharing.

The graphical user interface in myJXTA, shown in Figure 10.4, allows the user to create and join groups for chat. By default the client downloads a predefined set of Rendezvous and Routers that mediate such peer group contacts, but this list can be redefined. In addition, the local peer can be configured to act as a rendezvous and router peer itself. Not a polished application, albeit steadily improving build by build, the main purpose of myJXTA is to be a functional template for developers.

The *JXTA Shell* is an optional command-line interpreter application to enable users and developers to interact with the JXTA platform. The shell application can be used to monitor the status of peers or peer groups, to access and manage core platform objects (such as peers, groups, pipes), to communicate with "external" JXTA services and applications, and to debug for example communications problems. It functions in a manner similar to *nix-style system shells.

Gnougat is actually a fairly Gnutella-like "servent" (Chapter 7) implemented in JXTA technology. The crucial and innovative features of its protocol lie in how it identifies files and handles queries. Content ID is uniquely based on a hash of the content itself, which allows easy identification of duplicates for cases where parallel download of variable-sized fragments is feasible. Although queries (both for text and

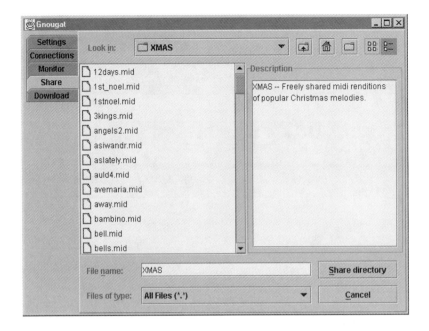

FIGURE 10.5 *Gnougat is an atomistic, Gnutella-like file-caching and file-sharing client for JXTA. Still very much in development, the implementation does showcase a number of interesting network-optimizing features.*

hashes) are broadcast and hits trickle back in the usual atomistic search manner, participating clients aggressively cache hit descriptor information based on visible demand and hit frequencies. The resulting adaptive behavior reduces overall network traffic in that more nodes can return valid hits that point to the correct source.

Figure 10.5 shows a capture from the sharing tab of the Gnougat client. Connection management and caching are not fully developed yet, so at the time of writing, it's more a proof-of-concept client than a deployable peer system. Like all things in this field, that status can change rapidly.

A number of the projects are still in proposal or planning stage but are interesting nonetheless. JXTA should be seen primarily in terms of providing an alternative, decentralized, peer framework with open source functionality that can match or surpass the centralized and proprietary .NET vision. It's far too early to say if one or the other, or neither, will come to dominate the future Internet. The open source aspect of JXTA however does suggest that the academic and Linux worlds will tend to support it more than any .NET solutions.

PART III

Voices and Visions

Peering Insights

I readily admit that this book is flawed. Any book on a subject as rapidly evolving and controversial as peer to peer and with as ill-defined scope as in this term will inevitably be both incomplete and unsatisfying to at least some readers. On the other hand, an attempt at greater coverage could easily have resulted in something approaching Gibbon's *The History of the Decline and Fall of the Roman Empire*—which empire, interestingly, exhibited several characteristics common to p2p models during several periods of its existence.

Although the selection of technologies and choice of perspective could have been made in other ways, with perhaps equal success in satisfying a reasonable portion of readers, I would be remiss in not taking space to include this last part about general insights, future and vision. Again, the scope and views may not be to everyone's liking, but surely it must at least prove thought provoking.

However, in the open and consensual spirit of true p2p, I offer it to you freely in accordance with the "Law of Two Feet" which pragmatically states: *"If you like it, you walk in. If you don't, then you walk away."*

Welcome then to Part III, which is less about p2p technologies as such and more about how they are used. Mainly, it's about the social contexts in which they are used—contexts that they have the power to profoundly affect, disruptively or constructively.

The first chapter in this concluding part looks at the "insights" aspect, and some practical conclusions are drawn regarding the use of p2p networks. Social themes, some hinted at in earlier chapters, become prominent from this perspective and deserve a deeper examination. The last chapter attempts to peer into the future, at best discernible as shadows rapidly moving in the mist.

CHAPTER 11 AT A GLANCE

This chapter looks at some of the social implications of peer technologies, and includes comments drawn from the experience and reflection of others.

Peer Community explores the social implications highlighted by p2p and relates some of the current commentary on these matters.

- *Technology Acceptance* is found to be a crucial factor in determining the success of a technology.

- In the *Social Criteria of P2P*, we take this analysis further by examining the different assumptions manifested in software as cultural expression.

- *The Content Control Wars* shows how diverging software cultures have come to be in conflict concerning control of digital content.

- *The Legal Challenge* outlines the current legislative mess surrounding copyright as applied to digital format usage.

- From the *Micropayment Solution* discussion, it seems clear that a micropayment infrastructure is the only viable way to effectively implement pay-for-use fees on digital content.

- *Free and Legal* provides a contrasting view, where digital content can both be free and be rewarding to the creators.

Visions of Sugarplum summarizes where we appear to stand in 2001/2002, after the fevered hype of the preceding years.

PEER COMMUNITY

A lot of p2p discussion is just about the technology, and one can see definitions of the term that fully reflect that view, such as the one given by Peer to Peer Working Group (www.peer-to-peerwg.org)—perhaps one of the better definitions, even though it seems to ignore the communicative aspect (that is, IM) altogether.

> *Peer-to-Peer Defined: Peer-to-peer computing is sharing of computer resources and services by direct exchange.*

I tried to go beyond this computer-limited view, even though most of this book (especially Part II) is very deep on technological detail, by sandwiching it between history, analogy, and legality views in Part I, and the social and personal views here in Part III. In fact, much of peer technology can be viewed as based on recognizing the *value of the individual* within a *community of users*. Realistically, this recognition involves both freedoms and responsibilities. Tim Berners-Lee, credited as creator of the World Wide Web, expressed a core freedom this way:

> *There's a freedom about the Internet: As long as we accept the rules of sending packets around, we can send packets containing anything to anyone.*

The rules he speaks about are the underlying technical conventions, the protocols that make the infrastructure communication at all possible. Packets of data are pretty impersonal entities until you can interpret and reconstruct the content—the transport medium doesn't care one way or the other what they represent.

Another freedom exists on the Internet as well, especially relevant to peer application equality. Call it the *universal interoperability principle*.

> **Bit 11.1 Standard Internet protocols are the universal level playing field.**
> So long as a device—any device—obeys the peer network protocols, its size, shape, form, and location are irrelevant. Anyone can play.

However, *social rules* are implicit in this situation, often unspoken, yet tacitly understood by the particular group that follows them. Like all social rules, they largely depend on your particular peer group's philosophical outlook. With regard to the Internet's common currency of content—*information*—the social rules are what molds how we use it—or conversely, restrict it.

Information might be neutral and free in theory, but in the human context, it is often subservient to other and more value-charged issues. Nor am I neglecting the commercial aspects by stating this relationship because few things are so emotion- and value-laden as money.

But let's return to the social dimension of interoperability for a moment.

Chapter 1 introduced Metcalfe's Law, which stated that the value of a peer network was approximately proportional to the *square* of the number of nodes (written as $n^2 - n$). The law can be seen as a value statement from a purely technical viewpoint, even though we are considering the perceived value of available resources.

From the community point of view, the important thing is groupings between people. The math tells us that the potential number of nontrivial groupings we find in this network is proportional to the *exponential* of the number of individual nodes (written as $2^n - n - 1$). This relationship is known as Reed's Law of networking.

> **Bit 11.2 Reed's Law: The social value of the network is proportional to 2^n.**
> The network represents the exponential value of interest group affiliations.

As the resource value (or intercommunication) of a network grows geometrically with a linear increase in the number of nodes, its potential social value (as grouping) therefore grows even faster. We may not always do the math, or be clear about how relevant it is, but intuitively, peer users do feel these value-rich aspects on some level.

Consider if you will the contrasting value of a network consisting of relatively few transmitters of information compared to a great many receivers—the common broadcast or server-to-client model. There, the network value increases only linearly with the number of nodes, because the information flow is unidirectional. This, incidentally, is Sarnoff's Law of networking. All good things come in threes.

So, transforming into a *peer group* a cluster of say 10 desktop clients that only connect to Web servers increases their aggregate resource value by about factor 100. However, the potential social value increases by about factor thousand (2^{10}) and can double for every additional node. These figures very quickly get mind boggling, if not absurd, with larger clusters, but the implications are clear. It's not much of a reach to assume that the *value experience* of the social aspects of peer networking, when people are involved, *comes to totally dominate all other considerations* even in very small networks. This grouping aspect also extends to all communicative peer situations, even automated ones, whenever such groupings confer added value.

Technology Acceptance

The things that transform the world are often *concepts*—simple concepts—that come from unexpected directions and somehow, without any real premeditation, end up being "the normal way" to do things. We tend to see only the changing shape of the technology detail, already there, ever more complex and sophisticated. However, look a bit deeper, and you'll realize that much technology expresses only a few, simple, human concepts—or let's instead say, much *successful* technology.

But what *is* success, really? Apart from anything else, a pragmatic indicator is that success generally means *social acceptance*. A technology can be "damned good" indeed, in the technical sense, seemingly deserving of instant recognition and adoption, yet fail abysmally. Why?

It's not just a matter of blind luck which technology succeeds and which is forgotten. The phrase "ahead of its time" is sometimes used for innovative curiosities consigned to a dusty attic, but often the answer is that the social context at the time was just not ready to accept it. In some way, the innovation "broke the rules" and paid the price for being too far away from the accepted social norms. Other variations, although less efficient or poorer designs, adhered closer to the rules and were instead accepted by a sufficient majority. (Yes, this is a generalization that ignores abrasive and antisocial innovator personality, or poor business sense.)

In this view, technologies are shaped by the social rules, and perhaps more succinctly, the result can be recast as: *Applied technology expresses the social rules* that are accepted by those who design and implement it. While innovation is about change, nothing really changes without the broader acceptance—if the tension is too great between the new and the accepted, the new is ignored. It puts constraints on the kinds of change that can happen based on the technological aspects alone. What good is a new technology that's deployed if nobody uses it?

Conversely, even old-fashioned or low technology can find new uses and become powerful catalysts for change under a new set of social rules. I believe that p2p technology to a large extent falls into this last category, notwithstanding the many innovative features a particular solution might showcase.

Internet and peer technologies are not exempt from social molding. Each significant group involved in developing and deploying the technology also shapes its design in its own image, so to speak. This book provides several examples, which is in part why the examined implementations are selected from both camps: open source and proprietary. Each has a different approach to the same basic p2p functionality, and the end result is also different in ways both obvious and subtle.

SOCIAL CRITERIA OF P2P

We can outline the main *social* criteria common to most of the open source p2p solutions presented in this book—consider how technical decisions often seem based on at least implicit reference to one or more of the following:

- **Consent.** Nothing happens without it.

- **Disclosure of information.** Censorship or exclusiveness is contrary to the purposes of a p2p network. Open information is necessary to the informed consent of the individuals in their participation.

- **Common ownership.** Content is shared freely across the network, not infrequently with a certain, shall we say, casual disregard for prevalent views on intellectual property ownership.

- **Empowerment.** Individuals are in full control of most aspects of their participation; their degree of collaboration, which content to be shared, and in general the behavior of the software. They are responsible for and control their own local resources.

- **Cooperation without vulnerability.** Individuals should be able to cooperate without fearing undesired exposure. The concept includes the possibility of full anonymity while still being able to verify a consistent source.

- **Distribution of storage or functionality.** In many systems, network resources are spread across many collaborating nodes, thus becoming more clearly community resources than strictly individual ones.

These social criteria all represent an expression of the attitude and philosophy held by the designers, and are examples of *software as culture*.

Consider then for each of the criteria, how socially acceptable the view is among the general population of users. Consider also for each, how acceptable the view is for business or government. Consider finally how much these respective measures of acceptance might vary between groups and countries. (Even the process of software localization involves far more than simple translation of the user interface.)

It's left as an exercise for the reader to formulate a corresponding list that characterizes the social criteria usually expressed by proprietary designs and therein to identify the main differences. For some, such considerations easily become overtly political issues, but for the purposes of this book, I won't go there, only look at it from the less value-sensitive social perspective.

The Content Control Wars

Peer technologies became very (and visibly) controversial in the wake of Napster's popularity. While a "new" battle rapidly evolved around music copyright and received media exposure, the battle lines already existed behind the scenes.

A sort of demarcation line has always existed between two different mindsets concerning intellectual property rights in general. On the one hand, the original academic setting of the Internet has long nurtured a strong "freedom of information" attitude that extended to free software and broad notions of fair use of otherwise copyright-restricted content.

> **Bit 11.3 The primary academic goal is to publish information openly.**
> The act of publishing information openly, subject to peer review, defines career advancement and is a prerequisite to funding success in the academic world.

On the other hand, the world of industry and commerce has constantly defended and strived to extend legal protection for the exclusive use of the protected product, content, or service—even to the point of it being counterproductive. It's inevitable that there is considerable tension between these two diametrically opposed views.

> **Bit 11.4 The primary goal of business is to sell something exclusive.**
> Protection of exclusive and proprietary rights maximizes short-term profits.

Add to this volatile mixture the interests of state and police control of content, made complicated due to the international nature of the Internet and uncertainties about the applicability of national laws to this new medium. Although it's still considered dubious whether one country's laws on content are applicable to providers or users in another country with other legislation, not to mention the confusion when many different jurisdictions are involved, pilot cases have already been pursued to that effect—successfully in first instances.

> **Bit 11.5 The primary goal of government and law is to control and regulate.**
> This means control of people, control of money, control of information, and control of rights. The tough part is to balance between too little and too much.

Both commercial and state interests therefore have a natural tendency to work against the spread of p2p technologies that undermine the very notions of central control and content censorship. It would simplify the legislative tangles for them if free access to content could simply be made technically difficult or impossible.

Although we can describe actors on both sides of this conflict as loosely belonging to a pro-p2p or an anti-p2p movement, such a simple dichotomy is a convenience only at a fairly superficial level. The respective actors have their own specific agendas and are just as likely to be opposed to their allies on particular issues.

The prospective peer technology user however must understand that the mere choice to use open p2p networks is practically by definition a subversive act, at least in the view of much of the business world and most of the world of authority. That said, significant sections of both worlds still see far enough beyond these narrow constraints to realize that open peer technologies can be both profitable and good for the national interest. This makes the entire show so much more entertaining, if at times more than a little confusing.

All About the Money

A prominent result of the different social views that came to expression in Internet technologies is the split between server-side content producers and providers, and the more, shall we say, *idealistic* peer-to-peer groups. The battle lines have come to center on, predictably, *money*—or as expressed at one remove, *ownership rights*.

The FreeWeb FAQ (freeweb.sourceforge.net/faq.html) puts it this way:

Sadly, modern technology has created a situation where privacy and copyright protection are now in direct conflict.

Both cannot exist at the same time.

Through much contemplation, the developers of FreeWeb and Freenet have concluded that the right to privacy and anonymity are fundamental human rights which morally transcend the principle of private intellectual property ownership.

The developers of FreeWeb and Freenet staunchly believe that artists and content creators do deserve compensation for their efforts. However, the existing system has proven itself to be a failure. Of the revenues generated from sale and licensing of works, artists throughout history have only received the tiniest percentage. Also, history has shown that many incredible works have been universally rejected by publishers, only to win accolades much later, often after the creator's death.

The P2P community is keen to usher in a new system of reward for artists/ creators, and a new system of contribution for consumers. The internet, as it evolves towards offering a platform for truly safe, secure, convenient (and even anonymous) payments, will make such a system possible.

Even though this particular community has rejected the social rules of the opposing camp in this context, they are by no means radical anti-socialites and are also concerned at some level with money and due compensation. This is not the same as another vocal group they are sometimes confused with, the "we won't pay" advocates of total freedom of software, content and bandwidth, at no cost.

The difference is that the main focus is the small-scale peer one—in this case, on the individual content *creator*, whom they feel is usually left out of the loop in the large-scale commercial models that are so intent upon preserving and extending content control for the aggregating *content publisher/wholesaler*.

It's not necessary to agree with one or the other view of commerce for the purposes of this text; that discussion leads far afield into the "new economy" and the nature of money—interesting enough, but surely worth at least a book on its own. Simply register the fact that the divide does exist and to a great extent is rooted in just the opposing social views described earlier.

Use of Technology

Another focus of the content control wars is on the technology itself, often seen as being disruptive and dangerous by simply existing as it does, free of any centralized control. This issue too has both commercial and political aspects, though it most often is expressed in legislative terms in attempts to control or ban the technology.

With Gnutella, for example, it can be argued that it is like any other Internet protocol, each of which is just as capable of "encouraging unlawful" purposes in addition to perceived legitimate uses—true for practically any technology, no matter how simple or otherwise innocent. The reactive tendency to repress p2p technology has come to a head in the increasingly harsh anticrime and antiterrorist environment of later years. Like strong encryption technology before it, p2p thus experiences ever more attempts by authorities to "control" it—or failing that, outlaw it.

Strong encryption technology was initially patented and classed in the United States as nontransferable weapons technology to prevent export. However, due to a technicality in timing between publication and patent, the algorithms were not deemed patentable in foreign patent law, allowing the technology to be developed as open source in Europe. The restrictions have largely fallen by now, because strong public key encryption is legally and easily available, despite attempts to mandate other, less-secure technologies that allow authorities back-door decrypting.

Just as the growing public key infrastructure (PKI) is now an inescapable part of the emerging new Internet, aspects of peer technology are being structurally built into it as well. Chances are decently good that a decade from now, p2p applications will be as natural a part of the landscape as the server-client systems, and hardly anyone looking back will quite see what the fuss was about.

It's an open question whether or not this will also mean an integrated global system for enforced control of content rights, according to an extended version of the regulation that the commercial interests are trying to erect now. It's simply too early to tell under which terms society will accept the technology in the long term, and what the ensuing social and economical consequences will ultimately be.

Business vs. Academia

Another view of the ongoing battle describes it as being between the "content faction" who want total control over digital media and its use in any kind of digital device, and the "tech faction" who feel such efforts are misguided.

This control issue is also socio-economic at root; we can note that the content industries always refer to *consumers*, while tech industries refer to *users*. Recall that the impulse to *empower users* was at the very heart of the microcomputer revolution. This same techie impulse is at the heart of the p2p movement.

A desktop in every home gives each individual the kind of computing capacity that IT-managers once would have waived their stock options for. In a different context, this situation would surely have been seen as both dangerous and subversive, and undermining the interests of business wishing to sell processing to consumers. As it happened, a consumer mass market for retail processing never emerged, hence there was little objection from that quarter. Never mind that the PC-revolution turned into a unprecedented and profitable global industry, far larger than anything anyone could have envisioned—first in computers, then components and software, and now spilling into games and entertainment.

What's to say the same can't happen to an emerging p2p infrastructure, nurturing an entirely new form of virtual economy based on network-distributed resources and services? The slogan *a peer-cluster in every home LAN* comes to mind, and it might be the appropriate battle cry for some new visionary.

Businesses continually seek to erect entry barriers to protect themselves and their particular markets from competition, and intellectual property is no exception. For them, copyright and patent law are often seen as the best (or just most cost-efficient) barrier—essentially a monopoly granted and enforced by government. A strong case could be made that the original intents of patent (that is, limited exclusive rights to innovators in return for publishing and licensing) and copyright (as ownership of created content and the right to derived revenue) have been subverted in the interests of unlimited control and corporate greed, supplanting the original creator interests.

The business view's desired future for digital content is quite simple: All digital content (such as books and music) will be tied to particular devices, and transfers between them will be difficult if licensed, or impossible if not. This tying down of content, by both legislation for digital content management (a euphemism for digital content control) and hardware implementation, actually ensures a far tighter control of content than for the traditional physical distribution forms that existed before digitized media. The goal is enforced scarcity to control revenue, which according to many is wrong in a digital content context.

John Dilmore of the Electronic Frontier Foundation wrote a lengthy analysis of the subject in his essay *What's Wrong With Copy Protection* (see www.toad.com/gnu/whatswrong.html), and it's worth reading. He answers the question in this way:

> *What is wrong is that we have invented the technology to eliminate scarcity, but we are deliberately throwing it away to benefit those who profit from scarcity.*

Supporters of open source and open content believe on their side that only excellence in execution constitutes a real barrier to market entry, much like a law of nature. They believe it not merely as a principle of theory, but as a practical truth firmly grounded in the traditions of the academic world of public funding: Any project that doesn't serve its constituency will either fail or be shut down. The artificial exclusiveness that much business seeks irrespective of excellence is therefore anathema.

On occasion, the proponents of this view have put their money where their mouth is, successfully generating revenue from value-added services based on freely distributed software, notably in the Linux and Open Source world. Such success leads us to believe that abundance economies are possible. John Gilmore thinks so (*ibid*):

> *I think we should embrace the era of plenty and work out how to mutually live in it. I think we should work on understanding how people can make a living by creating new things and providing services, rather than by restricting the duplication of existing things.*

Returning to this book's main focus, peer technology can be used for many things: collaboration, document sharing, distributed data, efficient distribution, and so on. The way it is implemented tends to assume that replication and distribution of existing data/content is open, unrestricted and free in the academic tradition—in fact, it proves very difficult and awkward to do otherwise.

Unfortunately, one very widespread use (and the *only* one in the case of the high-profile original Napster and its clones) was (and is) to share files with IPR-protected content in ways that are not allowed by the current "official" interpretation of content ownership laws. This casual disregard was provocative of course even to some of the content creators. It motivated the various commercial content interests groups to take notice when the usage becomes sufficiently commonplace, and it ultimately motivates them to seek to ban the technology completely if they can't regulate (profit from) its usage.

The objection is really on principle because, despite the vocal complaints by the industry about lost revenue caused by music and film swapping (or for that matter, software so-called piracy by individuals), the revenue projections always make the assumption that any individual possessing an illicit copy would otherwise have bought the same content through normal commercial outlets. For the most part, it's an unwarranted assumption, even ignoring the fact that many people download "illicit" digital copies of content *they have already purchased* but want in another, more convenient format. It also ignores the fact that the user might turn consumer by buying new content that they have previewed in downloaded format, something that reported increased sales of music CDs around university campuses would seem to bear out. Neither act is considered fair use by current IPR interpretations.

The issue is not an either-or situation, but one with infinite shades of gray.

Market Assimilation

The real issue lies elsewhere, however. It's not the abstract, potential *capability* of the technology that matters but *how people commonly use it*, and less often considered, how the social norms govern such usage. No modern country would ban telephone technology today, despite the fact that it is easily used by criminals.

While Internet technology has been subjected to such bans in some parts of the world, it's usually been partly due to the fact that it's only been used by a minority. Besides, banning legitimate use rarely stops criminal use. More commonly, it creates an artificial advantage for criminal use because ordinary people can't use it.

Forces are always at work that promote *adaptive* responses, even in the initially most adamant opponents. One of the more potent is the realization that there might be a market value in adopting a technology formerly seen as disruptive. Having assimilated the opposition, goes the thought, it can be possible to control as well. As an example of how it can work, I offer the following historic aside:

> *Does anyone remember when the tape recorder and VCR were both hotly disputed pieces of equipment?*
>
> *For a time, it was a highly controversial issue to copy music from radio or records to tape, or movies from TV to tape, and play these as often as you wanted, whenever you wanted, for free! The issue wasn't really about compensation to content creators and distributors, it was about control.*
>
> *The cinema interest groups fought the very concept of home recording with tooth and claw, striving to reserve movies for the big screen and later for television pay-per-broadcast. Ways to ban the technology and later to prevent illegal copying were considered but found inadequate or too difficult to fully implement. So what happened? Copying to tape for personal use, long seen as fair use by the general population, eventually became officially accepted, even though governments tried to apply special copyright taxes on blank tape media at the request of the music and movie industries.*
>
> *When the technology became commonplace enough, the content industry quietly adapted to the social consensus. Ubiquitous video rental stores and the rapid transition from cinema to rental media are a testimony to how the movie industry has changed its commercial model to fit the market. It now encourages everyone to own the technology, a VCR or DVD player, and for a pittance rent a legitimate copy of a movie at convenience.*
>
> *Copying from TV became a nonissue, and from other tapes less interesting because rentals are so cheap. Even legally purchasing your own copy is no more expensive than buying a book. Movie production is bigger than ever. Even the DVD system of region blocking is gradually fading. However, so far the ban remains on decoder software that can give DVD-movie support to platforms other than Windows, as view the DeCSS mess.*

The hope is that the music and movie industry will eventually want p2p technology to work *for* them, in much the same way. It should offer products and services attractive to consumers, instead of blindly attacking the technology and its supporters. This insight must have reached some quarters, as evidenced by the music industry's sudden and rapid acquisition of music p2p technology companies during 2001, even as competitors' lawsuits were still pending against the same companies in the courts.

Some details of the proposed music market changes still seem outrageous to the general public, such as limited playback of purchased music tracks, and inability to copy the tracks to other equipment that the buyer owns. Nevertheless, we can expect that aspect of commercialized p2p distribution to eventually mature under the pressure of the market. We hope.

As noted by John Gilmore in his essay (*ibid*), the copy prevention technology already being integrated into products on the market might before then leave the consumer-user in the single role of passive consumer. He asks

> *Being devil's advocate for a moment, why should self-interested companies be permitted to shift the balance of fundamental liberties, risking free expression, free markets, scientific progress, consumer rights, societal stability, and the end of physical and informational want? Because somebody might be able to steal a song? That seems a rather flimsy excuse.*

Bit 11.6 Resistance is futile. Prepare to be assimilated.
Even the most adamant resistance to new technology can vanish in an instant if there's an advantage to be turned by adopting it faster than the competition.

THE LEGAL CHALLENGE

Legislated digital content control is a thorny issue, highly politicized and steeped in vested interests. In America, the current efforts have also come into conflict with constitutional rights and widely accepted norms of fair use. There, one sees that the traditional balance between the rights of creators, on the one hand, and the rights of freedom of speech and the press on the other is being lost.

When copyright legislation has been unilaterally extended, the public domain has shrunk correspondingly. The right of criticism, even the right to dispute someone else's rendition of the truth, has been curtailed in practice, weakening the First Amendment's almost absolute right to publish. The active term of copyright kept getting extended by new legislation in the late 1900s, one consequence being that few works created after 1910 have entered the public domain, as was the original intent of copyright expiry. Now the content control rights created by technological restrictions are not even designed to end—they are made permanent and retroactive for all situations and all forms of media, even those not yet thought of.

Naturally, this has consequences for peer technologies.

Control and P2P

The various hardware and software implementations of digital content control, and the ill-considered legislative framework behind them, are all still very much on the advance, and some of them can critically affect or stop some forms of p2p technology before the media industry might itself segue into the p2p resale business.

Blocking the likes of Napster, Scour, and recently MusicCity and its affiliates was ultimately possible because a single center of operations could be held accountable for the transgressions of the users. Failing direct compliance by the center, one could then go after the hosting Internet provider or upstream connectivity provider and have them shut down the offending server connectivity. Once the central server is killed, clients stop functioning, and the network falls apart.

In the case of truly distributed p2p, no such identifiable center exists. It is nearly impossible to find and stop each offending end user. Trying to automatically detect such users and disrupt their connectivity with denial of service attacks for example, as has been done, is in general opinion seen as an action more reprehensible than the acts it tries to stop. The response is on the same level and intelligence as lobbing cruise missiles at post office branches found to have stored mail with illegal or suspect content. Besides, distributed networks are very tolerant of nodes dropping out.

The logical next target for those trying to stem the tide of free file exchange is therefore the developer community. Suing individual developers, and the companies that develop p2p technology is being tried, but it is a viable option only if the target is small and inconsequential. It's highly unlikely that you will ever see anyone try to sue Microsoft for the p2p sharing potential of .NET or Sun Microsystems for the potentially illegal actions that could be performed by users of JXTA. Promising innovations in p2p in smaller contexts however have been stopped by just the threat of legal actions, and venture capital made cautious about investing in p2p.

On the other hand, developers aren't exactly fleeing in droves. "Developers must continue to build software that makes copyright obsolete," is an expressed sentiment that's perhaps an overstatement, and developers (and their patrons) understandably don't feel comfortable about their ever more exposed position. As one posted:

> It is known that a number of Gnutella users share files they are not entitled to share according to RIAA and other interest groups. Whether you are one of those users is absolutely none of my business. But as a Gnutella developer, it IS my business that I could possibly be held liable for this.

But it's also true that technological advances always have a tendency to go beyond the bounds of legislation by providing functionality that the law formulators never envisioned. This is especially true of copyright when extended to digital content.

For some, it's become a vital issue, as numerous infoanarchy.org postings show.

Nothing but the idea of owning information will stop information technology from developing—nor should it, since your freedom requires it.

Such advocates believe that Gnutella, or networks like it, will inevitably become a huge part of the Internet—either that, or the Internet in its current form will be extinguished. The latter is generally seen as untenable (and not even possible in the short term), despite ever more rigorous and restrictive legislation. Note in this context that government is making itself ever more dependent on public Internet access, even as it is part of the organized movement to close down the very openness it needs.

What might some of the new and proposed legislation mean? A proposed next step in general p2p file sharing might mean that the receiving user must request a file from a *specific* user who must explicitly *agree* to provide it and store an audit trail. Such a consent method provides an individual accountability, of sorts, as opposed to the largely anonymous seek and download nature of most file-sharing p2p applications out there. Consensual sharing is already implemented in some messaging applications that added file transfer, such as mIRC (an IRC client) and ICQ.

This assumes that such transfers are not made meaningless by hardware blocks, as mandated by present and future legislation for digital content control. And mutual consent doesn't carry much weight if the transaction as such is made illicit. At its extreme, users might not be able to record or store any digital content at all, unless it is centrally authenticated that the user owns the copyright, or has purchased the (per-use) rights to replicate it—no hardware/software will exist that can do it otherwise.

The legislative backing for technology developments of this kind includes (in the U.S.) examples like the Audio Home Recording Act, the Digital Millennium Copyright Act, and the FCC ruling that it will be illegal to offer viewers the capability to record the new HDTV-format programs at all.

Hold the Laws, Please

Lawrence Lessig is a law professor at Harvard University and often profiled in media as a clear voice speaking out about the issues of intellectual property and freedom of information exchange. He encourages people to take a wait-and-see approach when it comes to legislation and p2p—as in a keynote speech at the O'Reilly P2P Conference:

Let's build it first. We can expect that there will be conflicts.

*The question is whether we stay committed to that initial ideal
... before we send in the lawyers.*

U.S. (and European) legislators would do well to adopt such a moderate approach, especially considering that the Internet is a global domain, not one dominated by a single nation or single culture, nor to be regulated by the laws of any one nation.

Bit 11.7 Open source is firmly in the build-now, regulate-later camp.

The main advantage to this approach is that at least one then knows what, exactly, one is trying to regulate, and if there's any point in doing so.

But then as we've seen, it's very much a question of short-sighted business interests pushing the implementation of such laws—and to a great extent, against the common sense attitudes of the general population. That doesn't mean legal protection isn't necessary even in what's termed cyberspace—the totally free and heady frontier days are over, and the Internet must become a safe place to visit and do real business in. That means serious *community* building, not empire building.

Even if the laws are not enacted, unfortunately, we still have the private agreements by manufacturers to embed copy-prevention technology in commodity media components. Examples of such efforts are **SDMI** and **CPRM/CPPM** submitted as part of new recording standards. Already, DAT and MiniDisc recorders treat all analog input as if it contains copyrighted materials that the user has no rights to.

While DVD recorders might be marketed for home movie editing and storage and digital photo storage, it seems clear that they will be internally blocked from the common VCR usages of time-shifting television recordings and recording streaming video from the Internet. Because manufacturers who attempt to offer more open functionality are sued, for example, for circumventing "copy protection" under the DCMA, competing noncompliant products are rapidly forced out of the market. Hence, the pragmatic "you have the right to record a copy of what you have the right to see" ruling (the Betamax case) defended by existing law is made irrelevant by largely undisclosed technological blocks.

Whether or not one agrees that manufacturers have the right to arbitrarily cripple the functionality of their own products, one must deplore the way the dominant players are redefining the global playing field for everybody.

MICROPAYMENT SOLUTION

Seen from another angle, much of the current problem from free digital content (interpreted as illegal copyright infringement) may stem from the simple and sad fact that a global payment system for the Internet, although long envisioned and awaited, has not yet materialized. If IPR interests get paid, then surely they'd be happy?

The many digital cash and e-wallet projects and proposals, all filled with promise, were ultimately left to fade away as footnotes. Why? The detailed reasons are many—often the lack of standards or transparent interoperability is blamed—but the fundamental reasons come to just two:

- *Lack of user convenience*, which in this case can be rephrased as a lack of a ubiquitous and transparent payment infrastructure for e-commerce.

- *Lack of user confidence and trust*, which is not solved just by making the system secure and trustworthy in the technical sense.

A solution that satisfied both of these requirements would quickly become an *ad hoc* standard, as other players quickly adopted it to have a share of the growing pie. As it is, we're stumbling along with a mix of sort-of-workable payment solutions in a sea of dubious advertising and user-free content.

The most accepted and common payment scheme on the Internet today is still the credit card details typed into a Web form, hopefully on a secure protocol server (using HTTPS). This form of transaction—which, by the way, is safer than using the same card physically in shops and restaurants—relies heavily on a really remarkable amount of consumer trust in the system and on the way the common cards are accepted around the world as a consumer convenient form of cashless payment. The global credit card infrastructure, already in place, made card purchases naturally translate well into the borderless Internet context. It's also relatively easy to implement over Web servers, from the technical point of view.

The major objections to credit card payment are that it's less convenient for the merchants (who pay the transaction costs), and that the current routing through banks makes card payment not feasible for smaller amounts. This also means that you have to have (and afford) a special merchant's account and a minimum volume to process card payments. Individuals with irregular sales, such as shareware authors, can use payment services such as SwReg.org for a cut of profits—typically a dollar fee plus 5 percent of the sale, but even offering "micro-commissions" for low-price items. With a stated annual sales at the $12 million mark, it's easy to see how such an established organization can meet the overhead of card processing.

In short, the state of Internet payments is at about the level of coin- or card-operated public telephones, except that the minimum charge is ridiculously high for that context. Returning to this telephony analogy to p2p makes sense even in the realm of e-payments. Telephony charges are accumulated as microcharges against a subscriber and billed periodically, like any consumer utility. User decisions are about higher service abstractions, such as which operator has the best rates and how high a periodic bill one can afford, not individual call charge blips or particular call-service fees.

Most operators work this way, and almost everyone accepts it.

Although the telephony network introduced and retains a per-minute style of charging for connectivity and services, it is less applicable to the packet-based kind of virtual connectivity that characterizes the Internet. The model is even becoming less relevant to telephony as its infrastructure also becomes more packet-based and service-subscriber oriented.

The Internet unfortunately lacks a metering and billing infrastructure for payments (disregarding the dial-up ISP by-minute model, which is essentially telephony in any case), so the closest thing now being deployed by the larger content providers is the fixed subscription model, monthly or yearly. Unfortunately, this addresses the revenue issue only from the provider's point of view. Subscriptions make sense only when people regularly rely on a single provider (or a handful): telephone operators, newspaper or magazine publishers, commuter cards, and so on. The advantage of the model lies solely in aggregating theoretical small fees into periodic sums that can be handled by traditional, out-of-band payment mechanisms (card, check, bank deposit, or transfer) and simplifying accounting by bundling access into all-or-nothing.

For freely roving Internet users, on the other hand, subscriptions are *site obstacles*, blocking their easy access to content. You can't hyperlink directly to subscription content, and search engines can't index it. The visitor is instead redirected to the entrance portal page to log in first. Session memory, cookie tracking, and recent, more intelligent login redirection to the original URL admittedly help usability there, but the site as such remains opaque to the outside world.

The main user objection to subscriptions is that the typical monthly fees for each site add up alarmingly fast, given the broad range of sites a typical user wants to visit. This model is roughly equivalent to telephone users being required to pay a monthly subscription fee for each and every telephone number they want to access. Put that way, it's clearly not a convenient solution, nor is it a viable one in the long run.

Subscriptions *might* make sense in a p2p environment, where the fee buys you access to the entire network for a particular time, but even here it doesn't solve the real issue of e-commerce: *how to make the payments* in the first place with minimal transaction costs. This issue ultimately makes the user look elsewhere. Out-of-band systems like Paypal (www.paypal.com) are only a short-term palliative.

> **Bit 11.8 Content subscriptions per site are not a viable e-revenue solution.**
> Let this stand for a prediction in the face of the projected rapid adoption of subscription solutions on the Web in 2002. As with the click-through advertisement funding it replaces, the subscription model must founder in the end when the expected flow of revenue devolves from a disappointing trickle to ever nearer zero.

But seriously, and allowing for the idea that digital content should have a price, the only realistic and lasting solution to some form of revenue model for content on the Internet has to be a very low pay-per-use model *built into the infrastructure*—in a word, a *micropayment* technology as transparent as telephony rates for phone users. Dial-up Internet users don't stop browsing the Web just because the activity is accruing charges to the operator or ISP by the minute. Neither should they conceivably object to similar sums going straight to the owners of the content they browse, as long as they aren't forced to do the detailed accounting.

> **Bit 11.9 Viable network agency will presume a micropayment infrastructure.**
> Let this be a longer-term prediction, that really useful p2p agency won't deploy until micropayment-based, scalable usage of distributed resources flies.

Given a decent infrastructure, micropayments make excellent sense because a characteristic of digital media is that the transaction costs can be made arbitrarily small, so even ridiculously small fees per item can be handled with no loss. The user-consumers see periodic sums charged to a real-world cash account; the user-providers see accrued sums deposited to their respective accounts. The micropayment system does the math either way, handles seamless transactions, and can cough up the item-specified lists for inspection on demand. The main design goal is to avoid needless detail for the user on either side of the transaction. Real microeconomics could do the same for Internet resources that virtual micropayment systems do for p2p resources, manage and scale them transparently on demand.

Free and Legal

The preceding discussion might give the impression that we'll have to pay and pay, but legal for-free alternatives keep turning up even in such a contentious area as the sharing of music files. A couple of recent examples are FurtherNet and RootNode, which might be seen as p2p versions of live-recording distribution channels such as Etree. Some artists also choose to distribute their music themselves, and releasing recordings for free trading is seen as a way of driving interest for their works.

Etree (www.etree.org) is a community of FTP servers that host and distribute lossless digital audio files (not degraded MP3 format) across the Internet. It's important to realize that Etree distributes concert recordings of bands that explicitly allow this. There is both a considerable amount of such legal material and a large community of music lovers that trade legal recordings. The primary focus is for users to be able to burn their own audio CDs with DAT-quality recordings.

FurthurNet (www.furthurnet.com) is a decentralized peer technology, called the first noncommercial p2p network for trading legal live music, and was created by fans for fans, with much support from members of Etree and Sugarmegs music-sharing communities. The client software enforces the sharing of only legal content by limiting search and sharing to a preselected list of bands. Music files are summarized in "sets" that make it easy to get complete collections by particular artists. Multisource download is supported, and reviews of the open source client developed in Java are favorable.

RootNode Live (RNL, www.rootnode.org) is another decentralized p2p network, descended from Gnutella. RNL is utilized for the legal, reliable trading of live concert recordings. It is open source, and rootnode.org itself is a music-magazine site made by some students from Georgia Tech. Running the client requires a registered account with the main RNL Web site, which provides a form of central accountability even in the serverless environment of the client. (Interestingly enough, Georgia Tech was a hotbed of person-to-person server technology in the form of the open Swiki, as detailed in my previous book, *The Wiki Way*, and the site encourages registered members to contribute to the content.)

Some concern has been voiced in the general p2p community that by moving into self-proclaimed "legal only" networks, these users are weakening the position of the free, general-content networks. This presumably means that the critics feel that by keeping a focus on a narrower segment of p2p file sharing, these users are unlikely to protest against new legislation, or the disruption and shutdown of the other networks, until too late. There is some historical precedent for that view.

VISIONS OF SUGARPLUM

As the recent hype about p2p as the solution to all problems faded in late 2001, along with many of the companies most vocal about this promise, we see a residue of practical solutions out there, hard at work or in the process of being deployed.

Despite the controversy, the single-source problem, the uncertainties about security and liabilities, many companies continue to pursue, sometimes aggressively, a deployment plan for p2p of one nature or another. Efficiency, better profit, better customer relations, staking out a future market—all are powerful motivations to take the risk, and their common element is some vision of revenue. Another, perhaps larger group is pursuing the open source implementations and further developing a generic infrastructure to transform the Internet as we know it. Their immediate goal is not revenue, though as it happens the infrastructure and software might make that more attainable, but to make p2p a natural part of the digital landscape.

Granted, the use of "p2p" as a descriptor has become less popular, and as noted previously, the spring 2002 O'Reilly P2P Conference was retargeted as "emerging technologies", without the peer focus. Perhaps this is an indication of a more considered approach to the technologies that are being discussed. Perhaps too, it is a realization that many p2p solutions don't function in a vacuum but depend on many layers of network and infrastructure, on interoperability with traditional centralized services, and even more importantly, on unforeseen social and legal dimensions that can derail even the most promising technology.

The situation is a far cry from the high-adrenaline days of 2000/2001, when most seemed to be convinced that the combined energy of emergent dot-com startups and new Internet technology would make the global economy go straight up indefinitely—shades of inexhaustible resources, in virtual space there are no constraints! Millions of PC users suddenly had the magic horn of digital cornucopia installed right on the desktop, with uncounted terabytes of music, film, software, and virtually anything at all at their fingertips, for free.

Well, that was fun while it lasted. The world is significantly more sober in 2001/2002, and other issues have largely dimmed the spotlight of attention of p2p. That may be a good thing, as now only the serious and committed innovators and developers remain in the field.

So, next, let's look at the implementations applied to practical situations and examine the usage patterns associated with p2p.

CHAPTER 12

P2P Case Studies

Practical peer technology experience to a large extent is as distributed as the technology itself. Many readers have no doubt already experienced some aspect of p2p in one situation or another, often without realizing it was p2p. File sharing, messaging, or some form of Web service at their best are just a natural and transparent extension of a user intention. And it's really quite amazing in how short a time we take a revolutionary innovation for granted.

Attempting to summarize the state of p2p with well-chosen case studies proves more difficult than anticipated, although one excuse is that most of the field is still highly experimental. Even widely deployed implementations frequently employ beta-test versions of the software, sometimes in the low minor digits. It takes highly optimistic (or foolhardy) companies to aggressively launch market campaigns based on little more than vision.

Or, at least it used to be so. Much of the dot-com bubble was just about just that: marketing the ephemeral visions of some innovator or hyped-up CEO. Sometimes the vision does in the attempt actually manifest a usable product, occasionally even with remarkable powers to change the entire playing field—imagine a world where the aggressive launch (multiple times, as it happens) of a beta-quality Windows operating system had failed and sunk into obscurity. Hmm, indeed....

Anyway, once the glowing testimonials and press release hype is filtered out, publicized deployment stories are relatively few and far between. Perhaps this lack can be rectified in a next edition, when this book has provided a focus for others, both in terms of potential deployment to relate and a realization that such stories have a value for others yet to take the plunge.

CHAPTER 12 AT A GLANCE

This chapter tries to tie together issues culled from practical deployment in the field, and make some observations about what to look out for.

Enterprise Goes Peer looks at what has happened in the vendor marketplace concerning p2p or peer-related technologies.

- *Intel and P2PWG* discusses how Intel is a strong supporter of peer technologies, primarily as hardware solutions.

- *Finance and Trading* is a brief look at areas most likely to be willing to deploy messaging and collaboration p2p technologies.

- *The Case of the Missing Material* speculates over why it can be difficult to obtain useful information about enterprise p2p solutions.

- *Brief Mentions* is an overview of several examples of application areas where p2p technologies have been tried or seem imminent.

Usage Cases attempts to define practical application issues.

- *Usage Patterns and Problems* takes an oblique approach by examining practical issues common to the different application categories, based on how they are used, rather than by looking at specific products.

Peer-to-Peer Journalism looks at p2p from the information angle, as solutions for people communicating with people.

- *Practical Trust Systems* outlines the current state of trust and reputation systems and their possible development in *Security Futures*.

- *Peer-to-Peer Politics* provides one deployment area where we've seen very little so far.

Peer Integration examines the potential for p2p to become ubiquitous and how it could totally transform our lives.

- *Integration with the New Web* mentions some areas where integration work is being done now.

ENTERPRISE GOES PEER

It seems likely that much enterprise functionality will migrate to p2p applications over time, as the technologies mature and are offered by multiple sources. While client-server model infrastructure will hardly disappear, at least some "mission critical" applications are destined to become peer distributed.

Analysts suggest that some server-based functionality should be decentralized sooner rather than later, and it's important for enterprise to figure out which they are in any given environment and what kind of p2p implementation to use. Tasks to be inventoried and scrutinized for such migration include critical problems in networking, communication, distribution, content sharing, collaborative work, community building, and information management.

Ideally, we want to see some practical user stories from the field. Trying to get an overview of peer technologies used in enterprise proved surprisingly difficult, and it is only partly due to the imprecise way "p2p" has been used as a descriptive term by various technology vendors and their customers.

In general, enterprise concerns about interoperability, security, performance, management, and privacy have seriously hampered the rapid adoption and implementation of new technologies. This is especially true for peer technologies that inherently deemphasize or even eliminate central control.

The easiest "peer" technology to clearly document based on case studies turned out to be a category I had largely excluded from this book, because practical implementations usually show little or no communication between peers. This is distributed processing outsourced to idle PC capacity in a network. DP resource sharing is most often entirely managed from central servers, and the distributed clients communicate exclusively with them, never their PC peers.

Other groups that have been documented in peer contexts turn out to be based on solutions for distributed resources, application logic, and storage. Again, in the enterprise context, control and management turn out to be centralized, with little or no control at the peer level. This fact makes these cases relatively uninteresting from the point of view of this book. At best, we see p2p communication between distributed central servers in an otherwise markedly server-client architecture.

That said, significant activity and experimental deployments have brought closer potential widespread adoption of different p2p solutions that will affect both corporate and individual users. In particular, work on standards and infrastructure, along with the heavy commitment of Microsoft to .NET, Sun to JXTA, and others, practically ensure that some forms of p2p will become as ubiquitous as e-mail, messaging and the Web are today.

This section therefore starts by examining a few of the enterprise-oriented efforts and moves on to some vendor solutions for enterprise.

Intel and P2PWG

Through the Peer-to-Peer Working Group (P2PWG, www.peer-to-peerwg.org), Intel is attempting to help set the standards for p2p computing applications and platforms. The P2PWG is a consortium for advancement of best practices for p2p computing that includes many major PC vendors. Note that P2PWG explicitly defines p2p to encompass desktop systems (from the Web site):

> Put simply, peer-to-peer computing is the sharing of computer resources and services by direct exchange between systems. These resources and services include the exchange of information, processing cycles, cache storage, and disk storage for files. Peer-to-peer computing takes advantage of existing desktop computing power and networking connectivity, allowing economical clients to leverage their collective power to benefit the entire enterprise.

Intel has been pushing fairly hard for a broad adoption of peer technologies for some time. This effort may be seen as a result of the success of the company's distributed processing effort, NetBatch, used in-house for over a decade. Not only did this technology increase Intel's average aggregate usage of processor capacity from 35 to 85 percent in its internal network, it saved the company hundreds of millions of dollars by allowing faster chip validation tests.

Intel is therefore advocating the adoption of standards so that the future Internet, seen as a mostly PC-based architecture, can become pervasive very quickly. A side-effect would be to accelerate the adoption of more powerful (and newer) client and next-generation devices. This in turn would naturally promote demand for Intel computer chips, and some of the distributed processing solutions it has developed.

The Peer-to-Peer Trusted Library (PtPTL), launched in February 2001, is one Intel-sponsored effort to provide the secure infrastructure components that business requires to confidently deploy true p2p solutions. PtPTL is a free open source library available for download, which is currently found at www.sourceforge.net/projects/ptptl. The stated goal of this project is to spur open innovation in p2p security.

The library allows software developers to add the element of trust to peer applications by providing support for digital certificates, peer authentication, secure storage, public key infrastructure, digital signatures, and symmetric key encryption. It also provides simple support for networking and some operating system primitives, such as threads and locks, to ease the development of applications that are portable to both Win32 and Linux.

So what business areas does P2PWG see adopting peer technology? Most. The organization doesn't really specify but instead presents the key activity areas, or scenarios common to many, where p2p will make a difference for enterprise.

- **File sharing**, which is glossed over a bit because P2PWG emphasizes that p2p is much more than just this popularized functionality. Nevertheless, it remains a major application in many distribution contexts by reducing network traffic, off-loading servers, and using aggregate storage.

- **Collaboration**, where individuals and teams are empowered to create and administer real-time and off-line collaboration areas in a variety of ways and locations. Collaboration increases productivity and enables teams in different geographic areas to work together. Requirements on servers and network are lower than corresponding centralized solutions.

- **Edge services**, which are billed as "Akamai for the enterprise"—in other words, p2p as a way to deliver services and capabilities more efficiently across geographical boundaries by local caching and adaptive distribution.

- **Distributed computing and resources**, where focus is on providing adaptive, large-scale computer processing and storage, and sharing the results among peer systems.

- **Autonomous agents**, which enable computing networks to dynamically work together. "Intelligent" agents reside on peer computers, exchange information, and initiate tasks on behalf of other peer systems.

All of these areas, coupled with inexpensive computing power, bandwidth and storage, lit a fire under the p2p movement, as the P2PWG puts it. Curiously, no explicit mention was found about instant messaging—whether due to an oversight, taking IM for granted, or simply not seeing it as legitimate enterprise p2p.

Towards the close of 2001, the focus more and more came to be on what's termed "Web Services" (in .NET), in part a reflection of the growing importance of p2p services deployed in a Web-XML context, in part as a reaction to the general hype associated with the generic p2p term. Perhaps too, it's a way of distancing the core of peer technologies from the ever more contentious file-swapping debate. A significant indicator is that the autumn O'Reilly P2P conference was named "Peer-to-Peer and

Web Services", while the corresponding spring 2002 event was renamed as the "O'Reilly Emerging Technology Conference". The latter's subtitle "Building the Internet Operating System" is even more indicative of the focus shift, and Tim O'Reilly notes in the Web information (conferences.oreilly.com/etcon/):

> *Peer-to-peer and Web Services are only the first steps towards the emergence of a distributed Internet operating system—a new platform for next generation applications that are device and location independent, and provide increasingly transparent services.*

While 2000 and 2001 saw the term "p2p" used everywhere, a more mature and business-oriented attitude seems more likely to refer to peers and distributed services. Even the individual areas (such as content publishing and sharing) have become more aware of the trust, responsibility, and legal concerns that are so vital to corporate deployment, so we see a convergence on more secure peer systems from all sides.

Finance and Trading

Business areas that require secure trust mechanisms are finance and trading. Mark Hunt, director of XML strategy at London-based information services company Reuters, said this in February 2001 (reported in an article at www.itworld.com/AppDev/4088/IW010212hnp2p/) about the future of peer technologies:

> *P-to-P is very key, mainly for building community and enabling a flow of good content. In the financial industry context, trading communities generate a lot of ideas. We can use p-to-p and instant messaging to connect that community together to form a feedback loop.*

This evaluation, that p2p would be of most interest in financial and trading contexts, which already depend on rapid and direct exchange of information in other media, suggests that companies in these fields would be in the forefront to adopt p2p.

While traditional information search paradigms are used by people to seek out information when they need it (for example on the Web or in databases), networks based on peer technologies have the capability to continuously track information relevant to a particular individual, in close to real time. Thus, asynchronous search is transformed into notification-driven information update, which is a major attraction for businesses that work in rapidly changing information environments and why they would be willing to adopt new technologies to this end.

All these p2p advantages are clear in principle, but practical deployment seems to have been very experimental so far. A keynote for 2001 has been large efforts to create standards, build infrastructure, and in other ways prepare the way for practical client networks in business. The next year or two should therefore prove a watershed in the way some of these interested companies do business.

THE CASE OF THE MISSING MATERIAL

It's been curiously hard to collect practical case material of explicitly p2p solutions from either business users or from vendors, despite some early, positive responses for contributions. The reluctance to produce may stem from several causes.

- P2P is seen as an outsider and rogue technology. In some corporate environments, it may have been deployed "under the radar" of the IT department. Those in the know can then be reluctant to attract the spotlight of attention by contributing material.

- The technology is being used in or around some more sensitive situations (such as military or mission critical). Inquiries coming from an author in a foreign country therefore are viewed with great caution, especially in the current anti-terrorist atmosphere.

- The technology or its application is viewed as cutting edge. Thus there is a natural reluctance to disclose detailed information that could end up in the hands of competitors.

- Some vendors may have fallen victim to their own hype or to the general market recession in 2001. Several companies that seemed promising early in the year were later no longer showing any activity, sometimes having dropped off the Web entirely.

- People perhaps have just been too busy or preoccupied to follow up on earlier responses or even to respond at all. Time after time, I followed published or forwarded contact links, only to run into consistently broken e-mail addresses, overfull mailboxes, or other discouraging signs that these people simply don't care about contact. *Hmm....*

This list of excuses aside, some general material could be gathered, or enough inferred, to make a case for shifting the focus to what's usefully known about the usage patterns associated with the different peer technologies. First, a few brief mentions of real p2p enterprise products and deployments.

BRIEF MENTIONS

In this section, a few peer-related enterprise solutions are noted. Small-scale solutions seem rare, perhaps because of the many free p2p implementations. The selection is somewhat arbitrary and is intended only to give an indication of where small business and enterprise p2p solutions are going. The examples are neither tested nor endorsed.

Distributed Storage and Content Delivery

Akamai (www.akamai.com) early made a place for itself on the market by deploying large-scale solutions for aggressively distributed and adaptive storage, and by extension, outsourced e-business infrastructure services and software. The solution is based on a central-server-based technology but in the form of peer clusters distributed geographically. The technology is fairly well documented, and it's used by Intel as a case study for successful use Internet technology (and of Intel hardware).

The guiding concept of Akamai Network Deployment sounds familiar from the p2p perspective: "The only way for Internet content services to work is to put content at the 'edge' of the public network, close to end users". In this instance, the company's perspective is global, with solutions to distribute storage and retrieval for multinationals and international service providers. The strategy is to put thousands of small, powerful, relatively inexpensive servers at thousands of locations around the world. It reportedly deploys several hundred new servers every month, and demand shows no sign of slackening. The rack-mounted servers provide a flexible clustering technique that can adapt to virtually any requirements. Akamai created its own suite of Linux-based management applications. As a counter to the extremely distributed architecture, it also set up a secure network operations center (NOC) that is staffed 24 hours a day. Network problems are found and fixed from a single location, in real time, no matter where the problem exists.

Another part of the strategy is a dynamic off-loading of central request-serving points with transparent redirection. While the user might see a single, central Web content provider, the content is actually being served from adaptive caches in any number of locations nearer to the user. High-load providers such as Yahoo!, CNN, and Amazon rely heavily on this form of storage and processing outsourcing, both to cope with loading and to provide redundant reliability in their core services.

To guide the future deployment of edge services, the W3C (World Wide Web Consortium) published a technical recommendation document that defines the Edge Architecture Specification (4 August 2001, www.w3.org/TR/edge-arch), derived from Akamai and Oracle work, which extends the Web infrastructure through the use of HTTP surrogates—intermediaries that act on behalf of an origin server.

Distributed Dispatch Management

Endeavors Technology, Inc. (www.endtech.com) has pledged its support of the Peer-to-Peer Working Group and contributed Magi, a p2p collaboration infrastructure, as a proposed world standard for the flow of information between Web-enabled devices using p2p technologies.

Magi Enterprise gives peer status to PCs, laptops, and Win CE handheld devices, allowing all to securely communicate and interact. Implemented as an end-product, Magi Enterprise securely links office and project teams together for such collaborative needs as file sharing, file searching, instant messaging, and chat. The system utilizes HTTP, WebDAV, and other open standard protocols to create a secure, cross-platform environment for collaborative-intensive applications. A MagiSeek component can search and index files across the community for rapid search and access activities.

One product built atop the Magi system, Magi Dispatch, manages the dispatch, tracking, and closure of field service repairs for service dispatch centers. Armed with no more than a WAP (Wireless Application Protocol) phone, a service technician can be alerted to a service call, obtain driving directions, place part orders, and file status reports. The Dispatch system includes a graphics-based, drag-and-drop development environment to establish work flows and distributed processes. One might also hopefully assume that service technicians can also directly update the support database, from field PDAs or some suitable desktop landing space.

Magi Enterprise for Devices is a p2p software development initiative to transform "unequal" computing devices, such as PDAs, PCs, servers, information appliances, and Internet-ready phones. The common infrastructure opens the door for the creation of collaboration applications for the mobile workforce, and it's perhaps the basic design for the Dispatch system.

Magi Express is a free version of its Magi P2P software, a fully operational peer infrastructure program that doesn't require any additional upgrades or equipment to function, with no trial periods or timeouts. It's billed as an easy-to-use thin server for users to create online collaborative communities.

All solutions are Windows only, although a Mac OS X version is promised.

Proposed is Magi Agent, an advanced process-automation software that is executed securely across peer-connected communities, intended for developing download and payment solutions for the music and video industries, or for creating business eProcesses, such as machine-to-machine commerce, auditing, and tracking in the utilities industry. Another proposed product is Magi E-Commerce software to provide for secure drag-and-drop transactions on the Web.

Home Management

Several vendors, including Endeavors, propose home management systems based on distributed peers for those people with an always-on Internet connection. A dispatcher application can then help homeowners to manage a variety of activities, including scheduling and deliveries. Security applications can also be added using agents that monitor or control motion detection and lighting.

Much could be done (and is) in do-it-yourself ways by individual home owners, given the availability of X.10 or LAN connectivity. What deters many is the lack of standardized structured connectivity, apart from power mains (explaining why X.10 is still around). Ideally, LAN or equivalent bandwidth and signal quality should be available throughout the home. The home owner is still effectively in the analogue position of trying to retrofit an electrical infrastructure given only the main fuse box as a connection point and lots of expanders and extension cords. Wireless networking (Bluetooth or other) might become significant, but physical wires or fiber is better from several points of view, not least the latter for inherent signal security, and cheaper if it can be installed already when the building is constructed.

Physical infrastructure aside, the client situation is better than one might expect. A great deal of Java development is about small clients and embedded, Internet-aware devices, which are inherently intended for p2p deployment. This fact means many home appliances are coming with network connectivity as natural to them as power connection. Separate client adapters can often be added to those that lack embedded clients, and such devices might become as common a commodity in the shops as socket expanders, dimmers, and switch blocks have been before.

Much of this technology is available *now*, ready to deploy for the home innovator, albeit in a somewhat haphazard way. The process is made difficult by a mix of protocols and a lack of unifying, ready-to-use control software for home PC management. Be prepared to write your own manual as you go.

Health Care Services

InterPro Global Partners (www.interproinc.com) aims to be a pioneer in building Web services with the solution it is implementing for Portarius, a services company that focuses on the health-care industry. In the spring of 1999, San Diego–based Portarius called upon InterPro to help build an e-marketplace for health-care communities.

The first analysis indicated peer technology: Instead of looking at a single hub and spokes model, where services are at the hub and the doctor is pushed out to the edge of the network, our model recognizes that the health-care industry is more granular than that; it puts the local physician at the hub. The selected Web services model gives individual doctors more control in the system.

The solution links medical professionals using devices such as PDAs and PCs to one another over a p2p network. They can share medical records, send lab and pharmaceutical orders, and perform other functions that traditionally create a long paper trail. InterPro installs proprietary server technology it calls a Services Gateway on each device, enabling p2p access to the network and allowing the devices to access information on the servers of other devices hooked up to the network.

The example is described both on the company's Web site and as an IBM case study of Web services (www-3.ibm.com/software/solutions/webservices/casestudies/interpro.html). It also uses aspects of Endeavor's Magi networking.

This ends the quick look at some examples of deployable enterprise solutions. We next consider usage cases for the different application categories to see how smaller-scale deployments function in practice.

USAGE CASES

In the application-specific chapters, the focus was mainly on the actual technology. In practical deployment, other issues tend to come to the fore. Some are inherent in the user community that build around the application, while others depend on the hosting network for the application.

Either way, they can come to dominate the practical deployment situation for any peer technology, at best rendering relative merits between competing implementations irrelevant by allowing only one solution, at worst making any p2p deployment impossible. So, although the basis for the following is in individual deployment cases, I have tried to generalize according to the patterns identified.

Realize that all networks in existence today started out small. Over time, some grew, gaining more users and resources, until a critical mass of users, content, or services was reached to make it genuinely useful (and popular). Somewhere along the way, critical problems were identified and addressed, and the simple designs evolved into more complex, and sometimes less p2p ones. Nevertheless, the simple solutions can be more than adequate in particular situations, as long as one is aware of the potential problems when (rather than if) the deployed network grows.

One useful by-product related to usage patterns is when existing peer implementations spin off entire libraries of peer-related code and best practice, which encourages both interoperability and modular design. FastTrack is an example of this, explicitly supporting Kazaa, Grokster and Morpheus, but with an easily licensed code base for rapidly creating other implementations. JXTA is another, even if its p2p aspect is only one component in a larger vision. This kind of architecture and open protocol benefits not only the applications that utilize the common infrastructure, but also the infrastructure itself, by increasing the rate of adoption, improving effectiveness, and providing more resources and services in the form of the new applications.

USAGE PATTERNS AND PROBLEMS

Each class of p2p application generally shows patterns and problems specific to that usage, so it perhaps can be valuable to examine them from this perspective and not so much as individual applications deployed in a particular environment.

We can take up some general scenarios to illustrate the concept, roughly grouped according to the peer-technology categories already defined. What's particularly interesting is the way each has given rise to a specific usage pattern.

Instant Messaging

IM clients are commonly deployed in environments where people are online for extended periods of time, usually over LAN or broadband. This doesn't mean that transient users, such as for dial-up, are rare by any means, just that their participation in live conversations is comparatively less frequent. In some sense, they form a subset category and rely heavily on any store-and-forward relaying feature provided by the particular technology deployed.

The usage pattern for IM thus divides into roughly three types:

- Extended conversations, one on one, where both individuals are devoting more or less constant attention to reading and typing. It can reach the point where the users grow weary of the delays and move to a voice channel, either phone or Internet. It's notable that the newer IM clients anticipate this and make it easy to place calls from within the interface. While video connections are often found intriguing, the small and jerky webcam images together with the perceived out-of-sync voice channel can prove distracting to serious conversations unless visual support is really needed.

- Short messages separated by extended periods when the session window is ignored. This frequently happens when attention at either end is mainly elsewhere. This exchange is more immediate than e-mail and conveys some important presence cues, yet is undemanding about relative timing of responses. This context may well be where IM functions best, and it's frequently associated with file transfer or other ancillary activities.

- Relayed messaging, when the users are rarely online at the same time. The usage is similar to the previous, except lacking in presence, and naturally requires a client-server model that implements store-and-forward. Extensions to this are message relays to other text-based technologies, such as SMS in cellular phones.

Connectivity is usually mediated through central servers, and is in the virtual sense one-to-one. IRC-like chatrooms and one-to-many modes might be available.

The identifiable practical problems with the popular clients are dealt with in Chapter 6 and include messages not being encrypted, dependency on a client-specific central server (external to corporate firewall), advertising relayed from third-party servers, unauthorized user profiling, proprietary protocol, and perhaps distracting features as the clients strive to become some kind of personal information manager.

A big issue is the lack of interoperability, where the so-far largest block of users, those using ICQ-AIM, are jealously walled in by AOL. The solution for the user is either to install multiple IM clients, or to hope that some multiprotocol client can keep in step. In either case, you need to define separate identities for each, and when searching for another user be prepared to fail due to the multiple directories and inconsistent identity mapping.

One thing to consider is whether the individual situation makes it meaningful to use a typed-message client at all. Even if motivated by other factors, the geographical spread of some companies can mean that the most likely benefactors of an IM system can't use it effectively because of time zone difference. A few hours skew can be enough that work hours when live messaging is likely rarely coincide, and in that case, e-mail is the better medium.

File Sharing

The history of the Gnutella network provides much material for studies of both usage patterns and network behavior under varying circumstances, but we must also look to the others for a more complete picture. These networks demonstrate some of the evolutionary aspects in making content sharing more efficient and reliable.

The usage pattern for file-sharing p2p is quite different from IM. For one thing, the other peers tend to be perceived as anonymous content repositories, so unless you specifically know who's at a particular node and want to chat, you don't really care if anyone is even sitting at the keyboard. File sharing is user asynchronous and frequently unattended for long periods.

There's generally a core of constantly online nodes, but some networks have a built-in drift in topology (as in Gnutella) so your system won't keep in touch with them indefinitely in any case. Other implementations encourage more permanent neighbor contact for various reasons, perhaps because of transaction rules and reputation systems. Local subnets will tend to be pretty static and always online, with largely equal client-LAN bandwidth, unlike many public nets that have a significant transient user base with widely varying bandwidth.

On public sharing systems, the "freeloader" issue always seems to come up sooner or later, and with it come various desired changes to the original open-to-all network behavior. In network terms, this means that the common resources are often heavily loaded by users who contribute nothing to the network, instead only causing congestion and problems for other users.

One popular modification in Gnutella was to deny access to Web-based Gnutella clients, in other words users who were not running a sharing application. Many clients are also configurable to drop connections or not share files with peers who themselves do not share or have further connectivity. A more sophisticated evaluation and filtering of peers is possible when reputation and trust systems are implemented.

Another strategy seen is to implement connection profiles to favor higher-bandwidth connections over slower modem connections. The result is that slow users are pushed to the outer edges of the network and no longer present a bottleneck to the core network maintained by a second tier of super-peers. An extension to this adds reputation tracking and other logic to evaluate peers. Another is the "reflector" principle of letting high-capacity nodes act as relay servers for slower or transient ones—similar to the common ISP-server-to-client hierarchy.

With these kinds of improvements, simple Gnutella-like networks can provide adequate performance in many situations, despite their intrinsic scalability problems. In more controlled environments, the usability focus is probably more on the search functionality, and how to optimize it for the particular content of interest. The related issue of storage strategy is also important—atomistic or distributed.

Some networks use dedicated central servers to index content while others use a hybrid architecture based on a large number of super-peers for this purpose. In this way, search performance can be made much faster than atomistic query broadcast or query route methods. In a similar way, distributed content-publishing systems also often rely on peer-cluster services to index and track content, and these services can be made more effective if they are located on super-peers. Otherwise, fully distributed searches are characterized by relatively long waits for search returns. In the public sharing networks, it seems that super-peer clusters provide a popular middle way between Napster-style architecture and the fully atomistic model, although there is some concern about the added vulnerability (legal as well as technical) that a super-peer model demonstrates compared to the latter.

File sharing can assert some unusual network demands. It's common to note in educational settings that uplinks are almost always oversubscribed—the sum of client bandwidth requirements is greater than Internet access bandwidth. Interpreted: lots of network node overhead, plus all those music, movie, and software transfers going on. Upgrade the access lines, and the users or clients increase their transfer throttles accordingly. Some statistics of dorm and lab usage at university campuses suggest that some few to 10 percent of the users stand for more than half of the bandwidth requirements even under tightly regulated conditions—in some cases, all the way to saturation. Similar if not so extreme usage patterns might apply to file-sharing clients used within a corporate setting that are allowed access to external networks.

Adaptive bandwidth management might be required, along with more targeted measures to stem inappropriate use or abuse. In practice, most campus and corporate systems were designed to and rely on statistically multiplexed "real life" loading expectations. These expectations build on the usual client-server usage patterns of Web surfing and FTP downloads. Introducing a significant amount of p2p traffic can seriously skew this loading, much as Internet dial-up for a time seriously skewed traditional telephony loading of POTS switching.

> **Bit 12.1 Granting free access to large and powerful unused network resources, even as a quasi-regulated p2p resource, is not without its risks.**
>
> As the adage goes, nature abhors a vacuum. Free Internet resources have a way of attracting usage to saturation much faster than the average system administrator can envision, and also of attracting misuse and abuse.

Bandwidth Management Issues

It might seem a little off topic, but practical p2p must factor in bandwidth management and the different ways that usage can be regulated. The observant user will note, for example, that this kind of awareness exists in the design of many peer technologies, especially atomistic file sharing, where clients have user-configured limits for upload, download, and general bandwidth usage, the sum of which is generally less than the user's total available bandwidth. Without this kind of overall control, it turns out that the p2p network as a whole suffers. In practical terms, this means that the p2p user can see the application as a background process and continue to use other, less demanding clients (such as Web browsing or IM) much as before.

From the administrative point of view, the following are various ways a host network might be bandwidth and usage controlled. Doing nothing generally means that either the network saturates to denial-of-service levels or the budget breaks under the pressure of bandwidth procurement to satisfy the essential services.

- Rate-limiting or blocking specific ports suspected of causing or having the potential to cause overloading. It is in effect the firewall approach, but directed inward to the LAN users. Any good firewall should filter and selectively block in both directions—the defining point is what.

- Rate-limiting total user traffic, which is difficult to do sensibly, even if scheduled or carefully rules-managed. It will assuredly prove a pain to some legitimate usage and to unforeseen requirements over time. There are router-based solutions for rate-limiting (for example, from Cisco), with a view to providing assured QoS levels to particular services or user groups.

- Category-limiting user traffic, which might for example give priority to particular services (for example a main server, or NetBIOS sharing). The solution thus lets everyone else use what bandwidth is left over, first-come, first-served. (A converse, less crippling approach is to enhance only some traffic with accelerated content-delivery technology.)

- Policy enforcement, which we see lately with broadband providers who actively police their customer networks for infringements on no-server or banned-application rules. In other words, they analyze traffic for specific patterns that identify applications which load the uplink (LAN to WAN) channel in unusual ways.

- Manual or automatic traffic monitoring, which is meant in a more general way to simply identify unusually "hot" users. Administrators then take measures based on what the analysis reveals for consistent loaders. So-called tail-trimming is probably quite common as an automated response here, meaning that the high-demand users will consistently see their traffic clipped first when bandwidth capacity saturates.

- Redefined network services. It's not unheard of for network providers to reconfigure critical services such as local DNS to deny (or "blackhole") requests that might trigger high-demand bandwidth usage.

- Aggressive caching for some kinds of traffic. While this lowers demand for outside bandwidth, relying on LAN bandwidth, usually higher, to carry some repetitive loading, it can seriously cripple certain clients.

- Natural filtering, which is an ironic way of describing the policy of just letting the existing bottlenecks in the network see to it that runaway bandwidth hogs choke. In rare cases, administrators might even retrofit lower-bandwidth components in critical paths. More commonly, a multitier transport is implemented so that some users (as determined by usage patterns or payment plans) end up with cheaper and less reliable routing options, or the available bandwidth partitioned in some way.

Chances are that one or more of these measures will be encountered by unsuspecting deployers of a new peer technology, discovered when the clients trigger network provider reprimands—or perhaps more typically, work sporadically or not at all.

It might be noted that there is an awareness in universities that p2p is something that's here to stay. Campus provisioning of connectivity, in particular in the context of Internet2 for American universities, must consider in this opinion various peering strategies to be able to meet the bandwidth demand from p2p applications. The awareness extends to the realization that while legal enforcement measures in the short term can reduce p2p client deployment on campus, the real solution is not to ban the applications, but to make the network work better and more cost-effectively at accommodating this kind of loading.

Publishing and Retrieval

The publishing to peers situation is sort of the reverse of file sharing (retrieval), although it can easily be combined with such applications. The main issue is whether publishing is from a single or centralized source, or whether it is a matter of arbitrary peers publishing to peers.

Implementations in earlier chapters address both sides of this issue.

Commercial distribution solutions tend to be the single-source variety along the lines of Swarmcast (although cost far more) or rely on Akamai-style outsourced, adaptive replication of server-hosted content. Which, depends on the usage pattern. Either way, publication tends to be to a central store and replicated on demand.

If the demand for given material peaks on publication, the Swarmcast model works well because most clients will be requesting the same documents at the same time, so publication becomes largely identical to distribution. If heavy usage is a more random demand, like at a typical Web site, then aggressive replication across many content servers with adaptive caching will be best.

Fully distributed publishing to a decentralized store seems rare as a commercial solution. However, the Freenet-based Karma purports to do so, and it seemed as if Mojo Nation was also trying to sell in its version of swarm storage. Encrypted decentralized storage is in theory an attractive revenue-generating solution for corporations with much unused disk space, but management is no doubt very hesitant to begin selling storage in that way. Likely customers might first be other, affiliated companies to spread the costs of reliable storage and backup. On the other hand, companies in the market for outsourced storage are more likely to opt for something like the Akamai solution.

The other factor to consider is geographical spread and overall connectivity. Akamai and others specialize in serving highly distributed customers in the global perspective, ensuring high-capacity replication and near-to-client adaptivity. Some of these performance benefits can be hard to duplicate without the same dedicated external resources. Home-grown solutions tend to work best within local LANs, where the company has direct control of all aspects of connectivity. Then, distributed search might also make better sense, because it's more likely that the entire network will be reachable with queries or that indexing mechanisms will work as intended.

It can be critical to see how publishing and retrieval meet in the area of search functionality. Search of a central store can be indexed and made both fast and efficient, but vulnerable to single points of congestion and failure. Distributed storage and search may have advantages, but unfortunately is often quite slow and may suffer from significant scope constraints. Most corporate settings probably choose just to leverage existing centralized storage as the least disruptive and demanding change. There's some indication that only new infrastructures seriously consider a fully p2p architecture for their connectivity and content needs.

The requirements for persistent storage and content management in general, including governance, can vary immensely. Swarmcast peer distribution is essentially transient because the peer meshes form on demand, although once downloaded to peers, content can remain available for subsequent requests. However, no peer is required to ensure that content remains stored or available; the central server is the reference (and final permissions arbiter). Fully decentralized storage can be harder to manage and requires some redundancy replication to ensure that content is always available even if some peers are not online. Governance is then also harder to implement, unless carefully built into the meta- and content-tracking services.

Libraries and public archives are potential adopters of this technology.

PEER-TO-PEER JOURNALISM

As a special focus theme on practical case studies, P2P Journalism (p2pj) combines many of the more interesting issues discussed earlier in the book, both in theory and in implementation. The p2p here isn't necessarily or specifically about the kinds of peer technologies described in this book, although these and others can certainly play an important role, rather it's about people as peers and the related trust issues.

How would one define p2pj? Perhaps something like this:

1. Original content is not generated by the centralized parts of the system (if there are any) but rather locally by the peers, mainly supported by, one might imagine, peer messaging and collaborative tools. This is in contrast to most modern journalism where a central editorial staff creates content from material culled from reporters, wire services, and archives.

2. Peers automatically host and reshare the content they produce and download from other peers. In other words, they are not only the content creators, but also at the same time the distribution system. This is supported by the peer technology relevant to sharing and distribution.

3. Peers also become the server source for disseminating content to a wider readership (or viewership), with access not just to the current material, but also the archive and reference links to related and background sources. Peer search tools or syndication digests might be common in this role.

From this point of view, each peer is a node in an automatic syndication network—both news "reporter" and access "library". Several important issues, not least of which is trust, must be dealt with in peer journalism.

Established news media have demonstrated reputations concerning how well or objectively they cover news, applicable by extension to the reporters and journalists that work for them. Most people base their trust of what they read or see reported on this association and perceived reputability, or lack thereof. A further extension is the trust given to the trust the media and their journalists have in their news sources. How would anyone know how to evaluate stories emanating from a peer network?

> **Bit 12.2 Viable network information content presumes a trust infrastructure.**
> As e-commerce development critically depends on a micropayment system, important growth in Internet's informational role depends on trust systems.

Practical Trust Systems

To summarize, practical trust systems have three distinct components in this context, which apply both to the journalist-peer and to the sources the journalist works with:

- **Authentication,** which asserts that people or agents are really who they say they are, and are in fact correctly representing what they claim.

- **Reputation,** which is a consensus evaluation ultimately based on perceived past behavior, possibly established by hearsay.

- **Trust,** which is the result of a personal evaluation of known reputation and other factors.

These issues are relevant to most any p2p situation, not just journalism. A peer system can resolve these issues in several ways, some of which have already been outlined in the earlier explanations of various technologies, especially the encrypted variations in the later chapters.

Authentication could establish identity with a distributed PKI web of trust or through central services such as Passport. Of special interest to journalists is the authenticated anonymous identity, the trusted anonymous source. Recall that public keys to establish identity, and digital signatures to authenticate content and sender, are intimately coupled through these products of strong encryption.

Reputation is determined by actual user behavior—history, not identity except to establish that a particular history is reliably linked to an established identity. Reputation determines whether or not people in general want to have transactions with that entity. In the peer context, reputation systems are very popular fields for development at the moment, as p2p networks move from connecting with anyone, to filtering out nodes that exhibit poor or unreliable behavior.

Trust is partly about reputation on the purely individual level, but it's moderated by the many other factors that an individual applies when deciding whether to deal with the entity in question. The individual trust shown in a particular context can run counter to what public reputation would dictate. The most important factor in personal trust are value judgements and things such as relative risk, expectation, greed, reward, and particular context. I might trust someone well in one context, but not at all in another. Based on known private history, I might trust someone not trusted by anyone else.

Both reputation and trust are typically managed at the application level, and several implementations are common in public posting sites, such as Advogato and Slashdot Friends and Foe lists. But they make much more sense in a decentralized network. Trust is there just an additional layer of information in your roster, something clearly seen in the key management section of PKI clients.

Combine trust with recommendation systems, and you can create quite interesting queries, along the lines of: "Show me all content that has been rated highly by people I trust in this category." Surely indirect relationships, web of trust style, can also be factored into the search result sorting, so that people who are trusted by people I trust are also automatically somewhat trusted by me (or my system). Such trust propagation could have quite massive effects on content propagation.

Nothing quite like it has been implemented yet, but it's something to be on the lookout for because it will be an important development for peer networks. Erik Möller, noted German freelance journalist, is quite keen on this idea:

> You can take this trusted recommendation concept even further. Form "teams" with other users who rate content, and assign teams reputations of their own. Thus, I could formulate a query: "Show me all content that has been rated highly by Team xyz recently."
>
> Then, the effects get even more massive.
>
> With massive, I mean that the network itself could create "hypes" on the scale of a "Slashdot effect", and more. If this is integrated with micropayment systems, these hypes could actually be turned into real money, for instance for an artist, an open source project, or a political action.

Some mention should therefore be made of projects to provide trust systems.

The Open Privacy Projects

One good resource for network-related trust and reputation systems is the OpenPrivacy initiative (www.openprivacy.org). This site is an open source collection of software frameworks, protocols and services that can provide a cryptographically secure and distributed platform for creating, maintaining, and selectively sharing user profile information.

The vision is to enable user control over personal data, while simultaneously at user discretion providing marketers with access to higher-quality profile segments— an incentive for a new breed of personalized services to provide people and businesses with timely and relevant information. While that might not sound too enticing as it stands, the practical projects provide a diverse mix of trust and reputation technologies that might, here presented roughly in order of completeness.

- **Sierra,** a reference implementation of the Reputation Management Framework (RMF), which is OpenPrivacy's core project. It's designed to ease the process of creating community with reputation-enhanced pseudonymous entities.

- **Talon,** a simple yet powerful component system for Java. Sierra is being developed using Talon and is expected to use Sierra's reputation manager to drive component selection.

- **Reputation Capital Exchange,** a secure mechanism for mapping between RCEs that use different trust metrics. Such mapping has important interoperability implications for unrelated reputation and trust systems.

- **Reptile,** an open source and free software Syndicated Content Directory Server (SCDS). It provides a personalized news and information portal with privacy and reputation accumulation, of significant interest to p2pj.

The RMF is primarily a set of four interfaces: Nym Manager, Communications Manager, Storage Manager, and Reputation Calculation Engine.

The implementation origins of OpenPrivacy are in the Broadcatch Project (www.broadcatch.com), which offers technology solutions for

- Portal and community building

- Infomediary agents (such as brokers)

- Pseudonymous publishing

- Reputation capital accrual

- Persona, profile, and reputation management

- Anonymous verification and authentication

GNU *Privacy Guard*

GNU Privacy Guard (GnuPG, www.gnupg.org) is a complete and free encryption replacement for PGP, the private encryption tool originally developed by Philip Zimmermann. Because it doesn't use the patented IDEA algorithm, GnuPG can be used without any restrictions. The application is compliant with ITEF standard RFC2440—that is to say, it's one of the OpenPGP implementations. Refer to the OpenPGP Alliance Web site (www.openpgp.org) for more information.

TABLE **12.1** *Comparison between different types of trust certificates seen on networks*

Certificate type	Certification authority characteristics	Kind of identification
X.509	Naming authority hierarchies. Cross-certification. CPS (Certification Practices Statement) required. (key bound to person)	Global by original definition, but local in practice (no single root, X.500 Distinguished Name is chosen by and hopefully unique to the issuing CA). Mapping failures security issue.
SPKI/SDSI	Single naming authority. No CPS is necessary.	Arbitrary local identity (keyholder or group) not bound to particular person.
SPKI without names	Authorization authority hierarchies; k-of-n lists. optional multiple holders	Global and persistent (public key or derived hash, globally unique). Could be anonymous group.
PGP	Web of Trust (multiple signers attest with own signature). Or, signer(s) trusted by user.	Global due to DNS-defined unique e-mail address, but not guaranteed persistent; some publication/revocation issues.

GnuPG can be freely used, modified and distributed under the terms of the GNU General Public Licence. Further development is funded by the German Federal Ministry of Economics and Technology.

The importance of public key encryption is evident in the many secure peer solutions that use it to secure and authenticate identity or content, and in the many derivative hashing and signature strategies that have been developed worldwide. OpenPGP is the most widely used e-mail encryption standard in the world.

In reputation and trust contexts, users rely on either personal evaluations or the distributed Web of Trust strategy. The latter involves multiple paths of certification to compensate for the fact that anyone can sign PGP/GnuPGP certificates. It is probably useful to have a summary comparison in this book between the common types of trust certificates seen on networks, and here seems reasonable, therefore Table 12.1.

A web-of-trust construction is a reasonably workable solution on the whole, as evidenced by the great amount of trust invested in it by people who use digital signatures and public keys. In reality, however, people rarely understand a web of trust or use it quite as intended, instead relying only on already known and trusted signatories. An interesting design feature is that the verifier sets the level of trust in keys and in principle can demand some number of independent signatures on a PGP certificate before that binding is considered valid. The working assumption here is that the different key signatures represent independent individuals, something rarely provable even assuming that the receiving user would go to that trouble.

At any rate, the construction is no worse than the hierarchical systems it's compared to, largely because as deployed, trust hierarchies are flawed (no single root directory, for example), or their mappings are vulnerable in various ways. Passport Kerberos authentication is no better in any respect. My reflection on the issue:

> It's been noted that the Internet domain name service (DNS) as a global map for Internet identities may have succeeded only because it was designed and implemented before larger political forces became aware of it or of its importance. Later turf wars surrounding the domain system, the registrar system and top-level domain (TLD) extensions tend to substantiate that view.

SECURITY FUTURES

As yet, a global public key infrastructure (PKI) for easy authentication and trust management is a vision—it's not clear what may or may not be deployed.

Microsoft wants us to sign on to the Single Sign-in Service on Passport for all our needs, and as usual, it is betting the proverbial farm on it in the current .NET paradigm. However, there are many reservations about that model. Apart from the fact that not everyone accepts the basic premise that everybody's identity profile be tied to a single vendor's server farm for all transactions on the Internet, there are concerns about the reliability and security of the technology offered.

A lack of global PKI means that transaction trust must be established in smaller communities whose members often collaborate, and possibly these communities in turn exchange trust information with others, as the need arises. This vision is rooted in a distributed view, closer to the basic p2p philosophy and could be deployed in terms of JXTA technology, for example. It's perhaps no accident that Microsoft and Sun, old adversaries, represent different ends of the spectrum here.

It's at least my view that local anchoring of webs-of-trust and transaction-trust mechanisms will be a natural and inevitable development as p2p matures. This process is likely to provide many definitions of "local" neighborhoods: physical, social, professional, and virtual. As in the physical world, our peer-based trust will be a context-driven metric with few (if any) absolutes, yet prove surprisingly robust and practical for the social situations in which we require it.

Private Key Management in .NET

Because the authentication system built into .NET is a central server model, it's to be expected that the core is a central Authentication Server (AS). The AS utilizes a somewhat modified form of the open Kerberos standard for private encryption keys.

The AS issues "tickets" to authenticated clients. When clients need to be authorized to use other services on the network, they submit the ticket to the service, which then authenticates it by passing it back to the AS on a back channel. To avoid repetitive transactions of this nature, the service might then grant the authenticated client a special local access authorization ticket good for a specified duration with the service, perhaps a day, called a *ticket granting ticket* (TGT).

The biggest vulnerability here is the central AS and the requirement for reliable real-time connectivity to it—services need to check authentication with the AS when the clients want to log in. Such a system can easily bog down for various reasons (peak demand, network congestion, server bugs, and so on) with serious consequences, as was vividly demonstrated when the Microsoft Gaming Zone shifted to this form of client authentication; some users were locked out for days. Even in good conditions, the authentication login process is bound to be experienced as slow.

The good point in the AS model is that the ticket can easily be revoked in a single location: the issuing AS itself.

An advantage of public key authentication is that it's easy and distributed. A signature is checked against one of many public keyring servers, assuming that the key holder has published it at some time on any one. Alternatively, the signature is checked against locally cached keyrings for frequent or known clients. In the latter case, no special connectivity is required. Keys can be generated individually or by an issuing authority, depending on the situation, which can be either an advantage or a problem. The real problem with distributed public keys and the associated certificates is that they are difficult to revoke. The signing key must be revoked in a published form, and everyone who might encounter the certificate advised of it.

The future prospects of both solutions are relatively good, because each caters to specific requirements in rather different areas. Still, it seems likely that the public key model (or PKI) has the clear edge as far as utility in p2p solutions is concerned and a probable edge for use on the Internet in general.

We might expect the central authority model to be the system of choice for central authority (for example, government), and thus be a key feature of any use of p2p in the political applications discussed next. But one can also image a scenario where a CA certificate mainly attests citizen authenticity of a PKI certificate.

Peer-to-Peer Politics

Speaking of politics, the effects of peer systems on democracy are also worth noting. After all, much of politics is about both reputation and trust, or their relative negative qualities when things come to mud raking and slinging.

The whole question of voting systems is not discussed elsewhere in the book, but it's rather interesting and ties in with the previous issues of secure identification, possibly authenticated but anonymous, of the citizen. Erik Möller and others have speculated in this area, and some main points are summarized here.

Can voting systems be combined with collaborative content creation and recommendation systems in such a way that "direct democracy" becomes feasible? Perhaps. Voting in such contexts becomes an active process of collaboration on concepts. Consider an interface that would show you all arguments from the pro-side, all those from the contra-side, consideration annotations by experts, moderated debates, and a (at least somewhat) editable collaborative (perhaps Wiki-style) discussion forum. Citizens could then decide whether to accept or reject a certain political proposal within a fairly asynchronous framework, until some predetermined threshold majority is reached one way or the other.

The binary yes/no vote is not the only option; what about "More information, please", "Don't care", or some other fine-grained expression from the constituency? After a political action has been agreed on, it could then be implemented or lobbied for using micropayment systems. Democracy could eventually become a massive collaborative exercise, run on decentralized p2p networks, with trusted meta-peers that collect votes.

Much could be done here. So far, we've seen mainly government administration trying to Web-disseminate information and forms to the general population (server to clients) and also provide access to centralized public archives. Some cases of information collection, such as taxes and the governmental equivalent of customer care services are in experimental deployment, and might benefit from deployed aspects of p2p infrastructure in the general Internet. However, voting and peer discussion applications would be a first major step into the p2p arena.

As noted earlier, this kind of massive change might come naturally when the p2p-friendly next-generation Internet infrastructure begins to dominate public usage and the services that can then easily be set up and integrated with it.

PEER INTEGRATION

Any really pervasive technology sooner or later integrates into the very fabric of our lives until we no longer really see it. A time-travel visitor from a century or two ago (in some cases, only decades ago), would marvel at some of the profound revolutions that we take for granted, even when they have drastically transformed our everyday environment. To gain some appreciation of this, it's enough to just look at some decades-old film and consciously enumerate all the things that are totally missing.

Some of these now-pervasive technologies have already been mentioned: telephony and the cellular handset, or the Internet and its services (Web and e-mail). Others have more been implied: the PC revolution, or computers at all for that matter, consumer electronics and always-available media (such as CD, tape, radio, TV), mass published books and magazines, mass transportation and its associated infrastructure (highways, service stations, the oil economy; suburbs, malls, and acres of parking lots; airports, let's not forget airports), and so on.

Harder to see are the social and lifestyle changes. Take, for example, shifts due to the year-round selection of produce culled from near and far in our supermarkets, or to the way people casually travel great distances for short vacations or make global business trips lasting only days.

It's more than likely that a few decades hence, the viewer of a film made today would be able to enumerate a large number of very basic things that are missing in that picture, a fair number of which would be directly or indirectly a result of the widespread deployment of p2p technologies and associated services. Many of these services would naturally have to do with communication in one form or another, yet for others, it might be very difficult to directly see this connection.

An off-the-cuff example: One can actually identify changes in how homes are both built and furnished that in one way or another reflect the central role that home entertainment electronics has come to play over the decades. It seems likely that integrated p2p could have similar far-reaching effects of at least the same magnitude, especially if it profoundly changes our work habits. Already, many people remote-work from home at least part of the time and hence have office space in their homes.

Major technology initiatives such as Internet2 have the stated goal of integrating the next-generation high bandwidth services with schools and business, something that will assuredly have great transformative effects there. The building blocks are visible to a great extent in the implementations that are covered in this book, as are the immediate uses, but it would be a difficult task to say with any degree of confidence what usage patterns we would see in only a decade or two.

INTEGRATION WITH THE NEW WEB

New Web services technologies are being deployed that allow Internet applications to communicate with each other in advanced ways. Microsoft's .NET and Sun's SunONE are the two main contenders at present.

In themselves based on many p2p concepts, either one can provide infrastructure options for new p2p technologies to develop. Interoperable XML-based protocols such as SOAP allow applications to expose local services to each another over the Web. New standards provide a feature-rich environment for managing such services—for instance, Web Services Description Language (WSDL) and Universal Description, Discovery and Integration (UDDI), along with a large number of collaborative possibilities. Others are more directly business oriented, such as Organization for the Advancement of Structured Information Standards (OASIS) and Business Process Modeling Language (BPML).

Other emerging specifications concern interoperability among autonomous systems, which were hinted at in the agency component summary for p2p implementations introduced in Chapter 2. The Foundation for Intelligent Physical Agents (FIPA, www.fipa.org) is one body that might play a pivotal role in this development by providing definitions of standards for common semantics for agent interaction, cooperation and coordination. One goal is to define complex tasks in a common way so that they can be distributed among multiple peers for execution. Another goal is to implement intelligent directory services, likely distributed as well, that will allow agents to locate and query available peers and other Web services.

FIPA's main emphasis is on practical commercial and industrial uses of agent systems. The development of intelligent or cognitive agents however is, as the name suggests, a long-term goal. This goal is perhaps unreachable, but no less noble—software systems that have the potential for reasoning about themselves and their environment. I, for one, suspect we have a long way to go before then. AI has been described as being "almost here" as much and as long as commercial fusion power. Yet decades of "not quite there" suggest that something fundamental is missing or wrong in the assumptions that the practical technology is trying to build on.

Having reached the edge of current development several times throughout this text, and ventured into future speculation more than once, perhaps it's now time to take that last step and wander freely into the visions, rosy or dark, that await us.

In a Screen Darkly

In this final chapter, we take out and dust off the crystal ball to discern where the current trends and ideas might lead. The view is necessarily dark, misty and unclear, both because of the difficulty in predicting which way critical events might go and because of the state of flux in which the entire field—for that matter, the entire world—finds itself.

Some of these imponderables have been touched on in earlier chapters. We however can't predict very well which technologies will "take off" and which will fall by the wayside. Nobody predicted, for example, the intense popularity of messaging or file sharing, although in hindsight, the development seems inevitable. Future changes in Internet infrastructure and general computing, in themselves hard to predict, can have enormous and unpredictable effects on the way people use and want to use the technology. All these factors affect any future application of p2p.

Other imponderables are the more general trends that affect the Internet or society as a whole. The ongoing commercialization of Web content—subscription or pay by view—and consequent tendency to move towards closed and proprietary systems for the sake of better content control is one such factor. The increased concerns over Internet security and content censorship in the wake of escalated terrorism, both in cyberspace and in the physical world, is another.

No matter. The following discussion looks at what is known, what can be guessed or conjectured, and opinions on the subject gathered from a collection of experts in the field who were willing to share their views.

CHAPTER 13 AT A GLANCE

This chapter looks into the future of peer technologies and related Internet issues by presenting a somewhat arbitrary selection of important topics.

Networking the Future examines if it is still a growth sector.

- *The Future of P2P* asks what factors will determine further deployment.

- *The P2P Vision* provides a glimpse of an idealized future that widely deployed p2p might mean.

- Much of the future hinges on *Embedded Peers* to provide seamless networking capability to appliances and homes.

- Behind *Collaboration Peers*, we find the requirement for well-defined transactions and change of work habits.

- *Distributed Processing* discusses the trends that promise transparently available extra resources on demand.

- *Superdistribution* is a component in a distributed resource market, and this section highlights two major research projects in that area.

- *Trust and Recommendation Peers* returns to trust systems from a different angle, this time as mechanisms for content recommendation.

NETWORKING THE FUTURE

The overall future of networking looks like a growth sector. We're familiar with Moore's Law as applied to ever-increasing computing capacity. And Gilder's Law for bandwidth increase suggests that this growth rate is even faster than that given by Moore's Law, albeit plotting the actual increases shows the growth to be more in periodic spurts than a linear increase. Although both were formulated as descriptive relationships, their predictive power is generally accepted as very good.

One might hazard to guess that this step-like growth reflects the slower turnover of bandwidth-related communication infrastructure—we don't rewire connectivity as often as we change computers, but when we do, it tends to be a large-scale upgrade. In addition, changes in infrastructure reflects larger shifts in technology—for example, a massive shift from dial-up to cable/DSL. One large-scale shift that's pending at the moment is that of wireless access and a whole new class of embedded devices.

Given ever more distributed computing power and storage, and ever more bandwidth to spend on connectivity, it seems a no-brainer to predict that networking technologies will become ever more pervasive. This seems especially true when device-embedded Internet connectivity promises to allow instant access of anyone and anything from anywhere, if we allow for a bit of hyperbole. The last great spurt of bandwidth increase provided by fibre optic cable deployment has been described as an "embarrassing glut" in light of the recent downturn in the dot-com broadband world and lackluster consumer interest in yet more cable TV. Nevertheless, history shows that added bandwidth, like any digital resource, invariably get filled by new uses. Peer decentralization and distribution on a large scale requires bandwidth.

Consider also network usage patterns. Network topologies have changed dramatically between 1995 and 2000, so much that the old rule-of-thumb usage pattern of 80 percent of network traffic over the LAN and 20 percent over WAN no longer applies. Typically, usage today is the opposite, so that 80 percent of a user's traffic is to off-LAN endpoints. Funneling this enormous traffic increase through the same central server and firewall conduits is rapidly becoming unrealistic. Granted there might be a return to more LAN-based traffic with newer technologies and more local caching, yet the trend is indicative of a radically different view of networking.

Surely, networking seems a hotbed growth medium for p2p technologies? On the face of it, yes, but recall what was said about the social dimensions (especially business and legislative) in Chapter 11. Other issues than the purely technological will determine what actually happens in the end.

THE FUTURE OF P2P

The future of public p2p technologies is inextricably bound up to a large extent with the future of free content, and the consequent disputes around the ever more restrictive control of intellectual property rights (IPR).

Thus, given the often contentious nature of the issues raised, reason to be less than sanguine about the general prospects for many of the current applications of p2p might be well-founded. Concerns for a number of other restrictive measures finding expressions in modern consumer electronics give rise to further doubts.

Similar worries might be held for the future of the Internet as a whole. Once seen as a free world repository for all human knowledge, significant sections of it are locked away now behind subscription barriers. In addition, the flow to fill the free part and extend public access reversed drastically in the face of terrorism concerns in late 2001. Content was quickly censored and sites taken down, the vain hope that doing so would somehow make it more difficult to plan new acts of terrorism.

Although not a popular concept among those in power, history shows regardless that simply repressing the free flow of information ultimately leads to worse situations than the repressive measures intended to combat. Besides, previous attempts to repress information on the Internet have had little long-lasting effects, because the system tends to route around censorship just like any other disruption of service. Both the design and prevailing philosophy of the network run counter to this kind of control. Taking the censored content mentioned earlier as an example, automatic caching and archiving services ensured that those who want to find the "removed" information can still do so, even when the original sites no longer provide it. At the very least, Internet search engines retain indexed copies for a long time. Add to this copies stored on local machines and other sites by individual users.

And none of these considerations even begin to take into account the situation that arises when virtual networks are deployed, actively designed to resist content censorship (as discussed in Chapter 9). Many censorship advocates clearly don't realize what they're up against when they seek to stem the flow of digital information. As noted in Chapter 11, people do whatever is socially and individually acceptable. Until it becomes totally unacceptable for the majority to access the information, there can be little in the way of effective barriers except closing down the entire system.

Erik Möller, freelance journalist and humanist from Berlin, Germany, who is prominently active in p2p discussions and review, made this observation in the course of one of our discussions about the future of p2p:

I'm ambivalent about the future of p2p technology. From the technological viewpoint, I have relatively little concerns—hackers have proven time and again that they can run circles around the most sophisticated technical achievements by the content industry. Their DoS attack is worthless with our reputation system, their spam-files are useless with our clever ratings and metadata. It's quite simple, more hackers are on our side than on theirs.

However, they have the lawyers, the lobbyists and the PR agencies, and the potential effects of certain legislation should not be underestimated. The DMCA already endangers cryptography research, but imagine a different scenario where you are only allowed to use cryptography with a license—this would be relatively easy to enforce and very effective.

It is not the technical, but the legal-social-cultural front where the geeks and hackers are losing ground. Insofar one might say that the progress of p2p will also be a race against ignorance and stupidity. But the amount of stupidity any civilization can handle before it collapses is finite.

Perhaps in hindsight we will say that the winner was already obvious at this time, entropy or order, but I prefer the view that we are at a historical juncture, and I see no evidence that contradicts this view.

Things are often obvious in hindsight, but rarely in the midst of sea-changes already in progress and never in advance. Quite the contrary, many if not most "obvious" predictions at any time turn out to be laughably untrue only a short time later. Such unpredictability is especially true when it comes to technology and its application, where "revolutions" happen rapidly and frequently. Sometimes revolutions can even reverse themselves due to new unforeseen factors.

It's not hard to picture a gloomy future, for that matter—not just for p2p, but for Joe and Jane Citizen in general as a result of all this fantastic technology. Some of these emerging factors are touched on in Chapters 4, 11 and 12—for example, in the sections about the content wars, new legislation, and threats to privacy. Science Fiction writers have long excelled at depicting various dystopian and apocalyptic futures based in misapplication of technology, cyber or otherwise. In the open source context, we can do worse than read Richard Stallman's "The Right to Read" essay (www.gnu.org/philosophy/right-to-read.html) from 1997—already dated in some aspects but with updated notes.

May we never reach the point of click-through waivers of constitutional rights at every virtual turn we take on somebody else's information superhighway.

THE P2P VISION

Let's recapitulate for a moment the idealistic vision for p2p.

Peer technology promises to grant any individual access to, and implicit "ownership" of, freely distributed content and services. The term "freely" doesn't necessarily mean without cost, for numerous payment and micropayment solutions are feasible in theory. This point is often misunderstood. We consider that we have "free" communication using fixed and cellular telephones, yet accept our periodic bills for these services and pay them to keep the providers in business. Yes, we might prefer the service without cost, but most of us are realists.

Individual ownership of content and information services is interpreted to mean direct personal access, freedom of use, and freedom of movement. As with the ownership of physical property, the assumption is that the individual may delegate or grant subsidiary rights to trusted entities.

The vision also encompasses the concept of *empowering the user*, which is an important ambition often lost in the many offerings promoted under the banner of increased "user convenience". The latter have a sad tendency to automate, obfuscate and hide functionality, thus constraining users in their options.

Some of the expressions of user empowerment are these user actions:

- Create content and services, and be able to locate them on any capable and available device
- Access content and services with any suitable device, no matter the source, location, time of day
- Administer and govern own content and services, and exercise this direct control anytime, from anywhere, and from any device
- Share with family, friends, colleagues, or the whole world
- Maintain the privacy, confidentiality and integrity of personal and proprietary information
- Steward the delivery of services and content
- Customize presentation, content and services

Not all of these user actions can be implemented yet, because they presuppose certain technical advances in numerous ways. Several p2p technologies however are moving in the direction of providing such services and potential.

The "any device" thought expressed here builds on the concept of embedded Internet access and device-agnostic protocols (for instance, XML). The ability to have 24/7, fixed address, Internet access from a cell phone is only a small part of this vision.

A Future Peer in Action

Just for fun, let's speculate on what a future day in the life of a peer-empowered individual might look like, assuming that most or all of the visionary items are generally available.

We might reasonably assume that I have a number of portable "devices" that can access the IPv6 Internet and other devices through wireless (typically, Bluetooth) or IR—for example, a PDA with about the capacity of a notebook of today, albeit a smaller screen. Some of these devices might be configured to function as primary authority delegators, probably by containing suitable public key certificates that I would have created and published with a local or global distributed trust system. Using the PDA and passphrase, I therefore could authenticate my presence and initiate authorized actions on the network. Consider the following scenario:

> *Having earlier set up a suitable appointment with a colleague by letting an agent query and match our respective agendas for when we were both available, I travel to his home for an informal meeting. The trip, by public transportation and taxi, is paid for with a smart card and reader system that has embedded access to a petty cash account managed by an e-commerce server run by the municipality—every so often I ensure a valid balance by transferring digital cash to this account from one of my normal accounts.*
>
> *During a cafeteria pause during the trip, I access my contacts list at the office and compose and send a few e-mails by using the PDA in its cellular phone mode (IPv6 24/7 Internet access). The inbox held a few personal messages that I move to the home network for later reading. I also check the online menus posted by a couple of favorite restaurants in town in case we decide to eat dinner out, making a preliminary reservation and bookmark.*
>
> *At my colleague's home, I am automatically announced and let in by the embedded receptionist service, which identifies me after an IR handshaking session between it and my PDA. Jim is working from home, as he so often does. As a matter of course, I interface the PDA with his home system to delegate some access authority that will facilitate access of work documents that I have stored in the corporate virtual file space.*
>
> *Our discussions go on for several hours, and a couple of times we have impromptu conferences with other colleagues located elsewhere. Shared*

workspace technology provides a virtual tabletop session with a mix of real and projected items that can be manipulated to illustrate key points, while real-time video provides acceptable presence cues between us all. My PDA automatically outsources several segments of heavy processing to provide real-time 3D simulation visualizations of some of the data sets pulled out by other agents during the session. These animations are seamlessly integrated into a presentation I decide to use to illustrate one of the topics discussed. I have a standard rules set coupled to a special company cost account that can handle the digital payments when all the microcredit transactions for such outsourcing are transparently called. None of this administrative detail intrudes on my awareness during the work session—preset rules sets rule.

Transcripts and recordings of our work sessions and conversations are made automatically, of all voice, video, and virtual actions, which allow later playback for details—and I won't have to regenerate those particular simulations on the fly again. Storage space for all this is automatically allocated (and paid for out of designated accounts) somewhere in the global virtual filespace, as it is needed.

Near the end, I receive two notifications marked urgent. One is a weather report service that warns of a sudden snowstorm that has begun in my home region, while the other is an agent alert from the home system that the power has failed. The home network has switched to backup systems and is shutting down nonessential components. Using the PDA to remote-control settings, I temporarily override part of the shutdown process to maintain access to the main home computer, while I upload the e-mails moved there earlier to global virtual storage, along with an unfinished document I've been working on. I also message my wife about the situation, assuming she is still at work but relying on our family messaging proxy to reach her no matter where she is, suggesting that she make other dinner plans and that I will probably remain in town for part of the evening. Needless to say, she can easily contact me at any time, no matter where I am. I also expand the scope for accepted weather and traffic notifications to my PDA. No sense in trying to go home until it was reasonable to expect I can get through.

After our work session, ongoing notification reports confirm my suspicions that the roads home will be impassible for at least a few hours. I update my personal journal and public weblog while we chat before dinner. I also show Jim the recent pictures from the family's trip to the mountains last week, which were in the family virtual store for events, but haven't been posted publicly yet. He likes one in particular, so I wave the PDA in his direction and authorize a content copy transfer to his system. Working in concert, our respective systems correctly interpret the intent of this from the context of the peer devices and the current display. We cowrite a relevant annotation to the image for his files and solicit signatures from the absent family members to add to my own. My daughter isn't online just now, but the context rules allow an agent proxy active on her system at university to send us a prewritten, signed greeting that seems appropriate. My wife's signature image comes with an acknowledgment that she's aware of the power outage at home.

Meanwhile, Jim has been scanning news headlines from a list that his home-system agents have compiled during the day. One breaking international story catches our attention enough that we spend some time to collaboratively research background and alternative reports. I set a custom program, resident somewhere in my custom services library, to sift through a copy of this material and present a summary that highlights divergencies between the many sources. That proves interesting reading, and Jim asks permission to relay the summary to friends of his abroad. I caution that part of the content might prove sensitive to send to the ones in Europe, because of the new EU e-mail legislation I've been reading about last week. In the end, we decide it's better to have him post the summary on a semiprivate section of his weblog, with due credit, and just pass along the hashed resource address key, the metadata descriptor, and a special key that would enable them to access the page at their own discretion.

Later, on our way downtown through the moderate snowfall even here, Jim's cellular notifies him that another colleague is unexpectedly free and soliciting dinner company through one of her agents, and that a preliminary accept for her to join us is pending. Her agent has evidently seen the peer group agenda information that Jim published about his whereabouts this evening, and based on her rules set, suggested she join us. I know that as a rule Jim is very open about this sort of thing, which is why he keeps that part of the agenda fairly public. We both think it's a great idea, and he messages her with the acceptance and our estimated time of arrival. Minutes later, he receives a brief message that she is on her way but will probably arrive slightly later than we do.

All and all, a whimsical flight of speculation, yet quite conservative because many of the things described can already happen in much simpler, verbal, and less automated ways. The technology as such does exist after a fashion, but what's lacking is the uniform protocols and infrastructure that would make the person-agent and agent-agent communication as natural and unobtrusive as implied by the narrative.

The reality will probably prove far more fantastic, with services, agency and behavior modes that we can't even begin to imagine. Just think of the changes we've experienced already in person-to-person communication due to only a relatively few years of ubiquitous access to both the Internet and the cellular phone, or the changes due to the Web, online booking and shopping, and existing p2p deployment. Implied in the narrative is also a fully digital economy—cashless, transparent, seamless. This goal is part of what the "Internet of Tomorrow" moniker is about.

The emphasis of embedded peers is intentional, because it is what many in the field have long felt is an essential component in the picture, and it will mean a pervasive and profound shift in our interactions with the network.

EMBEDDED PEERS

At the heart of the discussion of embedded peer devices is the realization that information and services are no longer just at the "hubs" of the network but increasingly on the periphery, on a large variety of smaller devices.

Despite their formal connectivity, such "edge devices" have remained largely inaccessible so far to the rest of the network, unable to share. The technology of embedding peers is intended to empower these devices with interoperability according to a chosen protocol, sharing on demand. Successful deployment of such embedded peers will have an incredible impact on network functionality and value.

One estimate suggests on the order of 10^8 desktop systems and server peers connected to the Internet in 2010 and some 10^{11} embedded peer devices. The communicative, and above all social value, of this network will be vast beyond comprehension—the math of Metcalfe and Reed give absurdly large numbers.

It's not hard to predict that an infrastructure of this nature is bound to become an essential aspect of our personal and working lives.

Business will experience a need to provide for mobile and instantaneous access to information in all products. Appliances and manufactured goods therefore will increasingly have embedded peer technology even for very simple information functionality. For example, I can easily foresee home thermostats, light switches, and some types of appliances supplied with embedded technology as a matter of course, able on demand to provide status information to a home network and be remote controlled from other devices held by the home owner.

> **Bit 13.1 Today's optional, premium feature is tomorrow's standard.**
> At some point in the development cycle of most products, optional features become embedded as standard components.

The extra cost of such peer-readiness is marginal in mass production items, but the extra value substantial to those who elect to use this functionality. This state of affairs is not far from the currently normal routine of prewiring a home or office with a standard number of power, phone, cable, and Internet outlets, with no initial regard for how a particular individual living there might later actually use them or not.

Peer-readiness is driven by a set of innovation demand factors acting in business and marketplace, which can be expressed in business terms, and they can be satisfied in efficient ways by embedded peer technologies.

- Demands for increasing efficiencies in resource allocation and consumption—**cost-driven** innovation

- Demands for more responsive and well-informed decision making—**business-driven** innovation

- Demands for more entertainment and education content providing revenue opportunities in peer distribution—**marketplace-driven** innovation

The net result of these factors is to compel manufacturers to add increasing amounts of "information" to their products to be able to adapt and scale to demand. In the current paradigm, this means embedded digital devices to all manner of common devices, no matter how little utility the consumer might initially see in this.

Factor in now the recent heavy emphasis on the "new architecture" of the Internet, of which JXTA and .NET frameworks are but the glow on the eastern horizon of a new dawn. We're rapidly moving from a world of standalone devices and local operating systems, to a situation where every device, however lowly, is network aware and based on interoperable standards. This new world will be one in which applications are routinely built as peer devices that rely on remote services.

> **Bit 13.2 The race is on to design a next-generation Internet operating system.**
> It's clear that whoever controls the infrastructure services and application framework for the new Internet will in effect control the entire industry.

The *peer infosphere* of the next decade could well prove as rich and diverse as any natural ecology. The key descriptors are *distributed*, *untethered* and *adaptive*, much like any life form when you add the magic ingredient *agency*.

COLLABORATION PEERS

The technology of peer architecture is one thing. How we actually come to use it is another. The technologies discussed in Part II of this book have been mainly two-fold in nature: messaging and file sharing, which is the picture at least when looking at the popular deployments and how people use them.

Less well known are the other applications, such as workspace sharing and decentralized collaboration. They undoubtedly will take the longest time to become widely used, if only because users then must change their way of working, learn new rules and conventions, and deal with unfamiliar interfaces. More critically, successful workspace sharing and collaboration depend on more than just technology—we here move into complex areas where technology can lessen but never remove the obstacles to communication that arise when people aren't physically near each other.

Well-implemented presence information is a minimum requirement, and possibly remote collaboration won't be really natural to us until we can recreate a complete virtual environment that faithfully reproduces critical nonverbal cues in person-to-person interactions, or for that matter, person-to-agent.

In general, I suggest that successful deployment of such solutions will depend on critical understanding of the semantics of the underlying information transactions between the people (and other agencies) involved.

> **Bit 13.3 A successful collaboration rests on well-defined transactions.**
> The chances of success are therefore greatest in small, closed groups (such as an intranet) with clear working contexts, and least in ill-defined, anonymous groups (typically, the public-access Internet) with no scaffolding.

These predicted transaction changes are relatively independent of the specific technology used. Community building based on special interests that define familiar social transactions go a long way to offset the lack of a formal transaction system— several Internet developments over the years have demonstrated scalability far beyond what was assumed workable in such an anarchistic environment.

There is also the issue of critical mass. With only a handful of registered users, IM would be about as interesting as telephony or e-mail in its earliest days, because there would be almost nobody to contact—most critically not the people you would need to contact. Many messaging technologies survive today due only to their established user base and thus the potential connectivity within a particular context.

DISTRIBUTED PROCESSING

The area of distributed processing is placed on the p2p periphery in this book due to the commonly implemented architecture that doesn't allow the clients to communicate with each other. The central server distributes piecemeal tasks that can be processed in parallel to large *ad hoc* clusters of processor nodes, over LAN or Internet, and then collects results. However, other more interactive forms of DP are possible and deserve inclusion in more mainstream p2p.

Some companies out there have long marketed various DP solutions of this traditional distributed computing nature: United Devices (UD, www.ud.com), Intel (www.intel.com), Entropia (www.entropia.com), and Parabon (www.parabon.com) to name a few. UD provided the technology that underlay the SETI@home project. In some cases, software developer kit (SDK) client-server distributions allow a company to set up customized DP networks on their own. The DP market is split between companies like UD or Intel that provide hardware or services for clustering processors and Entropia or Parabon that are essentially software vendors.

At present, the market for DP software seems limited to financial simulations and services, or more commonly, to computationally intensive areas of scientific research. Examples of the latter are now often found within the biosciences with projects for cancer research and genetics, a field sometimes called *bio-informatics*. DP deployment for load simulation, meteorology, and other more technical fields should increase in future as more solutions for harnessing idle resources become available.

In this case, the vision is for a free virtual market where idle processor and storage capacity, and perhaps other more complex services, can be offered in flexible micropayment increments on demand. Ideally, business logic on customer systems could automatically procure and release network-available resources, within user-configured constraints, in a way that would be totally transparent to the user. Needless to say, trust and reputation systems, plus secure encryption, would make these virtual resources at least as safe for personal data as using local ones.

Automated resource procurement is not a new concept—as noted in Chapter 1, it was being tested in university networks over 20 years ago, and it was even earlier one of the driving forces motivating the network research that eventually led to the Internet in the first place. What is new is how such resources could be made available at extremely small cost to any user device, anywhere. And furthermore, how corresponding idle resources in the local systems could be sold to other users, with perhaps enough revenue to support the external services consumed.

SUPERDISTRIBUTION

The ability of peer systems to adaptively provide efficient and reliable content distribution on demand was examined in earlier implementation chapters. The catch-all term for this aspect is superdistribution.

The concept is simple enough. However, effective management of this distribution, especially with regard to changing content, can be far from trivial and may require a complex mix of hardware and software solutions from different providers and vendors. We can expect more development to occur to provide more sophistication in caching, network monitoring, and routing algorithms. A commercial example of such emerging intelligent distributed storage technologies and services is provided in Chapter 12: Akamai.

A potentially vast market already suggested, which is possible but not yet implemented in any acceptable way, would be the sale of secure and redundant virtual storage to anyone. Perhaps the service could be based on a Freenet-like architecture deployed across the enormous amount of unused space available on corporate PCs. As noted in Chapter 5, anything from 80 to 90 percent of the aggregate storage capacity on current corporate PC hard disks is empty. However, to be at all realistic, such a commercial venture must use only encrypted and replicated virtual stores.

It seems that the large universities are currently backing much of the development in distributed storage. Two significant academic projects especially worth mentioning focus on globally distributed storage: *Interet2* and *OceanStore*. Both have a clear bias towards peer architectures, and both undoubtedly will have great influence on the future deployment of peer technologies.

Among other things, Internet2 is committed to helping develop a secure e-commerce/services infrastructure and promoting a wide selection of powerful new applications. OceanStore in particular belongs to the general p2p development class of scalable, decentralized, virtual filesystems, such as Mojo Nation (discussed in Chapter 8), Freenet (discussed in Chapter 9), and Free Haven, to name a few.

Internet2

Internet2 (www.internet2.edu) is formed around a consortium of 180 U.S. universities, working in partnership with industry and government, and was established to develop and deploy advanced network applications and technologies. As stated on the Web site, the mission statement is "to accelerate the creation of tomorrow's Internet"—elsewhere sometimes referred to as "Internet 3.0". Peer technologies are a dominant and recurring theme throughout the Internet2 effort.

The rationale behind this consortium is that university research and education missions increasingly require the collaboration of personnel and hardware located at campuses throughout the country in ways not possible over today's Internet. Extreme bandwidth requirements were an early motivator. Moreover, universities are a principal source of both the demand for advanced networking technologies and the talent needed to implement them. The effort is organized into initiatives and working groups around several focus areas:

- **Applications**, which means advanced network applications. They will enable people to collaborate and access information in ways not possible using the current Internet architecture and infrastructure. Tele-immersion, virtual laboratories, digital libraries, and distributed instruction are just a few examples of the kinds of projects being pursued.

- **Middleware**, which imbues the network with capabilities such as authentication, authorization and accounting. The intent is to allow advanced applications to operate seamlessly among many organizations. The Internet2 Middleware Initiative (I2-MI) is working toward the deployment of core middleware services at Internet2 universities.

- **Advanced networks**, which encompasses national, regional and campus networks. They will provide the end-to-end high performance required by advanced applications. This effort launched the End-to-End Performance Initiative (E2Epi) in the autumn of 2000.

- **Engineering**, which is currently represented by the working groups on New Networking Capabilities and on Advanced Network Infrastructure. Engineering efforts will provide capabilities to allow networks to work smarter and more efficiently, and to reliably support e-commerce. Some special focus areas are IPv6, measurement, multicast, quality of service, routing, security, topology, and the QBone Project.

- **Partnerships and Alliances**, which targets partners in industry, government, and other countries to work with Internet2 universities. The intent is to develop and test the technology of tomorrow's Internet.

Another major Internet2 initiative, complementing the E2Epi, is the Internet2 K20 Initiative. It brings together Internet2 member institutions, primary and secondary schools, colleges and universities, libraries, and museums to get the new technologies into the hands of innovators, across all educational sectors in the United States, as quickly and as "connectedly" as possible.

In a nutshell, what Internet2 intends to create is a distributed network of services to maximize the utilization of Internet resources. One concept here is that of *channels* or collections of content, which are seen as a superset of what we can access on the Web today. It's an aggregation of arbitrary forms of content (such as multimedia, applets, services, and resources) deliberately collected and made available to users. An example might be the entire ensemble of digital content used during an academic course, comprising documents, videos, software, data sets, simulations, online exams, and so on. Channels also express *policy-based applications of these resources*—a meld of content creator, infrastructure owner, and end user governance.

Critical to the concept is also *transparent delivery* to end users that can resolve any conflicts between the current DNS-based URI addressing scheme of content and user locality, with an access redirect mechanism that can convey conveniently nearby replicas from local caches to each requesting user.

The university-led Internet2 and the federally-led Next Generation Internet (NGI) are parallel and complementary initiatives based in the United States.

Through mutual agreements with similar organizations around the world, Internet2 establishes ties to ensure the continued global interoperability of advanced networking. The agreements enable collaboration between American researchers, faculty, students, and their overseas counterparts. International connectivity to Internet2 institutions is typically achieved by peering with the two Internet2 backbone networks, the vBNS and Abilene.

As a footnote to international connectivity, it must be noted that Internet users outside North America (or NATO countries) can't directly access Internet2 resources and sites—not unless they have Internet access through participating university networks in countries with close ties to the United States. Internet2 is seen as a strategic national resource, which might have dictated access policy. U.S. universities (and others) rarely realize that shifting access connectivity entirely to Internet2 makes them drop off the public international Internet. I ran into this problem when writing my last book, as I tried to research from abroad Wiki systems running on campus at U.S. universities. The "network unavailable" traces consistently returned from U.S. routers was not especially enlightening as to why entire subnets no longer responded to direct requests from abroad but remained visible to users in the United States.

Internet2 is not intended to replace the traditional Internet; it's to work in parallel to serve its particular constituents. Presumably, Internet2 will always be on the cutting edge of development. Much of the technology developed for Internet2 will most certainly also over time be deployed on the ordinary Internet.

OceanStore

The OceanStore Project (oceanstore.cs.berkeley.edu) has the goal of providing global-scale persistent data store designed to scale to *billions* of users. Currently hosted at Berkeley, the Web site incidentally sits on Internet2 and is not generally accessible directly from outside North America for the reason noted earlier. OceanStore is a component of the larger Endeavour project at Berkeley (endeavour.cs.berkeley.edu)—named after the ship James Cook used when exploring the Pacific Ocean.

> **Bit 13.4 For every Internet access obstacle, there are several workarounds.**
> Content from Internet2 sites is cached by the Internet search engines that can access Internet2. Search services like Google.com enable you to view cached content. An alternative route is to browse by way of a proxy server that can access Internet2—anonymizer services on U.S. servers will often suffice.

Future users will subscribe to a OceanStore service provider of their choice that provides access to a global, distributed, consistent, highly available, and robust storage utility. Storage is implemented on top of an infrastructure comprised of untrusted Internet servers, storage decoupled from the issues of intelligent content management that are resolved at a higher, encrypted abstraction layer—the servers are seen as mere bit buckets. Any computer can join the infrastructure, contributing storage or providing local user access in exchange for economic compensation.

Providers automatically buy and sell capacity and coverage among themselves, transparently to the users. The utility model thus combines the resources from federated systems to provide a quality of service higher than that achievable by any single company.

The OceanStore model caches data promiscuously, in that any server may create a local replica of any data object. Local replicas provide faster access and robustness to network partitions, and reduce network traffic by localizing access traffic. Migration algorithms also replicate data closer to points of demand and ensure a sufficient level of redundancy to meet overall data integrity goals. The content is thus modelled as *nomadic data*, free to roam anywhere within the network.

The working assumption is that any server in the infrastructure might crash, leak information, or become compromised. Redundancy and cryptographic techniques therefore are implemented to protect the data from the servers. A "Byzantine-fault-tolerant" commit protocol is used to provide strong consistency across replicas, although the OceanStore API does permit applications to locally weaken their consistency restrictions in exchange for higher performance and availability.

In addition, OceanStore implements versioning management, where each version of a data object is stored in a permanent, read-only form. The data object is encoded with an erasure code and spread over hundreds or thousands of servers. A small subset of the encoded fragments are sufficient to reconstruct the archived object. The design claim is that only a global-scale disaster could disable enough machines to destroy an archived object.

Internal event monitors collect and analyze information such as usage patterns, network activity, and resource availability, in order to improve performance and fault tolerance. The system can then adapt to regional outages and denial of service attacks.

The current status of OceanStore is that many components are already functioning in isolation. A complete prototype is under development. Anyone interested in tracking this project, or any other global-scale storage solution, might wish to join BlueSky, the Global-Scale Distributed Storage Systems mailing list, hosted at IBM (see www.transarc.ibm.com/~ota/bluesky/).

TRUST AND RECOMMENDATION PEERS

With all that global content out there, sloshing about in the infosphere, how does one go about finding anything, and more to the point, how do you find new stuff and figure out if you can trust it? These questions get to the heart of a really interesting and tricky subject.

The static Web is already filled with an enormous amount of content, of which a surprisingly large amount is trivia, in bad taste, false, incomplete, misleading, trying to get me to buy something or subscribe to see more, or just plain uninteresting.

Search and retrieval solutions are good and fine, but what's most lacking for average users is some evaluation mechanism for the quality of the information they can find and a *recommendability* feature that could point them towards unseen content that might interest them.

I'd wager that most people browse the Web based on a mix of traditional search for high-interest terms, less often digging in formal directories, and the occasional random recommendations by friends and colleagues who pass along URL addresses. Now it's been lamented that Web hyperlinks unfortunately contain no information except the address of the resource (usually a Web page), and in this context, such a one-dimensional pointer is woefully insufficient. Web creator Tim Berners-Lee early advocated a richer kind of hyperlink that can provide better information up front before you follow it. At the very least, one could wish for the equivalent of p2p presence; whether or not the target is actually available or valid.

> **Bit 13.5 Internet information flow must be more bidirectional to be useful.**
> The proposed new Internet HTTP version can provide mechanisms for better bidirectional information flow between client-server and client-client. Applications designed with this in mind will offer a whole new range of feedback to the user about what might be at the other end of a hyperlink.

The vision here is for much richer protocols to define and implement what is called the Semantic Web. An information infrastructure in which the underlying language allows data objects to describe themselves, the Semantic Web enables users and devices to do more with this self-descriptive data than just browse. All objects on the network are codified, data operates with a meaningful grammar so that data is organized more coherently—self-organized. XML and agent-agent implementations are moving in this direction, as is much work being done on the "new" Internet.

However, even fairly simple criteria can vastly improve the quality of Web hyperlinks. If you doubt that, consider the results generated by the search engine Google.com. Search engine results are typically presented in fairly simple dimensions:

- The "**hit**" itself, or the fact that a link is listed, which is pretty basic binary information—found, not found

- **Ranking**, which floats more "important" hits to the top of the list, according to some weighting or other

- **Relevance**, which grades results according to some other weighting—for example, how good the match is

Some might think that ranking and relevance are the same thing but it's not necessarily so. The weighting algorithms can be quite different, and they can be combined to provide a two-dimensional grading system. The usual problem is that the user doesn't know the ranking and grading criteria used by the presentation layer. Both ranking and relevance can also be saleable commodities—and thus bogus.

In Google's case, a relevance value is indicated indirectly by providing a context snippet with the match hits highlighted in bold. I personally prefer this kind of human-meaningful visual cue system to the more opaque styles of grading commonly found elsewhere—for example, "75%". A more complete view, and an alternate source for the content in case the target page is unavailable, is found by accessing the cached copy maintained by Google.

Google ranking is defined by "authoritative" weighting, which is determined by using the internal backlink index to compare how many other pages link to the currently considered hit. The more links that point to a given page, the more authoritative this page is assumed to be. Backlink information is given more visually as well, in that indented hits in the list are actually parent pages to the hit on the same site, which is often useful when less-precise search terms are used.

Absolutely, allowing backlink count to proxy "authoritative" is an extremely simplistic assumption! Even dangerous, but oh, so common in practical application.

> **Bit 13.6 Pragmatics: Information is authoritative if many sources quote it.**
> This is how many people do informal evaluation of information. At its extreme, it leads to modern myths and deplorable "everybody knows that" responses.

Yet, by and large, backlink count gives remarkably good ranking results. Why? It works because it's leveraging the aggregated assessments of all the many people who decided to put a link on their own Web site to a given external page. The hidden assumption is that most people, most of the time, make good quality assessments. Individually, they are *personally* recommending that page to their own readers. The method is not foolproof—urban myth snowballing through the Internet community can make the most absurd content "authoritative" in this model. Still, like the premise behind the PGP Web of Trust arrangement for attesting public keys, most of the time it does work. Google ranking is a form of multisourced, averaged *recommendation from our peers*—in fact, it's a peer architecture!

In the smaller scale, one occasionally sees experiments with "rate this article" or "annotate this content" mechanisms. As a rule however, they are constrained to only certain Web sites or to very specific browser applications. Many are simply feedback channels for support sites: "Was this KB article helpful to your problem?" Some review sites try to implement additional layers to confer some form of trust or rating of the reviewers, as mentioned in the trust section of Chapter 12, but the criteria appear diverse and arbitrary, not easily portable. That perception can change; note that the OpenPrivacy initiative has as one of its aims precisely to develop a system to make different trust metrics interoperable—that is to say, make trust value x in system A translate reasonably to trust value y for any other system B.

Until the general Internet supports a common infrastructure that transparently can convey more metadata, it seems clear that obstacles to deploying any meaningful trust system will be significant. This conclusion is motivated in a similar way to why we still don't have a transparent Internet system for payments.

Independently, peer technologies are implementing their own trust systems, simply because of the perceived need for them to better manage the dynamic connectivity issues and to counter disruptive influences—whether intentional or not. It's my guess that peer systems will lead the way in this field.

This reasoning might suggest that we can trust such peer systems fairly well, but that ultimately depends on how much you're willing to trust anonymous sources. Peer trust systems aren't so much about individuals (or the content providers) but about the nodes (and the transport layer). Therefore, trusted nodes can ensure that the content stored and retrieved at least is uncorrupted, but they can say nothing about the trust we can put in the content itself, the publisher of the content, and ultimately the creator. The most these trust systems allow is to consistently associate the content with an *authentic* source (either anonymous or identified).

Still, that's not bad, as such things go.

The public Internet is an unedited mess, to put it bluntly, and anyone can self-publish just about anything—there's precious little way to authenticate anything, or any reason to trust anything we read. We navigate Internet's "Cyberworld" by self-maintained trust beacons, sites we trust for their apparent integrity and known standing in so-called "Realworld". We also rely on recommendations by people we know and trust in some small way. At times such trust is misused, and such misuse generally is based on a misrepresentations of identity.

Trust abuse is nothing new, it's just so easy to do on the Internet. For example, school textbooks and other published, supposedly authoritative sources contain countless occurrences of urban myths and falsehoods. Tabloid journalism is just gossip or worse in many people's view, but even the respected media get things wrong often enough. The old rule of thumb is that *the veracity of a news story is inversely proportional to the reader's distance from the event*, sometimes formulated more succinctly as *the perceived veracity is roughly inversely proportional to how much you already know about the subject.*

A grassroots trust system grew up around PGP and the public key signature system, which is also peer technology on several levels. Public key servers are linked in a peer system to distribute stored keys according to fairly strict but agnostic rules. The construction of individual key trusts includes signing one key using another's signature. The main purposes of public keys and the associated infrastructure (as PKI) are to prove identity using digital signature authentication and verify the integrity of digitally signed content. Strong encryption of content, ensuring privacy, is part of the package but is a side-issue in this perspective.

Using PKI, we can establish a trust system for content and peer systems, and ultimately the public Internet by establishing either identity accountable for content or a verifiable and consistent, yet anonymous source for it. The public key model is not the only possible one, and the .NET approach to security relies on a private key model, as noted in Chapter 12. Looking into the future, we must be able to compare the key models and the trade-off each does for its own context of use.

The Final Trust

After some 400 pages, if you're still with me, you have shown trust in this book. As a reader, you did put trust on the line, based perhaps on a recommendation or a review, or perhaps on simple curiosity, to pick up this book and start reading it. What p2p can do for you in future might vary, but I'm sure that it can make your trust decisions quicker because you will have easy access to so much more peer recommendation and review to base them on.

As you see, trust is not new for the Internet or for p2p; it's always been an issue in human relations and communications. Reader trust in published books is one thing, but even the author must put trust on the line in advance—trusting that the book will be produced, and that the reader will be able to follow the discussion and structure in a book—a veritable leap of faith into the future.

Investigating the subject of p2p proves to be a remarkable journey—at least it did for me during the year I was researching and writing about this diverse and changing subject. It was "the book that would not end" because the subject matter never stayed put; the "final" text always needed further updates. Still does....

Anyway, I trust you enjoyed the ride.

Let me know what you think, reader-to-author, in true p2p spirit. Like many other authors, I can easily be contacted by readers through e-mail and other channels (see the Preface for contact information)—reader feedback always makes the effort feel more worthwhile. And in this case, it just confirms the value of peer technologies.

Technical Terms
and References

This Appendix provides a glossary of technical terms used in the book, along with the occasional technical references that didn't fit into the flow of the respective chapter. The latter introduce a number of computer and Internet terms that aren't necessarily defined in place or could benefit from some expansion.

24/7, shorthand for "constantly online" (24 hours, seven days a week). In common usage it less strictly means fixed-line connectivity as opposed to dial-up. When speaking of server uptime, for instance, 24/7 and 24/7/365 is taken in the literal sense, implying 99+ percent availability.

Actor, entity that can initiate activities—an actor can be a user, device, or software.

Analog telephone, or POTS ("plain ordinary telephone system") line. Digital data connectivity is by way of dial-up modem to an ISP modem pool and limited to a maximum 56Kbps, although substandard line quality causes a fallback to significantly less. Modem use blocks the line from accepting voice calls.

Architecture, a design map or model of a particular system, showing significant conceptual features.

Authentication, a procedure to determine that a user is entitled to use a particular identity, commonly login and password but might be tied much tighter to location, digital signatures or pass-code devices, or hard-to-spoof personal properties using various analytic methods.

Bandwidth, a measure of the capacity a given connection has to transmit data, typically in some power of bits per second or bytes per second.

Broker, a component (with business logic) that can negotiate procurement and sales of network resources. Discussed in Chapter 8, with Mojo Nation.

CD, Compact Disc, a Philips/Sony defined standard originally created for digital audio recordings (of one hour), but adopted as a storage medium for any data (about 600MB). **DVD** (Digital Video Disc, later renamed Digital Versatile Disc) uses the same physical form factor, but it has in its current version seven times the capacity of a CD, suitable for digital (usually compressed) cinema.

Checksum, a mathematical method for error or change detection.

Client-Server, the traditional division between simpler user applications and central functionality or content providers, sometimes written server-client—a seen variant is "cC-S" for centralized client-server, though cS-C would strictly speaking have been more logical to avoid thinking the clients are centralized.

Clone, a functionally similar and format-compatible piece of software. When the original code is proprietary, a clone can be reverse-engineered from analyzed traffic (output from original) and deduced protocols.

Convenience feature, an automated or default setting intended to make life "easier" for the casual user, but which often gets underfoot and makes it difficult to fathom how the application works.

CPRM/CPPM (Content Protection for Recordable Media and Prerecorded Media), a renewable cryptographic method for protecting entertainment content when recorded on physical media.

DAV (or **WebDAV**), Distributed Authoring and Versioning, a proposed new Internet protocol that includes built-in functionality to facilitate remote collaboration and content management. Current, similar functionality is provided only by add-on server or client applications.

Delta, math-jargon term for value or variable that conveys state change information, strictly speaking rate of change.

DHCP, Dynamic Host Configuration Protocol, is a method of automatically assigning IP numbers to machines that join a server-administrated network.

Directory or **Index** services, translate between naming and actual location. DNS is such a service for translating Internet domain names to actual IP addresses.

DoS, denial-of-service, a condition when a particular server or service is unable to respond to new requests, usually caused by bandwidth flooding or server overload. DoS is usually but not always due to malicious attacks. DDoS, Distributed DoS, is a malicious attack where many network nodes are remotely orchestrated to simultaneously flood designated targets with spurious requests, causing a massive DoS.

DSL, Digital Subscriber Line, usually known in its asynchronous form **ADSL**, a form of broadband access that works by aggressive multiplexing of many carrier frequencies on the last transport segment (or mile) of twisted-pair phone line to the user. Upstream of this last leg, connectivity relies on fiber-optic cable. DSL is always-on broadband, concurrent with any voice phone calls but sensitive to audible interference if line and connector quality is poor.

Dumb-terminal mainframe system, many clients with little or no logic communicating with a central server where all processing occurs.

End user, the person who actually uses an implementation.

Encryption, opaquely encoding information so that only someone with a secret key can decrypt and read or use it.

Exponential backoff algorithm, a way of ensuring that clients avoid repeated collisions of packets on a common line or channel. Each delays retransmit by a random time, and on failure, by a random time in a doubled delay interval.

Exposure (specifically **client exposure**), the degree that the user application enables remote endpoints to access information (possibly covertly) other than that which is freely and deliberately shared. Most clients pass along more information than users are aware of, although some of it is "needed" for client-server functionality. Some clients become downright invasive. Firewall and proxy filters can reduce the exposure.

Fat or **thin client,** reflects relative amount of resources built into or installed on a networked client (as hardware or software). Thin clients rely heavily on server or network services for functionality.

FEC, Forward Error Correction, a number of related encoding methods that allow reconstruction of a complete file despite packet losses. See Chapter 8.

Firewall, a packet-filtering form of gateway or proxy that allows connections only over approved protocols, on approved ports, to or from approved applications.

Freeware, software that is distributed free, but the author retains formal copyright unless the material is explicitly declared "in the public domain" or under some other IPR "free license".

FTP (File Transfer Protocol), is a common method to transfer files between server and client. It's considered more reliable than transfers using HTTP.

Gateway or **proxy,** network device (often a computer) that routes or bridges between LAN and WAN, or different network types, and frequently also provides NAT and firewall functionality.

Hash, a mathematical method for creating a numeric signature based on content; these days, often unique and based on public key encryption technology.

HTTP (HyperText Transfer Protocol), is the common protocol for communication between Web server and browser client. The current implementation is v1.1.

HTTPS (HTTP over SSL), a secure Web protocol that is based on transaction-generated public keys exchanged between client and server and used to encrypt the messages. The method is commonly used in e-commerce (credit card information) and whenever Web pages require identity and password login.

Implementation, a practical construction that realizes a particular design.

IP numbers, the Internet Protocol addressing scheme, written as four dot-separated numbers A.B.C.D, each originally representing a block range for subnets of varying size. A block that remains local to a LAN is reserved in each range.

ISDN, Integrated Services Digital Network, is a fully digital telephone line that supports voice and dual A-B data channels of 64 kbps each over standard twisted-pair phone lines. ISDN is more common in Europe where it was long marketed simply as "duo-com", two subscriber numbers for the cost of one line. The terminator adapter device supports both digital equipment and analog phones—data connectivity is by way of another adapter.

ISP, Internet Service Provider, a business entity that provides Internet access and hosting services. **IPP**, Internet Presence Provider, is an entity that provides Internet services, but only for customers who already have Internet access.

Journalizing, recording change information for delayed updates, rollbacks, or recovery purposes.

Kbps and **kbps**, measures of digital transfer rate. The abbreviations are used in the book in the international sense, as defined by ISO. Thus, 1Kbps = 1,024 bits/s (power of 2) and 1 kbps = 1,000 bits/s (power of 10). It's unfortunately common in U.S. writing to have Kbps also mean the latter.

Keyspace, a namespace for numeric keys, which are hashed from human-readable names.

LAN, local area network where the computer owner generally also is in full control of the physical network. LAN is distinct from **WAN**, wide area network, where at least some connectivity is through an external (or public) infrastructure.

Mailbox services, commonly implemented with POP3 (Post Office Protocol v3) or IMAP4 (Internet Message Access Protocol v4). The latter allows continued storage and manipulation of e-mail on the mailbox server after reading.

Market meme, a trendy term for "buzz" concept. An idea that is popular or widespread in current use—in the "meme market"—by virtue of being repeated the most. This is measured based on how often the idea pops up in the media, writings, or human conversations.

MB (megabyte), a measure of storage size. As used in the book, it's interpreted as true power-of-2 million—that is, 1,024 x 1024 or 1,048,576 bytes. (1KB is 1024 bytes.) In common usage elsewhere, however, MB might arbitrarily mean 1,024 x 1,024, 1,000 x 1,024, or 1,000 x 1,000.

Message, a higher logical unit of data, comprising one or more network packets, and defined by the implementation protocol.

Middleware, a third-party layer between applications and infrastructure.

Modem, modulator-demodulator, device to convert between digital data and audio-encoded data suitable for telephone lines. Also used more generally and less accurately for adapter devices to digitally encoded transports such as ISDN, DSL (ADSL or SDSL), and cable broadband.

NAT, network address translation, implemented by device or computer as a way of connecting a LAN, with local machine addresses, to a WAN, using typically a single external address.

NIC, network interface card, a device that physically connects computer to network, lowest level of the OSI model.

Node, a connection endpoint in a network, often a computer or the network client-server application, depending on one's perspective—physical or virtual.

Open protocol, the specifications are published and can be used by anyone.

Open source, opposite of proprietary "closed" source. Open means that the source code to applications and the related documentation is public and freely available. Often, runnable software itself is readily available for free.

OSI reference model (Open Systems Interconnect protocol layers), see Figure A.1, with reference to the OSI diagrams in Chapter 1 and 2, and to the native implementation examples. (.NET usually runs at the Application layer).

Out-of-band (OoB), a communications (or distribution) channel external to and independent of the considered or normal network.

Packet, a smallest logical unit of data transported by a network, which includes extra header information that identifies its place in a larger stream managed by a higher protocol level.

Persistency, the property of stored data remaining available and accessible indefinitely or at least a very long time, in some contexts despite active efforts to remove it

Platform, shorthand for a specific mix of hardware, software and possibly environment that determines which software can run. In this sense, even the

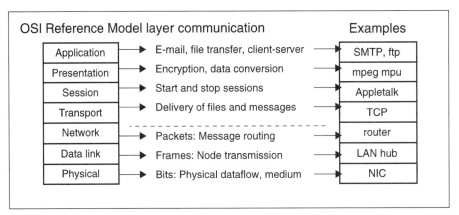

FIGURE A.1 *An indication of what kind of communication occurs at particular levels in the OSI model, and some examples of relevant technologies that function at the respective levels. The top four are "message based".*

Internet as a whole is a "platform" for the (possibly distributed) applications and services that run there.

Protocol, specifies how various components in a system interact in a standardized way. Each implementation is defined by both model (as a static design) and protocol (as a specified dynamic behavior).

Proxy (also see gateway), an entity acting on behalf of another, often a server acting as a local gateway from a LAN to the Internet.

Push, a Web (or any) technology that effectively broadcasts or streams content, as distinct from "**pull**" that responds only to discrete, specific user requests.

Redundancy, more information than is strictly required to retrieve or reconstruct the original data. Discussed at length in the section on FEC in Chapter 8.

Reliable and **unreliable** packet **transport** methods are distinguished by the fact that reliable transport requires that each and every message/packet is acknowledged when received, or it will be resent either until it is, or a time-out value or termination condition is reached.

Representational, when some abstraction is used for indirect reference instead of the actual thing—a name, for example.

RPC, remote procedure call, a protocol extension that enables remote software to directly invoke a host's local API (application program interface) functionality.

SDMI (Secure Digital Music Initiative), an encoding method that is intended to make it impossible to copy the protected CD music tracks or MP3 files.

Security is fundamentally in conflict with *availability* (I know that it's there) and especially accessibility (I can get it). Perfect security would deny both bits of information from the casual user. *Encryption* adds the further dimension that even if I can find it and get it, I won't necessarily be able to read it. Good security is finding the optimal balance for the situation and retaining a reasonable measure of convenience for the legitimate user.

Sendmail services, commonly implemented by the old but still prevalent SMTP (Simple Mail Transport Protocol) to transport e-mail across the Internet from sending server to mailbox server.

Shared workspace, when actions and data are shared over a p2p network.

Spyware, an application that includes software components that covertly collect information about a user and convey it to some collection endpoint.

Swarm distribution, when peers adaptively source downloaded content to other peers requesting the same material. Random offsets ensure quick fulfillment. Swarm services in general are network services implemented by cooperating nodes, often self-organizing in adaptive ways.

Swarm storage, when content is fragmented and distributed (with redundancy) to many different nodes. On retrieval, swarms adaptively cooperate to source.

TCP/IP, Transmission Control Protocol with Internet Protocol, the currently most common "reliable" network protocol—the protocol that defines the Internet.

Token server, a virtual bank that can issue digitally signed virtual currency in a secure manner. The server can allow withdrawal and deposit of tokens.

UDP, User Datagram Protocol, as UDP/IP is the Internet "unreliable" protocol that corresponds to reliable TCP/IP. UDP is transaction oriented with a minimum of protocol mechanism, and is defined in RFC 768.

Uniform protocol, all compliant clients can handle messages in the protocol; hence all these clients are interoperable and can freely pass messages to each other.

URI, Uniform Resource Identifier, is a complete and unique scheme for identifying arbitrary entities, defined in RFC 2396 (www.ietf.org/rfc/rfc2396.txt).

URL, Uniform Resource Locator, is a standard way to specify the location of a resource available electronically, as a representation of its primary access mechanism—the addressing notation we are used to from Web and other Internet clients (including e-mail). URLs are a subset of the URI model and are defined in RFC 1738. Another subset of URI, the URN (Uniform Resource Name), instead refers to specifiers that are required to remain globally unique and persistent even when the resource ceases to exist or becomes unavailable. It is thus a representation based on resource name.

Usenet, the peer-server network hosting newsgroups, defined by the protocols for posting, transferring and reading. A decent history is available from www.vrx.net/usenet/history/.

Web (World Wide Web, WWW), that part of the Internet accessed using HTTP-compliant clients—that is, the familiar Web browser.

Webmail service, a way to let users access server-based mailbox and sendmail services using an ordinary Web browser, and manage mail on the server rather than on a local machine's e-mail client. Webmail is useful for users who access e-mail from several machines or when travelling.

FREE SOFTWARE HISTORY

The following is from a summary by Florian Cramer.

The full text is available as "Free Software as Collaborative Text" (at userpage.fu-berlin.de/~cantsin/homepage/writings/copyleft/free_software/ free_software_as_text/en/free_software_as_text.html). The passage illuminates the Internet history section of Chapter 1 from a slightly different perspective.

It is not accidental that history of Free Software runs parallel to the history of the Internet. The Internet is built on Unix networking technology to a large extent. Academic institutions could get Unix for a "nominal fee" including its source code in the early 1970s, and it remains to be the historical base or model of the common Free Software operating systems BSD and GNU/Linux.

The affinity of the Internet and Unix technology still persists on various levels: e-mail is nothing but the Unix mail command. An e-mail address of the form xy@z.com is made up of what's historically a user name on a multiuser operating system and, following the "@", the system's host name. This host name is resolved via the free Unix software bind according to the Internet domain name system (DNS); DNS itself is nothing but a networked extension of the Unix system file /etc/hosts. Since the Internet has marginalized or even replaced proprietary computer networks like IBM's EARN/Bitnet, Compuserve, the German Btx and the French Minitel, Unix networking technology is standard on all computing platforms.

P2P Resources

This appendix collects references for further reading, which in some cases goes beyond what is mentioned in the text.

FURTHER READING

It's in the nature of hot new subjects that most resource material is in the form of scattered documents and resources on the Web. Much of this material is both very specific and narrow, dealing with only one or another implementation. This fact was one motivation to write this book, to try and collect useful information in one place for people who are looking for a concise technology overview.

BOOK RESOURCES

Not a lot of books are published specifically about modern peer technologies or how they function in a business context. Only the first O'Reilly essay compilation existed when this book was started. By the time of production, several new books had been published, and it's likely that more are in the pipeline for 2002.

- *Peer to Peer: Harnessing the Power of Disruptive Technologies*, Andy Oram, ed., O'Reilly & Associates, March 2001

- *Peer-to-Peer: Building Secure, Scalable, and Manageable Networks*, by Dana Moore and John Hebeler, McGraw-Hill Professional Publishing, November 2001

- *Cracking the Code: Peer to Peer Application Development*, by Dreamtech Software Team, Hungry Minds, December 2001

- *Discovering P2P*, by Michael Miller, Sybex, November 2001

- *JXTA: Java P2P Programming*, by Daniel Brookshier, et.al., Prentice Hall, 2002

- *P2P: How Peer-to-Peer Technology Is Revolutionizing the Way We Do Business*, by Hassan M. Fattah, Dearborn Trade, January 2002

- *2001 P2P Networking Overview: The Emergent P2P Platform of Presence, Identity, and Edge Resources*, by Clay Shirky, et.al., O'Reilly & Associates (industry report), 2001

The following book isn't strictly speaking about p2p at all, but I referred to it in Chapter 5 because of its wonderful insights about information flow and person-to-person communication. It has specific relevance when considering how peer technologies can be used to enhance collaborative teamwork and compensate for the lack of true face-to-face communication due perhaps to geographical distance.

- *Agile Software Development*, Alistair Cockburn, Addison-Wesley, December 2001

And then there's the parallel thread about the open source philosophy, for example:

- *Open Source: The Unauthorized White Papers*, by Don Rosenberg, Hungry Minds, January 2000

The preceding book is available online in its entirety from www-106.ibm.com/developerworks/opensource/library/rosenberg.html?dwzone=opensource.

Some legal aspects of p2p in the copyright realm are covered by the following book, part of which can be read online at www.digital-copyright.com.

- *Digital Copyright*, by Jessica Litman, Prometheus Books, 2001

A published, fairly comprehensive report that includes some aspects of the emerging p2p field in 2000 and 2001, albeit perhaps already dated in some areas, is:

- "Internet Infrastructure & Services", by Chris Kwak and Robert Fagin, May 2001, Bear, Stearnes & Co, Inc., www.BearSternes.com

The previous company (and report) has a main focus on equity research on new technology. Findings and details from this report can be found quoted or alluded to in many contexts on the Web, not necessarily attributed, but often using the term

"Internet 3.0". Reading it, you may not always agree with the take or conclusions of the report authors, but anyone serious about looking at the past few years of peer technology from the investment angle should at least look through the report. I provide three alternative sources for the report because it's not a trivial task to find it unless you know exactly what to look for and where to look.

- www.bearstearns.com/supplychain/infrastructure.htm

- www.bluefalcon.com/graphics/Interet3dot0-5-2001-FINAL.pdf

- www.storewidth.com/Reports/Internet3dot0-5-2001-FINAL-PDF.pdf

The report is not quite a book resource, but not exactly a Web resource either, so it provides a natural transition to the latter listing.

WEB RESOURCES

Some of the more active and comprehensive Web resources that deal with p2p issues in the broader sense are:

- O'Reilly Open P2P forum (also host to biannual p2p conferences, called the "Emerging Technologies Conference" as of 2002), www.openp2p.com

- Peer-to-Peer Working Group, www.peer-to-peerwg.org

Some relevant Internet search categories can be found in the Google Directory Listings—for example, directory.google.com/Top/Computers/Software/Internet/ Clients/. In particular, the subcategories "Chat" and "File_Sharing" list many implementations for these classes of applications. Corresponding lists are found in the Yahoo! directories—for example, dir.yahoo.com/Computers_and_Internet/Internet/ Peer_to_Peer_File_Sharing/.

Note that most implementation sites often provide links to further Web resources. They converge on the same resources that you might find from the higher levels of the hierarchical categories. Occasionally, site resource links point to resources that haven't yet made it into the proper category listings.

INTERNET HISTORY

Internet history is found in many places on the Web, both personal recollections and institutional archives. Some examples of comprehensive or historical sites that were alive and accessible at the time of final review are listed here.

- The Living Internet archives, www.livinginternet.com
- History of the Usenet, ww.vrx.net/usenet/history/

As always, properly cast searches on for example Google (www.google.com) turn up more sources than there is ever time to go through. Alternatively, valuable sites can be found through perusal of the different hierarchical category groups maintained by the major Internet search and indexing sites, portals, or enthusiastic individuals.

INTERNET INTEROPERABILITY AND RECOMMENDATIONS

Both these sites have many further links to specific issues:

- W3C, World Wide Web Consortium, w3.org
- IETF, Internet Engineering Task Force, www.ietf.org

ORGANIZATIONS

Several organizations turn up in the context of p2p, and especially in the context of disputed intellectual property rights when sharing content.

- Recording Industry Association of America (RIAA), www.riaa.org, the trade group that represents the U.S. recording industry. RIAA members create, manufacture, or distribute approximately 90 percent of all legitimate sound recordings produced and sold in the United States. The RIAA has intimate ties with corresponding national bodies in other countries that enforce music rights and collect performance fees.

- National Music Publishers' Association (NMPA), www.nmpa,org, with its watchdog subsidiary, the Harry Fox Agency (HFA), owns or acts on the behalf of those who compose music or write lyrics. Essentially ruling over published music, it doesn't always agree with the way the RIAA interprets how label royalties for recorded music are to be distributed.

- Motion Picture Association of America (MPAA), www.mpaa.org, and its international counterpart, the Motion Picture Association (MPA) serve as the voice and advocate of the American motion picture, home video, and television industries.

- Electronic Frontier Foundation (EFF), www.eff.org, a donor-supported, membership organization working to protect (American) fundamental rights regardless of technology.

- World Intellectual Property Organization (WIPO), www.wipo.org, instrumental in trying to harmonize (that is, strengthen and lengthen) copyright enforcement worldwide, albeit the purpose is expressed formally as "promoting the use and protection of works of the human spirit". WIPO treaty agreements are to be implemented through subsequent national laws passed by member states, while WIPO can act as international arbiter.

RECENT LAWS AND LAW PROPOSALS

The past few years has seen a number of laws and proposals in most countries that aim to regulate (read limit or roll back) traditional fair use of copyrighted material. Some examples from the alphabet soup:

DMCA (U.S. passed), The Digital Millennium Copyright Act

SSSCA (U.S. proposed), Security Systems Standards and Certification Act, renamed to CBDTPA, Consumer Broadband and Digital Television Promotion Act.

IMPLEMENTATION RESOURCES

The link fan-out ratio of most of the resource sites provided in this section is very high. It's a never-ending task to try and list all the many client and clone variations that exist at any given time. This area is one of very rapid change.

Instant Messaging

IETF, www.ietf.org:
RFC 2779, a messaging and presence "standard"

IM Unified, www.imunified.org:
A sort of anti-AOL alliance proposing a unified IM protocol

ICQ (original client, run by AOL):
www.icq.com

ICQ clones, links:
www.d.kth.se/~d95-mih/icq/ and www.icq-4u.com

AOL and AIM (AOL Instant Messenger):
www.aol.com, www.aim.com

Jabber (multi-protocol IM and XML transport infrastructure):
www.jabber.org

Psst (one-on-one p2p encrypted IM):
   netforth.sourceforge.net/psst/

Trillian (multi-protocol IM):
   www.trillian.cc

P2PQ (ask peers search p2p):
   www.p2pq.net

Windows Messenger:
   messenger.msn.com, go.msn.com, and other

File Sharing

Napster (MP3 sharing, now commercial but yet to reopen)
   www.napster.com

Gnutella (main source for clients):
   www.gnutelliums.com

Gnutella Web sites (news and info):
   gnutellanews.com, www.gnutella.co.uk, and others

Gnutella developer list (400+ strong community):
   groups.yahoo.com/group/the_gdf/

Madster (former Aimster):
   www.madster.com

Distributed and Encrypted Content

Mojo Nation: The original mojonation.net site went down in early 2002, taking
   the public net with it. Expect to see a new MNnet version later in the year.

Swarmcast (software now open source):
   www.swarmcast.com, sourceforge.net/projects/swarmcast

Freenet:
   www.freenetproject.org

Collaboration Spaces

Groove and user forums:
   www.groove.net, www.groove.net/forums

JXTA (open source infrastructure, all application types):
   www.jxta.org, www.sun.com/jxta/

Lists

This appendix lists all tables, "Bits", and figures in the book, and thus provides alternative entry points to the content. Bits are intended to highlight particular snippets of insight (see Preface).

TABLES

Bits

FIGURES

Page Figure Caption

Index

Also from Addison-Wesley

Bo Leuf and Ward Cunningham

Wiki is an open source collaborative server technology that enables users to access, browse, and edit hypertext pages in a real-time context. In one handy volume, *The Wiki Way: Quick Collaboration on the Web* compiles all of the information you need to set up, customize, and run a Wiki server.

0-201-71499-X • Paperback w/CD-ROM • 464 pages • ©2001

James Edwards

In this book you'll learn everything necessary to program applications as tools and tool sets on the Groove® peer-to-peer platform. *Peer-to-Peer Programming on Groove®* is written by one of Groove's early developers, under the full supervision of Groove's Technology team.

0-672-32332-X • Paperback w/CD-ROM • 504 pages • ©2002

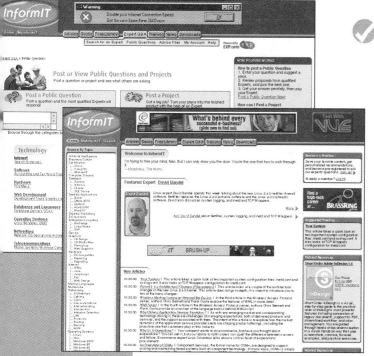